The Modern American Vice Presidency

THE
MODERN
AMERICAN
VICE PRESIDENCY

──────────────── ★

★————————————————————————————

The Transformation of a
Political Institution

JOEL K. GOLDSTEIN

Princeton University Press

278790

For my parents,
Milton and Merle Goldstein,
for Deborah, Ken and Alan, and
for Maxine.

Contents

viii ★ *Contents*

Tables

x ★ *Tables*

Acknowledgments

My interest in the vice presidency began in October 1973. I was looking for a paper topic for a course on Party Politics at Princeton University; Spiro Agnew was on the verge of leaving office in disgrace and President Richard Nixon would soon be nominating a replacement under the Twenty-fifth Amendment. My father told me of some of the potential problems of the nomination and confirmation process which that amendment prescribes, and suggested that I write my paper on them. Now, more than seven years (and four Vice Presidents) later, the undergraduate paper has grown into a larger project and I have accumulated many other intellectual debts along the way.

I would like to thank, first of all, the Rhodes Trust and its warden, Sir Edgar Williams, for the scholarship that allowed me to work on this book from 1975 to 1978 as part of my doctoral program at Oxford University, and Nuffield College for the benefits my studentship during 1977-1978 provided. I am also grateful to the Special Committee on Election Reform of the American Bar Association—its invitation to participate in a "Symposium on the Vice-Presidency," allowed me helpful contact with some stimulating students of American politics.

A number of scholars read all or part of my manuscript at various stages and commented helpfully on it. These include: Vernon Bogdanor, Nigel Bowles, Harry Bush, David Butler, Paul David, Louis Fisher, David Goldey, Stanley Kelley, Jr., Elizabeth Meehan, Graham Wilson, and Philip Williams. Parts of this book were presented to the American Politics and Government seminar at Oxford University, the Nuffield College politics seminar, and to an informal American politics study group at Nuffield College. I appreciate the suggestions the seminar participants contributed.

Brief excerpts have also appeared in *Fordham Law Review* 45. This manuscript was improved by the advice and editing of Sanford G. Thatcher and Marilyn Campbell of Princeton University Press.

Finally, I am most grateful to three friends for their generous help in this study. I wrote my first papers on presidential succession and on the selection, election, and campaign roles of vice-presidential candidates at Princeton University under the supervision of Stanley Kelley, Jr. He was a patient listener and meticulous critic who encouraged my first interest in the academic study of American politics. John D. Feerick, the leading authority on presidential succession, suggested the need for the present study. Conversations with him have greatly advanced my understanding of presidential succession and the vice presidency. This book is a revised form of a doctoral dissertation I wrote under the supervision of Philip Williams. He gave his time freely, his advise wisely, and his enthusiasm spontaneously.

The efforts of the above-mentioned helped greatly; I alone am responsible for mistakes and shortcomings that remain.

Cambridge, Mass.
April 1981.

The Modern American Vice Presidency

1

★ ★
─────────────────────────────────────

The Scope of the Problem

Since its inception, the American vice presidency has been
the target of more derision than any other national office.
Other major political figures—Presidents, Supreme Court jus-
tices, Speakers of the House of Representatives—have not
always served with distinction. But the legitimacy of their
offices has escaped serious challenge. Yet for most of its history the nation's second position has been seen, not unfairly,
as an accessory, both meaningless and menacing.

Time has not denied that view its popularity, only its ac-
curacy. The vice presidency has become an important component of American civic life. This book assesses the contemporary status of the office by focusing on the selection and
activities of its occupants from January 1953 to January 1981,
and relates the growth of the office to larger developments in
the American political system since the New Deal.

That the vice presidency has always received rough treatment is not surprising. To begin with, the office is a rarity.
As Richard M. Nixon pointed out, "Far more countries get
along without Vice Presidents than have them."[1] The Constitution grants it no significant permanent duties. Nor have
functions added by subsequent statutes imposed unduly on
the Vice President's free time. The history of the office is rich
in Washington folklore but poor in solid accomplishment.

The troubles of the vice presidency date from its creation.
The position was an afterthought, not suggested until the
closing days of the Constitutional Convention. Its reception

was not enthusiastic. "Such an officer as vice-President was not wanted," said delegate Hugh Williamson. Elbridge Gerry, later the fifth Vice President, opposed creating it. He and George Mason feared a weakening of the principle of separation of powers.[2] Alexander Hamilton defended it but admitted that "the appointment of an extraordinary person, as Vice-President, has been objected to as superfluous, if not mischievous."[3]

It is not entirely clear why the framers finally created the post, but three motives are commonly suggested. Most discussion of the office at the Constitutional Convention focused on the need for a president of the Senate.[4] Roger Sherman of Connecticut worried that lacking provisions for a presiding officer, some senator would lose his vote by having to chair the sessions. His state would accordingly be underrepresented.[5] And with an even number of members, Hamilton pointed out, the Senate might not always be capable of "definitive resolution."[6]

Neither argument is compelling. Abstention from voting is neither a prerequisite nor a guarantee of a fair chair, especially when, as is now the case, rulings are made along lines suggested by an appointed parliamentarian and are subject to appeal to the Senate. Nor does deadlock pose an insurmountable dilemma. Provision need only be made to handle tie votes. Further, during the debates Sherman noted that the Vice President "would be without employment" were he not the Senate's presiding officer.[7] This suggests that the duty was assigned to the Vice President to give him something to do rather than to solve problems facing the Senate.

The need for a means to fill presidential vacancies provides a second possible motive. Early plans suggested that the presiding officer of the Senate discharge executive powers in the absence of an elected Chief Executive. Other delegates proposed vesting those functions in the chief justice of the Supreme Court or in a council of state.[8] Yet, oddly, the delegates paid little attention to the question of succession. Their indifference makes it unlikely that they created the office primarily to solve that problem.

A third explanation of the creation of the office sees it as an expedient to faciliate the election of the President. A leading proponent of this position writes:

> The Vice Presidency entered the Constitution, in short, not to provide a successor to the President—this could easily have been arranged otherwise—but to ensure the election of a *national* President. For the United States had as yet little conviction of national identity. Loyalty ran to the states rather than to the country as a whole. If presidential electors voted for one man, local feeling would lead them to vote for the candidate from their own state.[9]

To counter this threat, Williamson proposed that electors be required to vote for three men. Two would be from a different state than the elector, he reasoned. Gouverneur Morris then suggested voting for two men, one of whom could not be from the elector's state. The extra vote, James Madison thought, would correct the tendency for provincial loyalties to guide voting. The second choice of the individual electors "would probably be the first, in fact," he predicted.[10] Acting upon this reasoning, the convention prescribed a single election to choose both the President and the Vice President. The individual with the majority of the votes would become President, the runner-up Vice President.

This is a plausible interpretation of the framers' motives. Indeed, Williamson claimed that the office "was introduced only for the sake of a valuable mode of election which required two to be chosen at the same time."[11] But even this explanation is insufficient. The scheme would have worked as effectively without the vice presidency. The "valuable mode of election" required only a second vote, not a second office.

The vice presidency was created, then, for reasons that are

at best obscure and at worst illogical. Yet initially the system seemed likely to fill the second office with persons of high caliber; John Adams and Thomas Jefferson were the first two Vice Presidents. But political change impeded its operation. Parties had begun to form in the 1790s; by 1796 they were selecting tickets, designating one candidate for President and another for Vice President. The electors were to support the ticket but at least one was to withhold his vote from the vice-presidential candidate to assure that the de facto presidential nominee became Chief Executive. In 1800 the system backfired. The same number of electors voted for Jefferson and Aaron Burr. Jefferson was clearly the intended standard-bearer. But it was not until the House of Representatives had held thirty-six ballots that he was chosen. Many were appalled that someone never intended for the presidency had almost been elected.[12]

The development of parties was incompatible with the system in other ways. Electors could have assured the victory of their opponent's running mate by giving him their votes. Or a President and Vice President of different parties could be installed, as occurred in 1796. Consequently the system outlined in the Twelfth Amendment was proposed. It provided for separate election of the two officers.[13] Fearing a diminution in the quality of Vice Presidents, some favored abolishing the office.[14] Since "the Vice President will not stand on such high ground in the method proposed as he does in the present mode of a double ballot," Samuel Taggart feared, it was likely that "so great care will not be taken in the selection of a character to fill that office." The Vice President will become a "secondary character," guessed Samuel W. Dana. William Plumer thought "the office of Vice President will be a sinecure [that would] be brought to market and exposed to sale to procure votes for the President." Roger Griswold feared it would be "worse than useless." Attempts to abolish the office failed by a vote of 19 to 12 in the Senate and 85 to 27 in the House of Representatives.[15] Despite these misgivings, Congress approved the Twelfth Amendment and it was ratified on 25 September 1804. The election of subsequent Vice Presidents proved these fears prophetic. No office could continue to claim occupants of the stature of Adams and Jefferson, but the remainder of the nineteenth century witnessed a sharp decline in the caliber of Vice Presidents.

Some prominent men still did accept the second office. John C. Calhoun and Martin Van Buren were among the early Vice Presidents. More often, however, the vice-presidential nomination was awarded as a consolation prize to a defeated faction of a party. The credentials of some nominees were ludicrous. George Clinton, Elbridge Gerry, and Rufus King were in advanced years and failing health. Others had scant experience. The prior public service of Chester A. Arthur consisted of seven years as collector of customs for the port of New York. Garret A. Hobart had never held a post higher than state legislator in New Jersey. Six of the twenty-three Vice Presidents in the century were not nominated to seek another term with the Chief Executive.[16] Six others died in office.[17] On four occasions nineteenth-century Vice Presidents succeeded to the nation's top job following the death of the elected Chief Executive.[18] Their administrations were largely undistinguished. None was nominated to seek an independent full term.

The experience of the first century no doubt gave reason to rue the creation of the office. Vice Presidents posed problems for many Chief Executives. Jefferson ignored Adams's entreaties to undertake diplomatic missions, viewing such activity as inconsistent with his leadership of the opposition party. Burr was no more helpful to Jefferson. Clinton refused to attend Madison's inauguration; Andrew Johnson came to that of Abraham Lincoln but in a state of advanced inebriation. Calhoun cast the decisive vote against Jackson's nomination of Van Buren as ambassador to Great Britain, exacerbated tensions in the administration over the Peggy Eaton affair, and split with the President on states' rights. Arthur denounced President James Garfield to a newspaper editor.[19]

Nor did Vice Presidents always meet a high standard of behavior. Burr killed Hamilton in a duel and was later charged with, though acquitted of, treason for allegedly conspiring to "liberate" the Louisiana Territory from the United States. Richard Johnson seemed more interested in presiding over his tavern than over the Senate. John Breckinridge became a Confederate general and later Secretary of War after his term ended. Schuyler Colfax was nearly impeached for improper financial dealings.[20]

The office rose in the early twentieth century but only incrementally. The first Vice President in that epoch, Theodore Roosevelt, was the most imposing figure to hold the post since Calhoun. Others, if not so prominent as Roosevelt, were already men of some stature when they became the nation's second citizen: Charles Dawes, Charles Curtis, John Nance Garner, Alben Barkley. Dawes had served under three Presidents and received the Nobel Peace Prize. Curtis and Barkley had been Senate Majority Leaders; Garner, Speaker of the House of Representatives.

The vice presidency was still not unduly challenging. But its occupants were occasionally being called upon to perform chores that transcended the constitutionally prescribed function. Thomas Marshall presided over the cabinet while Woodrow Wilson was in Versailles. "Until this administration the principal job of the Vice President was to preside over the Senate and dress up fancy and attend innumerable functions,"[21] wrote Garner. Cabinet meetings became a regular entry on the Vice President's schedule beginning with Garner in 1933 and Roosevelt enlisted his help in lobbying for early New Deal legislation. Garner became the first Vice President to travel abroad.[22] In 1941 Roosevelt appointed his second Vice President, Henry A. Wallace, as chairman of the

Economic Defense Board. Eight years later Congress made the Vice President a statutory member of the National Security Council.

By mid-century the vice presidency was not quite the sinecure of early years but it was still, essentially, a "hollow shell."[23] Herbert Hoover acknowledged no contribution Curtis made to his administration in his memoirs.[24] Garner eventually broke with Roosevelt and challenged him for the nomination in 1940. Wallace lost his chairmanship after frequent quarrels with Secretary of Commerce Jesse Jones and other cabinet members.[25] Other Roosevelt advisers knew of the existence of the atomic bomb, but Harry S. Truman was not informed of it until he became President.[26] Barkley recalls few vice-presidential duties in his autobiography; he seems to have devoted those years almost entirely to courting his second wife.[27]

The vice presidency has offered quipsters a ready source of material. But scholars have long ignored it. In *Congressional Government*, first published in 1885, Woodrow Wilson covered the vice presidency in less than one page. For, he observed, "the chief embarrassment in discussing his office is, that in explaining how little there is to be said about it one has evidently said all there is to say."[28] Seventy years later, Clinton Rossiter gave but seven of three hundred pages of *The American Presidency* to the second office "although even this ratio of forty to one is no measure of the vast gap between them [the President and Vice President] in power and prestige."[29]

Such indifference among scholars may once have been appropriate. It no longer is. Compelling arguments justify a detailed consideration of the vice presidency.

First, the possibility of presidential vacancy attaches importance to the procedures for maintaining the continuity of executive authority. The Vice President stands atop the line of successors in the event of the death, resignation, removal, or inability of the President. "I am nothing, but I may be everything," realized Adams, the first Vice President.[30] And history shows that Vice Presidents have become "everything" through succession with unhappy frequency. Nine Vice Presidents have succeeded to the presidency following the death or resignation of the Chief Executive. As Table 1.1 indicates,

TABLE 1.1
Vice-Presidential Successors to the Presidency

Successor	Date of Vacancy	Time Left in Term		
		Years	Months	Days
John Tyler	4/4/1841	3	11	0
Millard Fillmore	7/9/1850	2	7	23
Andrew Johnson	4/15/1865	3	10	17
Chester A. Arthur	9/19/1881	3	5	13
Theodore Roosevelt	9/14/1901	3	5	18
Calvin Coolidge	8/2/1923	1	7	2
Harry S. Truman	4/12/1945	3	9	8
Lyndon B. Johnson	11/22/1963	1	1	29
Gerald R. Ford	8/9/1974	2	5	11
Total		26	4	1

SOURCE: Adapted from Feerick, *The Twenty-Fifth Amendment*, Appendix D-I.

they have filled in as President for more than twenty-six years. Thus, 21 percent of America's Vice Presidents served as President by succession 14 percent of the time. Incumbency has provided a valuable asset to twentieth-century Presidents by succession. Four of the five have won terms of their own. If these years are added, Vice Presidents have served as Chief Executive more than 22 percent of the time.[31] On other occasions, particularly during the administrations of Garfield, Wilson, and Dwight D. Eisenhower, prolonged presidential illness raised the possibility that the Vice President might have to perform executive duties. The nine instances of presidential succession and three above-mentioned examples of incapacity top a pyramid of "near misses."[32] Presidents are mortals. There is no reason to expect death or incapacity to visit them less often in the future than they have in the past. The likelihood of presidential vacancy makes examination of the office of successor both valid and desirable.

The value of the vice presidency, and sometimes even of candidacy for it, as a political springboard offers a second reason for its study. Occupants of the office in this century have almost invariably been considered presidential timber. Of the seventeen men who held the position from 1901 to 1976, thirteen later sought the presidency or received consideration for the nomination near the time of the convention. The other four might well have, had not circumstances intervened. James S. Sherman died during his campaign for reelection in 1912. Curtis was defeated for reelection and died three years later. Agnew resigned from office and pleaded nolo contendere to criminal charges in 1973. Nelson A. Rockefeller was prevented from seeking the nomination in 1976 by Ford's decision to stand; he died in 1979. The office thus influences future choices for Chief Executive.[33]

The changing duties of the office also recommend review. The functions Vice Presidents discharge vary in each administration. Recent incumbents have performed important governmental and political tasks. The Vice President has opportunities to participate in the decision-making of the executive branch.[34]

Further, the vice presidency deserves study because it offers its occupant a prominent podium and a ready audience. With the exception of the President, presidential candidates, and an occasional cabinet member, senator, congressman or governor, Vice Presidents and vice-presidential candidates receive greater media attention than other public figures. The behavior of those who hold the office and of those who seek it affects the political climate. The rhetoric of Vice Presidents helps define the issues and tenor of political discourse. Their performances may sway electoral outcomes, including those of presidential races.

Finally, study of the vice presidency can illuminate important lessons about the theory and practice of American government and politics. The vice presidency is one lens through which to examine the relationship between different components of the American system.

The last quarter century has produced virtually all the literature on the vice presidency. This small corpus includes several good histories of the office,[35] some useful memoirs and journalistic biographies of recent occupants,[36] and two excellent studies of presidential succession.[37] Yet the published work has left major gaps. First, existing discussions do not include a careful analytical study of the office. The general works on the topic have capably reviewed the history of the office and occupants of the vice presidency, but have enhanced little our understanding of the operations of the position as a political institution. Second, they have virtually ignored the making of Vice Presidents. Studies have exhaustively described the initial electoral scheme but have skimmed quickly over the selection, campaign roles, and electoral impact of candidates for the second office. Finally, they have failed to relate the vice presidency and its recent evolution to changes in other political institutions and practices. Rather, they have typically examined the office as an isolated entity. Tunnel vision is an unfortunate characteristic of much recent American scholarship. But a satisfactory account of the development of the vice presidency depends on locating the office in the general landscape of American government and politics.

This book attempts to help fill a void. My mission is not to relate the history of the office from 1953 to 1981. Rather, I use the experiences and activities of Vice Presidents during that period to examine the modern vice presidency as a political institution. This book will argue that the vice presidency has evolved into a position of new importance. This view is neither novel nor universally accepted. The distinctive character of the present effort comes largely in its location of the factors promoting this rise in status. It is not sufficient to assign all responsibility to the frequency of presidential vacancy or to the personalities of particular Presidents and Vice Presidents, as is often done. These factors have certainly played a part. But the transformation of the office has depended primarily on dramatic changes in American political institutions since the New Deal. The nationalization of politics, the increased expectations of government, the rise of the presidency, the decline of parties, and the acceptance of an international role are prominent among the developments that have rearranged the terrain of civic life. The vice presidency could not stand remote from shifts of such consequence.

The periods chosen for this study, of Vice Presidents since 1953 and of changes in American politics since 1932, are neither arbitrary nor beyond challenge. Students of politics have assigned different dates to the growth of the vice presidency. Irving Williams traces the rise from the turn of the century. Nelson W. Polsby claims that "we can date the modern Vice-Presidency from April 12, 1945, the day Franklin Roosevelt died." Rossiter offers 1948 as the relevant year.[38]

It is not clear, nor crucial to this discussion, which, if any, of those dates is correct. I do not claim that the office did not gain in importance until 1953. Choice of that year allows this review to begin roughly where the last major published study ends.[39] Further, developments just prior to 1953 make it a genuine point of demarcation. Modern technology, particularly reliance on the airplane and television since then, has changed the nature of government and politics. Ratification of the Twenty-second Amendment in 1951 prevented future Presidents who had served six years or been twice elected from seeking another term as Chief Executive. Subsequent Vice Presidents have thus been able to plan their careers with some knowledge of when the President would leave office. The years since the beginning of the New Deal introduced radical changes in the bounds of government and the practices of politics. Few historical changes have precise beginnings and endings, but Roosevelt's election and subsequent four terms did inaugurate a new era.

The next chapter, an overview of changes in American politics and government since the New Deal, provides the context in which to assess the evolution of the second office. The selection, campaign roles, and electoral impact of vice-presidential candidates are the topics of chapters three through five. The next three chapters assess the major functions of the office. Chapter nine considers the Vice President's role as presidential successor. The filling of vice-presidential vacancies through the procedures of section two of the Twenty-fifth Amendment is the subject of chapter ten. Chapter eleven discusses the extent to which the office has become a presidential springboard. Chapter twelve evaluates various reform proposals, setting the stage for my summary and conclusion.

2

★ ★

The Changing Political Context

The New Deal years metamorphosed American political institutions. The blueprint designed by the founding fathers remained the underlying structure of American democracy. But the force of events dramatically altered the way government actually operated. Power flowed to Washington. The federal government absorbed some functions the cities and states had performed. Moreover, it assumed responsibilities previously thought outside government jurisdiction. It became more active in international affairs. These trends created a new political context that assigned the presidency greater prominence and debilitated the parties. These developments gave the vice presidency the opportunity to grow.

This chapter first outlines the historical process by which power accrued at the center. I then examine the consequences for the presidency and the parties. Space constraints prevent a comprehensive treatment; this brief discussion is intended merely to sketch the context in which the growth of the vice presidency occurred.

Overview

American government before 1933 bore faint resemblance to what exists today. Laissez-faire principles were dominant in the 1920s. Political institutions were weak at all levels, their activities covering a narrow realm. The federal government was particularly passive. Business was the god of the epoch, the federal government its eager and acquiescent servant. "The central theme of the politics of the 1920's," William E. Leuchtenburg has observed, was "whether the business interest, given full support by a co-operative government, could maintain prosperity and develop social policies which would redound to the benefit not merely of itself but of the whole American people."[1]

The presidency was no sinecure but neither was it the vital center of political life. Calvin Coolidge had once forecast that "four-fifths of all of our troubles in this life would disappear . . . if we would only sit down and keep still."[2] That philosophy summarized the strategy of virtually every Chief Executive after the Civil War save for Theodore Roosevelt and Woodrow Wilson.

Parties existed primarily on the state and local levels. National organizations were weak and fragmented. The Republican party was dominant. The protector of business, it also enjoyed the support of a "coalition of diverse elements"[3] that virtually spanned the electorate. It won six of eight presidential elections between 1900 and 1928 and thirteen of sixteen congressional contests between 1900 and 1930. The Democrats commanded little strength outside the South.

That political universe collapsed under new pressures. Increased domestic demands born of economic hardship heightened expectations of federal government. The inability to remain isolated from the perils of international affairs forced America to assume an active role in world events. Each factor merits separate examination.

The Depression brought new issues to the top of the political agenda. The trauma of massive unemployment, ruined fortunes, and bread lines shook confidence in traditional approaches. Economic collapse toppled business from the pedestal it had occupied and dissipated the longstanding antipathy to the state. The crisis required a coordinated program, not an independent solution by each state. Only Washington could engineer such a response. The failure of President Herbert Hoover to act effectively contributed to the landslide victory in 1932 of his opponent, Franklin D. Roosevelt.

Roosevelt proposed, and Congress enacted, programs designed to speed recovery. The legislation of the first 100 days of his term consisted of fifteen major bills devised to restore economic health. In 1935 a prolific Congress enacted a second series of administration proposals of lasting significance.[4]

The success of Roosevelt's response transformed the conduct of government. It gave respectability to the concept of activist national leadership. The extent of the federal intervention remained a contentious issue for some years. But the success of the New Deal committed the Democratic party to the active view and won some adherents among Eastern Republicans. By the 1950s, Eric F. Goldman has written, "a greater and greater percentage of the population decided that the Half-Century of Revolution in domestic affairs was here to stay and that it should be forwarded."[5]

Elections confirmed the popularity of the New Deal. In 1934 the Republicans expected the substantial gains that usually came to the out party. Instead, they lost thirteen seats in the House and nine in the Senate from already shrunken minorities. Two years later, Roosevelt's unprecedented landslide— with 60 percent of the vote he carried every state but Maine and Vermont (eight electoral votes)—offered further proof of support for active government. By 1937, only twenty-one Republicans remained in the Senate and eighty-nine in the House.

Not only did the concept of active government win popular acceptance in the elections of the mid-1930s, but it also gained legal ratification by the Supreme Court in 1937. The Court had presented the major obstacle to the success of the New Deal by declaring important statutes unconstitutional. Emboldened by his electoral victory, Roosevelt proposed his Judiciary Reform Bill to reconstitute the Court to provide a majority amenable to legislation he favored.[6] The attempt failed, but the Court, perhaps alarmed by the attacks, began to accept New Deal measures. It announced a double standard of scrutiny, by which it would *presume* the constitutionality of economic legislation while reserving its strictest review for laws alleged to violate civil rights and liberties necessary to the proper conduct of the political and judicial process.[7] The Court's shift in interest had a dramatic impact. It enabled an activist President with a malleable legislative majority to frame social and economic measures with little threat of judicial veto. And it suggested that civil rights and liberties, issues not likely to receive sympathetic treatment by Congress, might still find a prominent place on the national agenda. At once, the Court allowed political branches to deal with socio-economic problems and sowed the seeds of judicial activism in new fields.

The elephantine growth of federal bureaucracy was a second byproduct of the New Deal. Management of new programs required new structures. Government employment of civil servants increased dramatically, from 572,091 in 1933 to 1,014,117 seven years later.[8] Once established, bureaucracies grew, often regardless of the continued relevance of their functions. Interest groups pushed for extension of the departments in their areas. Congress organized its committees to parallel government agencies. Not only did this provide a rational arrangement for oversight, but also fertile fields for patronage.

Finally, the New Deal heralded a shift in the balance of power between national and state government.[9] Washington encroached on areas once considered the domain of the states. Congress extended the reach of the federal government by passing measures on health, law enforcement, education, working conditions, and welfare. The federal share of domestic expenditures rose markedly during the New Deal.

The accrual of power and responsibility to the center outlived the New Deal. The welfare state had become necessary for the fulfilment of the American dream. In 1949 President Harry S. Truman told Congress:

> The Government must work with industry, labor, and the farmers in keeping our economy running at full speed. The Government must see that every American has a chance to obtain his fair share of our increasing abundance. These responsibilities go hand in hand.[10]

President Dwight D. Eisenhower, too, accepted the propriety of governmental intervention. When recession threatened in 1953, he promised, "When it becomes clear that the Government has to step in, as far as I am concerned, the full power of Government, of Government credit, and of everything the Government has will move in to see that there is no widespread unemployment."[11] His Vice President, Richard M. Nixon, proudly told a Russian audience six years later:

> The day has passed in the United States when the unemployed were left to shift for themselves. The same can be said for the aged, the sick and others who are unable to earn enough to provide an adequate standard of living.[12]

The twenty years following Roosevelt's death witnessed a consolidation of New Deal programs. Truman, Eisenhower, and John F. Kennedy and the corresponding Congresses accepted, with differing enthusiasm, the viability of social legislation. Allotments for social security, education, and farmers increased. Government ventured, too, into new fields of regulation and new aid projects.[13]

Developments in the mid-1960s gave impetus to trends initiated by the New Deal. President Lyndon B. Johnson and a sympathetic Congress legislated Great Society measures that extended benefits to blacks, workers, the poor, and the aged. Expenditures on income security, health, education, and veterans rose sharply.[14] Government regulations proliferated and bureaucracy experienced modest growth. This second burst of government activity left states and cities more dependent on Washington.[15] Disillusionment with these events grew in the 1970s. But the institutional structures resisted dismantling.

Responses to the Depression initiated one centripetal pull. The coming of World War II provided a second lasting source of Washington's new power. Traditionally, America had avoided international involvement. The roots of isolationism stretched deep into American history. Introversion was possible so long as oceans posed impenetrable obstacles to those who might challenge American security. By the late 1930s geography was no longer so reliable a defense. German aggression threatened the safety of America's traditional allies and of her commercial vessels. The United States remained cautious in deference to prevailing sentiment. So strong was isolationist feeling that 188 congressmen voted for the Ludlow Amendment which, except when the United States was invaded, would have required majority approval in a referendum as a prerequisite for going to war.[16] The idea had impressive popular support, too; between 75 percent and 58 percent of the American people favored it in Gallup Polls between 1935 and 1939.[17]

German military aggression generated little new enthusiasm for internationalism. In 1939, staggering majorities opposed providing economic or military aid to England and France.[18] The attack on Pearl Harbor, however, made active participation inevitable, an effort which dominated American life for most of the next four years. America's involvement in World War II suggested that retreat from world affairs would not be among its future options. After the war, the United States and the Soviet Union emerged as the world's leading powers. They had submerged their ideological differences during the war when conflict with Germany made them temporary allies. With the war over, their animosity surfaced.

Exacerbated tensions with Russia gave America incentive to assume a world role. The Soviets sought, according to common American perceptions, to export widely their political and economic system. By the autumn of 1946, America was committed to an active policy in foreign affairs. Secretary of State James Byrnes announced:

> The people of the United States did their best to stay out of European wars on the theory that they should mind their own business and that they had no business in Europe. . . . They have concluded that if they must help finish every European war, it would be better for them to do their part to prevent the starting of an European war.[19]

The Truman Doctrine, articulated on March 12, 1947, stated, in part, "that it must be the policy of the United States to support free peoples who are resisting attempted subjugation by armed minorities or by outside pressures."[20] American foreign policy was no longer anchored in isolationism. When North Korean forces crossed the 38th parallel into South Korea, Truman promptly sent American soldiers to indicate that America would not be indifferent to communist advance. Domestic events, too, revealed the new interest in foreign affairs. Congressmen suspected the loyalties of various government employees. Representative Richard M. Nixon spearheaded an investigation by the House Un-American Activities Committee of Alger Hiss, a former State Department official. Senator Joseph R. McCarthy sprayed accusations of perfidy and conspiracy with abandon during the first half of the fifties.

With the advent of the Cold War, world affairs became the major preoccupation. Between September 1949 and September 1972, Gallup asked forty-eight times: "What do you think is the most important problem facing the American people today?" Some foreign policy issue headed the list on thirty-two occasions.[21]

The international responsibilities America assumed were undertaken amid, and necessitated by, the growth of the technology of war. At the end of World War II only the United States had atomic weapons in its arsenal. The USSR soon joined that exclusive club. "In an era of rockets and nuclear weapons," historian Robert Wiebe points out, America "was now uniquely vulnerable."[22] Both countries devoted inordinate resources to the development of more sophisticated missiles. The arms race accompanied the Cold War as a new reality of world politics. War had become increasingly dangerous, defense increasingly expensive.

America was conscious of the risk of nuclear war. It was not, however, reluctant to deploy forces abroad. The Truman Doctrine retained its viability as government policy well into the 1960s. Kennedy restated it in his Inaugural Address, using more eloquent language to convey a more absolute policy. He declared:

> We shall pay any price, bear any burden, meet any hardship, support any friend, oppose any foe to assure the survival and the success of liberty. This much we pledge— and more.[23]

This pledge produced, with mixed results, American military and economic intervention around the globe.

Reaction against American activities in Southeast Asia tempered enthusiasm for future military action. No longer was the United States willing to "pay any price" to prevent a communist advance. But the isolationism of the 1920s did not return. America's world prominence and the growth of technology denied such a course all feasibility. The United States pressed for detente with Russia and China, peace in the Middle East, racial justice in Africa, and resistance to Eurocommunism.

The Presidency

Washington's new eminence, brought on by domestic pressures and foreign responsibilities, modified the operations of major political institutions. The presidency was the chief beneficiary; its growth would later make possible the rise of the vice presidency. In both domestic and foreign affairs America looked to the Chief Executive for leadership. He became the embodiment of the nation. As George Reedy has written:

> Often the terms "nation" and "president" are used interchangeably without any awareness of the fact. When we say that "the nation" is doing something we usually mean that it is acting in accord with presidential directives. When we say that "a new national policy has been declared" we mean that it has been declared by the President. When we speak of a "buoyant confident" nation, our mental image is usually that of a buoyant, confident president. Conversely, when we speak of a "strong" president, we mean one who has mobilized the nation in his behalf and when we speak of a "weak" president, we mean one who is presiding over a divided nation.[24]

The rise of presidential power had a certain institutional logic. Of the three branches of the national government the presidency was the only true candidate for leadership. The Court, as indicated above, has given substance to the skeletal principles of American democracy in significant fashion. Often, it has outpaced the other two branches in guiding the shape of the future. Its decisions have helped form public morality. But the judiciary is a frail institution, lacking the power to coerce and the necessary political legitimacy to legislate too vigorously over too wide a spectrum. It depends on the other two branches and on public opinion for the acceptance and enforcement of its rulings. Moreover, the American Constitution seems, in its emphasis on decision-making by elected officials, to assign the judiciary a modest, though still substantial role.[25]

Nor could Congress be the fount of leadership. It has at times initiated domestic change. But a large assembly is ill-equipped to lead a nation. Its unsuitability is compounded when, as in the United States, power is diffused, parties are nonideological, and incentives to legislate are mitigated by the superior rewards of other activities.

But the President did not become the system's cynosure strictly by default. Institutional design and circumstance endowed his office with resources and reasons to assume such a position. The President had, first of all, most incentive to respond to group demands. The Democratic coalition first fashioned by Roosevelt in 1932 included segments of the electorate most dependent on government. Political survival required a Democratic Chief Executive to consider and act upon their pleas. But neither, until recently, could a Republican administration ignore issues of concern to these groups. Those with strongest attachments to the concept of the welfare state resided in the states with the most electoral votes. Their support became important to candidates of both parties. Since 1932, Democratic presidential candidates have endorsed activist domestic policies, a course Republicans also followed from 1940 to 1960. Further, the President was best equipped to coordinate federal programs. The difficulty and importance of synchronizing governmental outputs increased as Washington became more active. The President could best lend order to national policy consideration. He could assess the relative merits of competing programs and set priorities.

The increased salience of world events also contributed to the ascendancy of the Chief Executive. Here Presidents had commonly received greater deference than in the domestic sphere. But direction of foreign policy provided little power so long as isolationism prevailed. As external affairs assumed greater importance, so, too, did the officer who had to deal with them. Development of sophisticated weapons inflated presidential importance. The new technology of war modified the rules of international politics. A diplomatic blunder or misunderstanding could result in global destruction. Not only did the President have, as Wiebe puts it, "continuing access to the most formidable military resources in the world's history."[26] He also had the responsibility to prevent their use. In a sense, the President had become the direct custodian of the lives of all Americans.

Finally, the President was in the best position to mobilize support for his actions and programs. Three resources produced this capacity. First, the prestige attached to the presidency is unmatched by that of any other American office. The President is the best-known and most respected public figure. Adulation of the Chief Executive begins early; he is the first official of whom children are aware.[27] Unless they stumble badly, Presidents enjoy considerable public esteem. For most years, beginning in 1946, the Gallup organization has conducted a survey to determine the men Americans most admired. On twenty-four of thirty-four times, the President headed the list.[28] A 1958 poll found that of all historical figures, Americans would most like to invite to dinner five American Presidents—Abraham Lincoln, Franklin Roosevelt, Eisenhower, Washington, and Truman.[29]

Secondly, the President's control of important patronage helps him win assent from other politicians. He can distribute offices, funds, contracts, and honors to build majorities for his projects. No other politician has comparable resources to offer. Goods capable of allocation alone do not, of course, guarantee that a particular President will exert influence. "A President's persuasiveness with other men in government depends on something more than his advantages for bargaining," Richard E. Neustadt points out. "The men he would persuade must be convinced in their own minds that he has skill and will enough to *use* his advantages."[30] But control of "advantages" provides the Chief Executive with at least a head start over other political actors.

Finally, the President's easy access to the media has enabled him to build and exploit his prestige. Roosevelt first used the media for that purpose. Whereas Herbert Hoover held only 64 press sessions during his four years in office, Roosevelt conducted 337 in his first term, 374 in his second, and 279 in his third.[31] The radio gave Roosevelt an instrument of even greater value; it enabled him to communicate directly with voters.

Development of television has enhanced the position of the Chief Executive. Others clamor for a few seconds on the evening news. Their press conferences attract few auditors. But the President can claim prime network time for an address virtually at will, as the following data suggest.

TABLE 2.1
Prime Time Television Appearances of Some Recent Presidents

President	No. of Appearances	Period Covered
Eisenhower	23	96 months
Kennedy	10	34 months
Johnson	24	62 months
Nixon	32	first 40 months

SOURCE: Fred W. Friendly, Foreword to *Presidential Television* by N. Minow, J. B. Martin, and L. Mitchell, p. ix.

The changing context of American politics made the rise of the presidency inevitable. That he became the leading actor on the political stage was natural. Assumption of such a role had consequences for the operation of American government.

The founding fathers had expected Congress to initiate the legislative process by passing laws, and for the President to react either by signing or vetoing the bills. Roosevelt, in a sense, reversed this relationship. He submitted a program to which Congress responded. In doing so, Roosevelt advanced the power of his office not only well beyond that of other branches of government but also beyond that of any of his predecessors. Roosevelt preempted for his office the task of annually setting the national legislative agenda. His successors have followed suit. Each new Chief Executive was not, of course, entirely free to shape his own package of programs. He was compelled to accept and generally to expand popular programs. Not to have done so would, for most, have been tantamount to committing political suicide. Accordingly, Presidents from both parties have requested spending more on social security and veterans' benefits.

Different Presidents left their own distinctive gloss, too. Truman, for instance, called successfully for legislation on public housing and to raise minimum wages and unsuccessfully for civil rights laws, national health insurance, and federal aid to education. The Eisenhower administration proposed bills to construct highways and school buildings. Kennedy pushed the civil rights and tax reduction acts. Congress passed both following his death. Johnson offered the package of measures that comprised the War on Poverty.[32]

Increasingly, the public began to look to the executive branch for solutions both to problems government had avoided in the past and to those that changing circumstances now first presented. The creation of four new cabinet departments— Health, Education and Welfare (HEW) in 1953, Housing and Urban Development (HUD) in 1966, Transportation in 1967, and Energy in 1977—either recognized the involvement of the federal government in a new area or signalled its intention to assume a leadership role.[33] Other problems which did not merit a department were met with presidential committees—on water resources, youth employment, physical fitness and so forth. No matter that issues such as these would seem to have natural homes in the departments of Interior, Labor, and HEW respectively. Action by the President, not just by the executive branch, was expected; "Everybody now expects the man inside the White House to do something about everything," Professor Neustadt wrote in 1960.[34]

The increase of government activity gave the President new sources of leverage over other political actors. As government performed more services and spent more money, the executive branch had more goods to allocate. Possible sources of patronage proliferated. Presidents who marshaled these resources competently became more formidable.[35] But the expanded role the President assumed also increased his stake in legislative outcomes. The executive branch had added incentive to secure passage of projects it formulated. The President's programs and prestige depended in part on his success as a legislative leader. The Chief Executive and his lieutenants accordingly devoted more time and effort to congressional liaison.

The increased importance of foreign affairs not only necessitated the growth of the presidency but also altered considerably the nature of the job. Presidents became preoccupied with international issues, so crucial were they in the nuclear age. Advisers dealing with those matters—the secretaries of state and defense and the director of the National Security Council (NSC)—had easy access to the Oval Office. Domestic assistants, with rare exceptions, could claim little of the President's time. The feasibility of air travel enabled foreign leaders to visit Washington for long talks. The President reciprocated. Foreign policy rarely had entered into political discussion. It became a regular feature of political discourse from 1940. Presidential aspirants, accordingly, sought to develop and display impressive credentials in foreign policy and to project the image of a statesman. Senators with higher ambitions commonly sought appointment to the Foreign Relations Committee. Governors took trips abroad or spoke on international problems.

The rise of the presidency found its occupant pulled in diverse directions. To be an effective world figure he needed to protect his image as a diplomat. To be a successful legislative leader he had to engage in political bargaining. To discharge his executive functions he had to immerse himself in administration. To retain his political base he had to be attentive to party chores. To mobilize public opinion he had to be a credible spokesman.

These responsibilities provided the President with problems as well as power. Some conflicted. All demanded heavy commitments of time and energy. As Rexford Tugwell pointed out, "A president cannot be king today, prime minister tomorrow, and permanent head of the civil service all the time."[36] The Chief Executive could not fulfill all of his duties alone. The White House staff in March 1933 consisted of thirty-seven persons. Roosevelt augmented this meager work force by borrowing personnel from various departments.[37] "The President needs help,"[38] reported the Committee on Administrative Management, which was chaired by Louis Brownlow, in 1936. Acting on its recommendation, Congress authorized the President to create the Executive Office of the President and to appoint up to six administrative assistants. Congress, at once, confirmed what Roosevelt had been doing independently and enabled the further growth of the presidential office.

During the subsequent decades, the White House staff and the Executive Office of the President swelled in size and significance. The Bureau of the Budget employed forty-five people in 1939. Six years later it numbered 564.[39] The Employment Act of 1946 created the Council of Economic Advisers (CEA). The next year Congress produced the NSC. By November 1972, the White House staff had grown to 600 members.[40] Originally its members were generalists. But by the

1950s and 1960s specialized slots existed for a press secretary, legislative liaison, speechwriter and often a chief of staff. Development of the staff gave the President the capability to handle his increased responsibilities. Clinton Rossiter noted: "Thanks to the Executive Office, the Presidency has adapted itself to the exigencies of the modern state at least as well as the courts and far more successfully than Congress."[41] Staff support enabled the President to know, influence, and control more.

The evolution of the presidential staff produced other effects, some of which were not intended. Veterans of the presidential campaign soon populated the staff. Presidents came to rely on these aides as their chief advisers and administrators. After all, long and close political and sometimes personal ties linked the Chief Executive to these associates. Eventually, ranking White House aides gained an unintended predominance. Roosevelt's Executive Order establishing the White House office had stated explicitly that the assistants were not superior to cabinet members. It decreed: "In no event shall the administrative assistants be interposed between the President and the head of any department or agency or between the President and any one of the divisions in the Executive Office of the President."[42] In practice, most cabinet members found themselves subordinated to the top White House aides. The President's long ties to the staff were reinforced by their physical proximity. When the President wanted to discuss a problem or give a directive he was more likely to turn to the man whose office was a few paces away than to the cabinet official across town.

Ironically, by its very growth, the presidency produced one of its biggest problems. The executive branch had become too big by the 1970s, if not earlier. No longer could the President keep track of all or most of its activities. The bureaucracy swallowed presidential directives and frustrated his programmatic and administrative desires. As Tugwell pointed out:

> The theoretical ability to superintend the administrative establishment, when any novel initiations are undertaken, encounters the resistance of a huge bureaucracy; and if not resistance, then inertia. Orders from a president are smothered by interpretation as they pass down from desk to desk. There is delay, and, often, outright and organized opposition.[43]

The usual presidential response was to issue a clarion call for governmental reorganization.[44] Roosevelt commissioned the Brownlow Committee; Truman and Eisenhower, the Hoover Committees; Johnson, the Heinemann Committee; Nixon, the Ash Committee. The latter was most ambitious.[45] It called for redistributing the functions of the domestic departments among new departments of Community Development, Economic Affairs, Human Resources, and Natural Resources. This plan, like its predecessors, ran afoul of the congressional, bureaucratic, and pressure groups whose vested interests were jeopardized. Carter made the inefficiency of government organization a cornerstone of his campaign. Yet he, too, soon seemed reconciled to refashioning the rough edges rather than undertaking a wholesale assault.

The strong presidency bred imperious behavior in its occupants. Johnson disregarded the congressional prerogative to declare war by sending more than a half million soldiers to Vietnam essentially on his own initiative. He could justify that action, in part, by the Gulf of Tonkin Resolution. Presidential action could not have succeeded without tacit congressional approval. What made his actions magisterial was the self-righteous disregard of the formal constitutional requirements. Nixon, however, carried this defiant attitude further. He conducted secret bombing in Cambodia, impounded funds to frustrate the legislative will, and authorized and/or shielded the illegal acts loosely known as "Watergate."[46]

Congress began to redress the imbalance in the 1970s.[47] It imposed new constraints on the President. It passed the War Powers Act in 1973 forcing the Chief Executive to suspend military activity after sixty days unless authorized by Congress to continue. The Congressional Budget and Impoundment Control Act of 1974 introduced a larger legislative role in setting and overseeing national priorities. Congressional investigations of White House abuses of power produced Nixon's resignation and would almost certainly have resulted in his removal upon impeachment and conviction.

The Senate exercised a long-dormant power and rejected Nixon's nominations of Judges Clement Haynsworth and G. Harold Carswell to the Supreme Court, the first such refusals since 1930. More significant was the Senate's treatment of several Carter sought to name to high positions. Its recalcitrance forced Theodore C. Sorensen to withdraw as the proposed director of the Central Intelligence Agency (CIA). Griffin Bell and Paul Warnke gained their posts only after serious opposition. The three cases represented a break with the general practice of giving the President virtual carte blanche to choose his associates.

Factors that had prevented Congress from becoming the fount of leadership as government became more active also reduced the President's ability to act as legislative leader. The structure of Congress imposed one set of limitations. American legislative power is diffused. Presidential initiatives in most areas need the approval of both Houses. Committees are able to amend and block proposals. Until recently the filibuster offered a few senators the opportunity to prevent Senate action on a bill. The seniority system rewarded some of the most conservative members, the Southern Democrats, with committee chairmanships and the power to frustrate the will of more progressive Presidents; key committees were bastions of conservative strength. These institutions often prevented Truman and Kennedy from achieving their legislative goals. Recent assaults have made them less potent. Yet obstacles to presidential domination still abound.

The lack of ideological cohesion of American legislative parties not only prevents them from constructing and enacting a coherent program, but also makes them less likely to accept the one the President offers. Constituency, not party, shapes the programmatic inclinations of the lawmakers.[48] Party votes—those in which a majority of Democrats oppose a majority of Republicans—are the exception rather than the rule.[49]

Further, increasingly legislators have little incentive, other than ideological preference, to support presidential programs. The number of competitive seats in the House has dwindled. Legislators have voted themselves sufficient perquisites—larger staffs, more trips to their constituencies, use of the franking privilege—to make electoral defeat less probable. Increased committee and subcommittee assignments have allowed them to develop advantageous symbiotic ties with bureaucracies and interest groups.[50] Various forms of presidential patronage accordingly carry reduced value. Moreover, congressmen who do share the President's policy preferences generally have little incentive to perform the legislative chores necessary to move a bill to passage. As David Mayhew explains: "The congressman as position-taker is a speaker rather than a doer. The electoral requirement is not that he make pleasing things happen but that he make pleasing judgmental statements. The position itself is the political commodity."[51]

Despite successful efforts to check the power of the presidency, it remains by far the preeminent office. Reaction to Watergate and Vietnam, built-in structural features of American democracy, and the growth of bureaucracy and of legislative independence have made the job of the Chief Executive more difficult. But the office continues to be the focal point of government. No intelligible discussion of American politics can proceed very far without reference to it. All other political institutions necessarily adapted to accommodate the growth of the presidency.

The Parties

The parties were no exception. They had been formidable institutions during much of American history. Not only did they help structure campaigns, mobilize support and shape the alternatives offered, they also provided highly reliable indicators of the probable outcomes of elections. The events initiated by the New Deal that gave new stature to the presidency also brought three fundamental changes to the parties. They precipitated the decline of the party organizations, transformed their bases of support, and weakened partisan allegiances of voters. These affected the selection and activities of Vice Presidents and candidates for the office.

Traditionally, American political parties had been decentralized, with power residing in their state and local organizations. The immigrants who came to America early in the twentieth century, and the blacks who emigrated to the North, had provided the basis for the development of local machines. The machines had performed needed services for destitute groups—education, jobs and so forth—in return for political support. Political bosses controlled nominations at all levels of government, including the choice of the presidential candidates.

From the 1930s on, party declined. As federal government began to provide more services citizens began to look to Washington, not to City Hall. Washington was the source of social security checks and veterans' benefits. Indeed, as the notion of a managed economy gained acceptance, the federal government attempted to regulate unemployment and prices, too. Citizens expressed their grievances by mail to the

President. Increasingly, congressmen assumed the ombuds-
man function once performed by the local machine. The
strength of the machine depended upon its ability to provide
valued services for those dependent upon it. When party organizations could no longer deliver goods they could no longer
deliver votes. Candidates, accordingly, became less reliant
on party to secure office.

Development of technology contributed to the erosion of
the party base. Not only did the party machine have less to
offer candidates; other sources had more. The growth of mass
media, first radio, then television, offered an alternative route
to reach voters. As Stanley Kelley, Jr. has noted:

> The power of the boss depended in part on his monopoly,
> for political purposes, of ties with the electorate. He had a
> kind of independence, because, at any given moment, the
> relationships he had built with his bloc of votes could not
> be duplicated. The mass media of communication offer a
> channel through which leaders can appeal directly to the
> voter and over the head of the boss. His monopoly of power
> is broken.[52]

Exploitation of the media enabled candidates to challenge
the organization favorite in the primaries and to succeed in
the general election without the party. Development of survey research techniques in the 1930s gave candidates access
to information more reliable than that precinct captains and
ward leaders could provide. Specialists formed firms that offered campaign services for hire. They could provide the
strategy, organization, and other skills the party organization
once monopolized.[53] Finally, aspirants found independent
sources of campaign financing, eliminating yet another traditional party function.

In short, parties lost their exclusive control of the resources
necessary for campaign success. As Gerald Pomper points
out:

In elections, the parties are becoming only one of many
actors, not the chief contestants. Parties are wooed by ambitious candidates, but so are the mass media. Parties contribute funds to these candidates, but so do private individuals and interest groups. Parties campaign for their
nominees, but so do labor unions, and often more widely
and more effectively. Parties sponsor candidates, but so do
conservationists, business groups, and ideologues of various persuasions.[54]

These trends found encouragement at the presidential level
in the proliferation of primaries. Candidates used primaries
sporadically and with mixed effect for most of their history.
That changed in the 1960s. John Kennedy entered and won
seven in 1960. His success won him delegate support in those
states, but more important, it convinced leaders elsewhere to
back him.[55] Since then, the number of states holding primaries and the number of delegates chosen in this fashion have
increased markedly.

TABLE 2.2
Growth of Presidential Primaries, 1968-1976

Primaries	1968	1972	1976
Democratic Party			
No. of States	17	23	30
% of Convention Delegates	37.5	60.5	72.6
Republican Party			
No. of States	16	22	29
% of Convention Delegates	34.3	52.7	67.9

SOURCE: A. Ranney, *Participation in American Presidential Nominations,*
1976, p. 6.

The growth of primaries altered the rules of candidate selection, reducing the role of political leaders in choosing the
standard-bearers. First, primaries invited voters to participate

in the selection process. The outcome did not determine delegate distributions in all states. Nor did the candidate who did best in these tests always win the nomination. Turnouts were relatively low. But in any event, primaries involved more citizens in presidential nominations.[56]

Second, campaigning for the presidency became a four-year affair. Astute candidates began early to develop grass-roots support and skeletal organizations. Presidential aspirants could hardly hope to win the nomination by depending upon contacts with party leaders; after 1968 that strategy seemed especially obsolete. John Kennedy was the first to realize the new rules; he began preparing for the 1960 race before the 1956 returns were in. Senator Barry M. Goldwater, Nixon, Senator George McGovern, and Carter all followed suit. The failure of the candidacies of Senator Lyndon B. Johnson in 1960, Governor Nelson A. Rockefeller in 1968, Senator Edmund S. Muskie in 1972, and Senator Hubert H. Humphrey in 1976, and to some extent that of Senator Howard Baker in 1980 suggested the poverty of the old strategy.

The primaries helped open presidential politics to those previously excluded. Traditionally governors of major states, congressional leaders and cabinet members had dominated competition for nominations. They were most likely to have friendly relations with, or bargaining leverage over, the political leaders who determined the outcome. Their administrative experience was valued. They were most likely to be nationally known. The shift of power to Washington helped senators and hurt governors. Unlike members of the House, senators had some visibility; unlike governors, they were thought to be knowledgeable about national problems and foreign affairs.[57]

The primaries altered further standards of availability to favor those with little responsibility. Success in the preconvention tests required strenuous campaigning. Politicians with taxing duties elsewhere could not devote the time to electioneering. Thus, sitting governors fared poorly under these new rules; former governors, like Carter and Reagan, did well.[58] The ambitions of congressional leaders—Lyndon Johnson (1960) and Howard Baker (1980)—suffered; those of some backbenchers—John Kennedy (1960), Goldwater (1964), and McGovern (1972)—prospered. Aside from Presidents, the primary system seemed unsuited for members of the executive branch; some former members—Nixon (1968) and Bush (1980)—did well. Primaries provided events inviting national media coverage. They allowed some relative unknowns—McCarthy (1968), McGovern (1972), Carter and Udall (1976), and Bush (1980)—to gain wide exposure courtesy of the national news media.[59]

The attention given primaries accelerated the decline of the political convention. One perceptive analyst who foresaw this trend in the 1950s traced it to the development of mass media.[60] Parties were less likely to ignore the evidence the media provided concerning the relative strength of prospective candidates.

The convention once had been a veritable decision-making organ. By the 1960s, attention had shifted to the primaries. Conventions retained some decision-making significance; occasionally candidates collected the final votes necessary for nomination there. More often, the results of the primaries created a "bandwagon effect" which enabled one candidate to emerge before the quadrennial session began.[61] Some observers expected the convention to regain influence in the Democratic party at least, following that party's decision to allocate delegate support in primary states according to a proportional formula. These predictions may be realized in some future contests. The force of bandwagons suggests, however, that nominations probably will continue to be decided prior to the convention.

Finally, the primaries forced candidates to develop their own campaign teams well before the convention. The successful nominee tended to rely on his tested organization in the campaign as well. The party, accordingly, lost responsibility for managing the race.[62] Nor did it retrieve this function when its President sought reelection. The enlarged White House staff had ample room for those the Chief Executive had relied on through the primaries. Campaign direction came from 1600 Pennsylvania Avenue, not from party headquarters. Never was this so clear as in Nixon's reelection effort in 1972. Commented Senator Robert Dole, then the chairman of the Republican National Committee: "The Republican Party was not only not involved in Watergate, but it wasn't involved in the nomination, the convention, the campaign, the election, or the inauguration."[63]

Ironically, the proliferation of presidential primaries weakened the presidency in one sense. Without primaries, a President could use available patronage to control the party apparatus to assure his renomination. The preconvention tests encouraged challenges to the Chief Executive from within his own party. A poor showing by the President could prove sufficiently embarrassing to induce him to step aside. By 1976, both parties chose enough delegates through primaries so that a President's renomination was no longer automatic. Accordingly, both Ford and Carter had to overcome strong contests from prominent political leaders to secure the nomination.

Party organizations have declined since the New Deal. The state and local machines are mere shadows of their powerful ancestors. One recent development, however, suggests the possibility of some revival. Federal financing of presidential campaigns was first introduced in the 1976 elections. Candidates seem likely to accept the funds offered by government rather than soliciting their own resources. But receipt of federal money commits them to a lower level of campaign expenditure than was common in recent campaigns. Candidates can no longer rely on vast amounts of money for the general election. Accordingly, national leaders have new incentive to encourage at least to a point the growth of state and local organizations able to mobilize support. Such a development would infuse the party organizations with new importance. It would not return their past eminence.

The New Deal changed the relative positions and bases of support of the two parties. The Democrats had been very much the minority party throughout the 1920s. They dominated the South but ran poorly elsewhere. They broadened their appeal somewhat in 1928 by choosing Governor Al Smith of New York as their standard-bearer. Owing to his religion (Catholic) and appeal to urban dwellers and immigrants Smith carried 122 Northern counties his party had never won. He outran his Republican opponent, Herbert Hoover, by 38,000 votes in the nation's twelve largest cities. Meanwhile, Hoover won 200 Southern counties previously loyal to the Democrats and carried five states in that region.[64]

Roosevelt built upon Smith's gains to fashion a new Democratic coalition. The New Deal coalition consisted of the South, Northern workers, urban voters, immigrants, Catholics, and Jews. Blacks began to vote Democratic four years later. Loyalty of these groups made the Democrats the majority party. Since 1932 they have won control of the House of Representatives on twenty-three of twenty-five occasions and of the White House eight of thirteen times; put differently, the Democrats controlled the White House for thirty-two, and Congress for forty-four, of the forty-eight years between 1933 and 1981.[65]

Common to all the groups Roosevelt brought together was an interest in government intervention in the economy. So long as such issues prevailed the groups forming the coalition were cohesive at the electoral and legislative levels. Unity began to dissolve as other issues emerged. Civil rights was most disruptive. The rule requiring a two-thirds vote to choose the Democratic presidential nominee had prevented that party from supporting legislation to help blacks. That provision enabled the South to veto any candidate thought too progressive. The party reduced the threshold to a simple majority beginning in 1936.[66] Twelve years later, Northerners included a plank backing civil rights in the platform. The Southern wing of the party left the convention and supported a States' Rights ticket in the fall. The loss of four Southern states that year foreshadowed the end of that region as a Democratic bastion in presidential elections. The party received reduced levels of support below the Mason-Dixon line during the next three presidential elections.

Until 1963, voters attached relatively little importance to the civil rights issue. In March of that year, only 4 percent considered it the most important national problem. Six months and many televised demonstrations later, some 52 percent thought it most pressing.[67] Kennedy and Johnson committed the party firmly to civil rights; the latter shepherded significant legislation on the subject through Congress the next summer. Accordingly, the deep South deserted the Democrats for the first time and stayed away the following two elections as well.

Ratification of the Twenty-fourth Amendment to the Constitution that outlawed the poll tax and passage of the Voting Rights Act of 1965, enabled increased numbers of blacks to register to vote in the South. By 1976, a Georgian helped by substantial black support was able to return the South to the Democratic party.[68] Table 2.3 indicates the movements of the Southern vote during the period under study.

The election of 1932 made the Democrats the clear majority party, a position they have maintained. Data collected by the Survey Research Center at the University of Michigan suggest that the Democrats have generally claimed the identification of roughly 40 to 50 percent of the electorate since 1952, the Republicans 20 to 30 percent.[69] The relative positions have dictated the campaign strategies of the two parties. Democratic candidates emphasize their party and those

TABLE 2.3
Southern Support of Democratic Tickets, 1932-1980

Year	No. of States Voting Democratic	No. of States Voting Republican	No. of States Voting Third Party
1932	11*	0	
1936	11*	0	
1940	11*	0	
1944	11*	0	
1948	7	0	4*
1952	7*	4	
1956	6*	5	
1960	7*	3	1
1964	6	5*	
1968	1	5	5*
1972	0	11*	
1976	10*	1	
1980	1	10*	

SOURCES: Compiled by author from *Congressional Quarterly Guide to U.S. Elections*, ed. Robert A. Diamond (Washington, D.C., 1975), pp. 289-99 (for 1932-1972); Richard Scammon and Alice V. McGillivray, eds., *America Votes 12* (Washington, D.C., 1977), p. 15 (for 1976); *Congressional Quarterly*, 8 November 1980, p. 3299 (for 1980; unofficial returns).

NOTE: Southern states are Alabama, Georgia, Louisiana, Mississippi, and South Carolina (deep South); and Arkansas, Florida, North Carolina, Tennessee, Texas, and Virginia (rim South). Asterisk indicates majority of deep South.

economic issues on which their coalition is reasonably united. Republican candidates mention their party allegiance as little as possible since they must appeal to Democratic and independent voters. They encourage voters to consider foreign policy and the relative personal merits of the two presidential contenders. Further, they attempt to exploit the divisions among their opponents on the race issue by raising matters like crime, welfare, and bussing, all issues seen by some voters as synonymous with civil rights.

Democratic and Republican candidates alike rely for their electoral success on the support of voters who do not identify with their party. That suggests a third change in the nature and role of those institutions. From the 1930s through the 1950s, party identification was the single most critical factor in determining the vote decision.[70] That is no longer so. "Perhaps the most dramatic political change in the American public over the past two decades has been the decline of partisanship," note the authors of a leading recent study of voting behavior.[71]

The decline of partisanship manifests itself in three ways. First, voters have become more issue-oriented.[72] The growth of mass media over the last few decades has made possible the dissemination of information. Evidence suggests that voters know more about current affairs than was formerly the case. Party identification may prove decisive when a citizen sees as many reasons to support one candidate as the other.[73] It no longer automatically directs his vote.

Further, more voters consider themselves independents than ever before. Less than one-quarter of the electorate so classified themselves between 1952 and 1964. Since then, the proportion of voters who identify with neither major party has risen steeply. The increase in the number of independents has come primarily at the expense of the Republicans, although Democrats have suffered some attrition in the South. It also reflects the influx of new voters who have been unusually reluctant to associate with either party.

These and other factors have made voters more willing to split their tickets than were their ancestors.[74] Increased information about candidates, especially at the presidential level, has made citizens less likely to vote the party ticket. The incumbency effect has made voters less inclined to follow partisan preference in casting their ballots for senators and representatives. The greater willingness of voters to support members of different parties has increased the possibility that the White House and Capitol Hill will be controlled by opposing parties. Although Americans elected Eisenhower

TABLE 2.4
Party Identification, 1952-1974

Year	Democratic	Republican	Independent
1952	49%	28%	23%
1956	45	30	24
1960	46	28	24
1964	52	25	23
1968	46	24	29
1972	41	24	35
1974	42	18	40

SOURCE: N. H. Nie, S. Verba, J. R. Petrocik, *The Changing American Voter*, p. 83.

and a Republican congressional majority in 1952, they re-elected the President in 1956 while returning a Democratic Congress. Nixon failed to bring Republican majorities to Congress in 1968 and in the 1972 landslide; Reagan began his term with his party controlling only the Senate.

These developments have more than academic interest. They affect the operations of government. Some Presidents seem likely to serve with legislative bodies controlled by the opposite party. Moreover, Congressmen need not be so responsive to presidential requests since their electoral fortunes are not closely tied.[75] Not only has the presidency affected the parties; it has also been shaped by changes in voting behavior.

The behavior of governmental institutions is shaped in large part by the political context in which they operate. Changed expectations affect the conduct of civic bodies. As any important branch of government assumes a new role, other elements must also adapt. That the New Deal brought innovation to American government is not surprising. Development of the welfare state coupled with America's new involvement in world affairs ended the stage of American history in which federal government practiced laissez-faire principles. Instead, it became an active referee of social, legal, and economic events.

The transformed role of government produced the aggrandizement of the presidency. Its incumbent enjoyed vast power, but also encountered new duties and formidable constraints. The eminence of that office forced revisions in the status and role of political parties. Traditional leaders became less important in shaping electoral choices and in mobilizing support for candidates. Voters became less inclined to cast their ballot consistent with party identification. The cleavages that split the party coalitions contributed to the increased independence of voters.

Other institutions had to adapt to the new rules these developments produced. The vice presidency was one such office. So long as government had been inactive there was little for its occupant to do. The changed political context allowed the vice presidency to emerge as a more significant office. Its growth was most pronounced from 1953 onwards, the period under study here, and resulted from the larger changes discussed in this chapter. The remainder of this book explores the various aspects of the office, relating its growth to the argument and information just presented.

3

★ ★ ★

The Selection Process

*I*n many democracies, the United States among them, nominations are decisive in defining the electoral options available to citizens. Since American political actors are relatively unconstrained by rigid party programs, the personalities and philosophies of contestants for office loom large in determining the voter's choice. The process by which parties select candidates accordingly assumes considerable importance.

It is, therefore, unsettling, to say the least, that the way American parties designate their vice-presidential candidate appears, at first glance, to be so susceptible to criticism. Presidential candidates are chosen after arduous preconvention campaigns that test their ability to present themselves effectively to primary voters and to a lesser extent to party leaders. Selection of the running mate follows no such formal competition. Generally near the end of the quadrennial convention the standard-bearer recommends a ticket partner. The delegates ratify the choice with little or no dissent.

With varying emphasis, critics commonly decry four aspects of the process. First, they protest that the system is undemocratic in allowing the presidential candidate to be the sole decision-maker. Second, they describe the choice as being hastily made under adverse conditions. Third, they contend that the selection is based on political considerations, not the relative qualifications of prospective running mates. Consequently, they conclude, vice-presidential candidates are generally unsuited to be President.[1]

Although these criticisms identify unhappy tendencies, they overstate the case. Often the process works quite well. The faults are not inevitable; experience simply shows the likelihood that some will occur. Even so, these risks may be worth taking. The procedure for selecting candidates has facilitated the rise of the office and performs important integrative and stabilizing functions.

The current selection process sketched above is of recent vintage. Through much of the first half of the twentieth century the convention, not the standard-bearer, played the leading role in completing the ticket. Presidential nominees often were either unable or unwilling to dictate who would fill the second spot. For instance, William McKinley in 1900 and William Jennings Bryan in his three campaigns made no recommendations. Consequently, they ended up with running mates with whom they were unhappy. On other occasions, the convention actually rejected the preference of the presidential nominee. In 1920 delegates stampeded to Calvin Coolidge, then governor of Massachusetts, even after the senatorial colleagues of Warren G. Harding decided on Senator Irwin L. Lenroot. The 1940 Democratic convention was ill-disposed to Franklin Roosevelt's choice of Henry Wallace. The party grudgingly nominated Wallace only after the President made that a condition of his own candidacy. So great was the hostility to Wallace that he was persuaded not to deliver an acceptance speech.[2] Four years later, the Democrats took two ballots to confirm Roosevelt's choice of Truman.

Neither generosity nor belief in full participation prevented presidential candidates from seeking to impose their will on the convention. Rather, they lacked the necessary control over the body. Party caucuses controlled by state and local machines chose delegates. Provincial bosses, not presidential candidates, commanded the loyalty of these men. Tradition accustomed political brokers to regard the second nomination as an occasion to exercise influence, not to acquiesce.

An agreement among party leaders typically determined who would fill the ticket. They generally picked a vice-presidential candidate able to add balance to the ticket, to placate a faction of the party, or to carry a swing state. The balloting for the vice-presidential candidate often resembled that for the standard-bearer.

The modern process is a different event. Its structure can be exposed by examining four questions: Who is involved in the selection? When is the decision made? What criteria influence the choice? Are those chosen to seek the office qualified to be President? Such a discussion indicates that the criticisms outlined above paint too grim a picture. The selection system contains democratic elements and often allows sufficient time for rational deliberation. Although competency to serve as President is rarely, if ever, foremost among considerations, those nominated for the second spot since 1952 have, with a few exceptions, had impressive credentials and talents.

Who Chooses?

As the power of the Chief Executive has grown and that of the parties declined, the presidential nominee has come to play the decisive role in the choice of his running mate. Several factors help explain this change. Modern-day conventions consist of delegates whose chief loyalty is not to a state leader but to the presidential nominee. For as primaries and democratically run caucuses become prevalent, more delegates owe their positions to their early support of the eventual party standard-bearer rather than to the patronage of a party machine. Further, delegates are wary of opposing the wishes of a presidential nominee who controls ample resources as the new party leader and may wield far greater patronage if he gains the White House. Finally, conventions are reluctant to embarrass their standard-bearer before a national television audience by challenging his first major decision as party leader. Such a move would only damage his, and the party's, electoral chances.

Current practice is not, however, so autocratic as it seems at first glance. In fact, in only two of the sixteen cases since 1952 has the presidential nominee acted essentially alone in choosing his running mate. Nixon, in asking Agnew to run for a second term, and Senator Barry M. Goldwater in recommending Representative William E. Miller in 1964, seem to have relied almost exclusively on their own judgment. But in most instances, two features give the vice-presidential nominations some attributes of a competitive electoral process.

First, political figures interested in the vice presidency often "campaign" for the job. Serious contenders usually do not make formal declarations of candidacy. Overt efforts are thought likely to alienate the presidential candidate. Nor do they seek to bind delegates to vote for them. Rather, aspirants discreetly encourage public and private displays of support to convince the standard-bearer of their talent and popularity.

For instance, at least three serious Democratic contenders for the vice presidency waged such campaigns in 1956. More than two weeks before the opening of the convention, Humphrey advised allies that they could "work actively" on his behalf.[3] He encouraged Southerners, including Senators John J. Sparkman, Lister Hill, Walter George, Lyndon B. Johnson, and Richard Russell and the Speaker of the House of Representatives, Sam Rayburn, to press his case in talks with Adlai E. Stevenson, the Democratic nominee.[4]

Although publicly disclaiming interest in the post, John F. Kennedy privately campaigned for the 1956 vice-presidential nomination.[5] His Senate aide, Theodore C. Sorensen, began discussing the idea with political leaders early in the year. Many thought the party could not afford a Catholic on the ticket. To combat this sentiment, Sorensen prepared a paper arguing that a Catholic vice-presidential candidate on the Democratic ticket would add 132 electoral votes. The "study" was circulated during the summer by John Bailey, the leader of the Connecticut Democrats.[6] Sorensen corresponded with Stevenson aides Arthur M. Schlesinger, Jr. and Kenneth Hechler regarding tactics to advance Kennedy's prospects.[7] Schlesinger alerted Kennedy that his chances were being hurt by a story "going the rounds in various damaging versions" that Kennedy had contributed money to Richard Nixon for use in Nixon's 1950 senatorial campaign against Helen Gahagen Douglas.[8] Kennedy's brother-in-law, R. Sargent Shriver, assured Stevenson that Kennedy was healthy enough to undertake a national campaign and that the Kennedy family would lend its support to any such effort.[9] At their conference in early July, Governors Abraham Ribicoff, Dennis Roberts, and Luther Hodges endorsed Kennedy. So, too, did Senator George Smathers.[10] Other Kennedy allies—Representatives Edward Boland, Stewart Udall, and Frank Thompson among them— wrote Stevenson urging him to select Kennedy.[11]

The campaign of Estes Kefauver for the vice-presidential nomination was launched in early August shortly after Kefauver withdrew from the presidential race. In a meeting with Stevenson Kefauver voluntarily stated that his release of his delegates to Stevenson was not designed to secure him the vice-presidential nomination.[12] But Kefauver was plainly interested and his supporters were active.[13] Senator Richard L. Neuberger pledged Kefauver the support of the Oregon delegation if he sought the vice presidency. Robert E. Short, a Kefauver delegate, announced that some Kefauver delegates might not back Stevenson for the nomination unless Kefauver was his running mate. Kefauver delegates from several farm states unanimously endorsed Kefauver for the second spot after a meeting on 5 August. The campaigns were well advised as Stevenson declined to state a preference and asked the delegates to choose.

More conspicuous that year was the activity on the Republican side. Eisenhower failed to endorse Nixon unequivocally in the winter and spring of 1956. Rather, he suggested that Nixon might prefer a cabinet position. He was asked at his press conference on 7 March if he would be content to run again with Nixon.

> Well, I am not going to be pushed into corners here and say right now, at this moment, what I would do in a hypothetical question that involves about five ifs. I don't think you should expect me to.
>
> I do say this: I have no criticism of Vice President Nixon as a man, an associate, or as my running mate on the ticket.[14]

Harold Stassen went on leave from the White House staff to lead a move to drop Nixon from the ticket. According to one Eisenhower aide, the President encouraged Stassen on the condition that he did not purport to be acting for the Chief Executive.[15] Stassen commissioned a number of polls that reported that Nixon would cost Eisenhower votes in November. He lobbied actively for Massachusetts Governor Christian Herter as the replacement. Other prominent Republicans, including Governor Theodore McKeldin of Maryland and Governor Goodwin Knight of California, indicated their availability for the nomination.

The Nixon forces counterattacked aggressively. Senator Styles Bridges released a poll indicating voters preferred Eisenhower-Nixon to Eisenhower-Herter. Party leaders, especially party chairman Leonard Hall, rallied to Nixon's defense. Republican chairman in thirty-six of the forty-eight states backed Nixon in the winter. Of 110 state Republican leaders surveyed that summer, only one was as much as "leaning away" from Nixon. Nearly 180 (of 202) Republican congressmen signed a statement endorsing Nixon and condemning Stassen's move. Ultimately, Stassen dropped his attempt and seconded Nixon's renomination at the convention.[16]

More involved was the campaign Humphrey conducted for the Democratic vice-presidential nomination in 1964.[17] Early that year Humphrey began to meet with associates to formulate a strategy for obtaining the nomination. Friendly Johnson retainers advised him not to press the President publicly and not to fight Attorney General Robert F. Kennedy directly. Max Kampelman, a longtime Humphrey loyalist, contacted many potential supporters by mail. Humphrey supporters commissioned and leaked polls indicating their man's support among voters in general, and with farmers and laborers especially. Humphrey and his backers encouraged prominent officeholders to speak highly of the senior Senator from Minnesota in meetings with Johnson. Some forty senators endorsed their colleague as did virtually all major political leaders in twenty-six states and the District of Columbia.[18] Robert F. Kennedy backed Humphrey after he himself was eliminated from consideration, as did key White House aides, Larry O'Brien and Kenneth O'Donnell, and members of the cabinet.

Humphrey had long been a favorite of labor and civil rights groups but had not been popular on Wall Street. To mollify suspicions in the business community Humphrey arranged meetings with financial leaders in Chicago, New York, Washington D.C., and elsewhere. During these sessions he portrayed himself as a moderate not disposed to extensive government intervention.[19]

Friends of prospective candidates often conduct such efforts without the discernible involvement of the principal. Robert Kennedy realized he could not appear to be pressuring Johnson to designate him as his running mate in 1964. But a political ally, Paul Corbin, organized a write-in drive to indicate support for the Attorney General in New Hampshire. Kennedy received more than 25,000 votes, an impressive showing.[20]

In 1972, a petition drive spearheaded by Representatives Lester Wolff, Sam Gibbons, Wayne Hays, and Shirley Chisholm may have helped land R. Sargent Shriver on the Democratic ticket. Four years later Representatives Charles B. Rangel and Mario Biaggi sponsored a similar effort for House Judiciary Committee Chairman Peter Rodino which may have prompted serious consideration of him.[21] Although former President Ford had renounced any interest in running for Vice President in 1980, a number of Republican leaders sought to place him in the second spot on the ticket. Party leaders and Ford associates pressed the idea on Reagan and Ford. Although they persuaded Reagan to offer Ford the nomination, the ticket ultimately failed to materialize. Similar efforts may be waged against a prospective candidate. Representatives Paul K. Findley and William Cohen were among those who organized opposition to the choice of John Connally in 1976.[22]

These campaigns ensure that the choice of a vice-presidential candidate is not made in a vacuum. They allow potential candidates to demonstrate their strength with party leaders, interest groups, and, to some extent, the public. Moreover, they provide an attentive presidential nominee with useful information about possible running mates.

Virtually all presidential nominees introduce a second feature into the selection process, consultation. In almost every case since 1952, the presidential nominee has involved other party leaders in the choice. Although the power of state machines has declined, no race for the White House can succeed without their cooperation. In involving other party luminaries in the choice, presidential candidates hope, at the least, to ingratiate themselves to those consulted. They may also hope to attain information about the ability and acceptability of prospective choices. Inviting the views of leaders is common, but the nature of their participation has varied widely.

The most dramatic such attempt came at the 1956 Democratic Convention when Stevenson allowed the delegates to choose his running mate.[23] Stevenson probably had two motives: to present a contrast in the way the two parties chose vice-presidential nominees and to avoid offending those who wanted to be on his ticket. Twelve candidates received first-ballot support, the leaders being Kefauver (483½ votes), John Kennedy (304), Senator Albert Gore of Tennessee (178), Mayor Robert Wagner of New York (162½), and Humphrey (134½). Kennedy led Kefauver at the end of the second ballot 618 to 551½. But Gore's withdrawal triggered sufficient switches to give Kefauver the nomination.[24]

Stevenson's strategy contained risks, which helps account for the refusal of others to adopt it. An open convention might nominate a running mate unpalatable to the standard-bearer. It might also give the vice-presidential nominee an added measure of independence. Stevenson probably decided to allow the delegates a free choice only after deciding that all likely contenders were acceptable.

The approach of Dwight D. Eisenhower in 1952 allowed considerable input by party leaders while minimizing the danger of a choice he opposed. Following his nomination, a cross section of Republican leaders met to seek a consensus on the vice-presidential choice. Eisenhower did not attend the meeting but his close associates, Herbert Brownell, Senator Henry Cabot Lodge, and Governor Thomas E. Dewey, did. Eisenhower had given Brownell a list of acceptable running mates which included Nixon's name. So when Brownell phoned Eisenhower to report the group's preference for Nixon, the general readily concurred.[25]

That same year the Democratic nominee, Governor Stevenson, shared the choice with a small group of party leaders. Stevenson met with President Truman, Speaker Rayburn, and party chairman Frank McKinney following his nomination. After Truman vetoed Kefauver, and others opposed Russell, Sparkman emerged as the most acceptable choice.[26]

Candidates sometimes hold formal meetings to determine whether other party leaders will happily accept their preference for a running mate. In both 1960 and 1968 Nixon convened large gatherings of party leaders following his nomination. In 1960, Nixon invited more than thirty party leaders to his suite. Having previously discussed the matter privately with each, he knew that his preference, Lodge, would gain quick acceptance. A few favored a candidate from the farm states but eventually the group approved Lodge unanimously.[27]

The role of the 1968 meeting is more difficult to assess. Published accounts differ on important details.[28] Representatives of different factions of the party were invited. As Nixon expected, and apparently desired, conservatives objected to Mayor John V. Lindsay of New York, Senator Mark Hatfield of Oregon, and Senator Charles Percy of Illinois as too liberal; party moderates viewed California Governor Ronald Reagan as too conservative. Nixon was thus left with a choice between party moderates like Agnew, Governor John Volpe of Massachusetts, Senator Howard Baker of Tennessee, and California Lieutenant Governor Robert Finch. Finch apparently was favored by several Nixon aides but declined to be considered.[29] Once the choice narrowed to Agnew and Volpe the selection of the former was almost inevitable as more acceptable to the South.

It is not clear, however, that the 1968 meetings were intended to provide more than the appearance of broad participation in the choice. There is reason to believe that Agnew reached the final stages of consideration more through Nixon's support than through enthusiasm among party leaders. Senator Hiram Fong of Hawaii, a participant in the meetings, recalled:

We were asked as to who we wanted to be Vice President, who we thought would be a good Vice Presidential candidate. Many, many were named. Very few people brought up the name of Spiro Agnew; but the President [sic] kept on asking of us what we thought of him. Nobody knew that Spiro Agnew was in the running. Afterwards the nominee said that he wanted Spiro Agnew and Spiro Agnew was nominated.[30]

Indeed, Nixon writes that two weeks before the convention, he and John Mitchell "had tentatively—and very privately—concluded that the nod should go to Agnew."[31]

On the other occasions the consultation process has been less formal but important. At the 1960 convention John Kennedy met separately with different groups. A delegation of Southern leaders favored Johnson.[32] Party power brokers like David Lawrence and William Green of Pennsylvania, Wagner, Averell Harriman, Carmine de Sapio, and Michael Prendergast of New York, Mike Di Salle of Ohio, and Ribicoff and Bailey agreed that Johnson should have the first refusal of the nomination. At the same time, labor and liberal leaders including Governor G. Mennen Williams of Michigan, Walter Reuther, Alex Rose, Joseph Rauh, and Arthur Goldberg told Kennedy they opposed Johnson.[33] So, too, did members of Kennedy's campaign staff.[34] In the end, Kennedy overruled these objections and chose Johnson.

Johnson in 1964 and Carter in 1976, while clearly making the final decision themselves, discussed it widely with leaders beforehand. The broad support Humphrey had no doubt alleviated Johnson's fears of an adverse reaction from the South or the business community. Although Johnson reserved his announcement until the last minute it seems likely that he settled on Humphrey much earlier.[35]

Carter, sometimes through his associate Charles Kirbo, asked Democratic senators to evaluate their six colleagues whom

Carter was considering. Favorable references by Majority Leader Mike Mansfield and others apparently helped explain the inclusion of John Glenn in the final list.[36] Unflattering reports hurt the prospects of Senator Frank Church.[37]

Ford appeared to consult broadly in 1976.[38] He polled delegates to the convention for their preference for his running mate. The results were not decisive; the eventual choice, Senator Robert Dole, did not finish high on the list. Ford met with key advisers including Vice President Nelson A. Rockefeller, Senator Robert Griffin of Michigan, Senator John Tower of Texas, and Melvin Laird.[39] But Dole's support seems to have come from Ford more than his advisers. Reagan, Ford's convention rival, preferred Dole to others being considered.[40]

The selection of Senator Thomas Eagleton as McGovern's running mate in 1972 followed a large meeting of campaign staffers.[41] They winnowed an initial list of twenty-four names to six or seven that they presented to the candidate. McGovern's company was his staff but his decision was based partly on the advice of political leaders. He abandoned his preference for Mayor Kevin White of Boston after receiving objections from John Kenneth Galbraith and other members of the Massachusetts delegation. Kennedy, Mansfield, and Senator Gaylord Nelson urged him to pick Eagleton. After Eagleton's withdrawal from the ticket McGovern apparently relied more on the judgment of political leaders and less on that of his staff.

Humphrey, too, convened no gathering of leaders to participate in the selection of his running mate. Edward Kennedy could have had the second spot for the asking.[42] And on two occasions, Humphrey sounded out a Republican, Rockefeller, about joining him.[43] After these two, Humphrey had long leaned toward Senator Edmund S. Muskie of Maine. While continuing to consider others, including Senator Fred Harris of Oklahoma, Governor Richard Hughes of New Jersey, Ambassador Shriver, and former Governor Terry Sanford of North Carolina, Humphrey advised party leaders of his high regard for Muskie.[44] The views of other party figures narrowed his list. Humphrey eliminated Shriver after receiving indications that his selection would offend the Kennedy family or partisans.[45] Johnson apparently favored Hughes, Sanford, Governor Carl Sanders of Georgia or Senator Daniel Inouye of Hawaii. Humphrey made the eventual choice while closeted in a room with several top aides. He regarded much of the consultative process as a series of courtesies.[46]

The vice-presidential nominating process is like an iceberg: that part exposed to the public constitutes a small fraction of the entity. Certainly, the presidential candidate has far greater control over the choice than earlier in the century. He decides whose advice to seek and the format for the discussions. In the end, he determines the choice. But he faces important constraints. The campaigns and consultation broaden participation in the selection. And a standard-bearer who hopes to reach the White House can ill afford to alienate his party by disregarding preferences of its members.

Haste Makes Waste?

Especially since 1972, many writers on vice-presidential selection have concluded that the system operates hastily, allowing no time for deliberation. Wrote *Time* magazine:

> It is all done in a 3 a.m. atmosphere by men in shirt-sleeves drinking room-service coffee—elated, frantic politicians running on sleeplessness, juggling lists, putting out phone calls, arguing in the bathrooms, trying to make their reluctant minds work wisely as they consider an afterthought: the party's nominee for Vice President of the U.S. It is the worst kind of deadline politics. . . . Now a running mate must be chosen, checked out, signed on and presented to

the convention with a triumphant but seldom very credible flourish ("Tom who?" "Spiro who?")—all in a matter of hours. It is a procedure that invites error. Thus most vice-presidential candidates are too hastily chosen by only one man and his advisers, without any real democratic process or sufficient investigation.[47]

In fact, it is not *all* done in the nightmarish atmosphere *Time* depicts. Although some selections have been made under such unfortunate circumstances, others followed careful deliberation conducted over a period of time.

It is not unreasonable to expect candidates for the presidential nomination to devote some time to considering in a systematic fashion prospective running mates. Rarely do they. Until their nomination is secured candidates devote their resources to their own effort, not to choosing a ticket partner. The amount of attention given the choice of a running mate is closely related to the competitiveness of the battle for the presidential nomination.

On six occasions between 1952 and 1976 the outcome of the balloting for the presidential nomination was obvious before the convention began. In five of those cases—Goldwater being the exception—the successful candidate gave extensive consideration to the choice of his running mate.

With no doubt of President Eisenhower's renomination, the Republicans in 1956 focused attention on the choice of the vice-presidential candidate. Eisenhower's age and poor health made presidential vacancy more likely than usual; the ban against a President seeking a third full term which was embodied in the Twenty-second Amendment put his running mate in an auspicious position for the 1960 nomination. Eisenhower's unwillingness to endorse Nixon as his preferred running mate allowed open discussion of the choice. Although confused about Eisenhower's desires, Republican leaders considered possibilities. Much polling occurred. Nixon's renomination followed careful consideration of his popularity with voters and party members.

His nomination for the presidency assured well in advance in 1960, Nixon had ample time to consider possible candidates. Eventually, he constructed a list headed by Governor Nelson A. Rockefeller of New York, Ambassador to the United Nations Henry Cabot Lodge, Senator Thruston Morton, Secretary of Labor James P. Mitchell, Secretary of Interior Fred Seaton, and Representatives Gerald R. Ford and Walter Judd.[48] As discussed earlier, he consulted widely on his choice.

Johnson's nomination by acclamation in 1964 was a foregone conclusion. He used well the first eight months of the year to consider prospective running mates. He considered carefully the personal and political characteristics he wanted in his running mate. He polled extensively to determine the relative campaign strengths of possible choices. He questioned visitors and public figures on their preferences. He floated trial balloons for Shriver, Mansfield, Secretary of Defense Robert McNamara, and others. One month before the convention, Johnson eliminated Robert Kennedy and other cabinet members from consideration. After narrowing the choice, he sent Washington attorney James Rowe to ask Humphrey, and possibly others, probing questions concerning personal, political, and financial background and associations.[49]

Once he had overcome challenges in primaries by two obscure congressmen in the spring of 1972 Nixon's renomination was secure. It is not clear how much thought he gave to the question of retaining Vice President Agnew; it is clear that he had ample time to consider the matter. Newspaper speculation about replacements focused on Secretary of the Treasury John Connally, and, to a lesser extent, Rockefeller and Reagan. Nixon did, in fact, consider replacing Agnew with Connally.[50] Following McGovern's nomination and his selection of an equally liberal running mate, and a call by

Senator Jacob Javits for a new Republican Vice President, Nixon announced his wish to retain Agnew.

Carter clinched the nomination some five weeks before the convention by winning the Ohio primary, giving him time to consider vice-presidential candidates. In April aides constructed a list of 400 Democratic officeholders. Carter narrowed the list to fourteen whose relative strengths were tested by pollster Pat Caddell.[51] Carter's aide, Kirbo, interviewed seven members of Congress—Senators Frank Church, John Glenn, Henry Jackson, Walter Mondale, Edmund Muskie, and Adlai Stevenson, and Representative Rodino—and asked them to submit detailed information regarding their finances, health, and personal and political relationships. Beginning in early July, Carter interviewed the seven finalists. At various times he preferred Church, Glenn, and Muskie before settling on Mondale.[52]

In each of these five cases, the choice of the vice-presidential candidate followed much discussion and deliberation. No suggestions of undue haste dominated newspapers. The contrast with the manner in which the choice was made at closely contested conventions is telling.

The Democrats drafted Stevenson in 1952. Never declaring himself a candidate, it is unlikely that he began to consider potential ticket partners until after his nomination. Kennedy came to the 1960 convention short of the 761 pledged votes needed for nomination. His staff spent the convention securing sufficient delegates for victory; Kennedy gave his time to meetings with delegations to neutralize vigorous activity by Johnson and by Stevenson supporters. Little time was left to consider vice-presidential possibilities. Early vice-presidential speculation omitted Johnson. Kennedy had used the promise of consideration for the second spot as bait to win nomination. He had suggested to liberals that Humphrey would be his choice.[53] He told Clark Clifford that Senator Stuart Symington was his first choice just ten days before the convention.[54] At the convention, he told Minnesota Governor Orville Freeman that he was under strong consideration.[55] Senator Henry Jackson, too, was a prospective running mate. Rarely did the press mention Johnson as a possible running mate. Indeed, party leaders told the Kennedy camp that Johnson would not play second fiddle to his junior Senate colleague.[56] In the heat of the convention battle Kennedy could not question Johnson about his interest in the vice-presidential nomination. Based largely on subsequent conversation with Robert Kennedy, Schlesinger presents a persuasive case that John Kennedy offered Johnson the second spot as a courtesy, fully expecting the Senate Majority Leader to decline. When Johnson expressed interest, Kennedy found himself unable to withdraw the offer without damaging his electoral chances.[57] Other evidence suggests that Kennedy desired the eventual result. A memo Sorensen prepared in June 1960 ranked Johnson as Kennedy's best possible running mate.[58] Moreover, acting at Speaker Rayburn's request, Representative Thomas "Tip" O'Neill claims to have told Kennedy before the balloting for the presidential nomination that Rayburn would insist that Johnson accept an offer to run for Vice President. O'Neill reports that Kennedy indicated in no uncertain terms that Johnson was his first choice but that he feared Johnson would decline, thereby embarrassing Kennedy.[59] Kennedy aides were surprised by the choice. Some attributed it to haste. "The week of the convention had been too tense and chancy to give Kennedy time for serious thought about the Vice Presidency," wrote a former Kennedy aide, Arthur M. Schlesinger, Jr. Schlesinger claims that Kennedy felt it "terrible" to "have only twenty-four hours" to choose his running mate.[60]

Although Humphrey had long favored Muskie among those available to be his running mate in 1968, he did not make the final decision until the day after his nomination.[61] The possibility of a move to draft Edward Kennedy for the presidential nomination, the fight over the Vietnam plank in the platform, and the violence on the streets outside the convention hall preoccupied Humphrey and his staff. That same year Nixon went through four hastily assembled meetings following his nomination to reach agreement on a vice-presidential candidate.

The 1968 choices appear careful when compared to the process by which McGovern decided on Eagleton. McGovern had fully intended to choose his running mate carefully. Early in his campaign he told one newsman that "if, by some wild chance, I ever got the presidential nomination I would damned well avoid the messy way Vice Presidents had been picked in the past." And his campaign manager, Gary Hart, had thought, "if I ever get into a situation like that I am going to make sure the deliberations are careful, thoughtful, calm."[62] Unexpected events intervened. McGovern's good intentions were derailed by the Humphrey challenge to the California delegation. Court and convention battles on that question, which was critical to McGovern's success, cost him twelve days. But McGovern cannot be absolved of all blame. Despite Kennedy's repeated refusals to run for Vice President, McGovern continued to think he would accept. More than once during the eighteen hours immediately following his nomination, McGovern offered Kennedy the position. Each time Kennedy declined. McGovern was by no means the first, or last, candidate to have his offer rejected by his first choice. Rockefeller refused to run with Nixon in 1960; he and Edward Kennedy said no to Humphrey in 1968; Ford declined Reagan's offer. But whereas Nixon, Humphrey and Reagan had considered available alternatives, McGovern had not.

The final consultations on McGovern's running mate began after his nomination.[63] In a marathon session, some twenty staffers pared the initial list of twenty-four names to six or seven. Few of those with McGovern had met the leading contenders, Eagleton and White. Although their Senate careers had overlapped by four years, McGovern and Eagleton had rarely spoken. Rumors reached McGovern aides concerning Eagleton's alleged history of mental illness and alcoholism. A hurried investigation revealed nothing; no time remained to make a thorough check. McGovern spoke to Eagleton for approximately forty-five seconds during his call offering the Senator from Missouri the second spot on his ticket but apparently was unaware of the rumors. Frank Mankiewicz, a top McGovern strategist, asked Eagleton only the very general question, "Are there any skeletons in your closet? " Eagleton's answer was negative.

President Ford's selection of Dole also was a last-minute decision. Ford did ask a number of leading Republicans to provide information on their financial, political, and personal affairs.[64] In some instances White House aides interviewed prospective candidates. A good bit of public discussion had occurred. Opposition to Rockefeller among conservatives and to Connally among moderates was well known.

Reagan's strong challenge for the nomination made an early decision difficult. Ford did not know if Reagan's popularity with delegates would force his selection. Nor did he know, until the second night of the convention, whether he would have to announce his choice for a running mate before the balloting for the presidential nomination as Reagan forces had proposed. Thus, Ford did not settle on Dole until the morning after his own victory. Meetings running until 5 a.m. had focused on other possibilities. Senator Howard Baker was the front-runner, with Anne Armstrong, the ambassador to Great Britain, and William Ruckelshaus, the former deputy attorney general, also atop Ford's list. The choice of Dole surprised delegates, media, the public, and even some key Ford advisers.[65]

The 1980 vice-presidential selections deviate somewhat from the formula discussed above. Carter could not be certain of renomination until he prevailed in a rules fight to bind delegates to support the candidate they had backed in their state primaries. He had, however, announced Mondale as his selection well before the primaries. Voters and party leaders had ample time to register protests.

Reagan's success in the primaries assured his nomination before the convention opened. He had time to reflect on a running mate. That consideration apparently led him to favor a party moderate, first Ford, then Bush. Although Ford had announced that he would not run for Vice President, Reagan and other party leaders attempted at the convention to persuade him. Reagan and Ford associates met to negotiate terms under which Ford would run for, and serve as, Vice President. That effort failed, in part, some suggest, due to a lack of time. It may be that no amount of time could have produced such an agreement. In any event, Reagan had decided on a fall-back choice, Bush, who was anxious for the assignment.[66]

Recent history indicates that presidential candidates whose nomination is secured in advance of the convention can, and usually do, devote considerable time to choosing their running mate. Time is not the only helpful byproduct. An early decision allows the presidential nominee to meet prospective running mates on terms more favorable to a careful consideration. He can better determine which public figure would join him on the ticket. He need not use his selection of a running mate to win further delegate support. Finally, he can ask potential vice-presidential candidates, their peers and supporters, probing questions that might otherwise be ignored or resented. Carter's 1976 process, for instance, would not have been possible had his nomination not been assured early. He could not have determined whether rival candidates Church and Jackson, probable dark horse Muskie, or Humphrey ally Mondale were interested. Nor could he have solicited personal information from them.

Standards for Selection

Presidential Qualifications

If haste is sometimes a problem in vice-presidential selection, the criteria used for the decision are almost always an issue. Ideally, the test should be simple to define: presidential candidates should select as their running mate the available person who is best qualified to succeed to the presidency. Yet often ability seems at best a subsidiary consideration. Politicians are reluctant to admit that they use other criteria. It is, therefore, necessary to rely heavily on one's own judgment to assess the causes likely to have determined the choice.

Rarely is ability to be President the primary standard for measuring prospective running mates. The timing of the selection gives political considerations additional importance. The choice follows what often is a divisive competition for the presidential nomination. It precedes an electoral campaign. The most pressing business is winning the election. The vice-presidential nominee is chosen with an eye to maximizing the ticket's electoral prospects.

One recent presidential candidate, Barry Goldwater, has admitted as much. In an interview in 1972 he said:

> Well, let's be candid about it. Today, the way we do it, the selection of a Vice President is to get more votes. . . . You don't sit down and say: "Here we've got five men. Which of the five would be the best President?" Again, I don't particularly like this; it's: "Which of the five can get me the most votes?"[67]

Surely, few have suggested that Goldwater chose Miller because of his capacity to be President.

Similarly, the selections of Nixon and Sparkman in 1952, Agnew in 1968, Eagleton and Shriver in 1972, and Dole in 1976 do not seem to have been dictated by ability to serve as President. No doubt some of these men are quite able. In most cases the presidential nominee probably thought his running mate more qualified than his general election opponent. Still, judgments of the relative competence of alternative running mates seem to have received little weight in these instances.

The choice of Johnson in 1960 was more complicated. Kennedy had said that next to himself he thought Johnson most qualified to be President.[68] Yet Kennedy's assessment of Johnson's ability was not the foremost consideration. "Johnson was qualified, no question about that," Lawrence O'Brien, a close Kennedy aide, has said. "But he also was the best man available in terms of strengthening the ticket so you wouldn't be a footnote in history but in actuality would be able to seize the reins of government."[69]

On four occasions since 1952 the presidential nominee probably did give qualifications a prominent place. In 1960, Nixon's stated criteria, in order, were ability to serve as Vice President, compatibility with himself, and apparently ability to add strength to the ticket.[70] Certainly Lodge had distinguished himself through service in the Senate and at the United Nations. He was well known and highly regarded nationally. Despite his concern that Lodge's domestic views "were more liberal" than his own, Nixon believed Lodge could "serve as President with great distinction."[71]

Johnson said his "single guide" in 1964 was "to find a man best qualified to assume the office of President of the United States should that day come."[72] Johnson was perhaps giving himself too much credit. At times he had considered placing a Catholic on the ticket. He had polled widely to measure the popularity of his different options and found that none would affect the size of his landslide. Still, Humphrey seemed to fit nicely the test Johnson described. A Republican columnist called him "one of the two or three most skilled and brainy U.S. Senators of this generation."[73] A national Roper Poll found that voters rated Humphrey's ability to be President highly relative to other prospective running mates.[74]

Humphrey picked Muskie, he said, largely because "I saw a man of ability and of character . . . and I liked the man, so I felt here's a man I can trust."[75] That Muskie's political attributes were not as weighty as those of other possible choices lend support to Humphrey's claim.[76]

Carter pronounced Mondale best qualified of his prospective choices to be President. Carter aides expected Mondale to bring strength to the ticket as a fresh face with good standing among liberals and labor; they also were impressed by his credentials. "There were two or three other candidates who would have been a greater asset to me at this point if they had been on the ticket," said Carter at the convention, referring particularly to Muskie and Glenn.[77] In picking Mondale, Carter risked erosion of his Southern support. But that seemed a small gamble at the time as polls showed Carter well ahead of his Republican opponents.

Ticket-Balancing

Rather than emphasizing ability, presidential candidates usually seek a running mate who, minimally, will not *cost* them support, and who, ideally, will tap new sources of strength. Ticket-balancing is perhaps the major way presidential candidates try to expand their electoral base. Such considerations are made necessary by the pluralistic nature of American society and by the nature of the party system. Two serious candidates typically compete for the presidency. Neither can hope to attract a plurality by making a narrow appeal. Attempts at ticket-balancing generally involve four important factors: geography, ideology, religious background, and nature of experience.

That a presidential ticket reflects any or all of these balances does not indicate conclusively the criteria stressed by a particular presidential candidate. Coincidence may produce some balances. Further, a standard-bearer may have to settle for a running mate without the characteristics he would have preferred if higher choices decline to run. Still, Table 3.1, which indicates ways in which vice-presidential candi-

TABLE 3.1
Ticket-Balancing since 1952

Year	Party	Geography	Ideology	Religion	Experience
1952	D	x	—	—	x
	R	x	x	—	x
1956	D	x	x	—	x
	R	x	—	—	—
1960	D	x	x	x	—
	R	x	—	—	—
1964	D	x	—	—	
	R	x	—	x	—
1968	D	x	—	x	—
	R	x	—	—	x
1972	D¹	x	—	x	—
	D²	x	—	x	x
	R	x	—	—	—
1976	D	x	x	—	x
	R	—	—	—	—
	Reagan-Schweiker	x	x	—	x
1980	D	x	x	—	—
	R	x	x	—	x

NOTE: Dividing the country into Northeast (N), South (S), Border States (B), Midwest (M), and West (W), geographical balance is said to exist if ticket members come from two regions. A candidate's region is determined by the state in which he last sought public office. Residence becomes the relevant criterion for those who had not previously stood for office in a state; an asterisk denotes such cases in Tables 3.2 and 3.3. Judgments on ideological balance are necessarily subjective and may be open to some dispute. Religious balance indicates a Protestant and Catholic on the same ticket. Nature of Experience involves the source of a candidate's political background, e.g. legislative, executive. Under 1972, D¹ refers to McGovern's choice of Eagleton; D² to his choice of Shriver. The unsuccessful Reagan-Schweiker ticket is included here and in several other tables in this chapter since it demonstrated a rather dramatic instance of balancing. See Appendix for explanation.

dates since 1952 have balanced a ticket, offers some telling insights. In selecting a running mate, every convention or presidential candidate save one achieved some sort of balance.

The most common element balanced was geography. In all but two cases, presidential candidates chose running mates from different parts of the country. Regional combinations are indicated in Table 3.2. Regional balance makes sense

TABLE 3.2
Geographical Balance

Year	Democrats		Republicans		
	P	VP	P	VP	
1952	M	S	N*	W	
1956	M	S	N*	W	
1960	N	S	W	N	
1964	S	M	W	N	
1968	M	N	W	B	
1972	M	B	W	B	
	M	B*			
1976	S	M	M	M	
			W	N	(Reagan-Schweiker)
1980	S	M	W	S	

NOTE: Eisenhower's residence was New York in 1952, Pennsylvania in 1956. Shriver's was Maryland in 1972.

when an area of the country that is crucial to a party's success appears marginal. Republican tickets now typically include a Westerner. But they ignored that region in the early years of the century owing to its small electoral base. Similarly, until 1928, Democrats were confident of Southern support. They never needed to look to a favorite son from that region to fill their ticket. Governor Al Smith, the presidential candidate that year, was Catholic and opposed Prohibition, jeopardizing the party's chances in that key part of their electoral base. From 1928 to 1960, the second spot on the ticket, with one exception,[78] went to someone from the South or the border states.

In some cases, the ultimate regional balance may have been accidental. Although the vice-presidential candidate came from a different part of the country than the party's standard-bearer, other factors may have dictated the choice. Some evidence strongly indicates, however, that presidential nominees have sought some geographic balance. One test is the extent to which presidential candidates have considered running mates from their own areas. Table 3.3 indicates the geographic backgrounds of prospective vice-presidential candidates who were apparently given most serious consideration. Presidential candidates since 1952 appear to have given little consideration to prospective running mates from their own home territory. Indeed Ford and McGovern seem to be the only ones who did not discriminate on such geographic grounds.[79]

TABLE 3.3
Regional Distribution of Vice-Presidential Contenders

Year	Party	Region of Presidential Candidate	Regions of VP Contenders				
1952	D	M		4S	3B		2W
	R	N*				2M	4W
1956	D	M	2N	2S		1M	
	R	N*					VP
1960	D	N		1S	1B	2M	1W
	R	W	3N	1S	1B	3M	
1964	D	S	1N*		1B	3M*	1W
	R	W	2N			1M	
1968	D	M	4N	1S	2B		
	R	W	1N	1S	1B		1W
1972	D¹	M	4N*	1S	2B*	2M	1W
	D²	M	4N*	1S	1B*	1M	
	R	W			VP		

TABLE 3.3 (cont.)

Year	Party	Region of Presidential Candidate	Regions of VP Contenders			
1976	D	S	2N		3M	2W
	R	M		2S*	2M	
1980	D	S			VP	
	R	W	2N	2S	4M	1W

NOTE: N = Northeast; S = South; B = Border State; M = Midwest; W = West. VP refers to incumbent Vice Presidents who were renominated; where applicable, VP is placed in the column representing the Vice President's region. Numbers represent the number of individuals from a particular region who received most consideration as prospective vice-presidential candidates. Asterisks indicate instances in which at least one prospective running mate had not sought elective office; in those cases residence is used. It is impossible to know what potential running mates were given the most serious consideration. Computations here, and in Tables 3.5, 3.7, and 3.9 reflect my judgments based on primary and secondary material. See Appendix for explanation.

Regional characteristics have played a central role in several recent conventions. The choice of Sparkman in 1952 was designed to prevent a repetition of the Dixiecrat defection of 1948; Johnson was chosen in 1960 largely to carry the South. The prospects of Senator Thruston Morton and Secretary of the Treasury Robert Anderson in 1960, and of Senator Howard Baker in 1976 were hurt by the presence of a Southerner on the opposition ticket; the Republican standard-bearer in both cases decided to concentrate elsewhere. Their Northern origins may have helped Lodge in 1960 and Muskie in 1968. Bush, though a former Texas congressman, also had strength in some Northern states owing to his family ties to Connecticut.

Ideological balancing is far less common. It is probably impossible to construct a scientific test to place politicians along an attitudinal spectrum. Accordingly, discussion of this particular ticket-building strategy must rely on classifications that are subject to question. Table 3.4 reports my judgments of the ideological composition of tickets since 1952. It suggests that presidential candidates now generally select a running mate of similiar political philosophy.

TABLE 3.4
Ideological Balance

Year	Democrats		Republicans		
	P	VP	P	VP	
1952	M	M	M	C	
1956	M	L	M	M	
1960	M_L	C_M	M	M	
1964	L	L	C	C	
1968	M	M	M	M	
1972	L	L	C_M	C	
	L	L			
1976	M	L	C_M	C_M	
			C	L	(Reagan-Schweiker)
1980	M	L_M	C	M_C	

NOTE: L = Liberal; M = Moderate; C = Conservative. I have described candidates' ideologies based on my perception of where they stood relative to their own party when nominated. These judgments are subject to reasonable dispute; subscripts indicate an alternate classification that might have been valid.

Scholars often note that Goldwater declined to balance his ticket with a more moderate running mate, choosing instead another conservative. In fact, recent Republican tickets have generally joined candidates of like outlooks. Democratic pairings of Johnson-Humphrey, Humphrey-Muskie, and McGovern-Eagleton matched candidates whose positions on major issues were almost identical; those of Stevenson-Sparkman and McGovern-Shriver united men who differed on some subjects but who belonged to the same wing of their party.

On six occasions since 1952 tickets have indicated ideological balancing. Nixon in 1952 had supported Eisenhower on some convention votes. But he fitted more comfortably in the conservative wing of the party while Eisenhower was a moderate. Although Stevenson and Kefauver both appealed to the Democratic left, the former was essentially a centrist, the latter a liberal. Kennedy and Johnson are difficult to classify in 1960. But Kennedy probably fell somewhere between the moderate and liberal wings of his party while Johnson belonged between the moderate and conservative branch. Carter was widely regarded as a moderate, Mondale, a liberal in 1976. The same classifications probably held true in 1980, although four years as Carter's Vice President had probably given Mondale a slightly more centrist cast. Reagan and Bush were ideologically similar in many ways. They did differ on some issues which the Republican right viewed as litmus tests, the merits of the Equal Rights Amendment among them. Moreover, Bush was identified with the Ford wing of the party. Although some ideological balancing occurred in each of these instances, the differences between the candidates involved were not major.

In the past, party leaders more often selected a vice-presidential candidate whose views on major issues differed from those of the standard-bearer. The increased role of the presidential nominee on the selection makes ideological balancing less common. He is more likely to find merit in a running mate who shares his views. Further, the development of mass media makes it less feasible for members of a ticket to say different things in different regions. When campaign comments were not nationally reported, candidates could tailor their views to their immediate audience. This is no longer as possible.

Recent presidential candidates have often considered prospective running mates whose ideologies differed slightly from their own. But the information presented in Table 3.5 suggests that they rarely concentrated on prospective partners who did not share their views. Rather, they have often focused on those with similar ideologies.

TABLE 3.5
Ideological Distribution of Vice-Presidential Contenders

Year	Party	Pres. Ideology		VP Ideology	
1952	D	M	2L	5M	2C
	R	M		2M	4C
1956	D	M	3L	2M	
	R	M		VP	
1960	D	M_L	2L	2M	1C
	R	M	1L	3M	4C
1964	D	L	4L	2M**	
	R	C		1M	2C
1968	D	M	3L	4M	
	R	M	1L	2M	1C*
1972	D^1	L	9L	1M*	
	D^2	L	4L	3M*	
	R	C_M			VP
1976	D	M	5L	2M	
	R	C		1M	3C*
1980	D	M	VP		
	R	C		5M*	4C

NOTE: L = Liberal; M = Moderate; C = Conservative.

* Indicates a classification about which I am not confident; see Appendix for explanation. Subscripts indicate alternative descriptions that might have been valid.

Religion as a balancing consideration is a recent phenomenon. In 1960, Kennedy proved that a Catholic could be elected to national office. Since then, parties have occasionally combined a Protestant and Catholic on the same ticket. Kennedy in 1960 chose a Protestant running mate. Goldwater chose Miller, a Catholic, in part to attract Catholic voters in the Northeast. He also may have hoped that the presence of a Catholic on his ticket would induce Johnson to select Robert Kennedy as his running mate.[80] Humphrey chose a Catholic in 1968 whose ethnic background would also enhance the ticket's appeal to Polish-Americans. Both of McGovern's choices were Catholics.

TABLE 3.6
Religious Balance

Year	Democrats		Republicans		
	P	VP	P	VP	
1952	P	P	P	P	
1956	P	P	P	P	
1960	C	P	P	P	
1964	P	P	P	C	
1968	P	C	P	P	
1972	P	C	P	P	
	P	C			
1976	P	P	P	P	
			P	P	(Reagan-Schweiker)
1980	P	P	P	P	

NOTE: P = Protestant; C = Catholic; J = Jewish.

In several of these instances, the standard-bearer apparently treated religion as an important consideration. Table 3.7 presents the affiliations of those considered for Vice President. Kennedy considered only Protestants. Most of those Humphrey and McGovern gave thought to were Catholics. Neither Johnson nor Carter chose a Catholic but both weighed carefully candidates of that faith. At various strategy meetings Johnson suggested he needed a Catholic partner.[81] Religion seemed one of Muskie's major attractions to Carter. Democrats rely on the allegiance of large numbers of Catholic voters. It is not surprising that their Protestant presidential candidates perennially assess the need to appeal to those voters by choosing a running mate of that faith.

A fourth balancing factor is the nature of the candidate's political experience. A presidential nominee will sometimes choose a running mate with a different type of political experience to demonstrate the wide competence of his ticket.

TABLE 3.7
Religious Distribution of Vice-Presidential Contenders

Year	Party	Pres. Religion	VP Religion		
1952	D	P	9P		
	R	P	6P		
1956	D	P	3P	2C	
	R	P	VP		
1960	D	C	5P		
	R	P	7P	1C	
1964	D	P	2P	4C	
	R	P	2P	1C	
1968	D	P	3P	4C	
	R	P	3P	1C	
1972	D¹	P	4P	5C	1J
	D²	P	2P	4C	1J
	R	P	VP		
1976	D	P	5P	2C	
	R	P	3P	1C	
1980	D	P	VP		
	R	P	7P	2C	

Note: P = Protestant; C = Catholic; J = Jewish.

Table 3.8 indicates the types of experience presented by recent tickets. Symbols refer to the most recent kind of government work the candidate did. A combination of two different letters does not always indicate balance. Johnson and Ford, for instance, sought terms as President while Chief Executive but also had lengthy legislative backgrounds. In choosing senators as their running mates they did not achieve balance on this criteria; had they chosen a governor they would have.

Governors, in reaction to the growth of the role of national government, apparently feel a need to select a running mate with a Washington background. Stevenson twice ran with senators. In 1956, of course, the Democratic convention chose his running mate. Still, those Stevenson considered most carefully apparently included Kennedy, Kefauver, Humphrey and Gore, all senators. Both Carter and Reagan (in 1976) chose a running mate from the upper house; in 1980 Reagan chose a running mate with prior serivce in the legislative and executive branches. Indeed, Stevenson, Carter, and Reagan

TABLE 3.8
Previous Experience Balance

Year	Democrats		Republicans		
	P	VP	P	VP	
1952	S	L*	M	L*	
1956	S	L*	E	E	
1960	L	L	E	E	
1964	E$_L$	L	L	L	
1968	E$_L$	L	E	S*	
1972	L	L	E	E	
	L	E*			
1976	S	L*	E$_L$	L	
			S	L*	(Reagan-Schweiker)
1980	E	E	S	E*	

NOTE: E = Executive; L = Legislative; S = State Governor; M = Military. An L subscript is used when a presidential nominee, with substantial experience in both executive and legislative branches, chooses a legislator, i.e. Johnson (1964), Humphrey (1968), Ford (1976). In such cases, no experience-balancing can be said to have occurred. Asterisk indicates balancing.

virtually limited those they considered to individuals with backgrounds in Washington. Those with experience in the nation's capital generally do not feel compelled to choose someone with state experience; Nixon, however, apparently did prefer a governor in 1968. Table 3.9 suggests that experience balance often is not accidental.

Other Factors

Presidential qualifications and ticket-balancing are not the only factors affecting vice-presidential selection. Several vice-presidential candidates have been chosen to placate disgruntled factions of the party. Considerations of ticket-balancing and conciliating specific elements of the party often overlap but are not synonymous. Whereas the former approach generally seeks to attract support in the general election, the latter has as its immediate goal the appeasement of segments of the party. McGovern chose Eagleton and Shriver largely to

TABLE 3.9
Experience of Vice-Presidential Contenders

Year	Party	Pres. Exp.	VP Exp.			
1952	D	S	7L		2E	
	R	M	4L	2S		
1956	D	S	4L			1U
	R	E			VP	
1960	D	L	4L	1S		
	R	E	3L	1S	4E	
1964	D	E_L	3L		3E	
	R	L	2L	1S		
1968	D	E_L	3L	3S	1E	
	R	E	1L	3S		
1972	D[1]	L	6L	1S	2E	1U
	D[2]	L	4L	1S	2E	
	R	E			VP	
1976	D	S	7L			
	R	E_L	2L		2E	
1980	D	E_s			VP	
	R	S	5L		4E	

NOTE: E = Executive; L = Legislative; S = State Governor; M = Military; U = Urban. Many vice-presidential possibilities had varied experience. In such cases, only the most recent is indicated.

please labor and party professionals. Nixon in 1952 and Dole in 1976 were seen as bridges to the right wing of the party; Ford, and then Bush, in 1980, as bridges to party centrists.

Support for Mondale among labor and liberals helped Carter's standing with both.

Vice-presidential selection is sometimes dictated by a deal between political actors. A politician may endorse a presidential contender and deliver a bloc of delegate support in return for at least an implicit agreement to select him or someone he favors. The most famous instances of such trades came in 1912 when associates gave the vice-presidential nomination to Governor Thomas Marshall for Indiana's convention votes, and in 1932 between agents of Franklin D. Roosevelt and John Nance Garner.

The decline of the convention as a decision-making body has made such arrangements less common in recent years. One candidate now typically arrives with the nomination clinched or within easy reach. Since 1952 there is no concrete evidence of such a deal successfully taking place. Attempts have been made, usually before the convention. Kennedy, in effect, offered Symington the second spot for the votes needed to secure his nomination. McGovern, apparently, was prepared to offer the vice-presidential nomination to Muskie before the convention for his support. The Ford camp made repeated overtures to Reagan suggesting his early withdrawal would assure his selection as the President's running mate.

Such bargains are often related to conciliation. A candidate seeks to secure the nomination and to unify the party at the same time. This strategy was well-illustrated by Ronald Reagan in 1976. He tried a variation of the standard deal by inviting liberal Senator Richard Schweiker of Pennsylvania to be his running mate weeks before the convention. At the time Reagan trailed President Ford in the hunt for support. He hoped Schweiker would be able to swing enough votes in Pennsylvania and elsewhere to secure their nominations. Reagan also sought to convince the party that he would take the steps necessary to win the election and to unite the disparate wings.

Conventions occasionally select a running mate to exploit a particular issue or avoid one associated with an unpopular stand. By 1952, Nixon had established himself as an outspoken foe of subversive activity in the federal government. His choice indicated that Eisenhower wished to underscore that issue. Eight years later, Nixon chose Lodge to help focus the campaign on foreign policy. Indeed, Nixon's three top choices—Rockefeller, Lodge, and Morton—all had experience in international affairs. Democratic delegates may have supported Kefauver and opposed Kennedy in 1956 based partly on their records on farm policy. The choice of Dole over Baker and Ruckelshaus may have been an attempt to minimize discussion of Watergate.

Ability as a campaigner also figures into the calculus of completing a ticket. The men who chose Nixon knew of and admired his ability as a hard-hitting campaigner. And four years later, appreciation of Nixon's skill on the stump helped abort the move to replace him. Perhaps no vice-presidential candidate in recent years has owed his selection so exclusively to his campaign ability as Miller. "He drives Johnson nuts," explained Goldwater in justifying his choice to Republican leaders.[82] Dole was placed on the ticket largely because of his acerbic tongue. Humphrey, Eagleton, and Shriver were also regarded as unusually energetic and effective campaigners.

Popularity with party leaders provides another influence on vice-presidential selection. Nixon in 1956 and Agnew in 1972 had earned many campaign debts during their first terms. Dropping them would have alienated many loyal party workers. Many delegates liked past party chairmen Miller, Dole, and Bush. Humphrey, as mentioned earlier, enjoyed broad and enthusiastic support among party leaders in 1964. Similarly, Mondale finished first in NBC polls of delegate preferences for the vice-presidential nomination in 1976.[83]

Occasionally, though less often than in the past, a vice-presidential candidate is selected to help carry a swing state with a large body of electoral votes. Eisenhower aides thought Nixon might help bring California's bloc of thirty-two electoral votes into the Republican column in 1952. Kennedy hoped Johnson could contribute Texas's twenty-four votes to the Democrats in 1960. Nixon may have thought Lodge could help carry New York that same year. Otherwise, recent vice-presidential candidates have not come from large states, suggesting the decline of this as an important factor.

Such a strategy was popular in the past when few states were competitive. Parties often used the second spot to enhance the ticket's appeal in one of those states. Thus, Indiana, almost always a marginal state, produced five of the eight major party candidates for Vice President from 1904 to 1916; New York, then the largest source of electoral votes, was the home of four aspirants to the post between 1900 and 1920. Now most states are reasonably competitive. Candidates conduct national campaigns. A party can hardly afford to use one-half of its ticket to court a single state.

Which considerations prevail in any given campaign depends on changing circumstances. More promising generalizations can be made on the differences in likely behavior of the two parties in filling a ticket. Democratic and Republican presidential nominees generally seek different talents in their running mates owing to their divergent electoral needs.

The Democratic party is a broad church. Fragile bonds hold together the groups Franklin Roosevelt shaped into a winning coalition; Republicans invariably try to raise issues to disrupt their unity. The Democratic vice-presidential candidate is usually someone popular with that element of the New Deal formula—the South, blacks, labor, urban residents—to whom the party standard-bearer has least appeal.

Republicans must usually adopt a different approach. Their party is more homogeneous at the price of being much smaller. Victory depends on attracting independent and Democratic voters. While their presidential nominee pitches his appeal to these potential switchers, the vice-presidential nominee must maintain the loyalty of party regulars. Republicans generally fill the second spot with a candidate popular to the right wing which forms the core of the party. If, however, the standard-bearer himself is the favorite of the Republican right wing, as was Nixon in 1960 and Reagan in 1980, the second candidate is more likely to be someone with appeal to independents, as were Lodge and Bush.

That both parties pay such homage to political considerations rather than merit is proper grounds for some cynicism. Yet even expediency in this case has its virtue. Although no single overarching cleavage divides America, many smaller ones do exist. The willingness of parties to use the vice-presidential nomination partly to conciliate those not content with the presidential choice is not only politically pragmatic. It also helps safeguard the two-party system and the underlying consensus of American politics.

Qualifications of Running Mates

The equation varies from convention to convention but one thing is clear. Political calculations, not ability to be President, are the controlling factors in vice-presidential selections. This truth has not necessarily caused the selection of unqualified men, as many have contended. The running mate thought most likely to enhance the ticket's prospects may also be well-equipped to be Chief Executive.

No certain measure of ability to be President exists. Success in the White House depends on some shifting combination of talent, personality, popularity, experience, knowledge, and luck. Any attempt to determine whether running mates are presidential timber faces severe limitations.

Several tests do exist to help illuminate the question. Politicians and voters generally consider experience an important factor in appraising a candidate's merits. Length and breadth of government service are two relevant criteria. A third measure is whether a vice-presidential candidate had previously been considered for the presidency or vice presidency; a fourth, whether he subsequently was.

Vice-presidential candidates generally have had a considerable amount of government experience. Table 3.10 compares the total length of experience of presidential and vice-presidential candidates in Congress, as high officers of the executive branch, and as governors.

The quality of the experience of the vice-presidential candidates as a whole is impressive. In ten of the eighteen combinations since 1952, vice-presidential candidates had longer experience in important governmental positions than their party's standard-bearer.[84] The occupant of the second spot on seventeen of the eighteen tickets considered in this chapter had some previous contact with national issues through service in Congress or in the executive branch.[85] Of the fifteen individuals who ran for Vice President (including Eagleton and Schweiker, and counting Nixon, Agnew, and Mondale once each), thirteen had served in Congress,[86] four had been in state government,[87] three had held cabinet rank in an earlier administration,[88] and two had executive experience in local office.[89] Two, Johnson and Humphrey, had been elected by their colleagues to leadership positions in the Senate; three, Miller, Dole, and Bush, had been party chairmen.

Qualitative differences exist in the nature of the experience of various candidates, however. The backgrounds of at least five of the eighteen candidates seem insufficient to meet the assortment of demands made on a President. Nixon (in 1952)

TABLE 3.10
Experience of Presidential and Vice-Presidential Candidates

Year	Party	Presidential candidate Years experience	VP candidate Years experience
1952	D	4	16
	R	0[a]	6
1956	D	4	17
	R	4[a]	10
1960	D	14	24
	R	14	26[b]
1964	D	28	16[c]
	R	12	14[d]
1968	D	20	14
	R	14	2[c]
1972	D	14	4[e]
	D		9[bf]
	R	18	6[c]
1976	D	4	12[e]
	R	28	17[d]
	Reagan-Schweiker	8	16
1980	D	8	16[e]
	R	8	8[w]

NOTE: Numbers represent years experience in important civilian positions in the executive branch, as members of Congress or as state governors.

[a] These numbers are misleading to the extent they do not reflect Eisenhower's high-level military service through which he gained experience in foreign and defense matters and in administration.

[b] Includes service as ambassador or functional equivalent.

[c] Excludes service as local executive.

[d] Excludes service as Republican party chairman.

[e] Excludes service in state government as lieutenant-governor or attorney general.

[f] Includes executive service in sub-cabinet positions.

and Eagleton had concentrated on few issues in their brief legislative careers. Miller and Dole had somewhat longer experience but were excessively interested in issues related to their atypical constituencies. Agnew had only been involved with state and local issues.

Nine others seem to have had broad training. As Senate Majority Leader, Johnson dealt with a wide range of issues, worked easily with Eisenhower, and acquired some administrative training from planning and supervising the Senate's activities. Kefauver's and Humphrey's unharnessed interests and energies allowed them to gain expertise in an assortment of areas. Lodge's service in the Senate and as ambassador to the U.N. acquainted him with domestic and foreign affairs; similarly, Bush, after serving two terms in the House of Representatives, had under Nixon and Ford served as ambassador to the United Nations, liaison officer to China, and director of the CIA. Nixon and Mondale, as particularly active Vice Presidents, were exposed to virtually all major issues coming before the executive branch. Muskie and Mondale transcended regional issues, taking an interest in various urban and rural problems.

The four other candidates—Sparkman, Agnew (1972), Shriver, and Schweiker—are more difficult to classify. Sparkman and Schweiker had ample, and not undistinguished, legislative backgrounds. But neither had shown the leadership ability or broad interest in national issues found in those mentioned in the previous paragraph. Agnew probably gained some familiarity with national problems as Vice President but was not involved in decision-making. Shriver had impressive experience in foreign and domestic affairs but had never sought elective office.

Parties occasionally choose as their candidate for Vice President someone who they previously had regarded as a presidential prospect. Nine of the eighteen running mates from 1952 to 1980 had either sought the presidency or enjoyed frequent mention as a potential candidate. Nixon, Agnew, and Mondale gained wide following during their first terms as Vice President. Pundits viewed them as likely presidential candidates of the future by the time they won renomination.

Kefauver had been Stevenson's chief competitor in 1952 and 1956; Johnson and Humphrey had been Kennedy's main rivals at the convention and in the primaries respectively. Bush ran second to Reagan in the 1980 Republican primaries. Gallup Polls dating to 1937 indicated support for Lodge as a presidential candidate; he was among the handful of Republicans mentioned in public opinion surveys as a possible candidate in 1960. From 1972 to his withdrawal from the race

TABLE 3.11
Presidential Consideration of VP Candidates

VP Candidates	Presidential Nominee	Unsuccessful Presidential Candidate	Poll Strength
Nixon	1960, 1968, 1972	—	1956,* 1964
Kefauver	—	1952, 1956	1960
Johnson	1964	1960	1968
Lodge	—	—	1964, 1968
Humphrey	1968	1960, 1972	1976
Agnew	—	—	1976
Muskie	—	1972	1976
Shriver	—	1976	—
Dole	—	1980	—
Mondale	—	1976	1980
Bush	—	1980	—

SOURCE: Compiled by author from Gallup Polls.
NOTE: Poll strength refers to significant support (i.e. approximately 10 percent) in at least one Gallup Poll measuring presidential preferences of members of the individual's party within four years before the relevant election. An entry is given for poll strength only if the individual neither ran for, nor received, his party's presidential nomination that year.
* Refers to polls in which Eisenhower was assumed not to be a candidate.

in late 1975, Mondale was regarded as a leading liberal contender for the 1976 Democratic nomination. Other vice-presidential candidates during the period—Nixon and Sparkman in 1952, Miller, Muskie, and Agnew in 1968, Eagleton and Shriver in 1972, and Dole and Schweiker in 1976—had not been considered presidential timber prior to their candidacies.

Having been introduced to the electorate in their maiden campaigns, however, vice-presidential candidates generally have gained some significant followings. Of the twelve men who completed campaigns for the second spot between 1952 and 1976, ten later ran, or were considered, for President. Both Mondale and Bush seem likely to be considered in the future. Only Sparkman and Miller failed to become serious contenders for the White House following their vice-presidential campaigns.

Conclusion

The process for nominating vice-presidential candidates is not a bright spot in the American political system. But neither is it the disgrace typically depicted. The four criticisms sketched at the outset of this chapter must, to different degrees, be qualified. Most suspect is the suggestion that the system is undemocratic; varying degrees of participation are common in the selection. Nor is the process necessarily hasty. The amount of time given the choice is related to when the presidential nomination is secured. Although considerations of competence are generally secondary to assessments of political strength, vice-presidential candidates often are well prepared to serve as Chief Executive.

Developments in other political institutions are largely responsible for giving the vice-presidential selection process its distinctive, and oft-criticized, characteristics. The amount of influence a presidential candidate wields is a direct byproduct of the power inherent in the position to which he aspires. There is much to be said for allowing a President to guide the choice of the one subordinate he cannot replace. Such a procedure helps protect the presidency and increases the likelihood of an important role for the Vice President.

Nor is the predominance of political considerations odd or necessarily bad. A party facing an election of such great consequence as the race for the White House would be irrational not to weigh heavily the probable political impact of prospective running mates. A two-party system provides many advantages to a democracy. It simplifies voter choice, promotes consensus, adds stability to a society, and allows majorities to form. But every virtue has its costs. Compromise is part of the price. The use of the vice-presidential nomination to placate disgruntled factions is part of the mortar that holds the political system together.

Presidential nominees choose their running mates with their probable impact on the electoral outcome in mind. Vice-presidential candidates may contribute to the ticket's success by competently discharging their campaign functions. They may also help their party if some citizens consider preferences among vice-presidential candidates in casting their vote. The next two chapters address these considerations.

4

★ ★ ★

Campaign Roles

Discussion of campaign roles of vice-presidential candidates is touched with paradox. On the one hand, presidential aspirants consider carefully the political attributes of prospective running mates before making a selection. But then parties, media, and scholars tend to treat the second person as superfluous to the campaign. "Historically, an election campaign is not too hard an assignment for the vice presidential candidate," wrote Nixon, echoing the standard theme. "The presidential candidate wins or loses the election. The number two man goes along for the ride . . ."[1]

The role of the vice-presidential candidate once was as insignificant as Nixon attests. The second person was barely involved in some past campaigns. Garner, for instance, left his home in Uvalde, Texas, for only a handful of appearances during his two campaigns as Roosevelt's running mate.[2] Often the primary responsibility of the second man was simply to carry his home state. Arthur organized the Republican effort in New York in 1880. He never left that state nor did he make a single major campaign speech.[3]

Presidential candidates remain, of course, the central figures in national campaigns. The presidency has grown dramatically in importance since the New Deal; voters naturally pay more attention to the behavior of those who seek it. Development of mass media has made such information more easily attainable. The airplane has made extensive travel possible; changes in voting behavior have made it necessary.

Party identification no longer dominates the voting decision. Local organizations are no longer able to mobilize citizens to support their candidate. The nationalization of politics has left relatively few states safe for either party at the presidential level. Candidates, accordingly, have incentives to seek support throughout the country.

These changes have added prominence to the vice-presidential candidates as well. Campaigns have become national efforts in which both members of the ticket must travel widely and speak frequently to enlist support. Vice-presidential candidates are not superfluous. Rather, they play a unique role in presidential campaigns. Their activities may affect the outcome in ways not revealed by studies of voting behavior.

Elections are not won by a single person. Conducting a campaign requires diverse talents. Accordingly, presidential contenders enlist the help of specialists. A network of strategists, writers, publicists, and other expert advisers surrounds and assists every presidential candidate. A competent campaign effort may not be able to convert defeat into victory, but proper execution of a well-devised strategy can affect the returns.

The vice-presidential candidate, like the campaign manager, press aide, speechwriter, or treasurer is part of the campaign team. Differences do, of course, exist between the role of the running mate and that of the campaign staff. The former receives greater publicity, enjoys more prestige and has easier access to the public and politicians alike. Further, his name appears on the ballot. But like others in the operation, the primary function of the vice-presidential candidate is to help secure the victory of the party's standard-bearer. A campaign blueprint assigns certain roles to the second candidate. His performance in them can affect the election.

Not all campaign activity of the vice-presidential candidate or of others is directly and immediately oriented to gaining votes. A campaign is not a single entity. It is rather, as Stanley Kelley, Jr. explains, a set of efforts.

> A political campaign is, first of all, a campaign to win the support of the press. Secondly, it is a fund-raising campaign. It is, thirdly, a campaign to win or maintain the support of leaders of interest groups and of the interest groups themselves. Fourthly, it is a campaign to win or keep the support of local and state party leaders and their followers in the wards and precincts. And finally, it is a campaign to win the favor and the votes of the great mass of voters.[4]

This description reveals possibilities for the impact of vice-presidential candidates. Even if few citizens cast their vote based on the comparative merits of vice-presidential contenders, candidates for the post can affect the outcome by their behavior in the subcampaigns.

The remainder of this chapter explores the standard functions of vice-presidential candidates. The roles of the vice-presidential candidate in the first four subcampaigns Kelley has identified are discussed briefly next; more detailed treatment is later given to their function in the public campaign.

The Press Campaign

By winning favor among the reporters covering the campaign a candidate can help assure himself better treatment. Once citizens depended on party machines, local appearances by candidates, and the subsequent press coverage for their political information. The growth of mass media—radio, television and wire services—and the increasing number of reporters travelling with the candidates now provide alternative sources of campaign news. The images voters develop of candidates depend on what they read, hear, and see through the media. Candidates try to shape that content.

Nixon's pledge to avoid making personal attacks on his

opponents in 1956 was designed in part to help assure himself a better press. Some journalists commented on the improvement in his style.[5] Four years later reporters and editors reacted favorably to Lodge. They portrayed him generally as a rational statesman, an image that could not have hurt the Republican campaign.[6]

Humphrey was effective in dealing with the press in the 1964 race. A number of newspapers and magazines had called for his selection as Johnson's running mate. Some cited him as an additional reason for supporting the Democratic ticket.[7]

Of recent vice-presidential candidates, Muskie was unusually successful at creating a sympathetic press. Lewis Chester and his colleagues wrote:

> The press, eager to find something new to write about, lovingly fell upon the tidbit of comparing and contrasting the characters of the two newcomers to the national electoral scene: Ed Muskie and Spiro Agnew. And Muskie rapidly emerged as the journalists' favorite, almost their pet.[8]

Humphrey noted that Muskie "quickly became a hero to columnists and other press."[9] The *New York Times* suggested that citizens compare Muskie and Agnew in voting.[10] That Muskie received positive media play made the otherwise sputtering Humphrey effort look more attractive.

Carter improved his standing with much of the Washington press corps by his selection of Mondale. Columnist Joseph Kraft, who had endorsed Mondale for the second spot on the ticket, softened what previously was strong criticism of Carter.[11] During the campaign, favorable articles on Mondale received prominent play in a wide range of national publications.[12]

The Fund-Raising Campaign

Few vice-presidential candidates have been chosen because of their skill as fund-raisers.[13] And, given the Federal Campaign Act of 1974 that authorizes financing of major party tickets, it seems unlikely that this talent will loom large in future elections.[14] But bringing money into the campaign has been a significant contribution of some number-two candidates on the ticket. As Vice Presidents, Nixon and Agnew spent no small amount of time raising money to fill party coffers. Agnew raised considerable sums from the Greek-American community. Johnson helped Kennedy gain funds from Texas oil men. Part of the reason Eagleton was dropped from the 1972 Democratic ticket was the damaging effect his presence was having on the party's ability to raise funds from traditional sources. Shriver, as a member of the Kennedy family and former businessman, had access to people able to make substantial contributions.

Interest Group Campaign

Chapter three argued that appeal to particular interest groups is often a factor in vice-presidential selection. Not surprisingly, then, winning the support of specific organized bodies of voters often becomes an important role of vice-presidential candidates, especially those on the Democratic ticket. Not only does the Democratic party, particularly since 1932, depend on a more heterogeneous electoral base; many of its traditional voters tend to be more organized and less predictable. Humphrey, Shriver, and Mondale in particular concentrated much attention on this function.

Humphrey had close ties to an assortment of key groups in 1964. He was well-liked by intellectuals. Labor and liberals would have supported Johnson against Goldwater regardless of which prospective running mate he had chosen. But Humphrey was able to involve these groups enthusiastically in the campaign. Humphrey was friendly with black leaders, having long been in the forefront of the civil rights movement in Congress. Like Kefauver, he was popular with farm groups.

Shriver appealed to many of the same groups as had Humphrey. But his task was more crucial than Humphrey's had been. Labor leaders such as George Meany, the leader of the AFL-CIO, were hostile to McGovern. To Shriver fell the task of building bridges to this traditional element of the Democratic coalition.[15] Shriver gave much of his time to speaking before labor gatherings. He also focused on Jewish groups who were worried about McGovern's stance on Israel, Catholic organizations bothered by McGovern's position on abortion, and blacks who felt the McGovern campaign was concerned primarily with issues other than race and poverty.

Like Humphrey and Shriver, Mondale was popular with labor, and devoted much of his campaign effort in 1976 to winning its support. In contrast to 1972, Meany and other labor leaders worked energetically for Carter-Mondale. Their efforts to register new voters and bring citizens to the polls helped produce the margins by which the Democrats won in several states. Mondale also spent time wooing blacks, Jews and liberals to back Carter.[16]

The Party Campaign

State and local party organizations no longer play as critical a role in presidential campaigns as they once did. Still, they are not irrelevant. To be successful, a presidential ticket must motivate the party's powerful leaders not only to support the ticket, but also to commit them to mobilize resources at their disposal for use in the campaign. Restrictions on campaign spending should make local party efforts more essential in the future.

The role of mobilizer of party support is one of the more crucial jobs the vice-presidential candidate fills.[17] One way this task is performed is by frequent appearances at rallies and fund-raisers for candidates for Congress and state-wide office. Nixon in 1956 spoke for Republican candidates for the Senate and House of Representatives. That same year Kefauver stumped extensively for party candidates, and was especially effective in the Midwest. One of Johnson's earliest trips in 1960 was to Tennessee to help Kefauver win his primary race.[18] Muskie appeared with numerous congressmen; apparently he was particularly effective in helping those with Polish-American constituencies. A number of Republican candidates praised Dole as someone able to help them in their own races.[19] Mondale stumped for Democratic candidates in 1980. Visits by aspirants for national office provide local candidates with needed media exposure. The dividend the national ticket receives is the appreciation, and presumably the support, of the local politicians.

Vice-presidential candidates are also able to mobilize party support through direct sessions with state and local leaders. Nixon met repeatedly with conservatives in the Republican party to win their help for Eisenhower. Miller and Dole in particular tried to use their contacts in the party to the ticket's advantage. Dole, for instance, met several times with Reagan. Mondale's early September visit to Chicago in 1980 helped close a rift between President Carter and Mayor Jane Byrne.[20] Johnson played a crucial role in bringing party leaders into the 1960 campaign. It was only after a visit from the Majority Leader that Truman announced his complete support for Kennedy. Johnson worked vigorously and effectively to persuade Southern leaders to back Kennedy.[21] Similarly, Shriver was McGovern's bridge to party professionals disenchanted with the standard-bearer. He used his friendships with Johnson and Daley to arrange meetings with them for McGovern. He was constantly on the phone to Daley and other party leaders, seeking their advice and good will.[22] His speeches were peppered with flattering references to various branches of the party.[23] He brought together leaders of the rival regular and reform factions of the New York Democratic party. One party wheel horse put it: "Shriver gives us a sense of security. He makes up for the strangeness of McGovern."[24]

The Public Campaign

Regional Focus

Little effort has been made to describe the unique role of the vice-presidential candidate in the most visible part of the quest for office. Here vice-presidential candidates perform four fairly standard functions.

First, they often focus on one particular region, trying to carry it for the ticket. Whether a vice-presidential candidate concentrates on one section depends on strategic considerations and on the relative strengths and weaknesses of members of the ticket. After 1948, the Democrats could no longer expect to receive Southern electoral votes without investing some effort in that region. Accordingly, Sparkman spent most of his time in his native South in 1952 where his accent and ideology would be most persuasive.

More significant was the regionally-oriented effort Johnson waged eight years later. A sizeable portion of the 128 Southern electoral votes were essential to Kennedy's success. "The entire South depended considerably on Johnson," Sorensen has written.[25] Indeed, Louis Harris's polls, which Kennedy commissioned, found Johnson an asset in various Southern states. In Texas, 23 percent of those who favored Nixon for President preferred Johnson for Vice President. Similarly, Harris concluded that "it is highly important and urgent that Senator Johnson stump Tennessee heavily." There, 24 percent of Nixon voters preferred Johnson.[26] Johnson spent 43 percent of his campaign in the South, 50 percent during the critical last three weeks. By contrast, Kennedy allotted 15 percent of his time to the South, Nixon, 14 percent, Lodge, 21 percent.[27] It is generally agreed that the improved Democratic showing in the South—the party won eighty-one electoral votes there—was due largely to Johnson's efforts.[28]

In several other campaigns, the South seemed either secure for the Democrats or beyond their reach. The party chose a vice-presidential candidate with appeal elsewhere. Accordingly, the second man spent most of his time in some other region. Kefauver, for instance, concentrated on the farm states of the Midwest and West. Indeed, he spent all but two days of the last two weeks in September in that region. Following that tour, a reporter covering Kefauver's campaign wrote that the senator from Tennessee "has been given the mission of trying to win the farm vote which may be decisive in the November election." The Democratic ticket improved its 1952 performance only in the farm states of the West and Midwest, the result of Kefauver's efforts and the unpopularity of the Eisenhower agricultural program.[29]

Humphrey's campaign in 1964 assumed a similar regional slant. He spent approximately 20 percent of his time each in the Northeast, South, and West regions but devoted nearly 40 percent of his campaign to the Midwest.[30] He courted the farm vote by emphasizing issues concerning agriculture and trade. Except for Florida, Mondale ignored the South in his two campaigns, concentrating on the Northeast and Midwest.

Republican vice-presidential candidates occasionally focus on a particular region, too. In 1960, for instance, Lodge spent 47 percent of the campaign in the Northeast, compared to 36 percent for Kennedy, 31 percent for Nixon, and 21 percent for Johnson.[31] Lodge spent six of the last seven days of the campaign in the East. Dole began with a foray into the South and later focused on the Midwest. Bush conducted a national campaign, but concentrated on several industrial states where he was considered strong.[32]

The Echo

A second role the vice-presidential candidate performs is to underline the positions of the party standard-bearer. As mentioned in the previous chapter, vice-presidential candidates rarely make independent policy pronouncements. The reason is easy to appreciate. Spontaneous statements on is-

sues by the vice-presidential candidate may reveal differences with the presidential nominee. The growth of mass media makes it difficult for a ticket to take contrasting stances.
One way to avoid the embarrassment such splits often provoke is for the second candidate to follow the line the standard-bearer sets.

Nixon modified his stand on the McCarran Act to reflect
Eisenhower's views on immigration policy. Lodge's standard
speech sounded the same theme Nixon stressed—the need
for experienced leadership in foreign policy. Johnson in 1960
and Humphrey in 1964 did not make major policy addresses
but rather rehashed material from their respective platforms.
Muskie's standard theme was trust; Agnew underscored Nixon's interest in law and order. Although Shriver was assigned
several major speeches to make, he generally echoed Mc-
Govern's views on the war in Vietnam and domestic policies.[33] Carter and Mondale differed on two issues—the propriety of raising Ford's pardon of Nixon as an issue and the
wisdom of some Warren Court decisions. Otherwise, they
emphasized their points of agreement; in 1976 Mondale par-
roted Carter's statements about love, government reorganization, fiscal responsibility, and jobs.[34] Similarly, Bush's
speeches presented Reagan's views, not his own.[35]

Although repeating the ideas of the standard-bearer seems
an uninspiring task, vice-presidential candidates can contribute to the electoral outcome in this way. Presidential candidates cannot go everywhere. Nor can they speak effectively
in all parts of the country. The running mate can cover places
the number-one man does not reach. He can carry the party's
programs to a wider audience.

Salesman for the Standard-Bearer

Third, the vice-presidential candidate in some situations
can and does make a better case for the election of the ticket
than the standard-bearer. Studies indicate that in recent years

the personality and policies of presidential candidates have become more important in influencing voters.[36] This is not surprising. As the importance of the presidency has increased, so, too, has access to information about candidates. Rationality dictates devoting considerable resources to presenting the standard-bearer in the most favorable light possible.

Presidential candidates cannot sing their own praises publicly to the extent they might like. Their running mates need show no such inhibitions. They can be the unabashed champions of the presidential candidates, lavishing them with praise or defending them from attack. At times, this aspect of vice-presidential rhetoric, which one prominent columnist has called "the grovel factor," becomes ludicrous.[37]

Toward the close of his "Checkers" speech, Nixon performed this chore without restraint.

> I think my country is in danger. And I think that the only man that can save America at this time is the man that's running for President on my ticket—Dwight Eisenhower. . . . And remember, folks, Eisenhower is a great man. Believe me, he's a great man. And a vote for Eisenhower is a vote for what's good for America.[38]

He often hailed Eisenhower as "the one man" recognized internationally as being able to unite the free world. Four years later, Nixon emerged as the main salesman of the Eisenhower record. He told the American Legion national convention that "no man in the world today is more respected or more revered as a symbol of peace and liberty than the President of the United States."[39] A reporter covering Nixon paraphrased his standard campaign speech:

> He sings a hymn of praise for President Eisenhower as the "symbol of peace." He acclaims the President as a man who has given Americans "the best four years of our lives,"

a man Americans can "proudly hold up to their children, a man who has faith in God, faith in America, and a man who has restored dignity and honesty to the highest office in the land."[40]

Nixon told an audience during the closing days of the campaign that "this is not the moment to replace the greatest Commander in Chief America has ever had in war or peace."[41]

Lodge and Johnson performed this same selling chore for the party standard-bearer in 1960, but in different ways. Lodge was a thoughtful and effective proponent of the theme that Nixon's experience was needed. His standard campaign speech celebrated Nixon's maturity, talent, and background.[42]

Surveys indicated that many Americans, especially in the South, were reluctant to vote for Kennedy in 1960 because of his religion.[43] Kennedy faced the religious issue in a reasoned manner that would appeal to better-educated Americans. He did just that early in the campaign in a speech to a group of ministers in Houston. But it was Johnson who regularly addressed the issue in a way the average American could understand.[44] In Texas he concluded a lengthy narrative of Kennedy's war record with the comment: "When Jack Kennedy was saving those Americans, they didn't ask him what church he belonged to." In Hartford, Connecticut, he argued:

> If it develops that people do apply a religious test as a qualification for office, then we tear up the Bill of Rights and throw our Constitution into the wastebasket. In the next election, the Baptists will be out, and next a Jew or a Methodist or a Christian cannot be President, and soon we will disqualify everyone who believes in God and only the atheists will be left as eligible, and that's not the American way.[45]

Humphrey portrayed Johnson as a calm statesman. In Tennessee he suggested that Johnson was a great President who would be vindicated by history. At times he called Johnson "that great Texan." When Johnson's integrity was impugned Humphrey responded that "all his life President Johnson has been dedicated to [serving] the country. In fact, it has been at great sacrifice." Johnson was "intellectually and emotionally" equipped to lead the world for he was "a giant of a man."[46] Humphrey frequently drove home the statesman theme by portraying Johnson as a peacemaker.

While Humphrey was expounding on Johnson's virtues, Miller was doing the same for Goldwater. His standard speech described Goldwater as a soldier, family man, patriot, and man of peace; he praised his "strength" and "firmness."[47]

Four years later, Humphrey was the target of numerous attacks owing to his support of the administration's policy in Vietnam. Muskie could answer more effectively than the Vice President. In Cleveland Muskie urged:

Look at his whole life before him: It was a great life. It was a life of a great American, a man of courage. If you don't think he had courage, recall the '48 convention. He hasn't changed.

And I look into Hubert Humphrey's face, and what I see there is intellect, compassion, understanding and courage. I think he is a man. And I think he has proven it.

Two weeks later he characterized Humphrey as a peacemaker. "For a quarter of a century, his record has been the record of a man of peace. He's told us what he wants to do, he's put this problem at the top of his list."[48]

McGovern was hampered in 1972 by his widespread reputation as a radical. Shriver assumed major responsibility for presenting him in a better light. He sought to portray McGovern as a Democrat in the tradition of Franklin Roosevelt, Truman, and John Kennedy. He defended McGovern's patriotism by referring to his war record, and cast him as "a man of vision and courage." Shriver described McGovern as "sort of square, sort of rugged," "straight," "a Protestant pillar."[49]

Similarly, Agnew celebrated Nixon's virtues in 1972. His acceptance speech was a testimonial to the Chief Executive. Agnew's task was to "do everything in my power to help re-elect this great President." He portrayed Nixon as a peacemaker, a diplomat, and a man of insight.[50] Agnew continued to sound these themes during his campaign tours that fall.

Dole was Ford's leading salesman. He praised Ford as "a man of unparalleled decency and honesty and courage." He credited the President with having "given us a world peace."[51]

At the outset of his 1976 campaign Mondale seemed to know no limits in praising Carter. Carter was "this marvelous man who's from the soil himself." Mondale regularly referred to Carter as that "remarkable man from Georgia."[52] He continued to utter such praise, though in a less effusive manner as the campaign wore on. Four years later Mondale attempted to sell the Carter record rather than personality. Carter programs were producing economic recovery and employment, he argued. Mondale often found himself defending Carter by "explaining" some controversial presidential statement or action.[53] Meanwhile, Bush praised Reagan as "a decent, compassionate man" and one "who does care deeply."[54]

Laudatory remarks like many of those mentioned above may not seem credible to intelligent voters. It is likely, however, that constant repetition of specific praises helps enhance the image of the presidential candidate. The vice-presidential candidate is in an auspicious position to perform such a task. Unlike a presidential candidate, he need not seem arrogant in praising, nor too sensitive in defending his party's standard-bearer. Unlike other members of the campaign team, his presence commands a significant audience and his words receive conscientious media coverage.

The Hit Man

The most common form of propaganda in which vice-presidential candidates engage is not praise of their partner but abuse of their opponents. Since individuals, not programmatic parties, compete in American elections, strong incentives exist for politicians to make personal attacks on their rivals.

Republicans generally have greater reason to conduct a campaign based on personal attack than do Democrats. Victory depends on their ability to transcend their small base of loyalists. They must convince some Democrats and most independents to join them. The promise of new programs is not available as a means to lure this support, for recent Republican presidential candidates and their traditional voters have opposed further federal social measures. Accordingly, Republican tickets try to win backing by creating the impression that the Democratic ticket is headed by an unqualified or even dangerous person.

Democratic vice-presidential candidates attack the opposition less frequently. Their electoral success depends on their ability to maintain their traditional supporters and add a few independents. Personal attacks can help in these operations. But Democrats need not resort so often to such criticisms. Rather, they can rely on programmatic promises to hold these voters.

Intense criticism often becomes an attractive strategy for the party out of office. Its opponents have a record to defend. The "out" party may be able to win favor with some by focusing public attention on vulnerable aspects of the administration's performance. Further, a party well behind in the polls has greater reason to criticize. It must do something to pry voters loose from the opposition. The ticket running far ahead has little reason to attack. In fact, it may wish to ignore the opposition. Personal comment may alienate some voters.

Finally, the inducement to attack is greater when the opposing ticket includes a controversial or unpopular politician. Then supporters may be won by frequent reference to his attributes or views.

Presidential candidates spend *some* of their time blasting their rivals.[55] Yet generally they try to minimize exchange of personal invective, for it is the conventional, and usually wise, strategy for the standard-bearer to attempt to project a statesmanlike air. Such a posture is thought effective in winning support, especially given the increased salience of foreign policy issues. The first candidate would tarnish this image by engaging too frequently in vigorous personal attacks.

Someone must assume major responsibility for criticizing the other side. Citizens may be more likely to support a ticket if they are convinced they should not back the opponents. The vice-presidential nominee, to varying degrees since 1952, hurls abuse at the other ticket and party.

After controlling the White House for twenty years, the Democrats were vulnerable in 1952. Nixon described the Republican strategy:

> The plan was for General Eisenhower to stress the positive aspects of his "Crusade to Clean Up the Mess in Washington." I was to hammer away at our opponents on the record of the Truman Administration, with particular emphasis on Communist subversion . . .[56]

Nixon performed his role with relish. "If the dry rot of corruption and communism, which has eaten deep into our body politic during the past seven years, can only be chopped out with a hatchet, then let's call for a hatchet," he told one audience early in the campaign, mixing a strong criticism with a justification of his role.[57] He called Stevenson an "appeaser" and a "dupe of Hiss" who had gone "down the line for the archtraitor of our generation." He warned: "If Stevenson were to be taken in by Stalin as he was by Alger Hiss the

Yalta sellout would look like a great American diplomatic triumph by comparison."[58] Stevenson could not conduct foreign policy, proclaimed Nixon, for he was a disciple of "Dean Acheson's spineless school of diplomacy" which had "cost the free world 600,000,000 former allies." Yet Stevenson retained his "stubborn insistence on looking at the Communists through Dean Acheson's pink-colored State Department glasses." Not surprisingly, "Nothing would please the Kremlin more" than Stevenson's election.[59]

Nixon deplored the corruption of the Truman administration, too. "Every dollar that gang steals down there comes right out of your pocket," he told a New York audience. He suggested that dishonesty would be the undoing of the Democrats. "You know, as a matter of fact, this administration is going to go down in history as a scandal-a-day administration because you read about another bribe, you read about another tax fix, you read about another gangster getting favors from the government . . . and are sick and tired of it."[60] Nixon's attacks seem likely to have helped Eisenhower. A post-election survey found that 42 percent of Eisenhower's supporters considered "corruption in government" the major influence on their vote. "Communism in government" and "foreign policy" each determined the decisions of 9 percent.[61] Nixon's repetition of these themes on virtually every day of the campaign may have persuaded voters there was compelling reason to support Eisenhower.

In 1956 Nixon announced that he would take the high road. His reputation had been damaged by his tactics in the 1952 and 1954 campaigns. He sought to repair his image to position himself for a presidential race four years later. Thus, he announced that "I do not intend to . . . reply in kind with personal attacks on the integrity of our opponents in this campaign."[62] Within a few days his tone had changed. In a press release he declared that: "There is only one rule of the game as far as our tactics in this campaign are concerned, and that is to tell the truth. If the truth reflects unfavorably on our opponents, that is their fault and not ours." To be sure, the "truth" Nixon told reflected quite unfavorably on his opponents. He said Stevenson had "topped the world's record for demagoguery." He described Stevenson as "a jittery, inexperienced, novice who is eager to have the job but who is utterly unqualified" and as an "indecisive, how-not-to-do man, a pathetic Hamlet." The "butchers of the Kremlin would make mincemeat of Stevenson over a conference table."[63]

Kefauver, too, pledged to take the "high road." Yet neither positive enunciation of policy nor praise of Stevenson dominated his speeches. In his acceptance speech, he coupled his refusal to become a "hatchet man" with a subtle jab at Nixon. Kefauver declared:

> The chief function of the Vice President should not be that of a political sharpshooter for his party. . . .
> As your Vice-Presidential candidate, I promise you that I will never demean that high office to traduce fellow-Americans. I will never use it to sow division and distrust.[64]

The rhetoric Kefauver employed did not descend to the depths characteristic of Nixon's speeches in 1952 and 1956. Much of it was issue-oriented rather than personal; little could be gained by attacking the popular Eisenhower directly. Kefauver peppered his speeches with the charge that the administration favored the wealthy. In late September, for instance, he declared that "over and over again the Eisenhower administration has demonstrated that its heart does not lie with the plain ordinary citizen of America."[65] Such charges, and attacks on the Eisenhower farm policy, were tailored to have maximum effect in the small rural communities in which Kefauver spent much of his time.[66] At times, however, Kefauver did engage in personal attacks. In the closing days of the campaign he alleged that Eisenhower "turned back the clock on good government, and gave us an administration blotched and smeared with corruption among high government officials."[67] While Stevenson warned of the danger of Nixon succeeding to power, Kefauver mocked his Republican counterpart. After Nixon's pledge to avoid personal attacks, Kefauver said:

> I want to say . . . that I am delighted to hear, about this new Nixon. I think we will all be glad to welcome him back to the company of civilized men, of men who believe that it is possible in this great democracy of ours to differ politically without assassinating each other and to campaign against each other without the necessity of impugning the motives, the patriotism, the decency and loyalty of our opponents or of the leaders of the other political party.[68]

But perhaps no recent candidate has used sarcasm so skillfully at an opponent's expense as Johnson in 1960. The Republicans were seeking to persuade voters that Nixon was a seasoned and knowledgeable diplomat. Johnson dismissed that assertion in a variety of ways. He mocked Nixon for allowing Rockefeller to change the Republican platform in their famous secret meeting during the 1960 convention. Argued Johnson: "If the immature Governor of New York can take the mature, experienced Vice President forty-four floors up into the Waldorf Towers and strip him of his convictions and most of his platform between midnight and dawn, what would Khrushchev do to him if he got him in the kitchen all day?"[69] Johnson asserted that Nixon's foreign travels had cost America friends. He often charged that Nixon needed Lodge on the ticket because he did not feel capable of handling foreign policy. He accused Nixon of having a different position on civil rights for the North and the South.

Lodge, along with Muskie, engaged less in attacking opponents than other recent vice-presidential candidates. He generally limited his comment on the Democratic ticket to

the suggestion that Kennedy was too inexperienced to conduct foreign policy.

As mentioned in chapter three, Miller's ability as a hatchet
man was a factor in his selection for the second spot on the
Republican ticket in 1964. Circumstances at the outset of the
campaign made such a talent seem advantageous. Polls indicated that Goldwater trailed badly. Miller charged that
Johnson was "playing politics with the national security" and
was guilty of condoning street violence. He accused the
Johnson administration of using "Gestapo-state methods" to
discredit him and of countenancing conflicts of interest. Following China's first nuclear test and the ouster of Khrushchev
in October 1964, Miller charged Johnson with being naive
about Communism.[70] Senator J. William Fulbright, angered
by some of Miller's attacks, accused him of "the most foul-
mouthed vituperation and unrestrained misrepresentation of
any man in public life."[71] Not a single Republican congressman defended Miller.

Humphrey, too, had some incentive to attack. Goldwater
was not popular. His views on many subjects were unconventional. Early Humphrey talks painted Goldwater as "out
of step" with prevailing trends of history. Humphrey would
point to some popular measure that most senators supported,
"but not Senator Goldwater." He said Goldwater was "fis-
cally irresponsible." He called the Arizona senator "the Republican pretender to the Presidency" who did not know "the
difference between a ukelele and a corncob when it comes
to agriculture." He labelled Goldwater a "radical of the far
right" and warned that as President, Goldwater could "have
his finger . . . on the nuclear trigger."[72]

In his two vice-presidential campaigns Agnew fitted naturally into the role of "hit man." "I guess by nature I'm a
counter-puncher," he said, "You can't hit my team in the
groin and expect me to stand here and smile about it." One
of Agnew's virtues, Nixon said, was that "when it comes to

carrying the attack and resisting the attack, he's got it." In 1968, he sought to win Democratic and independent supporters for Nixon by challenging the record of Humphrey and the administration. Agnew called Humphrey "soft on communism," and on law and order. He compared the Democratic standard-bearer to Neville Chamberlain.[73] He frequently attacked peace marchers and hippies in his crowds. Four years later he capitalized on McGovern's controversial image. The "basic theme" of his 1972 campaign was "an unrelenting attack on Senator George McGovern and his proposals for national defense."[74]

Agnew's Democratic counterparts used different styles in attacking their rivals. Muskie was gentle and reasonable, criticizing Nixon for not debating, for misleading voters, and for choosing Agnew as his running mate. But his more vitriolic barbs were reserved for George C. Wallace, the candidate of the American Independent Party, for Wallace threatened to erode support for the Democrats among white blue-collar voters.

Shriver's taunts were more personal. His ticket was far behind; his rivals were vulnerable on several points. He said Nixon was "power mad and interested in power." He charged that the Nixon administration had tolerated crime in "the executive suites of government."[75] He called Nixon "the number one war-maker in the world today."[76]

Many speculated that Dole was chosen because of his ability as a hatchet man. The senator from Kansas did not disappoint such expectations, though he often coated his barbs in witticisms. Ford began far behind; he needed to cast doubt on Carter's fitness to be President. Dole frequently derided Carter for his *Playboy* interview. He warned that Carter and Mondale would weaken American defenses. He castigated them as liberals and big-spenders. He accused the Democrats of starting four wars this century.[77]

Mondale's attacks tended to focus more on issues. He frequently blamed Republicans for unemployment. Unlike Carter, he raised Watergate as an issue, criticizing Ford's pardon of Nixon. Mondale seemed to spend more time criticizing his opponents four years later. Then his ticket trailed in the polls from campaign's outset. Moreover, Reagan had long been a controversial figure. Mondale's acceptance speech portrayed Reagan as an extremist. Subsequent speeches echoed that theme, often in humorous fashion.[78] Still, Mondale's comment was largely issue-oriented; it was not infected by the personal invective characteristic of Nixon's speeches in 1952, Miller's of 1964, Agnew's of 1968, or Dole's of 1976. Meanwhile, Bush assailed Carter's record on the economy, foreign and defense matters, and suggested that Carter's "sorry" performance led him to conduct a "low-road" campaign.[79]

Personal criticism is an entrenched aspect of American presidential campaigns. Vice-presidential candidates are often responsible for making the most intense attacks. This seems prudent strategy so long as the comments stay within the standards the public expects of political discourse. It provides the President's deputy with a useful duty while allowing the standard-bearer to project a statesmanlike image.

The role of hit man carries risks. Vice-presidential candidates must keep their criticisms within the bounds of acceptable campaign discussion. Otherwise, their activity is likely to antagonize voters. The campaign performance of the candidate, particularly if he begins the race as a relative unknown, will shape voters' perceptions of him. Citizens may be reluctant to place him a step from the presidency if the nature of his attacks casts doubt on his own fitness.

A Concluding Remark

Vice-presidential candidates do not just "go along for the ride." Rather, they perform a fairly standard set of functions as an active and highly visible member of the campaign team. Their ability at these tasks may affect the outcome of the election. To a large extent, intuition must replace empirical evidence in reaching this latter conclusion. Yet it seems likely that Johnson's ability as a party organizer, defender of Kennedy, and hit man, especially in the South, was crucial to the Democratic victory in 1960; that Muskie's ability to gain favorable press treatment when the Humphrey campaign was otherwise faltering may have helped make the 1968 election close; that Mondale's ties to labor and liberals may have made the difference between victory and defeat for Carter in 1976. Others have also contributed to the margin of victory or defeat.

The previous chapter argued that political considerations generally dictate the choice of a running mate. But at times the factors weighed seem frivolous. Presidential candidates should consider carefully the ability of prospective partners in performing the campaign chores outlined above. Those who make an ill-advised selection of a running mate do so at greater political risk than often thought. The second candidate may also affect the outcome if his presence on the ticket itself helps some citizens decide how to vote. The importance of the choice between vice-presidential candidates is the topic of the next chapter.

5

★ ★

An Elected Official?

*T*he common justification for placing the Vice President first in the line of succession is that he is an elected official. Having run on the successful ticket he shares the mandate, according to the conventional logic.[1] Contemporary critics have questioned this conclusion. "Actually there is no evidence whatsoever to suggest that vice-presidents add or detract from the popularity of presidential candidates with the voters," wrote Nelson W. Polsby and Aaron B. Wildavsky, two leading students of presidential campaigns.[2] Or, as Arthur Schlesinger, Jr. put it, "No one votes for a Vice President *per se*. He is a part of a package deal . . ."[3]

An assessment of these theses is worthwhile. Chapter three argued, in part, that political factors dominate vice-presidential selection. Chapter four acknowledged the wisdom of considering such matters, as the second candidate may help the ticket by his successful performance of campaign assignments. Consideration of whether the relative appeal of competing vice-presidential candidates influences many voters provides further information useful in evaluating the extent to which parties act rationally in paying such deference to political concerns in completing the ticket.

Further, the extent to which the Vice President is elected helps locate the American system in democratic theory. The chief executive in any state that purports to be democratic should, it seems intuitively, owe his position to success in some fair and open electoral process. Vice Presidents often become President following death or resignation of the head of state. Such a succession is consistent with the American dedication to majority rule only if people "elect" the Vice President as well as the President.

Three obstacles obstruct treatment of these issues. To begin with, no consensus exists among political scientists as to how people decide which candidate to support. Some calculus of party, personality, and policy preference determines most votes. But the weights individuals assign the different elements are neither clear nor constant.

Second, the manner in which the Vice President is chosen impedes analysis of his influence on the outcome. Citizens cannot vote for separate slates of electors for President and Vice President. Rather, they cast a single vote for two offices. It seems safe to assume that most voters pay more attention to the competing candidates for President than to their running mates in arriving at their decision. After all, the importance of the Chief Executive far exceeds that of the Vice President. The person elected President is virtually certain to guide the country for at least some period of time; the chance of his running mate succeeding is relatively remote. It seems reasonable to expect voters to pay more attention to the second candidates than once was common. The second office has grown in recent years. Further, recent successions have increased awareness of the possible importance of the Vice President. Finally, the growth of mass media provides citizens with access to more information on the running mates. But it is not clear how much, if any, consideration is given competing vice-presidential aspirants.

Pollsters have provided little information concerning the impact of vice-presidential candidates on presidential elections. Only sketchy data exist concerning public knowledge of, and attitudes toward, the second persons on the tickets.

The materials presented in this chapter suggest that although the Vice President is not really an "elected" official his presence on the ticket may influence some votes. This chapter pursues separately four related inquiries: First, to what extent do voters know who the competing vice-presidential candidates are? Second, does campaign rhetoric include much discussion of their views and credentials? Third, does the media publicize the qualifications, statements, and activities of vice-presidential aspirants? Finally, do citizens consider their vice-presidential preferences in determining their votes? Of course, only the fourth question directly addresses the issue of whether the Vice President is elected. Unfortunately, responsive data is scarce. The other three inquiries measure the quality and quantity of information citizens have about those seeking the second spot, not how individuals use that knowledge. Still, these questions are instructive. The evidence they produce, though more impressionistic and less probative, is still suggestive of whether citizens consider vice-presidential candidates. Moreover, in identifying what voters know about the vice-presidential candidates, the first three questions help explain why citizens treat the vice-presidential choice as they do. That vice-presidential aspirants were generally known, widely discussed during the campaign, and well-publicized, were it true, would not alone guarantee that citizens would include the second candidates in their calculations. Rational voters might still find the presidential choice too important or the likelihood of succession too remote. Although knowledge about the vice-presidential aspirants is not a sufficient condition to assure their consideration, it is at least a necessary one. For the choice between the running mates can hardly affect voting if citizens lack information about them.

Recognition of Vice-Presidential Candidates

Available data measuring public name recognition of vice-presidential candidates is scarce. Existing information indicates, however, that vice-presidential aspirants often are relatively unknown when selected. They lose much of their anonymity during the campaign, but still are not so well known as the standard-bearers.

Few American political leaders enjoy widespread public recognition. The President and Vice President, many recent candidates for the offices, and a handful of other prominent politicians are known to large segments of the population. But some who have served in high office for lengthy periods of time remain almost anonymous. In January 1971, for instance, the Gallup Poll found that although many could correctly identify Senators Edward Kennedy (92 percent), Humphrey (87 percent), and Muskie (76 percent), only 11 percent were aware of their colleague, Henry Jackson.[4] At the time, Jackson was an influential member of the Senate, having accumulated eighteen years seniority. Many other prominent politicians remain similarly obscure. Without strong empirical or inferential evidence, it is not safe to assume that even an experienced public figure running for Vice President is widely recognized.

Eight of the seventeen vice-presidential candidates since 1952 were familiar faces when selected. Pollsters apparently did not measure Nixon's name recognition in 1956. But Gallup found that 82 percent could identify him in 1953 and that four years later 96 percent of Republicans had "heard or read about" him. In all likelihood, he would have scored somewhere between those two points when renominated for a second term. His rival, Kefauver, was also widely recognized, having been correctly identified by 83 percent of the public in June 1956.[5]

The competing vice-presidential candidates in 1960, Johnson and Lodge, also were well known. Two Gallup Polls in 1957 found that at least 67 percent of Republicans had "heard or read about" Lodge.[6] He gained wide publicity following those surveys owing to his confrontations with the Russians at the United Nations and his role as Khrushchev's escort during his visit to the United States.[7] Some 52 percent of Democrats were familiar with Johnson in November 1958.[8] The publicity he gained during his 1960 campaign for the presidential nomination certainly inflated that figure.

The other well-known vice-presidential candidates were Humphrey in 1964, Agnew in 1972, and Mondale and Bush in 1980. The Gallup Poll found 56 percent of Democratic citizens familiar with Humphrey in 1958.[9] His unsuccessful presidential campaign in 1960 and active role as Majority Whip in the Senate increased his fame. Agnew gained wide recognition during his first term as Vice President. His attacks on the press and on liberal senators received wide press coverage. He made strong showings in surveys measuring presidential preference for future elections and in Gallup's annual Most Admired Men study. Mondale's four years service as Vice President and Bush's unsuccessful campaign for the Republican presidential nomination had made them widely recognized political figures in 1980.

Evidence suggests that the other nine candidates since 1952 were relatively obscure. Agnew confessed in 1968 that his name was not a household word. Four years later Eagleton referred to himself as "Tom Who?" Similar, though less extreme, acknowledgements could have been made by Nixon and Sparkman in 1952, Miller in 1964, Muskie in 1968, Shriver in 1972, and Mondale and Dole in 1976.[10]

The public may know little about the vice-presidential candidates at the outset of the campaign, but awareness probably increases significantly before election day.[11] Still, midway through the 1976 campaign, 45 percent of the electorate knew little about Mondale and 50 percent felt unfamiliar with Dole.[12] Although data are again unhappily scarce, there is reason to suspect that a substantial part of the electorate may not be able to name the second half of the tickets. Surveys in 1944, 1948, and 1952 revealed that large numbers could not identify the vice-presidential candidates.

In October 1944, only 55 percent of Franklin Roosevelt's supporters could identify his running mate, Senator Harry Truman; 54 percent knew that John Bricker was the Republican vice-presidential candidate. Gallup found that 91 percent knew that Truman was the Democratic standard-bearer in 1948 and 88 percent that Governor Thomas E. Dewey was his rival. But only 49 percent and 58 percent respectively were aware that their running mates were Senator Alben Barkley and Governor Earl Warren. Following the 1952 conventions, Gallup discovered that only 45 percent could name the Republican vice-presidential nominee, less than one-third could identify the Democratic candidate, and only one-fourth knew both names.[13]

The increased use of television has probably boosted public awareness of vice-presidential candidates during the past two or three decades. Still, a large segment of the electorate generally knows little, if anything, about the holder of the second spot.

Discussion of Vice-Presidential Candidates

The public's ignorance of vice-presidential candidates should not surprise students of presidential campaigns. Both parties focus on explaining why policy and personality considerations favor their standard-bearer over his rival. Discussion of the qualifications and views of the running mates is minimal. Only three times since 1952 has a party made a concerted effort to influence the electorate by stressing attributes of its vice-presidential candidate.

The Republicans saw Lodge as an asset to the ticket in 1960. Eisenhower's speeches invariably praised Lodge, imploring voters to support not just Nixon, but the Nixon-Lodge ticket. Nixon's standard speech included the assertion that "I don't know of any man in the world today who has done a better job of standing up against the men in the Kremlin and representing the cause of peace and freedom than [Lodge] has."[14] Nixon promised that Lodge would oversee all non-military aspects of foreign policy in his administration. In the waning days of the campaign he pledged to send Lodge to Geneva to renew talks on the test ban treaty.

Humphrey strategists did not originally plan to use Muskie as a major selling point for the ticket in 1968. That changed once his ability to handle hecklers began to win him wide praise. As Theodore White observed, "Muskie had proven himself an almost immeasurable asset to the campaign, an asset amplified and made greater each time the Republican opposite number, Spiro Agnew, caught the headlines in contrast."[15] By mid-October the Democrats began to emphasize Muskie. President Johnson volunteered his belief that "Vice President Humphrey's choice of a running-mate—Senator Edmund Muskie—has shown himself fit in every way, to serve a heartbeat from the Presidency."[16] Humphrey called Muskie his "greatest asset." He argued that the high mortality rate of Presidents made it important to vote for the best team. He contrasted the succession of Muskie with the chance that Agnew might become President, a tactic pursued effectively in televised commercials. Two Muskie biographers note that "Humphrey praised [Muskie] so highly and warned so often of the mortality rate of American presidents that the joke sprang up that the presidential candidate was the first nominee to promise to die in office."[17] The Democratic media campaign sounded many of the same themes. Full-page newspaper ads featured Muskie. Though badly pressed for funds, the party purchased thirty minutes of network television time to present a biography of the senator from Maine. Muskie was much in evidence during Humphrey's election-eve telethon.

In the closing days of the 1976 campaign, Carter sought to capitalize on the popularity of his running mate. Private polls indicated that Mondale had a 44 to 27 percent positive/negative rating.[18] Carter gave few speeches during that

time in which he did not praise Mondale. He urged a Pitts-
burgh audience to remember "that you are voting for a ticket."
On other occasions he asserted that Mondale "would make
the greatest President." He spoke of the time "when Senator
Mondale and I are at the head of our Government" and con-
gratulated himself for his choice of a wife and a running mate.[19]
A Carter-Mondale televised commercial in 1976 attempted
to win favor by emphasizing Mondale's presence on the ticket.
It showed viewers, in succession, pictures of Mondale and
Dole. It then asked: "When you know that four out of the
last six Vice Presidents have wound up being President, who
would you like to see a heartbeat away from the Presidency?
Hmm?"[20]

Rarely are vice-presidential candidates given the opportunity to make independent policy statements. Although Nixon
allowed Lodge great latitude in discussing foreign affairs, he
did not encourage his running mate to offer his views on
domestic matters. To Nixon's regret, Lodge took at least two
risky stands on controversial issues—he advocated federal aid
to parochial schools and he promised that Nixon would appoint a black to his cabinet. In 1968, Agnew made some
proposals for rebuilding urban areas. Four years later, Shriver
made a number of speeches on governmental reorganization
and other domestic issues. But vice-presidential policy statements are rarities.

Discussion of the vice-presidential candidates more often
takes the form of attacks made by the opposition. Parties direct criticism at the second person on the opposing ticket
most often when the presidential candidate is unusually popular, when the public is particularly conscious of presidential
succession, or when the vice-presidential candidate is a controversial figure.

For instance, in 1956 the Democrats made Nixon their primary target. Eisenhower had suffered two serious illnesses
during his first term; surveys indicated that a sizeable seg-

ment of the electorate thought it likely that he would suffer a
third.[21] Not only did the possibility of succession seem to be
a real one, but Eisenhower was far more popular than Nixon.
The Democrats wasted little time in beginning their assault
on Nixon. In his keynote address at the Democratic convention, Governor Frank Clement of Tennessee called Nixon "the
vice-hatchet man slinging slander and spreading half-truths
. . ." In accepting the Democratic vice-presidential nomination, Kefauver denounced Nixon's deportment. At various times
in the campaign, Stevenson described Nixon as a "man of
many masks" who was "shifty," "rash," "inexperienced,"
and whose "trade-mark is slander."[22]

In several speeches, Stevenson sought to capitalize on voter
apprehension that Nixon would become President. He argued that Eisenhower was no longer in control. The dominant figure in a second term would be Nixon. He told a television audience on election eve that if the Republicans won
Nixon would probably be President before the term ended.[23]

Although Humphrey frequently made policy statements
consistent with the Democratic platform, the party strategy
called for little discussion of his credentials. More often, Republicans discussed Humphrey's record. Johnson was riding
a wave of popularity following his strong first months as President. Humphrey was thought more vulnerable. Miller accused Humphrey of having "one of the most radical [voting
records] in Congress."[24] "Hubert Humphrey's dangerous ADA
radicalism scares the daylights out of the voters," declared
Dean Burch, then Republican National Chairman. Burch said
Humphrey had a "curious affinity" for the National Lawyers
Guild, which he characterized as a Communist front organization.[25] More prosaic attacks on Humphrey were made by
private citizen Nixon. In a televised speech on "foreign policy" Nixon set out to "do something that he [Humphrey] has
not been to Barry Goldwater and that is to be objective and
to be fair."[26] Humphrey, conceded Nixon, "is a perfectly

loyal American, he's against Communism, and he's for peace, and he's quite a worker and he's quite a speaker." The problem with Humphrey, said Nixon, is that "he's just a very sincere, very dedicated radical." Referring to his record—"and we must judge men by their records"—Nixon charged that Humphrey had voted "100 percent down the ADA line." Indeed, "He's been a rubber stamp for Walter Reuther, he's in the left of the mainstream, on the left bank, for that matter of the Democratic Party, he's not representative of his party." Nixon contended that bills introduced by Humphrey and unsuccessful bills he supported would have increased the budget by $100 billion or $1,000 per taxpayer.

Four years later, Humphrey and his supporters chose not to ignore Agnew's presence on the Republican ticket. A series of early campaign blunders made Agnew a controversial figure. The assassinations of Dr. Martin Luther King, Jr. and Senator Robert Kennedy during the spring had reminded voters of the possibility of presidential succession, a reality the nation had experienced less than five years earlier. Humphrey frequently questioned Agnew's fitness to be President. His television commercials effectively sounded the same theme. One began with a picture of a television set with the words "Agnew for Vice President?" across its screen. A laugh slowly became more intense. Then the words "This would be funny if it weren't so serious" appeared on the screen. Another, which featured the sound of a heartbeat, reminded voters of the choice between Muskie and Agnew. "Who is your choice to be a heartbeat away from the Presidency?" it asked.[27] The Democrats ran large newspaper ads during the closing days of the campaign reminding voters of some of Agnew's outlandish statements.[28]

Other vice-presidential candidates have come under occasional attack. Republicans criticized Sparkman for his civil rights record and Muskie for encouraging civil disobedience. Carter and Mondale took issue with Dole for blaming the

"Democrat" party for leading the United States into four wars during the twentieth century. An early Ford strategy memo reasoned that "Carter's choice of Mondale can be viewed as a potentially serious mistake which opens his ticket to attack as being liberal, especially on social issues."[29] Accordingly, Ford and Dole attacked Mondale in some early speeches in the South as a radical and big spender. Introduction of a televised vice-presidential debate in the 1976 campaign provided voters easier access to information about the presidential qualities and policy preferences of Mondale and Dole. Discussion between the two senators exposed their disagreements on a range of foreign and domestic issues and their differences in style. Still, discussion of qualifications of the vice-presidential candidates in 1976 as in other years comprised a relatively minute portion of campaign propaganda.

Media Coverage of Vice-Presidential Candidates

Nor do vice-presidential candidates fare well in the third test, the amount of publicity they receive during the campaign. Presidential candidates receive premium media space during the weeks immediately prior to the popular vote. Their running mates are covered far less comprehensively.

One relevant indicator is the number of front-page articles during the campaign that deal with a candidate in a major way (mention his name at least twice on page one in the same story). The front pages of the *New York Times* and *Washington Post* in the presidential campaign years between 1952 and 1980 inclusive were examined. All issues of both papers were reviewed in each year from the day after Labor Day to election day.

The study indicates that vice-presidential candidates receive relatively scant coverage during a campaign. Every major party presidential candidate received between 55 and 151 front-page articles in the *Times*. The range for vice-presidential candidates was 2 to 27. The average number of stories for presidential candidates was 98; for vice-presidential contestants it was 9. Stated differently, stories about presidential candidates appear at the rate of about 1.5 per day or 11 per week. Candidates for the vice presidency make the front page about once a week.

The figures for the *Post* are not far different. The range of mentions for the presidential candidates was 162 to 60, and for the vice-presidential nominees, 37 to 1. The average figures were 93 and 9.5. In both newspapers, pictures of the presidential candidates were carried on the front page far more often than those of their running mates. (See Table 5.1 for complete data.)

TABLE 5.1
Number of Front-Page Stories about Presidential and
Vice-Presidential Candidates

Candidates	New York Times	Washington Post
1952		
Eisenhower	146	162
Stevenson	101	109
Nixon	27	37
Sparkman	5	5
1956		
Eisenhower	151	107
Stevenson	114	92
Nixon	25	23
Kefauver	13	11
1960		
Nixon	104	77
Kennedy	115	94
Lodge	18	13
Johnson	6	10
1964		
Goldwater	55	63
Johnson	87	74
Miller	4	4
Humphrey	9	5

TABLE 5.1 (con't.)

Candidates	New York Times	Washington Post
1968		
Nixon	107	72
Humphrey	108	93
Agnew	5	16
Muskie	8	6
1972		
Nixon	64	82
McGovern	57	60
Agnew	5	6
Shriver	2	5
1976		
Ford	89	95
Carter	79	86
Dole	4	4
Mondale	/	3
1980		
Reagan	67	90
Carter	120	134
Bush	2	1
Mondale	3	2

The nature of the front-page references vice-presidential candidates receive is revealing. They can make the front page if involved in some scandal. The 1952 controversy over Nixon's secret fund is the best example of an unusual event propelling the vice-presidential candidate to front-page attention. Between 2 September and 18 September neither paper carried a page-one story on Nixon. During the next eight days—the period in which knowledge of the fund became public, Nixon gave his "Checkers" speech, and Eisenhower decided to retain him on the ticket—Nixon was the major topic of twenty stories in each paper, more than either Eisenhower or Stevenson over the same period of time.

Twenty years later, Eagleton's announcement that he had undergone shock treatment for depression merited similar coverage. The story dominated the front page of both newspapers and was the cover story for *Time* and *Newsweek*.[30]

Other vice-presidential candidates have received front-page coverage owing to less significant "scandals." For instance, news that Miller had bought a home with a restrictive covenant received space on page one. So, too, did a number of stories identifying Dole as the recipient of illegal campaign contributions from Gulf Oil.

An unusual policy statement can also land the vice-presidential candidate on page one. Lodge gained wide publicity for his pledge in Harlem that Nixon would name a black to his cabinet. Agnew's assertion in 1972 that the White House had ordered the Federal Bureau of Investigation to look into the wheat deal with Russia produced front-page news, as did the later information that Agnew was wrong. Shriver's assertion that Nixon had missed an opportunity to end the war in Vietnam while Shriver was ambassador to France also produced a considerable amount of news.

A surprising amount of the vice-presidential candidates' front-page news grows out of some "blunder." The *Times* reported on page one that Nixon had used his franking privilege to poll his constituents on their preference for the 1952 Republican nomination. Nixon had earlier declared that he had never used government funds for political purposes. Agnew's apology for calling Humphrey "soft on communism" during the 1968 campaign was also reported on the front pages.

Finally, vice-presidential candidates are mentioned in front-page stories when their names are linked to that of the presidential candidate. Many of Lodge's front-page references came from references to the Nixon-Lodge team. Similarly, the Harris Poll, which the *Post* often carries, measures the popularity of the competing tickets, not just that of the presidential candidates. Humphrey, Miller, and Shriver received a major portion of their front-page mentions in this manner.

The study described above indicates that vice-presidential

candidates receive little news coverage. Two other surveys support this conclusion. Herbert Klein, Nixon's former press aide, cited a survey of the coverage given the 1960 campaign by seventeen newspapers. It found that the Kennedy-Johnson ticket had received 13,407 inches of coverage. Of that figure, 11,810 inches dealt with Kennedy, the balance presumably with Johnson. Of the 9,569 inches relating to the Republican ticket, 8,897 reported on Nixon's activities.[31] A study by Press Intelligence, Inc. of the 1956 campaign computed front-page headline mentions of the presidential and vice-presidential candidates in 650 daily and Sunday newspapers. While Eisenhower was mentioned in 50 percent of the headlines and Stevenson in 36 percent, their running mates were referred to in 9 percent and 5 percent respectively.[32]

The substantial difference in the amount of coverage given presidential and vice-presidential candidates suggests several tentative conclusions. First, it indicates that editors think information about the presidential candidates is more important and interesting to their readers than that about the vice-presidential aspirants. Second, the discrepancy in press treatment given candidates for the two offices suggests that individuals running for President say more newsworthy things than their running mates. Finally, the study implies that campaigns feature relatively little discussion of vice-presidential candidates.

Does Anybody Care?

The traditional view of the insignificance of the vice-presidential candidates to the electoral outcome was well expressed by John Kennedy in 1960. He told a "Meet the Press" audience:

> The vice-presidential candidate does not contribute. People vote for the presidential candidates on both sides. . . . They presume that the presidential candidate is going

to have a normal life expectancy. They don't say "We don't like the presidential candidate but we will vote for the vice-presidential candidate."[33]

Here again, evidence is scarce and disjointed. At first glance, it would seem that some useful conclusions could be drawn from study of the results in the vice-presidential candidates' home states. There, presumably, the candidate is well-known and his activities are likely to receive maximum coverage. Accordingly, his presence would seem likely to have most effect there. In fact, one scholar has found that vice-presidential candidates have had minimal electoral impact in their states from 1836 to 1972.[34]

Since 1952, vice-presidential candidates have carried their home states eleven of sixteen times. Tickets have fared better than the national average there just as frequently. Results are indicated in Table 5.2. In fact, these data tell little about the impact of the vice-presidential candidate. Results in the home states of vice-presidential candidates in specific instances may be useful but they encounter serious problems on an aggregate basis. Too many variables exist to determine generally whether the presence of a vice-presidential candidate contributes to the success (or failure) of his ticket in his home state. A ticket may win in the vice-presidential candidate's home state for reasons unrelated to his presence. Successful Democratic tickets usually win Minnesota; Republicans usually run well in California and Kansas. That Minnesota went Democratic in 1964 and 1976 cannot be attributed to Humphrey's and Mondale's participation any more than Nixon or Dole can receive credit for carrying California or Kansas. That a ticket lost the home state of the vice-presidential candidate may suggest voter indifference. But it might also suggest that the vice-presidential candidate was not admired there. Neither Miller nor Shriver ever won state-wide office; Lodge last won a Senate election in Massachusetts fourteen years before his vice-presidential race. There is no reason to believe that they were unusually popular in their home states.

TABLE 5.2
Results in VP Candidates' Home States

Candidate	Home State	Result in State	Relative to National Average (%)
Nixon	California	Won	+ 1
Sparkman	Alabama	Won	+20
Nixon	California	Won	− 2
Kefauver	Tennessee	Lost	+ 7
Lodge	Massachusetts	Lost	−10
Johnson	Texas	Won	+ 1
Miller	New York	Lost	− 7
Humphrey	Minnesota	Won	+ 3
Agnew	Maryland	Lost	− 1.5
Muskie	Maine	Won	+12.5
Agnew	Maryland	Won	+ .5
Shriver	Maryland	Lost	—
Dole	Kansas	Won	+ 4.5
Mondale	Minnesota	Won	+ 5
Bush	Texas	Won	+ 5
Mondale	Minnesota	Won	+ 6

SOURCE: Compiled from Richard M. Scammon and Alice V. McGillivray, eds., *America Votes 12* (Washington, D.C., 1977), pp. 3-15 (1952-1976); *Congressional Quarterly Weekly Report*, 8 November 1980, p. 3299 (1980).
NOTE: Percentages rounded to nearest one-half of a point.

Further, short-term factors may intervene to make certain results meaningless. Kennedy's presence on the 1960 Democratic ticket gave Lodge little chance of carrying Massachusetts or of lifting the Republican vote there above the national average. Although he failed to do either, it is possible that his presence on the ticket reduced the Democratic margin there. The feud among Republican leaders in California in 1956, rather than Nixon's candidacy, may have accounted for the ticket falling below the national average there. Although Table 5.2 does not so indicate, Johnson seems to have helped Kennedy carry Texas. A Louis Harris study, which the Kennedy campaign commissioned, found Johnson's presence was "of considerable help to the Kennedy cause . . . in Texas" since Johnson ran 4 percent better than the ticket there.[35] There seems reason to believe that Muskie's presence carried Maine for the Democrats in 1968. After all, that state had voted Republican in every presidential election but two (1912 and 1964) in more than one hundred years. Otherwise, lacking more data at least, it seems impossible to determine the electoral impact of vice-presidential candidates by studying the results of their home states.

Other evidence is more revealing. Evidence from the 1964 and 1972 National Election Surveys conducted by the Survey Research Center indicates that at least in those two elections few votes were affected by the vice-presidential candidates. Respondents were asked if there was something they liked or disliked about the parties and their presidential candidates. Only 3.9 percent mentioned Humphrey or Miller. Eight years later only 2.5 percent mentioned the vice-presidential candidate in answering the question.[36] These data suggest that voters in 1964 and 1972 either did not form opinions about vice-presidential candidates or discounted their importance. Yet 1964 and 1972 were unusual elections. Both offered a clear ideological choice. Both were decided by landslide proportions. Both involved incumbent presidents. And both presented vice-presidential candidates similar in policy preferences to their parties' standard-bearers.

In other contests, the personality of the vice-presidential candidates seems to have affected the attitudes of a number of voters toward the ticket. Emmet J. Hughes, a member of Eisenhower's White House staff, has reported that Eisenhower "was well aware of the almost tense reticence, in many sectors of public opinion, that denied him support for fear of the danger of Nixon's succession to the presidency."[37] A 1956 Gallup Poll showed that whereas Eisenhower was preferred to Stevenson 61 percent to 37 percent, Eisenhower-Nixon was favored over Stevenson-Kefauver by only 56 percent to 42 percent.[38] Apparently, 25 percent of the Democrats favoring Eisenhower and 12½ percent of the independents switched when the vice-presidential candidates were added, as indicated in Table 5.3.

TABLE 5.3
Impact of Nixon and Kefauver on 1956 Voter Preference

	Republicans	Democrats	Independents
Eisenhower	98%	29%	71%
Stevenson	2	69	23
Eisenhower-Nixon	97	22	62
Stevenson-Kefauver	3	76	31

SOURCE: Gallup, *The Gallup Poll: Public Opinion, 1935-71*, 2:1415-16.

Twelve years later, pollster Louis Harris found that a comparison of the vice-presidential candidates again affected a number of votes. Midway through the campaign, Muskie was adding 4 percent to Humphrey's total while Agnew was a 4 percent drag on Nixon.[39]

Eagleton's disclosure of his past psychiatric treatment affected the preferences of a sizeable segment of the electorate. Prior to Eagleton's withdrawal, a poll taken by Crossley Surveys Inc. reported that 9 percent of American voters seemed likely to change their votes; 76.7 percent said Eagleton's announcement would not alter their choice. Similarly, the Gallup organization found that 25 percent of the electorate felt less favorable to the Democratic ticket.[40]

Mondale's presence on the Democratic ticket in 1976 seems to have been crucial to the party's success. Harris and Caddell both found that the Democrats ran 3 percent stronger when the names of the vice-presidential candidates were included in questions. Eleven percent of voters leaving the polls cited the vice-presidential candidates as a factor in their decision; 80 percent of those voted Democratic. Gallup reported that 2 percent of Carter voters said Mondale's presence on his ticket explained their vote; 5 percent switched to Carter because they did not like Dole.[41]

In each of the four cases just cited, at least one of the candidates for the second office was controversial at the outset of the campaign (Nixon, 1956) or had made himself such by information produced since (Agnew in 1968, Eagleton in 1972, Dole in 1976). It may be that vice-presidential aspirants only affect many votes when they or their opponents arouse universally strong sentiments.

Even though some citizens are influenced by the vice-presidential candidates it would be inaccurate to conclude that the Vice President is really elected. At times, the preferred running mate is not the one who takes office. A Harris Poll taken after the 1964 conventions found that voters did prefer Humphrey to Miller by a 70 to 30 percent margin. And an NBC News survey found late in October that voters favored Mondale to Dole, 51 percent to 33 percent. But in 1968 it seems clear that the electorate preferred Muskie, not Agnew, for Vice President. A Harris Poll taken late in the campaign found that 41 percent favored Muskie and 24 percent Agnew. Four years later, a *Washington Post* survey indicated that voters were closely divided between Shriver and Agnew with the former preferred 42 percent to 41 percent. Only 27 percent of the electorate thought Agnew would be a good President; 57 percent thought he would not. In fact, only 39 percent of Nixon's supporters thought his Vice President would be a competent Chief Executive.[42]

Conclusion

Although data indicating the impact of the vice-presidential candidates on voting behavior is sketchy, several conclusions are evident. Some people running for the nation's second office have been widely recognized political figures, but the public has known little about many others. This is not surprising. Campaign rhetoric and coverage concentrates heavily on competing presidential candidates. Information about the running mates is less easily available.

This does not preclude the vice-presidential candidates from making some direct impact on the eventual returns. Surveys indicate that preferences regarding competing vice-presidential candidates affect some votes. An esteemed running mate can enhance his party's prospects just as an unpopular one can hinder them. But the suggestion that voters really elect a Vice President exaggerates his importance to the outcome.

That few voters weigh heavily the attributes of competing vice-presidential candidates is not necessarily cause for alarm. Presidential candidates often seek a partner least likely to hurt their chances. They avoid controversial choices apt to alienate supporters. A vice-presidential candidate may not affect the vote because he is broadly acceptable.

Nor would it be healthy for voters to emphasize the vice-presidential choice too heavily. The primary purpose of presidential elections is to pick a President, not a contingent leader. The presidency is so important that it would be unfortunate if Americans often rejected the Chief Executive they preferred because they disliked his running mate. It may be desirable that the vice-presidential candidates may only affect the vote more than marginally when particularly controversial, and that the system acts to eliminate such choices.

The general indifference to the vice-presidential candidates probably reflects, in part, the widespread belief that the Vice President performs few significant duties. That perception is not so clearly valid as it once was. The next three chapters assess day-to-day functions of the Vice President.

6

★ ★ ★ ───────────────────────────────────

Transformation of the Vice Presidency

*U*ntil recently the vice presidency was the most conspicuous sinecure in American government. Its occupants
presided over the Senate, their sole constitutional duty, and
did little else. No longer is the office so hollow. Changes in
American politics since the New Deal have drawn Vice Presidents into the presidential orbit. Vice Presidents now chair
Senate sessions only occasionally, concentrating instead on
a set of activities, assigned them by the Chief Executive, that
have become fairly standard from administration to administration. The importance of these functions varies with each
administration, for they depend on the relationship between
the two officers and on their relative strengths and weaknesses.

The Vice President relies on the President for assignments
that add substance to his office. Recent Presidents have given
the second officer seven types of activities. Some functions
involve the Vice President with the executive branch. He chairs
committees dealing with certain problems; he acts as a special envoy on trips abroad; he advises the President. These
might be called "institutional" duties. Other activities involve the Vice President in building support for the administration. He serves as a legislative liaison; he performs chores
for his party around the nation; he acts as a prominent
administration spokesman; he may become the Chief Exec-

utive's surrogate campaigner in presidential primaries. These pursuits might be called "political" duties.[1]

Distinctions between these activities are not always precise. Duties often are interrelated. Foreign travel or committee work, for instance, may make the Vice President a more effective adviser or spokesman. Legislative liaison and party work overlap. Further, activities identified as "institutional" have "political" aspects; the reverse is true as well. Still, the categories provide a helpful, if imperfect, framework to study the office.

This chapter and the two that follow examine the duties of the vice presidency. First, I provide the context and assess the causes of the growth of the office. The following chapter deals with "institutional" functions, the third with "political" roles.

Background

The earliest Vice Presidents acknowledged the vacuity of their office. Before his first term ended, John Adams wrote that "my country has in its wisdom contrived for me the most insignificant office that ever the invention of man contrived or his imagination conceived; . . . I can do neither good nor evil."[2] His assessment of the office led Adams to hope that his rival, Thomas Jefferson, would succeed him.[3] Jefferson did become the second Vice President, and was no more enamored of the position than his predecessor had been. He described it as "honorable & easy" and identified it as "the only office in the world about which I am unable to decide in my own mind whether I had rather have it or not have it."[4] Others found it no more taxing. Henry Wilson wrote more history than he made. Theodore Roosevelt hoped to use his term to study law.[5]

Circumstances in the early years of this century presented Vice Presidents with more to do, though not enough to relieve boredom. Thomas Marshall acceded to Wilson's request that he preside over the cabinet while the President negotiated the peace treaty in Versailles. Upon his return, Wilson asked Marshall to another cabinet meeting. At the invitation of Warren G. Harding, Calvin Coolidge became the first Vice President to meet regularly with the cabinet. Coolidge professed to find the experience valuable.[6] But Charles G. Dawes, his Vice President, declined that privilege before it was proffered. And Herbert Hoover apparently never asked Charles Curtis to join those sessions.

The vice presidency rose in status under Franklin D. Roosevelt. Garner regularly attended cabinet sessions; the President sought his advice privately as well. Garner acted as a legislative liaison to the Senate. He travelled abroad to the Philippines and Japan as president of the Senate, and to Mexico as Roosevelt's representative. Henry A. Wallace, Roosevelt's second Vice President, exercised greater powers. He chaired the Economic Defense Board, later renamed the Board of Economic Warfare. Roosevelt also used him as an emissary to Latin America, Russia, and China. But new duties presented perils which brought the political demise of Garner, then Wallace. Garner found the New Deal too liberal and openly opposed Roosevelt's decision to seek a third term. Wallace ran afoul of important Roosevelt advisers. His feud with Jesse Jones eventually cost him the chairmanship that constituted his major source of power. Secretary of State Cordell Hull disliked his involvement in foreign affairs.[7]

Owing perhaps to the unhappy experiences with Garner and Wallace, Roosevelt gave his third Vice President, Harry S. Truman, no special duties during the eighty-two days they served together. Truman did help secure Senate confirmation of Wallace as Secretary of Commerce. And he attended the few cabinet meetings that were held but found that the agenda contained "little of real importance."[8] Nor did Truman overburden his Vice President, Alben Barkley. Barkley did provide a useful link to Congress at times,[9] and was included in meetings of the cabinet by presidential invitation and of the National Security Council by law. But his term of office saw little significant activity.[10]

The seeds of an active vice presidency were planted, then, during the first half of the twentieth century as Presidents began to give their lieutenant duties. But these changes made little institutional impact; the position remained hollow until Nixon assumed office in 1953. Most remained indifferent to the plight of the vice presidency; in fact, the neglect was unfortunate. The office was attracting men of high quality, then wasting their talents.

Some reasoned that the Constitution precluded delegation of power to the Vice President. They advanced a two-part thesis. First, they argued that the Vice President is not an officer of the executive branch. His regular constitutional duties as presiding officer of the Senate are described in article one, the section of the Constitution which deals with Congress. Separation of powers principles, they reasoned, barred the President from delegating executive duties to him. This position had a long line of advocates. As Vice President, Jefferson wrote that "I consider my office as constitutionally confined to legislative functions, and that I could not take any part whatever in executive consultations, even were it proposed."[11] James Sherman declined the request of President William Howard Taft that he intercede with legislative leaders, saying "I am to be Vice-President and acting as a messenger boy is not part of the duties of a Vice-President."[12] Marshall accepted Wilson's invitation to preside over the cabinet during the President's absence with some trepidation. He emphasized at the first meeting that he was acting "informally and personally" and was "not undertaking to exercise any official duty or function."[13] Truman wrote that the Vice President "is not an officer of the executive branch."[14] Eisenhower, too, believed that the second man "is not legally a part of the Executive branch and is not subject to direction by the President."[15] Accordingly, Eisenhower would not direct Vice President Nixon to take specific assignments but would, according to Nixon, "wonder aloud if I might like to take over this or that project . . ."[16]

A second constitutional argument also found adherents. The Constitution provides that "the executive power shall be vested in a President of the United States of America." This suggests that he has final responsibility for executive actions. His right to delegate is therefore limited. The President could not assign tasks to the Vice President, the reasoning went, without abrogating his duties.

Perhaps some earnestly subscribed to these views, but the suspicion remains that the two constitutional defenses concealed other motives. Neither rested on sound logic. The first argument gave separation of powers a formality unsupported by common practice. The different functions government performs—legislation, administration, and adjudication—have, to varying degrees, been shared by the three branches. Presidents often consulted with members of the other branches and drafted them for special assignments. Why could they not have done the same with the Vice President? Further, the argument rested on the convenient, though not clearly correct, assumption that the Vice President was part of the legislative branch. Garner was closer to the truth in describing the office as "a no man's land somewhere between the legislative and executive branch."[17] If presiding over the Senate implicated the Vice President with Congress, standing with the presidential candidate in the election surely associated him with the executive branch. As Mondale put it, the Vice President is "the only officer of the federal government who breaches the separation of powers, being a member of both the legislative and the executive branches of government."[18]

That the President possessed executive responsibility need not have excluded his deputy from active participation. The

Chief Executive could have solicited his advice and asked him to undertake assignments while retaining authority to make decisions, or at least remaining accountable for them.

More likely, other factors produced the idleness of Vice Presidents. Government did little until the New Deal. The presidency was not itself very strenuous; there was little need for a second officer to relieve the Chief Executive of burdens he did not have. Even had work pressed the Chief Executive, he probably would not have turned to the Vice President for help. Rarely did the two get along. Party bosses, not the presidential nominee, played the leading role in filling the ticket. Considerations of balance, not of compatibility, governed the selection of the vice-presidential candidate. Not surprisingly, the modicum of trust necessary for a President to delegate tasks to his Vice President often did not exist when the two belonged to different factions. Occasionally, happy relations developed. Several pairs got along famously: Jackson and Van Buren, Polk and Dallas, and McKinley and Hobart. More often the association was stormy. Adams and Jefferson, Madison and Clinton, Jackson and Calhoun, and Garfield and Arthur were mutually hostile in the nineteenth century; McKinley and Roosevelt, Roosevelt and Fairbanks, Coolidge and Dawes, and Hoover and Curtis experienced strained relations in the twentieth.[19]

The futility of the vice presidency exacerbated tensions between the two. The office was a poor springboard; nor did its occupant have interesting duties. As Marshall put it, "The only business of the vice-president is to ring the White House bell every morning and ask what is the state of health of the president."[20] This was, Arthur M. Schlesinger, Jr. observes, "hardly the basis for cordial and enduring friendships."[21] Presidents must have suspected the motives of men who would accept an office whose sole appeal depended on their own death.

Finally, Presidents could expect to gain but little political capital from enlisting the help of their Vice Presidents. In a world in which power depended on control of resources, the second officer had little to dispense. "The Vice-President has no office whatever in his gift. If someone else makes an appointment for him, he has no way of repaying the favor," Theodore Roosevelt informed a friend seeking a government position.[22]

But the vice presidency was not immune to the effects of the fundamental changes in American government and politics that the New Deal began. Government became more active, with the Chief Executive assuming the leading role. His increased involvement created areas in which the Vice President, too, could take part. The White House became the active initiator of domestic programs. Groups directed demands there and expected a response. Presidents often expressed their interest by establishing committees within the Executive Office. Frequently they named the Vice President as chairman, at once giving him something to do and adding prestige to the effort. As Presidents began to submit legislative programs to Congress the Vice President became a useful liaison. America's increased involvement in world affairs also enhanced the vice presidency. Presidents were expected to travel abroad more, an activity simplified by the development of the airplane. They could not accommodate all invitations they received. The Vice President often served as a surrogate head of state, his high rank making him an appropriate representative.

As the presidency became so crucial, the credentials of the successor became a subject of greater concern. The Chief Executive could no longer ignore the Vice President. To do so would deny him the familiarity with problems he would confront should presidential vacancy elevate him. Presidents, accordingly, brought the Vice President into the cabinet; Congress made him a member of the National Security Council.

The rise of the presidency at the expense of party leaders also helped secure a greater role for the Vice President. The standard-bearer gained power virtually to dictate the choice of his running mate. This promoted compatibility between the two. Further, it provided an incentive for a President to use his lieutenant. The Chief Executive, not party leaders, would have to accept blame if the Vice President seemed a failure. Rather than appear to have made a mistake in the choice of the successor, Presidents preferred to praise their associate, underscoring their enthusiasm with assignments.

Close association with the executive branch also made the Vice President a useful administration spokesman. Presidents could not devote much of their time to defending their record or educating the public on certain issues. Nor could they often attack their critics without seeming too sensitive and unpresidential. Among the functions of the vice-presidential candidate were echo, defender of the standard-bearer, and attacker of opponents. Once in office, he performed these same roles. And by giving speeches at conventions of various interest groups, the Vice President could help the administration retain their favor. Moreover, as primaries became the decisive stage in gaining presidential nominations in the mid-1970s, the Chief Executive became increasingly susceptible to challenge from within his own party.[23] The Vice President was available to campaign for the administration in those races. Indeed, Mondale spent much of late 1979 and 1980 performing that chore.

The rise of the presidency made local parties more dependent on him. Local candidates enlisted his help in their campaigns. Air travel made possible forays to help office-seekers around the nation. But Presidents sought to restrict their partisan activity. Time presented one constraint. Further, Presidents like to present themselves as statesmen, an image tarnished by frequent political activity. That the party that controlled the White House usually fared poorly in midterm elections also discouraged presidential activity. Presidents are not usually inclined to associate themselves with losing efforts. The Vice President helped solve this dilemma by assuming heavy responsibility as a party worker.

President of the Senate

As Vice Presidents have become increasingly active in their institutional and political roles, they have devoted less time to their constitutional function of presiding over the Senate. They chair Senate sessions rarely. Nixon said he averaged a half-hour to an hour daily in that role, 5 percent to 10 percent of his workday; Agnew made a similar estimate.[24] So negligent had most Vice Presidents been in their prescribed role that when Rockefeller presided on four consecutive days, Senate Majority Leader Mansfield praised his dedication.[25] During his first year in office, Mondale presided on nineteen days for a total of eighteen hours.[26]

In fact, there is little reason for Vice Presidents to pass their time in the chair. The powers of the presiding officer are meager.[27] Senate rules allow him little discretion; as Johnson pointed out, "The Chair acts under the direction of the Senate."[28] He cannot participate in Senate debates. The Senate elects its president pro tempore, by custom the senior member of the majority party, to preside during the absence of the Vice President. He, too, avoids the duty; generally, junior members assume the chore as part of their initiation.

Only occasionally can the Vice President play an important part by presiding. The Constitution empowers him to break tie votes. In practice, this prerogative confers little power. Deadlocks rarely occur.[29] When they do, the Vice President's vote is significant only if he favors a measure. Otherwise, an even division defeats the bill. Nixon, for instance, cast only eight votes during his two terms. Most tie votes—seven of ten according to one informed estimate—favor the administration's position.[30] It usually has sufficient patronage resources to swing an additional vote if needed. The opposition has little to offer wavering legislators.

The authority to make procedural rulings provides a second source of minimal power. Vice Presidents make few such decisions; when they do, they generally follow the prompting of the parliamentarian. Occasionally, however, they can issue judgments that will affect policy outcomes.

For many years, the first controversy facing the Senate each session involved Rule 22, which until its amendment in 1975, required a two-thirds vote to limit Senate debate. The difficulty of achieving cloture enabled small minorities to prevent votes and thereby frustrate majority preference by talking continuously. By the 1950s, the filibuster had become a favorite tool to prevent passage of proposed civil rights legislation. Liberals regularly sought to relax requirements of achieving cloture.[31] Conservatives repeatedly defeated such attempts by filibustering. To succeed, reformers needed the help of the Vice President. The specific ruling they sought varied according to the parliamentary tactics being employed. Essentially, however, they wanted him to rule that debate at the beginning of each new Congress could not be continued to prevent the majority from framing new rules.

The issue came before Nixon in 1957. Senator Hubert Humphrey asked the Vice President "under what rule is the Senate presently proceeding?" Nixon stated his belief that the Senate acted under those rules carried forward from the previous Congress except that no provision could prevent a majority from framing new rules. Nixon emphasized that his statement constituted merely an expression of his own opinion and not a ruling "because under Senate precedents, a question of constitutionality can only be decided by the Senate itself, and not by the Chair." Nixon's view was praised by opponents of Rule 22, but as it was an opinion rather than a ruling it made no direct contribution to their efforts. Nixon took the same position during debates in 1959 and 1961.[32]

Johnson was less helpful to reformers when the Senate considered Rule 22 in 1963. He declined to give advisory opinions as had Nixon, and announced that he would submit any inquiry regarding a constitutional question to the Senate.[33] The practical effect of such action would be to end any chance of change. Senators could filibuster the question submitted to them. The debate generated a discussion of the powers of the Vice President as president of the Senate. Senator Jacob Javits, a leader of the reform group, urged Johnson to act to force a vote. He argued:

> The Vice Presidency is not a hollow shell. . . . History shows that it is a great and vital office in our Government. Here is an opportunity to demonstrate that it is.

Other senators, Keating, Clark, and Case among them, suggested that Johnson take some action. But when Johnson asked Keating to cite some rule or precedent that would allow the presiding officer to limit debate, Keating was silent. Johnson justified his inaction by pointing to the poverty of his office. He told the Senate:

> This is not a question, as the Chair sees it, of whether the Vice President is a figurehead. It is a question of whether the Vice President is going to arrogate to himself a responsibility and a power which he does not have.

Senator Mike Mansfield assured Johnson that he "need have no worry that any extraordinary powers will be allocated to the Vice President." Several senators, including Mansfield, Russell, McCarthy, and Ribicoff, agreed that Johnson had no power to act.[34]

As a senator, Humphrey had always advocated relaxing the two-thirds requirement. When called upon in 1967 to rule Humphrey did not act as his Senate record suggested he would. He cited his new position ("The Chair is now the Presiding Officer of the entire Senate and stands as a servant of the Senate, rather than as an advocate within it.") and precedent ("It has not been considered the proper role of the Chair to interpret the Constitution for the Senate.") as reasons for submitting the debatable constitutional question to the Senate.[35] Two years later, Humphrey ruled that the Senate could pass new provisions by simple majority. But his decision was reversed by the Senate, 53 to 45.[36] His successor, Agnew, declined to rule in a manner favorable to the reformers' position.[37]

Humphrey had acted decisively in 1969 but was reversed. But the Senate sustained Rockefeller when he ruled to the same effect in 1975 by a vote of 51 to 42. This decision did not clinch victory for Senator Walter F. Mondale and others seeking to reduce the cloture requirement to three-fifths. Senator James B. Allen attempted to prevent a vote by manipulating the rules. He called for numerous quorum calls, advanced new motions, raised points of order, and appealed decisions successfully for five days. The Mondale proposal prevailed only after Rockefeller refused to recognize Allen, who was trying to make a parliamentary inquiry, and put it to a vote. Rockefeller was acting within Senate rules, though not according to customs of the body.[38] Rockefeller played a critical role in amending the cloture rule. The reform effort could not have succeeded without his help. But it prevailed because a majority wanted it to do so. Had most senators opposed the reforms, Rockefeller's rulings, like Humphrey's in 1969, would have been overturned. The Vice President has little independent authority as presiding officer; his rulings are subject to appeal.

Of the roles Vice Presidents play, that of president of the Senate is least rewarding but most secure. The duty has little to recommend it in terms of power conferred, potential for favorable publicity, or intrinsic interest. It is, however, the one assignment bestowed on Vice Presidents by constitutional grant.

Presidential Grants

Elsewhere vice-presidential activity depends on presidential generosity. The types of roles Vice Presidents play are fairly standard. But the extent and significance of functions Presidents give their Vice Presidents depend on the relationship between the two individuals. As Humphrey observed:

> What the Vice President will do or is permitted to do, in the main, is determined by what the President assigns to him or permits him to do and the power and authority that he is willing to share with him. The President can bestow assignments and authority and can remove that authority and power at will. I used to call this Humphrey's law— "He who giveth can taketh away and often does."[39]

Past alliance does not, as Humphrey discovered, guarantee that a satisfactory relationship will continue.[40]

One factor which plagued past relationships has already been mentioned. Since the sole attraction of the vice presidency was the possibility of succeeding to the White House, Presidents suspected the motives of those who accepted the second office. Some astute observers believe that that impediment strains the relationship still. As Henry Kissinger put it, "The relationship between the President and any Vice President is never easy; it is, after all, disconcerting to have at one's side a man whose life's ambition will be achieved by one's death."[41] Indeed, Lyndon Johnson observed of his vice presidency that "every time I came into John Kennedy's presence, I felt like a goddamn raven hovering over his shoulder."[42] Arthur Schlesinger, Jr. argued that "antagonism is inherent in the relationship." He explains, "Presidents inevitably resent the death's head at the feast; Vice Presidents equally resent the monarch who stuffs himself at the banquet table while they scramble for leavings."[43] To be sure, the situation is awkward. Yet it is not clear that incompatibility is inevitable. First, there is less reason for modern Presidents to suspect the good will of their Vice Presidents. The second office is no longer bereft of interesting duties. Moreover, it offers a sufficiently attractive springboard to a presidential nomination that capable leaders seek it even when their chances of becoming President by succession might be thought slight.[44] Second, the extent to which resentment hampers relations between the President and Vice President would seem to depend upon the personalities involved. Nixon and Johnson, prone as they apparently were to find conspiracies nearby, may have felt uncomfortable with the arrangement first as Vice Presidents, then as Chief Executives.[45] Yet there is no indication that similar mistrust colored the relations between Ford and Rockefeller or between Carter and Mondale.

Rather, the nature of the relations between President and Vice President rests on four factors. First, the President and Vice President must be personally congenial. "The most important factor is personality, the trust factor that exists between the two men," observes Senator Birch Bayh.[46] Presidents are less likely to assign important tasks to Vice Presidents they do not like, trust, and respect. Formation of an amicable association does not depend on the President alone. The Vice President must recognize that he is, in fact, a subordinate. He must act as part of the President's administration. This in itself will not assure him the confidence of the Chief Executive. But failure to behave in such a fashion will almost surely result in ostracism. The President and Vice President must be comfortable in their relationship. Kennedy liked Johnson and extended many courtesies to him. Johnson often responded effusively. "Where you lead—I will follow," he wrote Kennedy on one occasion; "I am constantly amazed, amidst all you have to do, that you never overlook the extra kind-nesses," he wrote on another. He sent word to Kennedy that he felt himself treated better than his predecessors. Still, the association was not happy. During the eight years they had served together in the Senate, Kennedy was a backbencher subject to, and dependent upon, Johnson's power. Neither found the sharp role reversal easy.[47]

Second, the two officers must be politically compatible. They need not agree on every issue, but Presidents are less likely to entrust meaningful responsibilities to a subordinate who will not execute them in the manner desired.

Third, the President must believe the Vice President has something to offer him. This varies with the relative strengths and weaknesses of the administration and of the Vice President. Some Vice Presidents may have links to particular groups that can prove useful to the Chief Executive. Nixon's ties to the Republican right made him a valuable intermediary to deal with Senator Joseph McCarthy. Humphrey's long association with liberal groups made him a logical spokesman for the Johnson administration's conduct of the Vietnam War. Ford's popularity on Capitol Hill made him an emissary to congressmen hostile to Nixon. Mondale's credibility in the Washington community enabled him to promote Carter to a constituency unfamiliar with, and suspicious of, him. Others may have expertise valuable to the administration. Nixon, Johnson, and Mondale, for instance, possessed greater legislative experience and acumen than did the Presidents under whom they served; Rockefeller had extensive schooling in domestic affairs and administration. Some have little to recommend them. Presidents will use their Vice Presidents more if they are dependent on their skills or reputations for achieving desired goals.

The relationship beween the President and the Vice President affects the way in which others treat the second officer. Members of the executive branch take their cues from their leader. If the President looks favorably on the second officer, subordinates are more likely to do so, too.[48] Yet a qualification needs to be made. A fourth factor shaping the association of the two highest officers is the relationship between the Vice President and the White House staff. That the President treats the Vice President with respect encourages his aides to do so; it does not guarantee that they will. For White House staffers may view the Vice President as a competitor. As his influence rises theirs may decline. As he receives assignments and authority they lose out. As he spends more time with the President less remains for them. Further, he is an outsider. White House aides are largely committed to serving the President. But the Vice President may have other interests. The staff may not trust or respect the second officer. Accordingly, relations between the White House staff and Vice President are usually strained and often impede a meaningful role for the second officer. Backbiting is common. Although Kennedy treated Johnson graciously, the White House staff showed the Vice President little deference.[49] Humphrey encountered resistance among Johnson's associates; Joseph Califano and others worked to deny him a meaningful role.[50] Nixon's top aides viewed Agnew with hostility.[51] Ford subordinates, especially Donald Rumsfeld, placed obstacles in Rockefeller's path.[52]

Mondale maintained excellent relations with Carter's top aides during his years in office. Ranking White House staffers like Hamilton Jordan and Jody Powell publicly praised Mondale and declared themselves his subordinates.[53] In 1977, Mondale's principal assistant, Richard Moe, traced the unprecedented harmony to two factors:

> The principal aides are very secure in their relationships with the President and Vice President. They're not threatened by the Vice President playing an important role. The President has made it abundantly clear that he wants the Vice President to play an important role.[54]

"The President was determined to make this relationship work and he made it clear to everyone in the administration," Moe repeated in January 1981.[55] The harmonious relationship apparently continued throughout the Carter administration.[56] Mondale and his staff worked closely with Carter's aides. Mondale's assistants performed assignments that Presidents normally would assign to their own appointees. Moe, for instance, headed a White House task force on hospital cost containment, supervised administration efforts to uphold the presidential veto of the defense authorization bill, and directed lobbying against the proposed constitutional amendment to balance the budget. In many of these efforts, Carter's primary staff members functioned in subordinate roles.[57] Smooth contact between the Vice President and his staff and the White House staff contributes to good relations between President and Vice President.

The dramatic changes in American politics and government since the New Deal have created a context that provides new outlets for vice-presidential activity. The Vice President is no longer limited to the tedium of presiding over the Senate. Rather, he has become, in practice, a member of the executive branch. The responsibilities that he undertakes upon assignment by the President give his office what substance it has. The following two chapters discuss in turn the institutional and political duties of the Vice President.

7

★ ★

Institutional Roles

*T*he institutional responsibilities that Presidents have attached to the vice presidency since 1953 have lent respectability to the office. That recent Presidents, unlike their predecessors, have allowed their Vice Presidents executive duties is not accidental. The increased role of the presidential candidate in choosing a running mate and the heightened visibility of his subordinate have created incentives for the Chief Executive to involve him; the new importance of the President in foreign and domestic affairs since the New Deal has provided opportunities for vice-presidential activity. Presidents have appointed Vice Presidents to chair commissions, sent them on trips abroad, and used them as advisers. The importance of these assignments has varied according to the relationship between the two officers. Some tasks have been make-work;[1] others have involved the second officer in useful activities.

Commission Chairman

Presidents have appointed their Vice Presidents to head various commissions on domestic problems. Such supervisory activities have brought the Vice President into the executive branch in a formal way but at risk to both officers. The Vice President is the one major figure in the executive branch who the Chief Executive cannot remove at will. Presidents are accordingly reluctant to delegate important areas to them.[2] Vice

Presidents often receive many assignments but little authority, responsibilities but no power.

The process of making these roles a regular vice-presidential activity began with Eisenhower. On 13 August 1953 he signed Executive Order 10479 creating the Government Contracts Committee with Nixon as its chairman. Its charge was to end racial discrimination in companies holding government contracts. The committee, Eisenhower later wrote, "performed an invaluable service" in persuading companies to end bias against blacks.[3] That assessment exaggerates its impact, for the committee was limited by its small budget and staff and its lack of enforcement power.[4] Eisenhower later asked Nixon to head the Cabinet Committee on Price Stability for Economic Growth, a group devised to recommend policies to control inflation. Nixon apparently did not regard these as significant duties: he ignores them in his books and mentions them without elaboration in an extensive interview on his years as Vice President.[5]

Kennedy gave Johnson greater responsibilities in the government's efforts to combat racial discrimination. He combined the President's Committee on Government Contracts and the President's Committee on Government Employment Policy into the President's Committee on Equal Employment Opportunity with Johnson as its head. It retained the same purpose as the Nixon body; as Kennedy put it, "to ensure that Americans of all colors and beliefs will have equal access to employment within the government, and with those who do business with the government."[6] But the new entity had greater enforcement powers and was more active than the earlier body. It could terminate government contracts with companies that discriminated on racial grounds. It solicited complaints from government workers of such mistreatment; in its first two years it handled more such allegations than its predecessor had in seven and a half.[7] It successfully encouraged companies to sign "Plans for Progress" and labor unions to agree to "Plans for Fair Practices." Kennedy praised its work in his 1962 State of the Union address and elsewhere.[8]

Initially, Johnson was reluctant to undertake the assignment.[9] Some Johnson associates were pessimistic about its prospects; a memo his staff prepared for him judged that "this committee probably has more potential harm than good."[10] But Johnson actively pursued the committee's goals. According to Roy Wilkins, then the director of the NAACP:

> Mr. Johnson began to emerge during the Kennedy Administration wholly unexpectedly and to the delight of the civil rights forces in areas that we didn't expect him to be active as Vice President. For example, he took a very personal concern on the fair employment business. He used the inevitable telephone, without which he is never seen or heard, and he called all manner of people—unions and employers and all over the country on the matter of increasing their employment of Negroes. Now, for a Vice President of the United States to do this, and especially a man who knew his way around and where the bodies were buried, so to speak, in Washington, this was very effective.[11]

Johnson wrote letters to heads of government departments urging them to cooperate with the committee. The response was favorable.[12] He communicated frequently with black leaders.[13]

Some administration officials found fault with the committee's conduct. "The President's Commission is operating without direction," Ralph Horton, Jr. wrote Robert Kennedy. "The Vice President sees the program as an opportunity to build his image as a liberal."[14] The Attorney General also criticized what he regarded as the slow pace of the committee's efforts.[15]

Johnson apparently increased his control over the committee late in his term as Vice President. Secretary of Labor Arthur Goldberg appointed the first two Executive Vice Chairmen but Johnson was sufficiently in command by late 1962 to name Hobart Taylor, Jr. as the third occupant of the post.[16] Still he faced constraints. Taylor recalls that President Kennedy and Attorney General Robert F. Kennedy occasionally advised Johnson to ignore discrimination in states represented by important senators. Johnson would later take the public blame for his apparent indifference.[17] Johnson occasionally implied that he was frustrated at being under reins.[18]

A second assignment given Johnson and subsequent Vice Presidents was direction of the National Aeronautics and Space Council. Johnson had long been interested in this area. On 10 April 1961 Kennedy sent a draft bill to Congress proposing that the Vice President replace the Chief Executive as its chairman. The measure passed Congress ten days later. Kennedy occasionally referred publicly to space studies Johnson was directing.[19] Johnson seems to have had a measure of control at NASC as its director, James Webb, was an old friend.

Johnson had few formal assignments. But race and space were among the most pressing problems America faced in the early 1960s. By associating Johnson and the vice presidency with them, Kennedy gave both prestige. Vice-presidential functions proliferated in the Johnson administration. Humphrey, one journalist wrote, "wears more hats than Hedda Hopper."[20] Yet some roles were so trivial that they demeaned the office. Humphrey chaired President's councils on youth opportunity, Native American opportunity, and recreation and natural beauty; he headed a cabinet-level task force to promote tourist travel within the United States. By statute he headed the NASC; Congress added a second such post when it made him chairman of the Council on Marine Resources and Engineering.[21] More assignments did not necessarily suggest more prestige. There was truth, as well as humor, in Humphrey's suggestion that the only assignments Congress gave him were "out of this world or down under the seas."[22]

At the outset of his term, Humphrey seemed likely, as chairman of the President's Council on Equal Opportunity, to coordinate the administration's civil rights program. He soon lost that assignment ostensibly of his own volition. In a memorandum to Johnson made public on 24 September 1965, Humphrey "concluded that the reasons for creating the council no longer exist," and suggested "that it be terminated."[23] Senator William Proxmire praised the recommendation as another Humphrey contribution to civil rights.[24] In fact, the memorandum was a face-saving device. Humphrey wished to keep the assignment. But Johnson "wanted to stay on top of everything"[25] and was persuaded by his chief domestic assistant, Joseph Califano, to take it from Humphrey.[26]

Humphrey was active in many of his assignments. He successfully contacted public and private employers in search of jobs for youth. He energetically promoted domestic travel and marine programs. These efforts were useful but they did not involve Humphrey in major problems of the period. His only role in an area of real significance was as liaison to the nation's mayors.

Agnew inherited most of the responsibilities Humphrey had held. In addition, Nixon named him to head the new Office of Intergovernmental Relations. Federal departments were to view Agnew as Nixon's "personal representative to smooth out any rough spots in their relations with state and local government," Nixon instructed. It would be Agnew's responsibility "to help make the Federal executive branch more sensitive and receptive to the views of state and local officials." Agnew would help "move government closer to the people and to make it more responsive to their will."[27]

The agency did not perform up to its advance billing. Agnew tried to relay positions of the governors to the administration. But he found himself helpless to act on their grievances. The office was abolished in December 1972. So slight was its impact that "few tears were shed over its demise and its passing was scarcely noticed."[28]

Few of these chairmanships still existed when Ford took office in December 1973. Aside from directing a Committee on Privacy, he remained aloof from the executive branch during his abbreviated term.[29]

Rockefeller, however, undertook some assignments of potential substance. Ford asked him to oversee the Domestic Council as its vice chairman.[30] The President agreed, over the objections of members of the White House staff, to allow Rockefeller to appoint its staff director. Rockefeller's choice, James Cannon, was to be responsible to Rockefeller while reporting directly to Ford. But Rockefeller met with frustration in his involvement with the council. The Vice President had viewed it as a vehicle for long-range planning. But Ford's top aide, Donald Rumsfeld, assigned it problems demanding immediate attention.[31] The major function of the council became channelling paper to and from the White House. These projects diverted the council from the role Rockefeller preferred. He soon disengaged from it, and during his last year in office was relieved of supervisory responsibilities at his own request.

Ford also named Rockefeller to head an investigation into the activities of the Central Intelligence Agency. Rockefeller and his associates were to examine allegations of "massive violations or infringements of civil rights" and the suitability of statutes in the area.[32] Fearing that this assignment would intrude upon the time he could spend in domestic policy formulation and would inject him into controversy, Rockefeller narrowed the scope of the commission's review. The final report did not focus upon past CIA plans to assassinate foreign politicians, although Rockefeller did apparently undertake a confidential investigation on this matter, the findings of which he forwarded to congressional committees.[33]

Rockefeller's committee lost credibility in some circles for its narrow focus and conservative composition.

Rockefeller also served on a number of other commissions. He chaired the National Commission on Productivity and Work Quality, the President's Panel on Federal Compensation, and the National Commission on Water Quality, and was a member of the Commission on the Organization of Government for the Conduct of Foreign Policy. These roles had limited significance.[34]

Most recent Vice Presidents have pointed proudly to their chairmanships as evidence of their stature. Mondale, however, largely avoided these positions.[35] He explained: "In the past, Vice Presidents have often taken on minor functions in order to make it appear that their role was significant when, if they were President, they wouldn't touch them at all. I decided to stay away from that."[36] These duties posed problems common to the experience of many of his predecessors.

First, Vice Presidents who directed presidential committees with operational responsibilities became adversaries of some part of the bureaucracy. Many of the functions they assumed normally resided elsewhere. Their committees impinged on other jurisdictions. Hostility ensued.

Secondly, Vice Presidents could not afford to move their committees in directions likely to prompt presidential rebuke. Such action would embarrass both officials. As Charles Kirbo has observed:

> There is one thing that troubles all of us and that troubles me, and that is that you can't put the Vice-President in a position where the President will have to reverse him. If you put him in an executive function on a regular basis where you have got the risk of him doing something and then having the President go in there and turn it around, well, that is a bad relationship.[37]

Presidents gave the second officer only minor assignments;

Vice Presidents generally conducted themselves in a subservient manner.

The possibility of reversal suggests a third problem—Vice Presidents lacked authority. The Kennedys restrained Johnson in dealing with employment discrimination; Agnew could not satisfy the demands of governors; solutions Rockefeller developed received little attention.

Fourth, many tasks demeaned the vice presidency by their insignificance. Topics like marine resources, Indian opportunity, domestic travel, and so forth were appropriate perhaps for an assistant secretary but not for a Vice President. Government officials and observers could hardly think the Vice President important so long as his activities were so clearly peripheral.

Insignificant though these chores were, they consumed time. They filled the Vice President's day with secondary problems, preventing him from focusing on major concerns. Mondale sought to escape this trap. Early in the Carter administration, Richard Moe explained: "Mondale wants to stay unencumbered by any institutional responsibilities that would tie him down to a particular space and time. . . . He wants to be left free to float to the problems."[38]

Finally, Vice Presidents generally lack the staff support to undertake major operational duties. For instance, Kennedy's secretaries of labor, not Johnson, assumed much of the responsibility for directing the President's Committee on Equal Employment Opportunity. They could call upon a department for support; Johnson commanded but a small staff.[39]

Chairmanships of presidential committees offer Vice Presidents some opportunity for useful service. Johnson made a contribution through his work on the equal employment opportunity committee, as did Humphrey in various roles, and Rockefeller through the Domestic Council. Yet often these assignments created only the illusion of work. The committee chairmanships were significant in identifying the Vice President as a part of the executive branch. Ironically, they also constrained his useful involvement.

Special Envoy

Foreign travel has provided a second institutional activity for recent Vice Presidents. They have covered much of the globe in frequent journeys abroad. Table 7.1 suggests the extent of their peregrinations.

TABLE 7.1
Foreign Travel of Vice Presidents

Vice President	Trips	Countries Visited
Nixon	7	54
Johnson	10	26
Humphrey	12	31
Agnew	7	28
Ford	1	1
Rockefeller	6	12
Mondale	14	35

In foreign travel as elsewhere, the Vice President depends on the Chief Executive for his assignments. Eisenhower helped Nixon's image by sending him to each inhabited continent. Kennedy gave Johnson extensive opportunity to travel. Carter indicated Mondale's importance to his administration by sending him to major countries during their term.

Other Presidents were more parsimonious in allowing travel. Johnson ignored or rejected several apparently reasonable trips for Humphrey. Early in 1965, Chester Bowles suggested Humphrey visit India, where Bowles then served as American ambassador. The White House staff, acting for Johnson, scotched the idea. A year later two Humphrey trips were proposed—a visit to Latin America and another to England where

Humphrey would participate in the installation of Oliver Franks as chancellor of East Anglia University and receive an honorary degree. Johnson instructed an aide to "relay to the Vice President that he should slow down on his travelling." Nor did a projected trip to East European nations materialize.[40] Still, Johnson at times allowed Humphrey to undertake major missions. Some were, in fact, designed to help Humphrey's sagging popularity. Nixon, however, was consistently inconsiderate to Agnew in this regard. He rarely allowed Agnew to visit a major ally, sending him instead to battle zones in Asia.

Use of the Vice President as an envoy offers several advantages. Presidents and secretaries of state cannot satisfy all the diplomatic demands made on them. Vice Presidents can ease part of the burden. As Humphrey contends, "He can perform assignments that the President feels would be unwise for him to take on himself, but for which an official lower than Vice President would be unsuitable."[41]

Nor are Vice Presidents usually reluctant to travel abroad. Foreign trips invariably maximize their public exposure. The media, which pays little attention to the daily calendar of the Vice President, find much that is newsworthy every time he steps on foreign soil. Further, these missions help establish foreign affairs credentials for Vice Presidents. They cite the number of countries visited as evidence of their diplomatic expertise.[42] Finally, international voyages offer one of the few chances the Vice President has to appear, as well as to be, busy. Neither President nor Vice President appreciates the recurring suggestion that the second person is inactive. Such commentary makes the former appear foolhardy, the latter foolish. Trips help silence these assertions.

Vice-presidential travel is advantageous for America's two top officers. That these trips serve some vital national purpose is often less evident. But various journeys have been important. First, they often allow some significant communications. Occasionally, the trip may produce merely an exchange of polemics. Nixon, for instance, visited Russia in 1959 for meetings with Premier Nikita Khrushchev. Their sessions produced direct discussion at a high level of central issues of the Cold War. Neither side budged from previous ideological predispositions.[43]

More often, the mission may be designed to convey some message likely to produce a tangible result. Kennedy sent Johnson to southern Europe and to the Near East in the summer of 1962 to discuss military needs of allies there. The mission was delicate; some of the countries—Greece, Iran— were upset over reductions in American military and economic aid. Johnson handled the discussions skillfully for which he won Kennedy's commendation upon his return.[44] Nearly five years later Johnson sent Humphrey to Western Europe. With some success, Humphrey discussed a range of topics including nonproliferation of nuclear weapons, the Kennedy round of tariff talks, and the future of NATO with Prime Minister Harold Wilson in Great Britain, President Charles de Gaulle in France, and Chancellor Kurt George Kiesinger in West Germany.[45]

Mondale, too, took important messages with him on some trips. Less than seventy-two hours after taking the oath as Vice President, Mondale embarked on a ten-day mission to confer with America's major allies. In announcing the trip, Carter said Mondale's agenda would include discussing coordination of NATO policies and of a response to increased oil prices; Mondale would also advise allies of the administration's policies regarding the Mideast, South Africa, and problems relating to Cyprus.[46] Other economic issues were also raised.

In part, the mission was designed to illustrate Carter's intention of consulting friendly nations rather than acting unilaterally. Mondale underscored this point at the outset. He said that his trip to Europe and Japan indicated Carter's interest in "early consultations aimed at progress on the interests our peoples share."[47]

But Mondale went as a purveyor of policy, too. He urged France and West Germany to join voluntarily in a moratorium on sales and purchases of nuclear breeder devices. He helped arrange the economic summit meeting between Western leaders. Mondale won wide praise for his handling of the mission.

Mondale's second trip abroad was also significant. The nineday excursion through five European countries in May 1977 provided ample occasion to echo Carter's emphasis on human rights. Mondale praised Spain for its democratization and discussed human rights with Marshal Tito in Yugoslavia. But the most meaningful exchange on human rights came during Mondale's meetings with South African Prime Minister John Vorster in Vienna. Mondale's assignment as manager of administration policy toward Africa had become known a month earlier. This added force to his warning that policies of apartheid jeopardized relations between America and South Africa. American officials reported that Mondale gained concessions from Vorster regarding holding elections in Rhodesia.[48]

At times a vice-presidential visit may carry important symbolic value in communicating support for a regime or policy. Nixon, for instance, celebrated the second anniversary of Diem's government in Saigon where he promised "the warm support and admiration of the American people."[49] He also visited Austria in 1956 to demonstrate American concern for, and support of, Hungarian refugees.[50] Johnson's stop in Taiwan in 1961 confirmed continuing American support for that island. Mondale's visits to Spain and Portugal indicated solidarity with newly democratic polities.

But never has a vice-presidential visit provided so effective a demonstration of commitment as did Johnson's to Berlin in August 1961. Kennedy sent Johnson there to calm fears occasioned by the construction of the Berlin Wall. Johnson spoke movingly before the Bundesrat and before crowds numbering as many as 250,000. His presence signified American support and his performance earned effusive praise. Kennedy termed the mission "remarkably successful and important" and "this most important service."[51] Majority Leader Mansfield referred to Johnson's "great tact and diplomacy" and his "deep perception of the complexities of the situation." The Minority Leader, Senator Everett M. Dirksen, thought Johnson "performed superbly and did a great job for the President and for his country." Senator Albert Gore labelled it a "signal service." The media joined in the tributes.[52]

Promoting good will is a second purpose vice-presidential trips serve. Nixon, for instance, took an extended trip to the Far East in the autumn of 1953 in which he made himself visible to crowds in all nations he visited.[53] In 1957 he took a similar trip to Africa. His visit to England in 1958 included more ceremony than substance. One columnist proclaimed Nixon the most popular American visitor in years.[54]

Johnson's second mission abroad was designed to boost American popularity in Asia. He succeeded. "The Vice President undoubtedly scored a personal hit with most Asians who saw him, including the man in the street," wrote one reporter.[55] Humphrey went to Western Europe "to convince the doubting Europeans that the Johnson administration is still interested in them."[56] He later visited nine African countries to assure them that American involvement in Asia did not connote indifference toward Africa.

Vice-presidential trips occasionally take a third form, factfinding missions. Nixon's initial foray was characterized this way. He presented a lengthy report to the National Security Council upon his return.[57] Kennedy described Johnson's trip to Asia as "a special fact-finding mission."[58] The trip did have an information-gathering function which Johnson emphasized in South Vietnam. "I have come to listen to your ideas and to discuss with you our ideas so that together we may find better ways to preserve the independence of security of your nation," he told President Ngo Dinh Diem, whom he somewhat exuberantly called the "Churchill of today."[59] Johnson later told Kennedy that Diem was a complex man with many political problems and suggested that America might have to fight Communism in his country.[60]

Humphrey's trips to Southeast Asia were invariably described as fact-finding ventures. The experiences apparently did shape his view of the war. On his first trip there in February 1966, Humphrey received most of his information from briefings conducted by Ambassador Henry Cabot Lodge and General William C. Westmoreland. These contacts convinced him of the propriety of the American effort. He returned home more hawkish than when he left. But considerations of propaganda, not policy, produced the trip. Johnson wanted Humphrey's "report" to identify the Chinese as the aggressors, a "fact" Humphrey's staff had not found. The fifty-page memo Humphrey sent Johnson did not meet with approval; the White House ultimately issued an abbreviated report devoid of substance.[61] Before Humphrey returned, members of the White House staff concocted ways to maximize the political capital of the trip. One Johnson aide proposed that Humphrey brief members of the Senate Foreign Relations, Armed Services, and Appropriations committees.[62] Such a session, the memo argued, would divert attention from the Senate Foreign Relations hearings while excluding such vocal critics of administration policy as Senators Gruening, Hartke, and McGovern. Humphrey emerged from the trip as an active advocate of the war before congressional groups and on public platforms.[63]

The motives behind some vice-presidential trips have been suspect. Indeed, Arthur Schlesinger has identified the trips' design as "getting Vice Presidents out of sight."[64] Although some trips have produced useful dividends, others have seemed superfluous. Vice Presidents have often toured obscure and insignificant countries at a leisurely pace with little apparent purpose.

Several of Johnson's trips seem well-described as makework. The primary purpose of his first diplomatic mission was representing the United States at independence celebrations in Senegal. Kennedy added luster to the tour by asking Johnson to meet with Arthur H. Dean, the American representative at talks on a nuclear test ban in Geneva, and with Ambassador James Gavin and the NATO commander, General Lauris Norstad, in Paris. Secretary of Defense Robert McNamara asked Johnson to inspect military installations in Spain. Kennedy greeted Johnson upon his return and pronounced the mission an important success. Yet so senior a representative was not needed for the festivities in Senegal and whatever Johnson absorbed in Geneva, Paris, and Spain could have been conveyed by telephone or cable.

Like other Vice Presidents, Johnson attended inaugurations and funerals of foreign leaders. He helped install Juan Bosch as president of the Dominican Republic and helped bury Dag Hammarskjold and Pope John XXIII. Kennedy attempted to give substance to the Hammarskjold assignment. He wrote Johnson that "there is much going on in our discussions with our major European allies and I shall be glad to have the advantage of your own account of discussions which you might have in Paris with our senior people there. . . ."[65] Johnson met with Norstad, Gavin, and Thomas Finletter in sessions designed to project the appearance of involvement.

Johnson's last two trips abroad as Vice President were equally marginal. He spent nearly two weeks visiting Sweden, Finland, Norway, Denmark, and Iceland in September 1963. None were major countries; indeed Johnson was the highest-ranking American official ever to visit any of them. He gave a number of speeches and conferred with leaders but the trip was devoid of any tangible purpose or result. Less than two months later he performed ceremonial chores in Luxembourg, the Netherlands, and Belgium.[66]

Yet the Johnson trips were not so inconsequential as some Agnew took. His debut in diplomatic travel included some important stops—South Vietnam, Taiwan, and Australia—and had the ostensible purpose of explaining the Nixon Doctrine.[67] Yet his three-and-a-half-week mission also took him to Nepal (which never before merited an American of higher rank than senator), Afghanistan, Malaysia, and Singapore, hardly major stops. Agnew had little authority to negotiate; his primary role was to listen.[68]

Nixon later found foreign travel an expedient way to help Agnew escape some domestic controversies. He sent him on a month-long trip to eleven countries in Asia, Africa, and Europe. The journey began with the inauguration of South Korean President Chung Hee Park and included stays in Singapore, Kuwait, Ethiopia, Kenya, the Congo, Morocco, and Portugal. Agnew's schedule was sufficiently open to allow time for thirteen rounds of golf.[69]

The perceived importance of vice-presidential trips depends largely on actions of the President. A vice-presidential trip seems more significant if the President identifies the Vice President as his personal representative. Kennedy, for instance, conveyed this message by letter to foreign leaders and by word to the public and often rearranged his schedule to meet with the Vice President before his departure. Carter followed this example. He saw Mondale off to Europe with the assurance that "The agenda is the same as if I were making the trip myself. . . . All the leaders know that when they see Mondale, he is coming there as my personal emissary."[70] Before Mondale's meetings with Vorster, the White House disclosed that the Vice President was in charge of African policy. Presidents lend dignity to the mission when they greet the Vice President upon his return and hear his report soon after.

Presidential Adviser

Nowhere is the Vice President so dependent on the Chief Executive as he is in a third institutional role—that of presidential adviser. The cost to the President of giving the second officer committee chairmanships and travel opportunities is relatively low. But presidential time is precious. The President will spend it conferring with his Vice President only if he anticipates some valuable return. The ability of the Vice President to influence important decisions is contingent almost entirely on his relationship with the President.

Attempts have been made to institutionalize the Vice President's role as policy adviser. Presidents have invited him to cabinet meetings; Congress has made him a member of the NSC. These steps have helped establish the office as part of the executive branch and have improved its image. Occasionally these memberships may offer the Vice President an opportunity to contribute. But the Vice President does not become an important adviser merely by attending these sessions. He may not participate. Or the President may ignore his advice.

Further, Presidents rarely use such bodies as forums for meaningful deliberation. Eisenhower was an exception. But most recent Presidents have questioned the efficiency of engaging cabinet members in meetings outside their area of competence. They resist attempts to impose upon them advisers whose views they are not anxious to hear. And they realize that their control increases in informal sessions. Cabinet and NSC meetings are often called to announce decisions, not to make them. They have symbolic rather than substantive functions.[71]

Eisenhower's emphasis on large meetings worked to Nixon's advantage. Meetings of the cabinet, NSC, and legislative leaders occurred frequently and provided the arena for discussions producing decisions. In his first seven and a quarter years in office, Nixon attended 163 cabinet meetings (19 of which he chaired), 217 NSC sessions (presiding over 26), and 173 conferences with legislative leaders. From all accounts he participated actively. Private talks with Eisenhower, in person or by phone, occurred less often.[72] Nixon was able to carve a niche for himself as a political adviser during Eisenhower's first term. He was a skilled politician in an administration whose top personnel came from other backgrounds. Accordingly, he advised Eisenhower and cabinet officials on dealings with Congress in general and with McCarthy in particular.[73] Nixon assumed a broader portfolio in his second term. Others solicited his views on policy as well as tactical matters. He helped Secretary of Labor James Mitchell negotiate a settlement to the 1959 steel strike. Eisenhower asked him to investigate allegations of misconduct on the part of White House Chief of Staff Sherman Adams.[74]

Johnson lacked some of the advantages that had enabled Nixon to play an important advisory role. Kennedy disliked long meetings with large groups and so did away with the formal sessions of the cabinet and NSC that had guaranteed Nixon a role. Nor were Kennedy and his associates political novices dependent on the expertise of the Vice President. Further, the reversal in roles from their Senate days when Kennedy was Johnson's subordinate complicated their relationship.[75] Kennedy and his aides may have felt threatened by Johnson's past dominance and accordingly consulted him less often than they should have. Johnson was uneasy in his unaccustomed role. He rarely spoke in meetings unless asked to do so by the President.[76]

Yet Kennedy made a conscious effort to involve Johnson. Sorensen describes Johnson as one of six senior advisers who was "particularly close" to Kennedy; "his advice was particularly sought by the President on legislative and political problems." Schlesinger asserts that Kennedy "liked the Vice-

President, made an effort to include him in the discussions, and so on . . ."[77] O'Brien recalls that "it was clear to me that for any meeting in the White House that I structured it was automatic that the Vice President was invited." Douglas Dillon, secretary of the treasury under Kennedy, remembers Kennedy as being "very strong" about the necessity of including Johnson in discussions. Roswell Gilpatrick recalls Kennedy sending McNamara and him to Johnson for advice. Kennedy's interest was partly pragmatic; Sorensen relates that Kennedy often asked Johnson for his advice in the presence of others so Johnson could not later claim "that he had not been consulted or had not been in agreement."[78]

Recollections of Johnson associates add credibility to the portrait the Kennedy men sketch. Kennedy "went out of his way to keep his Vice President informed and to seek his judgment on important issues . . . ," wrote George Christian. Reedy thought "that President Kennedy was rather generous to Vice-President Johnson." Kennedy and Johnson saw each other several times a week and maintained a good relationship, according to a member of Johnson's vice-presidential staff.[79]

Johnson became an important adviser on civil rights. According to one black leader, Johnson "played a very key role" in 1963 in drafting the civil rights proposals "and was actually more supportive of some of the measures than some of the Administration, the other Kennedy people, were."[80] Johnson's advocacy of a massive job-training and vocational education program and of the establishment of a community relations service secured their inclusion in the Kennedy proposals.[81]

Johnson was a less successful adviser in other instances. He favored a "firmer" response during the Cuban missile crisis and opposed the wheat sale to Russia. He was not invited to play a role during the steel crisis; at other times, he did less than administration officials had hoped.[82]

Humphrey, too, had sporadic chances to contribute to decision-making, varying with Johnson's disposition. Occasionally Humphrey's presence in the Oval Office was constantly demanded. Johnson would invite him for lengthy talks in the early morning or late afternoon. Publicly, Johnson was gracious. On 21 August 1965, he told a gathering:

. . . I guess if we had a man-of-the-year poll . . . the Vice President would be voted the one person in the Government that is everybody's best friend. If the Secretary of State, Defense, or Labor or any of them had a peculiar and particular and delicate situation on their hands, I imagine they would want to talk to him—and they usually do—to get not only sympathy and understanding, but to get some energy and some effort and some constructive leadership. I know that is true of the Cabinet. It is particularly true with me. In a very wide range of fields and complex subjects, I find the Vice President specializes in practically all of them.[83]

Less than two weeks later, Johnson responded to Humphrey's birthday letter in a similar manner. He wrote, "I cherish the solid feeling that when the day becomes gray and somber, and time seems out of joint, I know I can count on your loyalty and your energy, and most of all your generous patriotism."[84]

At other times, "everybody's best friend" was neglected and abused, his wide specialization and "generous patriotism" insufficient credentials to gain entry into important councils.[85] Johnson relieved Humphrey of his duties as civil rights coordinator only days after the flattery of August 1965. Johnson often consulted Humphrey on civil rights and used the Vice President as a liaison to black leaders. Humphrey often submitted memos in this area which apparently were well received. But Humphrey played little role in formulating policy on Vietnam. He opposed bombing North Vietnam in administration councils early in his term, and argued for a political settlement in a lengthy memo to Johnson on 15 February 1965. After that his opinions were rarely solicited.[86]

Humphrey probably offered Johnson his views on the war in their private meetings. Neither principal disclosed the nature of that advice. He did occasionally discuss the war in memoranda; after a visit to West Virginia State College in November 1965, for instance, he reported that "there is a rising tide of support for your policy on Vietnam amongst the college students."[87] But Humphrey was not party to the discussions at which war policy was evolved. As George Christian, one of Johnson's press secretaries, has written, "The critical decisions on the war were made at the 'Tuesday lunch' and supplemental meetings, especially in the last two years of the Johnson Administration. Humphrey was only rarely a participant in these sessions."[88]

Kennedy and Johnson solicited, and apparently respected, the opinions of their Vice Presidents in domestic matters. Nixon, however, displayed little interest in knowing the views of Agnew or Ford on particular matters. Agnew saw Nixon in meetings but rarely alone. "I don't try to get in to see him alone, because I don't feel the insecurity that would require me to have to open that door," he explained. It seems unlikely that either Agnew or Ford could have opened that door had they tried. Nixon apparently had little respect for either. He did not seek Agnew's advice on many important matters, the decision to visit China among them. He ignored Agnew's advice on taxing municipal bonds and on the funding of a mass transit program and Ford's on congressional relations.[89] By 1970, one Nixon aide wrote, Agnew had "been frozen out by Nixon for almost two years."[90] And well into 1973, Agnew acknowledged that "the President hasn't defined my role yet. . . . I don't know exactly what I'll be doing and it's up to the President to define it."[91]

Unlike Agnew and Ford, Rockefeller found his primary role as a presidential adviser for domestic affairs. He considered himself a "staff assistant" to the Chief Executive. Rockefeller had a regular private meeting with Ford each week and had easy and frequent access to him.[92] He developed programmatic recommendations and advised Ford on numerous issues ranging from domestic policy generally to the establishment of a White House science office. Ford adopted some Rockefeller initiatives, most notably the Vice President's proposal for legislation to create a public corporation to help the United States achieve energy self-sufficiency. Ford's acceptance represented a notable achievement for Rockefeller since the President's ranking economic advisers opposed the plan. On other occasions Rockefeller was less successful. Rumsfeld sought to restrict his access to Ford. Moreover, Rockefeller's advice on various issues diverged from Ford's inclinations. The Vice President suggested providing direct assistance to help New York City out of its financial crisis at a time Ford favored a more limited approach. Rockefeller proposed nineteen major domestic policy initiatives for Ford's 1976 State of the Union address; Ford adopted only six, some in much diluted form.[93]

No previous Vice President had ever approached the importance as presidential adviser Mondale achieved while in office. From the outset, Mondale's role was to be Carter's "general adviser."[94] Conventional wisdom identified Bert Lance, Carter's first director of the Office of Management and Budget, as the President's closest associate at the outset of his term. Carter challenged that conclusion. He told one interviewer:

> With the exception of actual budget hearings and Cabinet meetings which Bert and I both attended, I saw Bert one or two hours a week. I see Fritz four to five hours a day. There is not a single aspect of my own responsibilities in which Fritz is not intimately associated. He is the only person that I have, with both the substantive knowledge and

political stature to whom I can turn over a major assignment.

Carter told a press conference that "there is no one who would approach him in his importance to me, his closeness to me, and also his ability to carry out a singular assignment with my complete trust."[95]

Regardless of Mondale's relative position among Carter's staff, the stature he achieved as an adviser was unprecedented for a Vice President. He helped choose cabinet members and influenced the appointments of several ranking figures—Secretary of HEW Joseph Califano, Secretary of Agriculture Bob Bergland, Secretary of Education Shirley M. Hufstedler, Secretary of Transportation Neil E. Goldschmidt, and Chairman of the Council of Economic Advisers Charles Schultze.[96] He participated in most major decisions. His views did not always prevail; he opposed Carter's decision to retract the proposed fifty-dollar rebate and to deliver the "malaise speech." He favored higher minimum wages and farm supports.[97] But he was a driving force in the decisions to cancel production of the B-1 bomber, to revise the government brief in the Bakke case and to slow the schedule for submitting the tax revision message.[98]

Mondale's influence as a policy adviser was made possible by his close relationship with the President. It is not unusual for Presidents to praise the second officer publicly even while privately exiling him to a political Siberia. Yet there are grounds for accepting Carter's words as sincere. First, unlike other Presidents, he apparently made no derogatory comment about his Vice President; his only publicized complaint was that Mondale did not criticize him enough.[99] Second, other members of the administration commended Mondale highly. Veteran Carter aides, like Hamilton Jordan, insisted that they considered Mondale their second boss.[100] There was little of the traditional backbiting. Relations apparently did suffer dur-

ing the latter part of 1979 following the disagreement over
the "malaise speech." "There was some stress but it passed
quickly," according to Moe.[101] Third, Mondale and his associates attested to the harmonious interaction between the
two principals and their staffs. "I have been closer to a President than maybe any Vice President in history," said Mondale during the last five weeks of his term.[102] "The President
and Vice President continued to have a close and fruitful relationship," according to Albert A. Eisele, Mondale's press
secretary. "They did more with that fairly awkward office
than anyone else had done."[103] Moe observed that tensions
had been "very few and very minor" and that there had been
"a unique relationship" which "could not have been better."[104] Finally, Carter's conduct suggested his regard for
Mondale. He gave him impressive and dignified assignments
and created conditions under which Mondale could be an
effective counselor.

Carter helped assure his Vice President a successful advisory role. He gave Mondale a White House office only steps
from his own. This proximity encouraged contact, not only
between the Vice President and Chief Executive but between
Mondale and other ranking Carter associates.[105] Second, Carter
gave Mondale the right to participate in any conference unless asked to leave. Third, he allotted one lunch a week to a
private conference with the Vice President. He frequently saw
Mondale in small group sessions, too, including his weekly
policy meetings with his foreign and domestic advisers.[106]
Fourth, Carter made available to Mondale the same information that crossed his desk. Fifth, he refused to fill Mondale's schedule with trivial, but time-consuming, tasks. Finally, during the first years of his administration he placed
Mondale in charge of the group that determined long-range
priorities.[107]

Mondale's influence apparently "persisted right until the
end." According to Eisele, "if anything it grew." Mondale

assumed major responsibility for campaigning for Carter's renomination during late 1979 and the first half of 1980. These
travels, of course, took him away from the locus of presidential decision-making. To preserve the Vice President's involvement and value as a presidential adviser, Mondale's staff
scheduled him to be away from Washington on campaign
trips for only a few days at a time. Indeed, Eisele suggests
that the political activity may have enhanced Mondale's value
as an adviser. "It gave him almost constant contact with the
public so that he became a pipeline for grassroots feelings to
the President," he said.[108]

Conclusion

Changes in American politics since the New Deal have made
the participation of the Vice President in the executive branch
politically feasible and practically possible. Presidents now
have incentive to use the second officer. The two are more
likely to be compatible now that the presidential candidate,
not party bosses, designates his running mate. But the selection process gives the Chief Executive reason to involve the
Vice President even if the relationship is not wholly satisfactory. Having chosen his partner, the President would rather
give him assignments than acknowledge tacitly his poor judgment by ignoring him. Further, the increased importance of
the presidency requires that its occupant appear to keep the
successor informed; otherwise, he will seem cavalier about
his country's future.

The rise in the presidency since the New Deal has created
opportunities for the Vice President to assume institutional
roles within the executive branch. The President cannot alone
satisfy all demands made on him. But he can indicate his
interest in certain issues by appointing the Vice President to
chair various commissions. He can maintain good will abroad
by using his deputy as his emissary. He can stay abreast of a

job becoming regularly more complex by relying on the Vice
President as an occasional adviser and trouble-shooter.

The extent to which the President uses his Vice President
depends largely on the relationship between the two and on
the ability of the second officer to contribute skills the administration otherwise lacks. At times, Presidents assign their Vice
Presidents superfluous activities which create only the sem-
blance of involvement. Proliferation of titles does not necessarily signify increased power or responsibility. Constraints
are inherent in any activity assigned the Vice President. But
many vice-presidential duties have been significant. Johnson
performed important service on the equal employment committee; Rockefeller in investigating the CIA and in overseeing
the Domestic Council. Some foreign travel of Nixon, Johnson, Humphrey, and Mondale has been substantively worthwhile as well as ceremonial. Most Vice Presidents have been
valuable advisers in at least some areas; Mondale seems to
have been most successful in this role.

Even when institutional roles give the Vice President little
power within the executive branch he still may exert some
influence outside it. Political functions offer him a second set
of activities. It is to these that we now turn.

8

★ ★ ─────────────────────────

Political Roles

*T*raditionally the Vice President was seen only in the Senate and heard nowhere. Since the New Deal, the political fortunes of the Vice President have become more closely tied to those of the Chief Executive. Consequently, Presidents have assigned him necessary political chores. Vice Presidents have become lobbyists for selected legislation, energetic party workers, frequent administration spokesmen, and presidential surrogates in primary campaigns. The mix varies according to the goals of the Chief Executive and the talents of the Vice President. But in all of these duties, the Vice President acts for his superior. The second officer can produce important results, and in performing these functions he relieves the Chief Executive of time-consuming, and often undignified, responsibilities.

Legislative Liaison

The major activity of the Vice President on Capitol Hill is not in his official capacity as president of the Senate but rather in the informal role as an administration lobbyist for selected legislation. Vice-presidential involvement in building legislative majorities is a development of relatively recent date. For only since the New Deal has the President assumed responsibility for offering a comprehensive program to Congress and only since that time has the second man become truly a member of the executive branch.

The Vice President is well suited for this role. His occasional presence in the Capitol brings him into contact with legislators. Further, most recent Vice Presidents have had legislative experience. Six of the eight Vice Presidents since 1953,[1] and nine of the twelve since 1933,[2] had served previously in one or both Houses of Congress. Accordingly, they were well acquainted with Senate mores and personalities. Finally, the Vice President may be more attuned to the problems and attitudes of elected politicians than are other administration figures. Unlike most cabinet members and White House staffers, he shares their experience of running for and serving in elective office. He is more likely to be sensitive to the considerations that motivate politicians than an appointed adviser who has never himself faced a democratic test.

Vice Presidents have known some success in representing the administration to the people's representatives. Nixon mediated between the Eisenhower administration and Senator Joseph McCarthy. He convinced McCarthy to withdraw a letter demanding an explanation of Eisenhower's position on trade with the People's Republic of China; he persuaded McCarthy to drop plans to investigate the CIA and to oppose some Eisenhower nominations; he urged Republican senators to press for a meeting between the Wisconsin senator and one of his targets, Secretary of the Army Robert Stevens. He informed Eisenhower of sentiment for the resignation of Sherman Adams. Along with other administration figures, he negotiated changes in the Bricker Amendment with its author.[3]

Johnson, too, had some impact behind the scenes. He used his friendships with congressional leaders to advance Kennedy programs. John McCormack, the Speaker of the House during most of the Kennedy presidency, recalled, "I would say that on many occasions with his many friendships, that he did everything he possibly could in a proper way as Vice-President to try and help the leadership in the House, and the President in the White House and himself as Vice-President to get through progressive legislation recommended by the President that was hotly contested and where the vote would be particularly close."[4] Johnson brought together the feuding Senator Carl Hayden and Representative Clarence Cannon, then chairmen of the relevant congressional committees, to resolve their differences on an appropriations bill. He helped in the administration's battle to enlarge the House Rules Committee. Senator George McGovern recalled that Johnson prodded him, and others, to speak in favor of Kennedy's proposed wheat sale to the Soviet Union. Senator Clinton Anderson remembered Johnson as having lobbied Senator Robert Kerr to advance the space program. Lawrence O'Brien, the Kennedy aide responsible for legislative liaison, acknowledges that Johnson was "involved," "helpful," and had some "impact."[5]

Humphrey appears to have been more active. In its early years, the Johnson administration was concerned primarily with pushing domestic measures through Congress. Humphrey said he spent most of his time in 1965 lobbying for Great Society legislation. He urged key legislators to support Johnson's immigration bill. Later that fall, the Vocational Rehabilitation Bill and farm measures occupied some of his time. He spoke to important senators about the rent supplements bill in the spring of 1966. Indeed, his top aide credited him with assuring the four-vote margin of victory in the House by persuading three representatives to abstain and another to switch his opposition to support.[6]

For a variety of reasons, both institutional and political, the three Republican Vice Presidents who followed—Agnew, Ford, and Rockefeller—were less involved in lobbying. The conservative Presidents they served had more modest legislative goals, given the Democratic Congress. Split control of government narrowed the scope for legislative work. Circumstances peculiar to each further reduced their roles.

Agnew lost any chance to be effective by his obtuse lob-

bying for the administration's position on the proposed anti-
ballistic missile and on the income tax surcharge extension.
His tactics on the latter so upset Republican Senator Len Jordan that he promulgated a rule: "Whenever I am lobbied by
the Vice President, I will automatically vote the opposite
way."[7]

Many expected Ford to mediate between Nixon and Congress. Instead, Ford took the advice of associates that he avoid
that precarious role. He spent little time in Washington as
Vice President and rarely interceded with Congress.[8]

Rockefeller occasionally tried to sell administration programs "on a very informal basis." But he was not active in
this role; he would lobby, he said, only if asked to do so; he
implied that he was rarely asked.[9] Rockefeller did attempt to
persuade several key committee chairmen to conduct hearings on the proposed energy corporation. His efforts met with
little success.[10]

Mondale proved more active in Congress. According to
Representative Robert Young, Carter "was using Mondale as
a Majority Whip." Senator Daniel Patrick Moynihan judged
Mondale as "worth 10 votes to the President in the Senate."[11] Although both claims seem exaggerated, Mondale was
a useful liaison to Congress. Early in their first year in office,
Carter assigned Mondale to supervise his electoral reform
legislation. The package was largely unsuccessful despite
Mondale's active efforts. Mondale worked with congressional
leaders on Carter's gas regulation bill and helped secure the
confirmation of Paul Warnke as America's negotiator at the
Strategic Arms Limitation Talks.[12]

Two factors produced Mondale's early involvement in legislative work. Initially, Carter's staff had little experience dealing
with congressmen; the Vice President helped fill this void.
Stuart Eizenstat, Carter's chief domestic adviser, credited
Mondale with a "terrific sense of both Congress and Congressional reaction."[13] Mondale's role subsided as the White House

staff gained some expertise.[14] Mondale also provided Carter with a credible conduit to liberal legislators. Senator Gaylord Nelson, for instance, told Carter that he would not bother him. "The Vice President is my good friend, and if I have anything to say—I'll just tell Fritz."[15] Senator Birch Bayh, too, said that "I call Fritz Mondale sometimes instead of bothering the President."[16]

The above synopsis of vice-presidential activity suggests that the second officer can help advance administration programs. Unfortunately, the nature of the office impedes a complete assessment of its legislative role. Here, as elsewhere, the Vice President works for the Chief Executive. The latter receives credit for any legislative successes. Thus, Humphrey's complaint that "my role in helping to get this [Great Society] legislation passed has never been made public" may well be justified.[17]

Still, the feeling persists that vice-presidential efforts produce scant legislative results. They may be helpful[18] but the Vice President faces serious constraints which circumscribe his ability to affect the legislative process.

Johnson's experience as Vice President suggests the limited influence that officer can exert on the legislative process. Johnson had built a reputation as a skilled and powerful Majority Leader of the Senate. He clearly hoped to maintain some legislative authority in his new position. O'Brien observed:

> I think that Johnson, in the first days of the Kennedy administration, had hoped to play a unique role as Vice President. He thought he could serve as Kennedy's ambassador to Congress, and also, although no longer Senate majority leader, he could in effect continue as the Democratic leader in the Senate.[19]

Humphrey shared O'Brien's assessment of Johnson's expectations.[20] Two developments dashed Johnson's hopes. A proposal that he continue to preside over the Democratic Conference provoked sharp controversy. Some seventeen (of sixty-three) Democratic senators, including several who had backed the Texan for the party's presidential nomination, opposed the motion. Humiliated, Johnson declined the tarnished honor. Further, Johnson discovered that the White House had no intention of relying on him to handle legislation, for Kennedy made clear that O'Brien was his chief liaison to Congress. Johnson demonstrated little effectiveness in helping Kennedy's legislative program. He once observed that O'Brien's assistant for the Senate, Claude Desautels, had greater influence than he.[21]

Vice-presidential lobbying is necessarily limited. To begin with, Congress is not a malleable institution. On most issues, relatively few legislators are susceptible to executive influence. Not only the Vice President but the President is unable to engineer many shifts. Benefits of incumbency have produced a proliferation of safe seats. Electoral security has further insulated congressmen from presidential persuasion. Presidents and their legislative staffs must work hard to achieve even marginal gains in legislative votes.

The Vice President may assume a supporting role, but he generally is not a crucial actor in these endeavors. His legislative roles give him little bargaining power. Lacking favors to trade he can have little influence. As a former congressman put it, "The guy has to have some oomph. If he doesn't have a vote and if he isn't on any of the committees he doesn't have any oomph."[22] Or, as O'Brien put it, "You can't take a fellow off the Hill when he becomes Vice President and expect him to march up to the Hill and continue to have the same influence."[23]

Lacking patronage of his own to distribute, the Vice President depends on the Chief Executive for his influence. Presidents make parsimonious grants; they have little reason to be generous to their number two. The Vice President has his own political future to consider. His interest and that of the President are not always identical. His actions are likely to reflect that discrepancy. Presidents cannot make legislative lobbying their full-time occupation. They can, however, maintain a large measure of control by entrusting that responsibility to tested aides whose employment depends on their continued loyalty. Thus, the anonymous Desautels achieves greater influence than the man who stands a heartbeat from the presidency.

The staff member who acts as chief legislative emissary may, as indicated above, ask the Vice President to undertake certain assignments. Such occasions rarely occur. The legislative staff can handle regular dealings. Occasionally high-level persuasion may be valuable. But as O'Brien points out, "If you're going to have that kind of contact, you'd use the President."[24] The second officer usually gets lost in the shuffle.

The situation the Vice President confronts is delicate and requires discreet behavior. He is an outsider in a xenophobic club. He must be sensitive to senatorial folkways. His relationship with the Senate becomes precarious if he lobbies too energetically, or at the wrong time and place. Such activity might jeopardize his role, limited though it is, as president of the Senate. Mondale articulated this potential dilemma:

. . . I don't assume responsibilities for congressional liaison. That is one job I don't want, because it would create a suspicion that I might use my role as presiding officer of the Senate to prejudge or try to influence an issue. The presiding officer is supposed to be neutral.[25]

The Vice President may offend congressional leaders if he appears to compete with their operations. Humphrey's efforts apparently upset Senate Majority Leader Mansfield.[26] The Vice President must approach legislators with great tact. Agnew's failure to observe expected etiquette provoked Jordan's rule.

That Agnew damaged his position by lobbying need not mean that all Vice Presidents should forego the activity. Bayh observed:

> The reaction of senators to Spiro Agnew isn't typical of reactions of a normal senator to a normal Vice President. I cannot imagine very many members of the Senate who'd be turned off if Fritz Mondale approached them. . . . Anybody who's Vice President if he's reasonably astute would be an asset if they went about it the right way.[27]

Recent history indicates that the Vice President can help with legislative liaison. But his activity must complement that of the White House staff and of the congressional leadership. Lacking plentiful sources of political currency, the Vice President must guard the influence he has by conducting himself in the "right way."

Party Worker

The Vice President must step cautiously in his legislative work; he has little to trade in a hazardous market. The situation differs, however, in his partisan activity. Here resources are ample and rewards available. Vice-presidential activity in party affairs helps a variety of political actors. Presidents assign it because it allows their administrations to win support without spending their time or prestige. Candidates appreciate it because it attracts attention to their campaigns and funds for their coffers. Nor are Vice Presidents oblivious to the advantages it offers them. A campaign speech or appearance for a local organization or candidate is one of the few resources a Vice President has to barter. The promise of partisan activity can provide the second man with present influence and the possibility of future favor.

Nixon fulfilled the role of party leader capably. Eisenhower was not interested in partisan activity. His major electoral asset was his image of being above politics. Sherman Adams recalls: "He [Eisenhower] told Nixon and others, including myself, that he was well aware that somebody had to do the hard-hitting infighting, and he had no objections to it as long as no one expected him to do it."[28] Eisenhower's reluctance to engage in party activity created a void that Nixon filled.

Nixon was most visible during midterm elections. His forty-eight-day schedule during the 1954 campaign included visits to ninety-five cities in thirty-one states, 204 speeches and more than 100 press conferences.[29] He preached unity to the divided wings of the Republican party and denounced the Democrats in vitriolic fashion as the party of Korea, Communism, corruption, and controls. The cumulative impact of Nixon's effort is difficult to assess. The Democrats won control of Congress and added eight governorships to the twenty-one they already held. Some swing in their direction was to be expected. Eisenhower's coattails had been long two years earlier; his absence from the ticket no doubt hurt his party, as did high unemployment. Some Republicans who received generous allotments of Nixon's time did well while others fared poorly.[30] Party leaders appreciated Nixon's work. "No man could have done more effective work" to help Republican candidates, Eisenhower wrote Nixon near the end of the campaign.[31]

Nixon undertook a strenuous effort on behalf of his party in 1956 and again carried the Republican banner in 1958. His position in 1958 differed from that of four years earlier. As the heir apparent Nixon could hardly repeat his 1954 performance as the Republican "hit man." He sought to help his party but not at the expense of his own ambitions. The election was disastrous for Republicans but the campaign helped Nixon consolidate his hold on the party.[32]

Johnson assumed many of the party duties but little of the political power of his predecessor. Unlike Eisenhower, Kennedy enjoyed partisan activity. He was not about to delegate party strategy to his Vice President. Rather, he retained control of the party apparatus and exercised it through such trusted lieutenants as Attorney General Robert F. Kennedy and White House staffers Lawrence F. O'Brien and Kenneth O'Donnell. Still, Johnson spoke frequently at Jefferson-Jackson Day dinners and at other party functions around the country, praising Kennedy and local Democrats and raising campaign funds. He labored to maintain the support of party branches in the South. He was active in the 1962 campaign until the Cuban missile crisis aborted partisan efforts. As Vice President he made about 400 speeches in thirty-five states.[33]

Humphrey was perhaps more active than Johnson had been in his role of party cheerleader. But he, too, acted essentially as surrogate for the President in his party duties rather than as its leader. He observed:

> I always thought, of course, that a Vice President might very well have assisted with, even fulfilled that role of political leader. It was not to be so. While the President listened to my political ideas and analysis, and seemed to give them credence, he had conflicting emotions when it came to my political initiative or possible prominence. After all, by the very nature of things, the President was the political leader. There couldn't be two.[34]

Unless the President was willing to delegate authority as party leader to him, the Vice President could only be a partisan functionary. A memo Humphrey directed to Marvin Watson suggested the frustration of that role. Humphrey wrote:

> I've been in over thirty states for the DNC since January, attended dozens of receptions which, at best, are tiresome and frequently exhausting. I am not complaining. I like my work. But it must have taken some figuring on the part of someone at the DNC to exclude the Vice President on the two major publications of the Committee for 1965.

Watson replied sympathetically and promised Humphrey better treatment in the future.[35] But the incident would not have occurred had Humphrey been a true leader rather than just another campaigner.

Humphrey's activity was most conspicuous during the 1966 campaign. He scheduled visits to thirty-eight states, freely associating himself even with Democratic candidates predestined to lose. Humphrey worked hard for his party even when no election date stood near. In 1965, for instance, he made thirty-six political appearances, and spoke at local and President's Club dinners in twenty-seven states, the District of Columbia, and Puerto Rico.[36] He obliged legislators looking for an attraction at their fund-raisers. Humphrey was particularly anxious to assist the freshmen Democratic representatives elected in the 1964 landslide.[37] He rarely let pass an opportunity to praise a local Democrat in appearances around the country.

Less visible was the role Humphrey played as a funnel for information from party members to Johnson and his top political aides. For instance, Humphrey reported that Representative Lester Wolff feared political repercussions from the proposed closing of a naval training base in his district. He suggested that Representative William R. Anderson, the skipper of the nation's first nuclear submarine, receive a special assignment relating to national security. He urged Johnson to provide a high-level public briefing on Vietnam for Nebraska Governor Frank Morrison who was seeking a Senate seat. He relayed a comment from Governor Harold Hughes that the lieutenant governors had not been invited to a White House conference and suggested that such an event occur after the 1966 primaries.[38]

Finally, Humphrey offered suggestions concerning campaign strategy in 1968. For instance, he advised the President early to enlist the help of California Attorney General Thomas Lynch for the 1968 campaign.[39] Lynch later headed the delegate list committed to Johnson. Humphrey also participated on a four-man task force designed to deal with the presidential candidacy of Senator Eugene McCarthy. "We are making life interesting for Eugene," John P. Roche, the organizer of the group, told Johnson.[40]

Both of Nixon's Vice Presidents embraced the partisan role. In fact, they were merely imitating Nixon's behavior as Vice President. Unlike Eisenhower, Nixon was not disposed to delegate partisan strategy to his deputy. But both Agnew and Ford spent much of their time on the circuit, raising money and support for Republican candidates.

Much of Agnew's early effort was devoted to expanding the Republican base in the South. He delivered 36 percent of his political speeches during his first nine months in office in that region.[41] His political work assumed prominence, as well as a national flavor, during the 1970 midterm elections. Agnew raised $3.5 million for Republican candidates and campaigned in thirty-two states.[42] His job was "to purge the Congress of dissident doves," legislators he referred to as "radical-liberals."[43] Those he attacked were Democrats, with the exception of Senator Charles Goodell of New York. The campaign against Goodell served two purposes. It suggested to other Republicans the political hazards of opposing Nixon's Vietnam policy. Further, it helped elect James Buckley, the Conservative party candidate, by suggesting to Republican voters that he was a more appropriate representative of their party. The impact of Agnew's campaign is difficult to measure. He does appear to have helped Buckley; Republicans ousted two other Agnew targets, Senators Joseph D. Tydings (D. Md.) and Albert Gore (D. Tenn.). In all, the Republicans lost nine seats in the House and eleven governorships but gained two senators. Yet the last result was disappointing. Those up for reelection to the Senate had won their seats in 1958 and/or 1964, both heavily Democratic years. Several Democrats were vulnerable. Agnew's tactics may have alienated enough voters to cost his party additional places in the upper house.

Ford did little but campaign during his eight months as Vice President. Republican candidates were eager to enlist his help since Nixon's unpopularity jeopardized many seats. Moreover, travel allowed him to dissociate himself from Watergate. In all, Ford made nearly 500 public appearances (approximately fifteen a week) in forty states.[44]

Rockefeller was not so politically active as his predecessors. His time in office did not include a midterm election. He was more interested in policy and less in politics than either Agnew or Ford. Further, he was anathema to the dominant wing of his party. His major political efforts as Vice President were to help Ford win the nomination and election. He assured Ford the support of the crucial New York delegation and canvassed other Northeastern delegates on his behalf. He may have raised as much as $3.5 million for the President's campaign.[45]

Mondale was, however, politically active. He arranged briefings for freshmen congressmen.[46] During his first year, he campaigned for Michael Sullivan, the unsuccessful Democratic candidate for the Minnesota congressional seat vacated by agriculture secretary Bob Bergland; for Edward Koch, the victorious candidate for mayor of New York; and for Brendan Byrne, the surprise winner in his race for reelection as governor of New Jersey. He appeared at numerous fundraisers—in California (for Senator Alan Cranston), in Arizona (for Representative Morris K. Udall), in New York (for Moynihan), in Minnesota (for Donald Fraser), and elsewhere. He campaigned actively for Democratic candidates in the 1978 elections. Before he had served three years as Vice President, he had visited forty-eight of the fifty states, often to promote members of his party.[47]

Vice Presidents perform partisan chores that otherwise might occupy the President's time and dissipate his prestige. Political work may be dull and taxing but Vice Presidents regard it as time well spent. The effort invested in party work pays dividends. It creates political IOU's redeemable, perhaps, when a Vice President lobbies for an administration measure, perhaps when he seeks renomination, perhaps when he seeks the presidency on his own.

Such activity poses dangers, too. A Vice President who engages too frequently or too vigorously as a partisan comes to be seen as a party hack. He may attract the full wrath of the opposition. He may be viewed as a politician and nothing else, an image that may be unappealing to a President contemplating a running mate for his reelection campaign or to a party seeking a new standard-bearer.

Administration Spokesperson

When Vice Presidents engage in their party duties they rarely just appear. They also speak, at political functions and at nonpartisan events. A third political role the Vice President has inherited is that of prominent administration spokesman. He plays parts similar to those performed during the campaign; he attempts to mobilize support for presidential initiatives and he attacks administration adversaries. Further, he cultivates the good will of certain interest groups by appearing at their events. The substance and style of the addresses varies with the tenor of the times and the temperament of the Vice President. But all speak principally as a surrogate for the President.

A favorite Nixon topic during his first term as Vice President was Communism. His speeches would commonly explain the virtue of, and need for, Eisenhower's leadership and contrast his policies with those of the previous administration, themes not very different from those Nixon had developed during the 1952 campaign.[48]

One of Nixon's most important performances as spokesman came in March 1954 when he answered criticisms made by Adlai Stevenson. Eisenhower had made it clear that Nixon was speaking for the administration and the Republican party.[49] Nixon began by reminding his national television audience that "we found that in seven years of the Truman-Acheson policy 600 million people had been lost to the Communists and not a single Russian soldier had been lost in combat."[50] Further, America was involved militarily in Korea and had already lost 125,000 soldiers there. Eisenhower, Nixon said, had ended the war and brought troops home while placing "the responsibility where it belongs—on the Communists— for blockading the road to peace." Unlike his predecessor, Eisenhower had not been blind to the menace of domestic communist subversion, Nixon insisted. "We don't agree with Mr. Truman in kissing off that danger by calling it a 'red herring.' Nor do we agree with Mr. Stevenson, referring as he did to the investigations of that danger as 'chasing phantoms' . . ." said Nixon. Accordingly, Eisenhower had taken steps to keep Communists off the government payroll and to remove from government jobs "those of doubtful loyalty." Nixon went on to decry the tactics of Senator Joseph McCarthy. He ended with ringing praise for Eisenhower ("I have never seen him mean; I have never seen him rash; I have never seen him impulsive. . . .") and a plea for unity. Other Nixon speeches sounded similar themes.[51] In the second term, Nixon more frequently discussed other issues. Fear of communist subversion had subsided with McCarthy's fall from power. Further, Nixon sought to cultivate a presidential following of his own.

Johnson covered a variety of topics in his public addresses as Vice President. The threat of world Communism was one favorite subject ("I do not believe that this generation of Americans is willing to resign itself to going to bed each night by the light of a Communist moon.");[52] space was another.

But on no issue were his words so eloquent and his thoughts so important as civil rights.

Johnson spoke on the subject from the outset of his term. He made an impassioned plea for civil rights, for instance, at an Equal Opportunity Day dinner in November 1961. Johnson's talk, one black leader recalled, "made mine sound like the moderate."[53] But he made race his common topic in the summer of 1963. The issue was gaining in saliency and the Kennedy administration had committed itself to seeking enactment of a civil rights bill. Johnson's job was to help mobilize sentiment behind such a measure.

Most conspicuous was a speech he gave during Memorial Day ceremonies at Gettysburg. Liberal legislators praised it lavishly. Senator Hubert Humphrey called it "eloquent and challenging" and "the second Gettysburg Address." Senator Wayne Morse, a frequent Johnson critic, pronounced it "the greatest speech on the civil rights issue that has been delivered in this country in the last quarter century." Senator Edward M. Kennedy praised Johnson for his "liberal statesmanship." Senator Alan Bible called it "one of the truly great speeches of our time." Senator Philip Hart found the speech "as eloquent as any which we could recall having heard."[54]

In it, Johnson argued that America could no longer ask patience of the Negro. He urged blacks to use lawful means to attain civil rights and called on all to work to achieve racial justice. He concluded:

> Until justice is blind to color, until education is unaware of race, until opportunity is unconcerned with the color of men's skins, emancipation will be a proclamation but not a fact. To the extent that the proclamation of emancipation is not fulfilled in fact, to that extent we shall have fallen short of assuring freedom to the free.[55]

Johnson preached that same creed often in all regions during the spring, summer, and fall of 1963. His Southern accent added poignance to his words and force to his message. The *Washington Post* commented:

> Vice President Lyndon Johnson has been speaking out on civil rights issues with increasing frequency, force, and clarity. He is doing a great deal to shape public opinion and alter public outlook. Frequently he gets to the gist of the matter with a directness and vigor that pierces the fog of legal dispute into which we so frequently become mired. . . . The Presidency always has been known as a great platform from which to appeal to the mind and heart of America. The Vice Presidency is being made into a great platform by Vice President Lyndon Johnson.[56]

President Lyndon Johnson also helped make the vice presidency "a great platform" by using Humphrey as a champion of administration programs, whatever they were. During his first year in office, Humphrey spoke most often on domestic issues. Johnson was inundating Congress with his Great Society legislation; Humphrey's task was to help mobilize public support for it and to make sure the administration received full credit for it. He spoke often on civil rights, poverty, creative local government, farm problems, and labor issues. His speeches were useful discussions of important issues, saturated with data and analysis. This did not obscure their political content. For Humphrey was not merely a salesman for the Great Society but for its architect, too ("And what is new to America today is the energy, vision and faith of Lyndon B. Johnson as he challenges us to join with him in building the Great Society.").[57]

The escalation of American involvement in Vietnam changed Humphrey's role. He continued to speak on domestic issues. Increasingly, however, he acted as an advocate of administration policies in Vietnam. The advantage for Johnson in assigning Humphrey this role was obvious. Liberals were most critical of the President's conduct of the war; Humphrey's credentials with this group were impeccable. After a trip to Southeast Asia in early 1966, Humphrey became the chief defender of the war. He insisted to one audience:

> Make no mistake about it. If aggression succeeds in one part of this world, it will quickly follow elsewhere. If we fail to stand today, we shall have to stand tomorrow even closer to home.[58]

One journalist called Humphrey the "fastest flying object in the U.S." since he travelled so much to generate support for the war. Senator Fred Harris termed the new Humphrey role as "the most important, most needed, most useful task of his life to date." After Humphrey delivered six speeches on the war in two weeks, *Newsweek* called him "the scrappiest warrior in the White House phalanx."[59] As the election year approached, Humphrey returned to domestic issues with greater frequency. He recited the litany of successful Great Society programs which remained the administration's best selling point. But Vietnam remained a common topic of his talks.

No Vice President, however, devoted so great a proportion of his time to speech-making as did Agnew. Nixon and his associates were relatively inaccessible to press and public alike. Agnew had little else of substance to do.

The major topic, and target, of Agnew's talks were critics of administration policy, especially on Vietnam. Agnew denounced them as "an effete corps of impudent snobs," and as "ideological eunuchs whose most comfortable position is straddling the ideological fence."[60] Intellectuals, young people, and antiwar activists were his primary victims.

But Agnew made his biggest splash in his indictment of the national media, first in a televised speech to the Midwestern Regional Republican Conference in Des Moines, Iowa, on 13 November 1969, and then elsewhere. Analysis of a presidential statement on the war immediately following its delivery had upset Agnew. He blasted "a small band of network commentators and self-appointed analysts, the majority of whom expressed in one way or another their hostility to what [Nixon] had to say." Agnew challenged their political views and professional credentials. He continued this line of attack a week later but expanded it to include print as well as broadcast media. Then, in Montgomery, Alabama, he asserted, "The American people should be made aware . . . of the trend toward the monopolization of the great public information vehicles and the concentration of more and more power in fewer and fewer hands."[61] Agnew clearly spoke for the administration in delivering these addresses.[62] The speeches ended any chance that Agnew would be a quiet Vice President. They made him a lightning rod for many of the complaints against the administration. Like Agnew, Ford often defended the Nixon administration. He differed, however, in technique and topic. The denunciations of administration critics which had formed the core of Agnew's talks were absent from those Ford delivered. Instead, Ford exonerated Nixon from any involvement in the planning or cover-up of Watergate.[63]

Rockefeller and Mondale were probably not as prominent in the role of public spokesman as were their predecessors. But neither were they inactive. Rockefeller gave a major speech in Chicago five weeks after becoming Vice President. He apparently wanted to avoid the assignment but eventually relented to pressure from Ford and his top aide, Donald Rumsfeld. "I don't think that with the problems that exist that there's going to be as much speech-making," Rockefeller told the press.[64] Rockefeller later gave a speech in which he suggested that should Congress refuse to appropriate funds for South Vietnam it would bear responsibility for a Communist takeover there.[65] His most controversial speeches were a series on major issues which he delivered independent of the administration during his last year in office.

Mondale's speeches lacked the thematic cohesion and

headline appeal characteristic of those of some of his predecessors. He explained administration policies on a number of important issues. One early speech explained administration proposals for tax, foster care, and welfare reform. Others stressed the validity of Carter's approach to the energy crisis. He told the annual convention of the American Federation of Teachers of plans to give "classroom teachers a real voice in setting education policy in our country." He spoke on civil liberties and reform of the judiciary. He attacked the proposed constitutional amendment to balance the budget.[66]

At times he boosted Carter's international policies; in July 1979, for instance, he promoted the proposed SALT II agreement in seven states (with a total of ten uncommitted senators). As well as discussing issues of importance, Mondale's purpose, like that of other Vice Presidents, was to convince his audience of the friendship, concern and wisdom of the Chief Executive. He told a branch of the AFL-CIO: "I am proud to serve with a man like Jimmy Carter who has the courage to make the tough decisions, who believes it is his job to face the difficult problems that have been ducked and ignored for so long: in the economy, in energy, in taxes and welfare reform, health costs and Social Security and illegal aliens and labor law reforms." Such words would probably not persuade the average person. But they may have influenced the immediate audience since Mondale had solid labor credentials. Similarly, the Carter administration often sought to capitalize on Mondale's good relations with Jewish groups by having him defend controversial policies on Israel.[67]

Delivering a speech is hardly an onerous task. Yet the Vice President may encounter a variety of problems in this role. The content or delivery may make him a controversial, even a divisive figure. Nixon by his speeches on Communism, Humphrey by his talks on Vietnam, and Agnew by his expressed views on dissenters all became contentious. In fact, the Vice President has some incentive to make provocative speeches. The press generally ignores the Vice President when his comment is sane and sensible. It covers his speeches, if at all, "back with the corset ads."[68] An unconventional or inflammatory statement, however, may land on prime time or in premium space.

Further, a Vice President is largely constrained in what he can say. Presidents expect members of their administrations to support publicly policies they oppose privately. Only on rare occasions does the second officer openly disagree with a presidential position. This does not mean that all Vice Presidents have to clear speeches with the President before giving them. Rather, most Vice Presidents exercise self-censorship. As Rockefeller put it, "the fact that I exercise discretion is why I've got it."[69] But Vice Presidents must resist the temptation that occasionally must arise to voice their disagreement with particular policies.

Finally, use of the Vice President as a spokesman may obscure, rather than clarify the President's positions. That the Vice President rarely criticizes administration programs does not mean that his words always indicate presidential policy. He may speak on a subject where the administration has no clear stance. He may suggest an embellishment on or interpretation of current policy which, it subsequently appears, is not acceptable to the Chief Executive. It was not obvious in 1954 whether Nixon spoke for the administration when he blamed Dean Acheson for the loss of China and the Korean war. Eisenhower did not clarify the matter when asked to comment at a press conference.[70] When Agnew attacked dissenters and the media, it was not immediately certain whether he spoke for himself or whether he was venting Nixon's views. It later became clear that Agnew did, in fact, speak for the administration.[71] But Presidents preserve the luxury of disowning statements the Vice President makes. Vice-presidential discourse may, therefore, obfuscate rather than clarify issues.

Yet use of the Vice President as a spokesperson has value beyond the political capital it secures for the administration. His speeches may contribute to the political education of the public. Recent Vice Presidents have discussed important topics. The quality of the presentation sometimes left something to be desired. Nixon and Agnew could have been less bombastic in their attacks, Humphrey and Ford less simplistic in their defenses. But all raised important subjects, and some stimulated their consideration.

The public benefits in a second way from seeing and hearing the Vice President. Voters rarely have the opportunity to measure the performance of the Vice President. His public speeches offer the few occasions. The policy content may not be exactly as the Vice President would like. Still, citizens can learn much from the delivery, reasoning, and nuances of the talk. As Agnew put it: ". . . I believe that the people of the United States would like to know their Vice President for what he really is and what he really thinks."[72]

Finally, public appearances help acquaint the Vice President with various issues. Humphrey, for instance, spoke on a range of topics in depth. His speeches were replete with data. Public speaking brings the Vice President into contact with people and issues around the country.

Chief Surrogate in Presidential Primaries

In the role of prominent administration spokesman, the Vice President seeks to mobilize support for the President and his policies generally; the effort is not directed to a particular election. Vice Presidents undertake a fourth political role the exclusive purpose of which is to promote the President's renomination. The recent growth of presidential primaries allows other politicians to challenge with some prospect for success an incumbent's renomination. A sitting President may find that his opportunity to serve another term may depend upon his ability to win delegates in the preconvention tests. The Chief Executive may not wish to undertake an extensive campaign effort owing either to the press of work or to the possible damage to his image by partisan activity. The Vice President thus may become a logical surrogate.

Mondale performed this role exhaustively during the 1980 primaries. Carter curtailed his campaigning following the hostage crisis in Iran and the Soviet invasion of Afghanistan; Mondale and Mrs. Carter accordingly became the chief surrogates in the primaries. From September 1979 to April 1980, Mondale travelled 103,500 miles, visited thirty-two states, gave 175 speeches, 170 news conferences, and attended 125 fund-raisers.[73]

A Vice President's role in the presidential primaries resembles the one the second person performs in the general election campaign. He raises money, appeals to party leaders and other interest groups, praises the President, and criticizes the opposition. The latter role is precarious. The President and his staff are likely to want the Vice President to attack rivals. The Vice President may be reluctant to risk alienating fellow party members with direct assaults.[74] Mondale focused part of his rhetoric on Kennedy. He suggested that Kennedy had no ideological reason for challenging Carter. He implied that Kennedy's criticism of the grain embargo was unpatriotic. He suggested Kennedy withdraw to avoid splitting their party; he derided Kennedy's call for a debate with Carter.[75] Generally, Mondale avoided, or tempered, attacks on Kennedy.

Not all Vice Presidents will perform the role of surrogate campaigner in the primaries. That job becomes superfluous if a President chooses not to run or if he is not challenged. Moreover, it is conceivable that the Vice President may oppose the President for the nomination. Even if the President runs again, the Vice President is less likely to act as surrogate campaigner if the Vice President will not again be the running mate or if the Vice President is unpopular with constituencies to which the President must appeal. Rockefeller, for instance, made some appearances for Ford in 1976. He raised funds and appealed to friendly delegates. Political considerations made a larger role inadvisable. Ford faced a more conservative challenger, Reagan, in primaries where voters tend to disproportionately represent the right wing of the Republican party. Since Rockefeller was unpopular with these voters, his efforts were circumscribed.

A Concluding Remark

Political roles of Vice Presidents, especially those of party worker and administration spokesperson, have engendered much controversy. That Vice Presidents should act as partisans is neither surprising nor reprehensible, for they are politicians, not civil servants. Their role is to help assure the operation of democratic processes by offering alternatives and executing policies.

Were Vice Presidents to forego political activity they would, no doubt, experience a decline in their influence. These tasks are sources of power for an officer permitted few. Communication with legislators provides the second officer with information; party work produces the gratitude of politicians; public speaking, attention and perhaps a following; primary surrogacy, the reliance of the Chief Executive.

Yet the nature of the vice presidency may push the behavior of its occupant in unfortunate directions. The Vice President has benefited from his closer association with the executive branch. But he still relies on the President for his assignments; he generally acts and speaks as a presidential puppet, not as an independent agent. The President may be tempted to use his Vice President to do the gutter fighting inappropriate to the top office. The Chief Executive can at once vent frustrations and achieve desired ends without dirtying his hands. The Vice President has reason to accept such demeaning assignments, for the nature and extent of his future role depend on the President's satisfaction with his loyalty and ability.

The President's favorable assessment of his Vice President may come at great cost to the operations of American institutions. The kind of vice-presidential activity that Presidents may be inclined to encourage may debase the level of political conduct and discourse. Further, it may make the second man a controversial figure among politicians and public alike. Such a turn would make the Vice President less able to unify the country should presidential vacancy install him in the White House. Ideally, vice-presidential activity should make a politician better suited to act as a presidential replacement. The role of presidential successor is the topic to which we now turn.

9

★ ★ ★
The Vice President as Successor

Whatever logic supports the continued existence of the vice presidency must reside in its ability to handle problems caused by the absence of a functioning Chief Executive. No matter how valuable the duties a particular occupant of the office performs, as Woodrow Wilson realized, "his importance consists in the fact that he may cease to be Vice-President."[1] Wilson's assessment, far from disparaging the vice presidency, confirms its significance. For an unexpected presidential vacancy produces one of the telling tests of American government. A country can ill afford an unreliable means of replacing its chief political officer. The problem assumes weighty proportions in the United States where the importance of the presidency, especially as it has developed since the New Deal, permits no hiatus in executive leadership.

Five types of contingencies may produce a presidential vacancy. A President may leave office through death, resignation, or removal. He may be temporarily unable to perform his duties, or the electoral system may fail to produce a Chief Executive able to take office on inaugural day. The Constitution provides that the Vice President is first in line to succeed in each of these cases. The office provides a solution to the problem of presidential vacancy that is both workable and consistent with basic principles of American democracy.

This chapter first sketches the constitutional provisions governing presidential succession. It next considers why

America finds it necessary to designate in advance an officer to complete an unexpired presidential term. The chapter then assesses justifications for the Vice President as that successor.

The Constitutional Provisions

The founding fathers originally provided:

> In case of the removal of the President from office, or of his death, resignation, or inability to discharge the powers and duties of the said office, the same shall devolve on the Vice President, and the Congress may by law provide for the case of removal, death, resignation or inability, both of the President and Vice President, declaring what officer shall then act as President, and such officer shall act accordingly, until the disability be removed, or a President shall be elected.[2]

That clause failed to handle adequately the problems of presidential vacancy.

To begin with, its language is ambiguous. It defies certain determination of what devolves on the Vice President—the "powers and duties" of the presidency or the office itself. The question posed a problem of more than semantic interest. If "the same" referred to the "powers and duties," the Vice President would merely substitute for the Chief Executive during the hiatus. If the office were transferred, however, the President would lose it permanently.

The first test of the meaning of the provision came upon the death of President William Henry Harrison in 1841. Informed opinion was divided but Harrison's Vice President, John Tyler, insisted that he became President, not acting President. The seven other Vice Presidents who succeeded under the clause echoed his claim.

In fact, the Tyler interpretation was incorrect. Study of the records of the Constitutional Congress makes clear that the framers intended the Vice President merely to "discharge the powers and duties" of the President in all situations.[3] Then a Chief Executive could step aside during a period of inability without surrendering his office. But the Tyler precedent prevailed.

Consequently, when Presidents Garfield, Wilson, and Eisenhower suffered from clear disabilities their Vice Presidents refused to assume executive responsibilities. They feared that action on their part would supplant the incumbent. Their reticence was compounded by the lack of guidelines defining disability and providing for its determination. As Eisenhower told a news conference audience: "The reason that a Vice President is so reluctant to act in this case is because our Constitution does not provide now whether he would become the President, whether he would be the Acting President, when the President and how the President would take over again, all of those things are cloudy."[4]

The first step toward dealing with the problem came on 3 March 1958 when Eisenhower and Nixon formulated a set of extralegal guidelines. They agreed that the President would advise the Vice President of his inability, if possible, at which point the Vice President would act as Chief Executive. If such communication was not possible, the Vice President "after such consultation as seems to him appropriate under the circumstances" would decide whether to act as President. In any case, the President would decide when to resume his duties. The same arrangements were subsequently adopted by Kennedy and Johnson, Johnson and McCormack, and Johnson and Humphrey.[5]

This arrangement was an improvement over the previous lacuna but was inadequate nonetheless. It lacked legal sanction so that the right of the Vice President to sign a law, appoint or dismiss officials, or act as Commander in Chief was not beyond challenge. Further, the plan assumed that the President and Vice President were the only relevant parties. "I think Mr. Nixon knows exactly what he should do in the event of a Presidential disability of the kind that we are talking about," Eisenhower had assured a press conference audience.[6] But, as Senator Wayne Morse argued, "The Constitution does not make the Office of the President of the United States the private preserve of the incumbent to dispose of as if it were a quail-hunting lodge."[7] The plan imposed little restraint on the Vice President. It relied on a close relationship between the two highest officers. As Eisenhower pointed out, "Such a plan, of course, presupposed that the President and his Vice President were mutually trustful; it would scarcely work if for any reason they were personally unfriendly to, or distrustful of, each other."[8] Perhaps more seriously, the Eisenhower-Nixon pact relied solely on the President's judgment that he could function.

The Twenty-fifth Amendment was designed to solve many of these problems.[9] Section one separated the case of inability from those of death, resignation, and removal. It stated: "In case of the removal of the President from office or of his death or resignation, the Vice President shall become President." Section three provided that the Vice President would serve as Acting President if the President declared himself unable.[10] Section four provided an elaborate mechanism by which the Vice President and "a majority of either the principal officers of the executive departments or of such other body as Congress may by law provide" may declare the President disabled.[11] The Vice President would act as President only until the Chief Executive could again discharge his duties.

The President can regain his position by his written declaration of his ability to perform his duties. Should the Vice President and a majority of the cabinet (or of an alternative body which Congress can establish) within four days of the President's statement declare again that he is unable to govern, Congress would then be required to meet within forty-eight hours to decide the issue within twenty-one days. The Vice President would act as President during this time. He would continue to do so if each house of Congress by a two-thirds vote within the stated time limit found the Chief Executive unable "to discharge the powers and duties of his office." The President would resume the discharge of his duties if less than two-thirds of the quorum of either body believed he was disabled or if the issue had not been decided within the twenty-one days. The provisions contained in section three and, especially, section four are not perfect. Loopholes remain.[12] The mechanism does, however, fill a troublesome gap.

The Twenty-fifth Amendment, then, provided a mechanism for handling the first four contingencies—death, resignation, removal, and inability of the President—mentioned earlier. The Twentieth Amendment, which was ratified in 1933, was designed to handle failures of the electoral system to produce a Chief Executive able and qualified to assume office. It provides that if the President-elect dies; the Vice-President-elect becomes President. If the President-elect is disabled or if none qualifies, the Vice-President-elect acts as President until the disability ends or a Chief Executive qualifies.

Under authority vested in it by the Constitution, Congress has constructed a lengthy line of successors.[13] Following the Vice President are, in order, the Speaker of the House of Representatives, the president pro tempore of the Senate, and eligible members of the cabinet beginning with the secretary of state.[14]

The Logic of the Solution

Providing for the succession may seem a weak peg on which to hang an office, especially one so controversial as the vice presidency. Indeed, America is unique among the major nations of the world in having an officer whose chief purpose is providing a ready successor. Other leading democracies either await a vacancy before designating a new leader or make some officer a caretaker pending the result of a special election.[15] Only America indicates the successor in advance and has him serve the remainder of his predecessor's term.

American history and institutional arrangements indicate the prudence of providing some easy formula of succession. The problem of presidential succession, of course, does not regularly find itself on the agenda of government business. But the possibility of executive vacancy haunts the American experience. Nine Chief Executives have been unable to complete their terms. Their Vice Presidents have directed the nation's course as Presidents by succession for twenty-six years.[16]

But these statistics tell only part of the story. Table 9.1 presents twenty other instances in which presidential power barely escaped interruption. With one exception, every pres-

TABLE 9.1
Near-Instances of Vice-Presidential Succession

President	Date of Crisis	Nature of Crisis
Jefferson-Burr	2/11-2/17/1801	Electoral deadlock
Madison	8/24/1814	Threat of capture by British
Jackson	1/30/1835	Assassination attempt
Tyler	2/28/1844	Gun salute misfired
A. Johnson	2/24-5/16/1868	Impeachment proceedings
Hayes-Tilden	11/7/1876-3/2/1877	Electoral deadlock
Garfield	7/2-9/19/1881	Shot by assassin, unconscious
Cleveland	7/1/1893	Cancer operation
Wilson	9/29/1918	Stroke, disabled
F. Roosevelt	2/15/1933	Assassination attempt
Truman	11/1/1950	Assassination attempt
Eisenhower	9/24/1955	Heart attack
	6/8/1956	Ileitis operation
	11/25/1957	Stroke

TABLE 9.1 (cont.)

President	Date of Crisis	Nature of Crisis
L. Johnson	1/23/1965	Chest pains, hospitalized
	10/5/1965	Gall bladder operation
Ford	9/5/1975	Assassination attempt
	9/22/1975	Assassination attempt
	10/14/1975	Automobile accident
Reagan	3/30/1981	Assassination attempt

idency from that of Franklin Roosevelt to that of Ronald Reagan faced some real or potential crisis of succession. During twenty of the first thirty-eight presidencies, the Chief Executive either left office prematurely or completed his term only after surviving some threat to his incumbency. These statistics cannot be viewed as curiosities of casual interest. Such an attitude might have been appropriate in earlier days when the President did little. It no longer is.

Events since the New Deal have added importance to procedures handling presidential succession. Heightened expectations of government have pushed the Chief Executive to center stage. He is the recipient of public adulation and the trustee of the national fortunes. His international responsibilities dwarf his domestic duties. The means of filling so crucial a position is an integral feature of the political system.

These considerations—the frequency of presidential succession and the increased importance of the presidency— make clear the need for satisfactory procedures to deal with presidential vacancy. They do not, however, explain why the United States should have a successor designated in advance. The features mentioned above are not peculiar to recent American experience. Other countries have not been immune from the hazards of sudden vacancy at high levels.

Since 1963, for instance, two British Prime Ministers— Harold Macmillan and Harold Wilson—resigned while their parties continued to hold majority support in the House of Commons. Their successors were soon selected through procedures involving different degrees of participation by the members of Parliament of their respective parties. During the same period, the French presidency has fallen vacant twice—when Charles De Gaulle resigned in 1969 and when Georges Pompidou died in 1974. In both instances the president of the Senate acted as a caretaker pending a special election within thirty-five days. The chief political officer in these two countries, though not so powerful in some respects as an American President, remains important within their own systems.

A first glance nourishes the suspicion that the approaches of Great Britain and France for replacing a leader are superior to the American method. Of course, comparison has its difficulties even when systems of government are roughly similar. When they rely on diverse institutional arrangements as do the nations in question, attempts to relate elements of one political structure to those of another become even more treacherous. The temptation remains to prefer a system of succession that relies on some form of election to one that does not.

Elections quite obviously play an important role in the American concept of democracy. They are not, however, without proper limit. Too frequent elections, the founding fathers realized, would jeopardize other goals. The framers of the Constitution gave elected officials fixed terms to mitigate the influence of popular opinion and to lend stability to government.

The Role Assessed

Rather than reflecting absolute devotion to popular sovereignty the American democratic tradition incorporates several values. Effective democratic government requires stability, popular consent, and competent leadership. Far from being undemocratic, the system of succession built around the Vice President well serves the diverse values upon which American democracy depends and operates harmoniously within the political institutions.

Stability

Not the least of the virtues of the vice presidency is its ability to provide a smooth transfer of power. In the best of times, transitions brought on by the quadrennial election can be difficult.[17] The outgoing President may be hostile to the new man. Party change may force sweeping personnel shifts at all levels. No important, neutral civil service exists to pave the way.[18]

But Presidents who gain office through electoral victory have two advantages over those who replace a fallen leader. An elected President has two-and-one-half months to plan programs and select subordinates; a President by succession is confronted, without warning, with one of the most demanding jobs in the world. Moreover, an elected President *may* begin his term amid some crisis, but he may also enter office in days of relative calm. A President who succeeds almost certainly does so during a national trauma, for presidential vacancy is in itself one of the chief crises the American system faces.

The impact of a vacancy in America's highest office can be gauged in part by the amount of news coverage given a change of leaders. The assassination of Kennedy and elevation of Johnson merited the first sixteen pages of the *New York Times* on 23 November 1963 and thirty-nine primary news pages the following three days. The *Times* gave its first fifteen pages to news of the Nixon-Ford transfer on 9 August 1974. The attempt on Reagan's life on 30 March 1981 occupied the first seven pages of the next day's *Times*.

The successions of Johnson and Ford came in time of trauma.

In both cases, the transfer was smooth even though the circumstances differed. Johnson became President under inauspicious circumstances. Kennedy's standing in public opinion polls had, predictably, declined since his inauguration. But he remained a popular figure at the time of his death. The latest Gallup Poll had found that 59 percent approved of his presidency, while only 28 percent disapproved.[19] Succession occurred without warning, amplifying the atmosphere of crisis.

Ford entered under more advantageous conditions. Nixon's departure was expected. Investigations culminating in the hearings to consider proposed resolutions of impeachment had been underway for more than a year. The Committee on the Judiciary of the House of Representatives recommended three articles of impeachment by 30 July 1974. The release of a new set of White House tapes on 5 August established Nixon's knowledge of the cover-up within a week of the break-in. At this point, the Republicans who had defended Nixon during the Judiciary Committee hearings abandoned him, as did other high-ranking legislators.[20] The next day, Alexander Haig, Nixon's chief of staff, advised Ford to expect to become President within three days.[21] Ford, accordingly, had warning of the succession. A few associates had been preparing for a Ford administration independently some time before. Ford authorized a larger group to make transition plans early in August.[22] Ford entered the White House with some personnel and policy moves already decided.

Further, Americans welcomed Ford's succession. Nixon's popularity had declined sharply; his approval rating stood well below 30 percent. A few days before the transition, Gallup found voters preferred Ford to Nixon, 45 to 32 percent.[23] The public reflected the view of opinion leaders. In May 1974, a survey of 100 leading newspapers found that forty-seven favored resignation or removal. Only nine backed Nixon.[24]

The day before Nixon left, Senator Barry M. Goldwater told him he had only fifteen supporters in the Senate.[25]

Presidential vacancy produces uncertainty. The quick succession of the Vice President has a calming effect. Americans may not be pleased with their new leader; they may have preferred his predecessor. But at least citizens and politicians, in the United States and abroad, know who the new leader is and who it will be for the remainder of the term. Further, Americans are reassured that their government works. As Chester A. Arthur observed following his succession, "No higher or more assuring proof could exist of the strength and permanence of popular government than the fact that though the chosen of the people be struck down, her constitutional successor is peacefully installed, without shock or strain, except the sorrow which mourn the benevolent."[26] Or, as *Newsweek* put it following the Kennedy-Johnson transition, "The loss was momentous [but] *the fabric was preserved.*"[27]

The primary virtue of succession of the Vice President is not, however, reassurance. More important is the likelihood that the vice presidency as it exists today will provide a successor who will not disrupt the operations of government. Modern Vice Presidents share party identification and, generally, ideology with the Chief Executive under whom they serve.

One way in which recent accidental Presidents have promoted stability has been by retaining officials appointed by their predecessor for at least a transition period. Earlier practice was often very different. The cabinet Tyler inherited, with one exception, resigned within five months. In little more than two months, Fillmore ousted all those President Zachary Taylor had named to the cabinet. Andrew Johnson achieved smooth relations with three of Lincoln's seven chief advisers; Arthur had replaced six of the seven department secretaries within five months. Theodore Roosevelt and Coolidge kept the previous administration largely in place but Truman made seven cabinet changes within six months.

The most recent Presidents by succession, Lyndon Johnson and Ford, have shown a greater willingness to retain members of their predecessor's cabinet. In the first days of his tenure, Johnson circulated among Kennedy appointees imploring them to stay. All of those who served in Kennedy's cabinet on 22 November 1963, save for Attorney General Robert F. Kennedy, remained in office for at least thirteen months.[28] Four secretaries—Dean Rusk (State), Willard Wirtz (Labor), Orville Freeman (Agriculture), and Stewart Udall (Interior)—continued in their posts for Johnson's entire term; another, Robert McNamara (Defense) lasted all but the final year.

With a presidential election within a year of his succession, Johnson quite naturally was anxious to associate himself with his predecessor's popularity by retaining Kennedy's most visible associates. The circumstances under which Ford became Chief Executive bore little similarity to those surrounding Johnson's succession, and accordingly, presented different political imperatives. As Richard Neustadt has observed, "Succeeding a disgraced man, but not himself legitimated by a popular election, Ford needed to assure the continuity of office by his demonstrated *difference* from his predecessor."[29] Still, Ford demonstrated similar inclination to continue able personnel in office. He retained Nixon's entire cabinet for several months.[30] His first announcement as Chief Executive was that the widely admired secretary of state, Henry Kissinger, would stay on.[31] Kissinger and Secretary of the Treasury William Simon did remain for the entire term; Ford continued Secretary of Agriculture Earl Butz in office until Butz's racial slurs made him a campaign liability. Defense Secretary James Schlesinger and Rogers Morton also stayed for more than a year though Schlesinger was later dismissed and Morton switched from the Interior to the Commerce Department.

It is not surprising that Johnson and Ford were more disposed to retain incumbent cabinet members than were many earlier Presidents by succession. The increased role of the President in selecting his running mate promotes compatibility between the Vice President and cabinet. Earlier Vice Presidents owed their positions to party leaders who chose them to provide ideological balance for the ticket. Their relations with the President and his cabinet were strained. But Kennedy and Nixon handpicked their Vice Presidents. Ford's political philosophy, if not his tactical approach, was similar to Nixon's. Kennedy and Johnson differed somewhat on issues at the outset, though never so much as had nineteenth-century teams. But Johnson was a loyal Vice President, giving unmeasured support to Kennedy's programs.

The declining importance of the cabinet offers a second incentive for a new President to retain advisers he inherits. The American cabinet has always been a different institution from its British counterpart. Collective decision-making has not been among its standard functions. But until the creation of the Executive Office of the President in 1939, its members served as the President's chief advisers. As recent Presidents have come to rely more heavily on the White House staff for guidance and execution, the costs of retaining cabinet members have lessened. Yet continuing previous cabinet members may help the departments operate smoothly. Presidents by succession have relied heavily on some inherited cabinet members. Rusk, McNamara, and Wirtz were among Johnson's closest associates. Ford depended on Kissinger and Simon. More often, an accidental President can retain a cabinet official but ignore him.

The White House staff presents a more difficult proposition. It consists primarily of long-time associates of the Chief Executive. Their loyalty is to their patron, their function largely personal and political. Members are unlikely to feel the same devotion to the successor; the new Chief Executive will want to surround himself with trusted intimates. Further, conflicts between presidential assistants and Vice Presidents are common.

Still, Johnson and Ford made efforts to retain intact the staffs their predecessors had designed, at least for a brief period. Lawrence O'Brien told Johnson he need not feel he had to keep Kennedy's staff.[32] But Johnson persuaded Kennedy's aides to stay for the transition period, in part by ignoring attempted resignations. Rather than dismissing Kennedy appointees to make room for his own, he supplemented the existing staff with his associates.[33] This arrangement could not last long. Many Kennedy people found adjustment to Johnson difficult. He had not been close to Kennedy's staff. Kennedy had treated Johnson circumspectly. His aides had not been so kind. They had paid little attention to the Vice President. Sudden subordination did not come easy.[34]

Further, relations between Johnson and top Kennedy aides were strained by events immediately following the succession. Johnson, quite properly, sought to surround himself with symbols of the presidency. He decided to return to Washington on the President's plane, Air Force One, which the Kennedy party was also using, rather than on the similar carrier he had flown previously. Physical proximity to Kennedy's casket, widow, and aides would emphasize the continuity of government. Kennedy aides wished to depart from Dallas immediately. Johnson ordered that takeoff be delayed until a judge had arrived to administer the oath. These actions upset the Kennedy people. As Lawrence O'Brien has admitted, "There was, as is well known now, some feelings of bitterness by me and other of the Kennedy people during the flight back from Dallas."[35] Some members of Kennedy's staff retained their influence by successfully shifting their loyalties to the new chief. Most prominent among this group were

O'Brien, McGeorge Bundy, and R. Sargent Shriver. Others—Theodore Sorensen, Kenneth O'Donnell, Pierre Salinger—soon left.[36]

Ford asked all but one of Nixon's senior aides to remain at least briefly.[37] It was not in his interest to extend them a permanent invitation owing to their identification with Nixon's Watergate defense. Some, like Brent Scowcroft, Alan Greenspan, and David Gergen, did find places in the Ford White House. Ford added to the executive staff officials like Donald Rumsfeld and James T. Lynn who had held important posts under Nixon.[38]

Succession of the Vice President lends further strength to government by creating the likelihood that policies followed by the previous Chief Executive will be pursued. Modern Vice Presidents reflect the views of the Chief Executive. As the role of the presidential nominee in selection of the running mate has grown, tickets consisting of ideological opposites have become rare, perhaps obsolete. It was not surprising that Tyler, Fillmore, Arthur, and Theodore Roosevelt departed from the policies of their predecessors given the manner in which they were chosen for the second spot. But Johnson and Ford were chosen by their predecessors and generally shared their views.

Johnson was no mirror image of Kennedy when their alliance was formed. Their differences were not great, but Johnson's Senate record had a more conservative cast. Their outlooks reflected, in part, the demands of their constituencies. Kennedy came from urban Massachusetts, Johnson from more conservative Texas. As a presidential contender, Kennedy needed support from liberals; as Senate Majority Leader Johnson had to retain the confidence of a diverse coalition. Both had tailored their conduct accordingly.

Some Kennedy insiders initially feared Johnson would move the country to the right. These fears proved unfounded. Occasionally, as Vice President, Johnson assumed a more conservative stance than Kennedy. He argued for a more aggressive response at the time of the Cuban missile crisis, for instance. But he had supported Kennedy's liberal overtures—the test ban treaty, Russian wheat deal—and had pushed for more progressive administration measures on civil rights. In his first speech to a joint session of Congress as President, Johnson called for the "earliest possible passage of the civil rights bill for which [Kennedy] fought so long" and the "early passage of the tax bill for which he fought all this long year."[39] He worked for, and signed into law, both measures.

Ford, predictably, followed closely Nixon's policies with few exceptions. While in Congress, Ford had ranked among Nixon's most reliable supporters. He had reaffirmed his agreement with Nixon's programs during his confirmation hearings.[40] Ford distinguished himself from Nixon by departing from unpopular administration attitudes on executive-legislative relations and by adopting a more conciliatory posture toward public, press, and Congress. And he implemented a limited program for amnesty for draft evaders.[41]

Continuity of policy is not, of course, always desirable. Presidents by succession may be led to accept policies of their predecessor without reflection. Johnson may have wandered into Vietnam for fear that early withdrawal would seem to reverse a Kennedy policy.[42] Continuity is no virtue when ill-conceived policies are perpetuated. The responsibility of the Chief Executive is to use his best judgment, not to mimic the views of his predecessor. Still, general policy continuity, like retention of personnel, has strategic value in reassuring interested parties and restoring stability.

Acceptability

By following policy lines drawn by his predecessor, an accidental President associates himself with the popular will as expressed at the last election and so legitimizes his inheritance. The Vice President is not, after all, elected on his own right. He may add some strength to the ticket. But voters may support a ticket in spite of the running mate.

In fact, voters have doubted the presidential qualities of some recent Vice Presidents. Nixon, as Vice President, fared well in the public's estimation. Gallup found a majority of voters gave him a favorable rating; relatively few described themselves as "mildly" or "highly" unfavorable to the Vice

TABLE 9.2
Voter Assessment of Vice President Nixon

If Vice President Nixon takes over the presidency, do you think he will do a better or worse job than President Eisenhower?

Better	8%
Worse	26
About the same	45
Don't know	21

Do you think Vice President Nixon would do a better or worse job than former President Truman?

Better	44%
Worse	22
About the same	15
Don't know	19

SOURCE: Gallup, *The Gallup Poll: Public Opinion, 1935-71*, 2:1535-36.

President.[43] Late in 1959, Gallup reported that about one-half of the electorate thought Nixon would be as good or better a President as Eisenhower; most felt he would be better than Truman.

The public has regarded other Vice Presidents less sympathetically. In November 1965, the Gallup Poll found little sentiment for a Humphrey presidency. Of those asked whether they would "like to see him become President sometime," 23 percent responded "yes," 58 percent, "no."[44] Four-and-one-half years later, Gallup found that Agnew scored marginally worse when the same question was asked about him.

Only 19 percent favored an Agnew presidency at some point while 61 percent opposed it.[45]

American voters are becoming more issue-oriented, but elections still do not produce a clear programmatic mandate. Electoral outcomes provide faulty barometers of the views of citizens under the best of circumstances. When, as in the United States, parties are nonideological, information imperfect, issues varied, and personalities influential, the result offers little guide to citizen preferences. Elections in America are devices to select leaders, not referenda on policy.[46]

Still, accidental Presidents are wise to continue the popular policies which their predecessors had put forward. The notion that the previous presidential election directed certain programmatic outcomes may be myth, but political systems depend on illusions as well as realities. Whether or not the electorate dictated a given policy is not crucial. The country is more likely to view as the legitimate heir a successor who follows the general policy outlines of the previous Chief Executive.

TABLE 9.3
Initial Popularity of Presidents

President	Approve	Disapprove	No Opinion	Net Popularity
Truman	87%	3%	10%	84%
Eisenhower	68	7	25	61
Kennedy	72	6	22	66
Johnson	79	3	18	76
Nixon	59	5	36	54
Ford	71	3	26	68
Carter	66	8	26	58

SOURCES: Gallup, *The Gallup Poll: Public Opinion, 1935-71* and *The Gallup Opinion Index.*

Indeed, recent Presidents by succession have won impressive initial support. All new Chief Executives enjoy a honey-

moon period of strong public approval. But the initial read-
ings of accidental Presidents have been unusually high. Table
9.3 lists the first measure of public approval of Presidents.
The difference between approval and disapproval ratings is
greatest for the three Presidents by succession.

Further indication that accidental Presidents have secured
popular support comes from their success in seeking terms of
their own. None of the four Presidents by succession in the
nineteenth century won an independent term. Since then,
four of the five have. The only one who lost his own election
bid—Ford—nearly won despite severe disadvantages.

Competence

A final justification for the vice presidency as the first station of succession is its ability to provide competent leaders.
A person who becomes Chief Executive under the adverse
conditions under discussion here must be prepared to assume
control immediately. There is no provision for a regency and
no time for a course on the arts of government. As Truman
recalled:

> I felt as if I had lived five lifetimes in my first five days as
> President. I was beginning to realize how little the Found-
> ing Fathers had been able to anticipate the preparations
> necessary for a man to become President so suddenly. It is
> a mighty leap from the vice-presidency to the presidency
> when one is forced to make it without warning.[47]

The formula for effective presidential performance is elusive. Success in the White House depends on some shifting
combination of personality, experience, ability, acceptance,
and luck. Not all of these criteria lend themselves easily to
objective analysis. Available evidence, presented in chapter
three, indicates that recent Vice Presidents have had extensive background in government and have achieved wide followings.

At the time they enter office, Vice Presidents should be qualified to be Chief Executive, for the vice presidency is not a finishing school where frail political saplings mature into presidential timber. There is no training ground for Presidents. The vice presidency can, however, provide its occupant with information and experience valuable to a sudden successor. Most recent Presidents have been attentive to their responsibility to make sure the Vice President is well-acquainted with information necessary to the discharge of executive responsibilities. As Eisenhower remarked in a news conference:

> I believe that it is almost showing indifference to the welfare of the American people, unless you keep the Vice President aware of everything that is going on. Even if Mr. Nixon and I were not good friends, I would still have him in every important conference of Government, so that if the grim reaper would find it time to remove me from this scene, he is ready to step in without any interruption and, certainly, without being completely unaware of what is going on in the Government.[48]

Recent Vice Presidents have had access to information important in executive decision-making. Nixon, for instance, was party to high-level discussions by virtue of his participation in meeting with cabinet, NSC, and the legislative leadership. Johnson received the same economic briefings from the CEA as did Kennedy.[49] They and other Vice Presidents received frequent military and intelligence briefings. Never did the process go so far as during Mondale's four years. He received the same material as Carter and had carte blanche to join any presidential conference.[50]

Such participation is highly desirable. Inactivity is likely to have an adverse effect on the ability of a Vice President to succeed. Arthur Schlesinger contends that the vice presidency "is much less a making than a maiming experience."

He argues that since Vice Presidents are not often involved in decision-making, they are likely to draw erroneous lessons. He attributes Johnson's unfortunate moves in the Dominican Republic and in Vietnam to his exclusion from foreign policy consultations under Kennedy.[51] It is not clear that these factors contributed to Johnson's mistakes. His foreign policy may have reflected the hawkish outlook he brought with him from Congress. Further, his vice-presidential years seem to have strengthened his commitment to civil rights. Indeed, Johnson was probably better prepared by having served as Kennedy's Vice President. Richard Neustadt observes that:

. . . what appears beyond dispute is that, once chosen, Johnson was so treated by [John Kennedy] as to ease his way enormously when he took over there. Johnson may have suffered great frustration as Vice-President, but his public standing and his knowledge of affairs were nurtured in those years. From this he gained a running start.[52]

The vice presidency need not be a destructive experience.

Temporary Succession

The cases of death, resignation, and removal of the Chief Executive are most conducive to simple resolution. Then the gap is permanent; the successor takes office for the remainder of the term. The other two contingencies—presidential inability and failure to qualify—pose more complex problems. The considerations already discussed in this chapter generally apply to them as well. But as they involve slightly different situations they merit brief separate treatment.

The distinctive element of presidential inability and failure to qualify is that the duration of the vacancy is uncertain. The case of disability involves a further complication. In the other four contingencies the Vice President automatically assumes presidential powers. In case of presidential incapacity, he acts only if the provisions of section three and four of the Twenty-fifth Amendment are first satisfied. A Chief Executive may clearly be incapable of performing his duties, but if both he and the cabinet refuse to acknowledge his inability the Vice President cannot act.

Until the shooting of President Reagan on 30 March 1981, there had been no occasion for problems associated with presidential inability to arise since the provisions described in sections three and four of the Twenty-fifth Amendment took effect in 1967. In the first moments following the shooting, Reagan's top assistants considered the advisability of invoking the disability procedures to vest presidential power in Vice President Bush. Many, though not all, of the "principal officers of the executive departments" gathered in the White House in case cabinet action under section four of that Amendment would be necessary. Bush abbreviated a speaking tour in Texas to return to Washington. Ultimately, Reagan's associates determined that no formal transfer was necessary during Reagan's operation and recovery.

Although Reagan did not return to his normal work schedule for several weeks, he signed a bill and met with top administration officials the day after the shooting. During Reagan's convalescence, Bush assumed a more prominent role, chairing some executive councils (including the cabinet) and acting as an administration spokesman.

The experience of Eisenhower's two serious illnesses, though prior to the adoption of the Twenty-fifth Amendment, is also instructive regarding problems that might confront the Vice President and system of government.

Eisenhower's heart attack occurred at a time when no important problems pressed for immediate resolution. The President's recovery was lengthy; two months passed before he again met with the cabinet, five before he resumed his regular schedule. But he was conscious and able to make major decisions for most of that period. He suffered his stroke at a less opportune moment. The Russian launching of the first Sputnik into outer space in October 1957 intensified Cold War anxieties. Eisenhower was scheduled to attend a meeting of the NATO allies in December. The economy was in recession. Fortunately, Eisenhower was soon able to resume his duties. In both instances, government functioned in Eisenhower's absence in a manner close to normal. It was able to do so, in part, because Eisenhower had organized his administration to allow subordinates a wide range of decision-making authority. Nixon presided over several meetings of the cabinet and NSC at the President's request. In public statements, Nixon and others emphasized that government was proceeding almost as it would have had Eisenhower not been incapacitated.[53] But it was not clear how long the disability would continue nor how government would handle an emergency that might arise. Nixon's position was precarious. He subsequently recalled:

> My own position as Vice President called for maintaining a balance of the utmost delicacy. On the one hand, aside from the President, I was the only person in government elected by all the people; they had a right to expect leadership, if it were needed, rather than a vacuum. But any move on my part which could be interpreted, even incorrectly, as an attempt to usurp the powers of the presidency would disrupt the Eisenhower team, cause dissension in the nation, and disturb the President and his family. Certainly I had no desire or intention to seize an iota of presidential power. I was the Vice President and could be nothing more. But the problem was to guard against what I knew would be easy misunderstanding of any mistake, no matter how slight, I might make in public or private. The crisis was how to walk on eggs and not break them. My problem, what I had to do, was to provide leadership without appearing to lead.[54]

Future Vice Presidents facing situations similar to those that confronted Nixon and Bush should find their position less tenuous owing to the adoption of the Twenty-fifth Amendment. Once the provisions of section three or four are followed, the Vice President will be empowered to exercise all powers of the presidency. The acting President will still be in a weaker position than those who succeed permanently. He must either rely on those administration officials he inherits or replace them. He may lack confidence in key officials yet fear that replacing them would disturb the President upon his return. He may not know when his service will end. He will not want to take actions that the Chief Executive will subsequently reverse. He must act in a cautious and circumspect manner.

But the possibility of presidential inability strengthens the case for the Vice President as the successor. A President would probably be less likely to declare his inability if that action would bring a congressional leader of the other party or of a different part of the political spectrum to power. Nor would the cabinet be as likely to sanction the rise of such a replacement or to work comfortably with him. If the Chief Executive has acted responsibly in selecting a running mate and in keeping him informed about the affairs of state, the temporary succession of the Vice President should bring an acceptable and competent leader to power in a manner likely to protect the stability of the executive branch.

No President-elect has ever failed to qualify. Such a contingency could arise in any of three circumstances. The President-elect might be unable to take the oath of office for some reason. He might fail to meet some eligibility requirement. Or the electoral system may not have produced a Chief Executive by inauguration day. In each case, the service of the Vice President would probably be temporary pending the qualification of a President-elect. Accordingly, the association of the two would probably help assure the smooth conduct of government.

In one situation, however, succession of the Vice-President-elect would not satisfy the criteria of stability, acceptability, and competence. The Constitution provides that if no candidate receives a majority of the votes of the electoral college, the House of Representatives, voting by state delegation, elects a President and the Senate, balloting as individuals, chooses a Vice President.[55] The two bodies might elect members of different parties. Such a result could occur in a number of ways. For instance, the Senate could elect a Vice President of one party before inauguration day and the House, a President from the other party some time after the new term began. The Vice President would establish an administration until the House chose a President. In that case, use of the Vice President as the substitute Chief Executive would create an awkward situation.

That such an event might occur is hardly a serious indictment of the vice presidency. First, the likelihood of the contingency is very remote. Further, it is not clear what plausible arrangement would guarantee that the person who acts temporarily as President and the eventual Chief Executive would share party identification. The problem resides not in the vice presidency but rather in the electoral system that could produce such a result.

The nature of the vice presidency makes it peculiar among government positions. Its central importance lies not in the activities its occupant commonly pursues but rather in the possibility that he will become or act as the Chief Executive. Any system of government must have some procedure to fill a vacancy in its ranking political position. The vice presidency provides an answer capable of satisfying the demands of presidential succession. Events since the New Deal that have brought the vice presidency into the executive branch have enhanced its ability to provide an informed leader who is regarded as the legitimate heir and whose succession lends stability to government. Whether a particular transfer of power conforms to those standards will turn largely on the competence of the second officer and the extent to which the Chief Executive has acted responsibly in selecting a compatible Vice President and preparing him to succeed.

10

★ ★ ★

Filling Vice-Presidential Vacancies

*A*lthough the United States has always had provisions to assure presidential succession, it did not, until 1967, have any means to fill a vice-presidential vacancy. The absence of any such arrangement for so long says much about the second office. The founding fathers and subsequent legislators were content to designate others to perform its functions of presiding over the Senate and standing next in the line of succession and to leave the office itself open.

Congress and the states implicitly recognized both the growth of the office and its necessary connection with the presidency by amending the Constitution to provide a procedure to replace a Vice President who had left office prematurely. Congress proposed the Twenty-fifth Amendment in 1965; three-fourths of the states ratified it less than two years later. Section two of that measure provided that "whenever there is a vacancy in the office of the Vice President, the President shall nominate a Vice President who shall take office upon confirmation by a majority vote of both Houses of Congress." The two initial exercises of the procedure demonstrated that section two, though not free of problems, provides a means of choosing an acceptable and able successor in a reasonably democratic fashion. This chapter first sketches the historical background of the amendment, then discusses the theory behind section two. It proceeds to assess the first two applications—the selection of Ford, and then Rockefeller, to be Vice President.

Historical Background

The legislative effort to produce a means of filling a vice-presidential vacancy began in full force in 1964.[1] The succession of Lyndon Johnson following the assassination of President Kennedy left the second office unoccupied. This did not, of course, present a novel situation. The vice presidency

TABLE 10.1
Vice-Presidential Vacancies

Vice President	Reason for Vacancy	Length of Vacancy		
		Years	Months	Days
George Clinton	Death		10	12
Elbridge Gerry	Death	2	3	9
John C. Calhoun	Resignation		2	4
John Tyler	Succession	3	11	0
Millard Fillmore	Succession	2	7	23
William R. King	Death	3	10	14
Andrew Johnson	Succession	3	10	17
Henry Wilson	Death	1	3	10
Chester A. Arthur	Succession	3	5	13
Thomas A. Hendricks	Death	3	3	7
Garret A. Hobart	Death	1	3	11
Theodore Roosevelt	Succession	3	5	18
James S. Sherman	Death		4	5
Calvin Coolidge	Succession	1	7	2
Harry S. Truman	Succession	3	9	8
Lyndon B. Johnson	Succession	1	1	29
Spiro T. Agnew	Resignation		1	26
Gerald T. Ford	Succession		4	10
Total		37	9	8

SOURCE: This table is a slightly modified version of that provided in Feerick, *The Twenty-Fifth Amendment,* Appendix D-II.

had been left vacant on fifteen occasions prior to 1963. By then, the vice presidency had been empty for thirty-six years, roughly 20 percent of the nation's existence. During those periods, some other officer designated by Congress stood first in line of succession—the president pro tempore of the Senate, 1792-1886; the secretary of state, 1886-1947; the Speaker of the House, 1947 onwards.

Five factors made the mid-1960s a propitious time for the change embodied in section two. First, the importance of the presidency was clearly established. Congress was, accordingly, concerned about the quality of provisions to assure the continuity of executive power. Interest was intensified by recent reminders of the possibility of presidential vacancy. Eisenhower's three illnesses had increased public consciousness of the importance of the issue. The assassination of President Kennedy in November 1963 revived interest in succession provisions and made all guarantees of presidential safety less convincing. Further, Johnson's health was suspect; he had suffered a heart attack less than a decade earlier.

These two considerations would not have produced a change had existing arrangements seemed satisfactory. But Kennedy's death left Speaker John McCormack and Senate President pro tempore Carl Hayden heading the line of successors. Both were well beyond the usual age of Presidents. Neither had ever been prominently mentioned as a prospective Chief Executive. That McCormack and Hayden were so unsuited for the presidency stimulated interest in devising an alternative plan, but prevented action, in the House at least, until 1965. By then, a new Vice President had been elected; congressional action to make the succession of the Speaker less likely would no longer be construed as an insult to its occupant.

Part of the appeal of section two came from the help it gave the provisions in sections three and four of the Twenty-fifth Amendment. Presidential inability, not replacing the Vice President, was the main concern of those who pushed the measure. Indeed, the procedures ultimately adopted to ensure executive continuity in case of presidential incapacity bore strong resemblance to plans discussed in the House in the mid-1950s following Eisenhower's stroke and in the Senate Subcommittee on Constitutional Amendments in June 1963. But those required a Vice President to participate in declaring the Chief Executive disabled. Section two was designed in part to make sure that a vice-presidential vacancy would not make the disability provisions inoperative for the remainder of the term.

Finally, passage of section two indicated a belief that the vice presidency had become a worthwhile office. At the outset of the discussion of S.J. Res. 139, the proposed Twenty-fifth Amendment, its sponsor Senator Birch Bayh argued that "the office of Vice President has gone through a period of development, perhaps to a greater degree than any other office in the history of the country." He described it as "a full-time, highly responsible office." He argued:

> I submit that reason dictates that we take steps to assure that the Nation shall always have a Vice President. He would lift at least some of the awful burden of responsibility from the shoulders of the President and make the most important office in the world perhaps a little bit less burdensome. His presence would provide for an orderly transfer of executive authority in the event of the death of the President—a transfer that would win public consent and inspire national confidence.[2]

Others echoed his sentiments.[3] This assessment of the second office, so different from traditional comment, reflected recent experience. Nixon and Johnson had been relatively activist Vice Presidents. Further, Johnson had lent the vice presidency added prestige by his masterful performance upon leaving it. In the spring and summer prior to consideration of S.J. Res. 139, most leading Democrats had made no secret of their interest in occupying the second spot on their party's ticket.

The House did not act on the measure in 1964 but it passed

the Senate by voice vote on 28 September 1964, and 65 to 0 the next day.[4] Johnson promised to propose laws on presidential succession in his 1965 State of the Union address on 4 January;[5] less than four weeks later he urged quick action on identical proposals (S.J. Res. 1 and H.J. Res. 1) introduced by Bayh and Representative Emanuel Celler which, with minor alterations that did not touch section two, subsequently became the Twenty-fifth Amendment.[6] The Senate again approved the measure on 19 February 1965, 72 to 0; the House acted favorably on 13 April by a vote of 368 to 29. The report of the conference committee passed the House by voice vote on 30 June and the Senate, 68 to 5, six days later.[7]

The legislative debates included little criticism of section two. Most who opposed the measure found fault with the provisions for handling presidential disability. But several congressmen, even in 1965, regarded section two as an affront to the House since it made the succession of the Speaker far less likely. Representative Roman C. Pucinski feared it might lead to "palace intrigue"; he and Representative John D. Dingell attacked the procedure as dynastic, too.[8] Representative Charles McC. Mathias argued that the Vice President should remain "an elective office" and predicted that "congressional confirmation of a vice-presidential nominee would be only a mild check and, in my judgment, would be a mere formality in a period of national emotional stress."[9] Senator Mike Monroney expressed similar doubts.[10] Fearing that Congress might delay action on a nomination by a President of the opposite party, Senator Ross Bass believed section two should require congressional action "immediately." Bayh and Senator Sam Ervin argued that Congress would not act in so partisan a fashion; Bayh and Senator Roman C. Hruska urged that Bass's proposal might cause Congress to act too swiftly, perhaps without hearings. Bass's plan was rejected.[11]

The Theory of Section Two

Section two attempted to combine two political values that have been associated with many recent discussions of the vice presidency.[12] Some congressmen sought to maximize presidential control of the selection of a new Vice President. Others preferred a process that would allow wider participation. Generally these assigned Congress the leading role. Bills embodying seven different plans for filling a vice-presidential vacancy were introduced in Congress in 1964 and 1965.

Five plans, including Bayh's, called for congressional participation in the process. Ervin proposed that a joint session of Congress elect a Vice President whenever the office was vacant. Mathias and his colleague, John V. Lindsay, modified Ervin's plan to allow the President a veto. Senator Frank Church suggested that whenever the vice presidency were unoccupied, the President, with the advice and consent of the Senate, would nominate between two and five persons; the House would select from that group. Senator Stephen Young would have allowed the President to appoint his successor with the Senate's consent.[13]

None of the four plans was thought satisfactory. Ervin's proposal allowed a high risk that the Vice President would be personally and/or politically incompatible with the Chief Executive. The veto that Lindsay and Mathias proposed would theoretically have given the President a measure of control. In practice, the Chief Executive could not reject the person Congress chose without offending the individual, who would probably be an important politician, and perhaps antagonizing Congress. The Church and Young plans, conversely, offered Congress little control. The President could manipulate Church's system by offering one serious candidate and several implausible ones. The House would have no option to reject all. The advise and consent procedure generally provided only a cursory treatment.

Two other plans gave Congress no role in the choice. Monroney and Senator Kenneth Keating proposed creating a second vice presidency whose occupant would be elected in tandem with the President and his traditional running mate.[14] But the second vice presidency would probably have difficulty attracting able candidates. Its occupant would receive little scrutiny.

A curious collection of public figures suggested that the President submit a nomination to the Electoral College for consideration. Proponents of the plan included former President Truman, Nixon, and Senator Strom Thurmond.[15] They pointed out that Congress might be controlled by the opposite party from the President; the Electoral College, however, would reflect the outcome of the last presidential election. Yet that body is not equipped to perform the role they envisaged for it. It has no investigative machinery. Nor are its members chosen to exercise discretion. Further, electors are generally anonymous and are not in a position, as are legislators, to be held accountable for their acts.

Bayh's proposal sought to reconcile the two values. It gave the President a leading role in choosing a new Vice President to help ensure compatibility between the two officers; it required congressional participation to introduce an element of democratic control. As Bayh put it, "We [are] guaranteeing that the President would have a man with whom he could work. We were also guaranteeing to the people their right to make that decision."[16] Others, too, spoke of the provisions of section two as involving a balance. Senator Alan Bible, for instance, commented:

> By this means, it is virtually assured that the Vice President will continue to be a man in whom the President has full confidence and a man of the same political party and po-

litical philosophy. At the same time, congressional confirmation gives the people of the United States a voice through their elected representatives.[17]

Paul A. Freund, a prominent legal scholar, observed:

The Vice Presidency should have a popular base and at the same time be in harmony with the Presidency. These objectives can best be achieved by associating the Congress and the President in the selection, with the opportunity for informal consultation to be expected in such a process.[18]

Attorney General Nicholas deB. Katzenbach predicted:

Permitting the President to choose the Vice President, subject to congressional approval, in the event of a vacancy in that office, will tend to insure the selection of an associate in whom the President has confidence, and with whom he can work in harmony. Participation by Congress in the procedure should help to insure that the person selected would be broadly acceptable to the people of the Nation.[19]

The two principles are more easily combined in statements than in practice. The President was entitled to a Vice President who shared his views. That would promote a meaningful role for the second officer. Further, it would help ensure that a Vice President who succeeded to the presidency would honor the policy preferences implied by the results of the last presidential election. Yet confirmation was not to involve a perfunctory review. Congressional participation was designed to "enable the voice of the people to be heard" through their elected representatives, Bayh said. "What better opportunity is there for the people to express their wishes than through those who serve in Congress?"[20]

A nominee in harmony with the Chief Executive, however, might not represent the "wishes" of the people as reflected by their representatives in Congress. The ambiguity of their role posed a necessary dilemma for many members of Congress and a potential problem for the aggregate body. Individuals with constituents whose views differed from that of the Chief Executive and his Vice-President-designate could not satisfy their representative role if they voted to confirm the nominee. Further, the majority of Congress might hold views quite different from the President. The likelihood of such a division is increasing and presents a problem especially for Republican Presidents who have occasion to use section two of the amendment. Elections for the two branches have become more independent of one another. Voters are more likely to decide between competing candidates in the presidential race; at lower levels, party assumes greater importance. Incumbency enables many members of Congress to win reelection even while their constituents vote for a President of the opposite party. Accordingly, Democrats controlled both houses of Congress for twenty-four of the twenty-eight years from 1953-1981 but held the White House for only twelve.

Congressmen took little notice of the problem the dual standard could present during the initial debates on section two in 1964 and 1965. But the ambiguity in the standard gave rise to a number of interpretations when in 1973 and 1974 Congress was called upon to consider presidential nominees. Representative Ketchum exaggerated only slightly when he complained that "there are as many interpretations of that amendment as there are points on a compass."[21]

For instance, Joseph Rauh, then vice-chairman of the ADA, thought the appropriate test was whether, partisan considerations aside, the nominee was "among the group of persons that a majority of the Members of both Houses of Congress want to see as President of the United States." Representative Jerome Waldie (D. Calif.) implied an even stricter standard. He suggested that Congress had "a choice between [the nominee] and a multitude of others."[22] Accepting these standards, a number of congressmen argued that disagreement with the nominee's views was proper ground for opposition.

Others believed the political philosophy of the Vice-President-designate irrelevant to congressional consideration. Liberal Republican Senator Mark Hatfield pronounced the important question as "Is this man capable of performing the duties? Not whether or not he agrees with me or I with him . . ." His conservative Democratic colleague, James Allen, agreed. He suggested:

> The woods might be full of people who are qualified of [sic] being Vice President. But under the Constitution now, it is up to the President, not the Congress, to make the initial choice.

Representative Martha Griffiths (D. Mich.) told the Senate Committee on Rules and Administration:

> . . . It is not within the province of this body to say, because we do not agree with [the nominee] on the issues, we will not support him. We are here to check . . . integrity, . . . ability, . . . leadership ability, and with any confirmation, to give the stamp of approval upon these items.[23]

Ford thought that the congressional investigation "should be of the broadest possible scope" and should include the voting record of the nominee but that "one's political philosophy is not necessarily the criteria [sic] by which a person is approved or disapproved."[24] Representative Burt Talcott (R. Calif.) interpreted the congressional role far more narrowly. He felt "unless there is a reason for finding the nominee guilty of charges presentable for impeachment, the nominee should be confirmed."[25]

The above survey indicates the diversity of suggested standards. Most are unsuitable. Talcott's view, for instance, would accept ignorance, incompetence, and a range of horrific characteristics so long as the nominee had committed no impeachable offense. Rauh and Waldie err in the opposite direction. Their standards could prevent a President from selecting a compatible heir if his political philosophy differed from that of a majority in Congress.

It is probably impossible to purge section two of ambiguity. It attempts, properly, to balance two principles which do not lend themselves to such a compromise. It is possible, however, to define with more precision a proper standard consistent with legislative history. The President is entitled to nominate a successor whose views approximate his own. The discussion of the provision prior to its ratification indicates clearly that Congress was not to refuse a Chief Executive his choice purely on philosophical grounds. This constraint does not consign Congress to an inactive role. To begin with, Congress can explore a wide range of personal characteristics. It can reject a nominee as incompetent, inexperienced, or immoral. It might also refuse to confirm if polls indicated a clear majority of the public opposed the nominee. As the surrogate of the public, Congress could reasonably reject a nominee out of step with public sentiments or one whose succession was likely to create some unsettling problem for government.

Although general ideology might normally be irrelevant, considerations of issues relating to the operation of government institutions might be germane. Senator Howard Cannon suggested that it would be improper to oppose a nominee because of his views on foreign policy, social welfare, "or other burning issues of the day." But he believed Congress should properly inquire into the nominee's views on presidential power and prerogatives and the relationship of the executive branch to the courts and Congress.[26] Answers to these sorts of questions suggest whether a nominee is likely to commit offenses which might later justify impeachment.

Finally, the rationale for not considering ideology is weakened seriously once the person nominating the Vice President is not an elected Chief Executive. A Vice President might succeed to the presidency and nominate someone whose views approximated his own but differed markedly from those of his predecessor. Congress would at least be expected to determine whether the views of the nominee were in general harmony with those of the public. Such a consideration would be especially important if a Speaker of the House from the opposite party was called upon to discharge the duties of the presidency and submitted a nominee under section two.

Although section two limits the extent to which legislators can properly consider ideology in evaluating a nominee, it retains other virtues of a democratic procedure. The investigative process allows extensive scrutiny of a prospective vice-presidential candidate. The process may not allow the electorate the option of directly rejecting the nominee, but at least it makes voters familiar with his credentials and allows them to communicate their opinions to their representatives.

No occasion arose to use section two from the ratification of the Twenty-fifth Amendment in 1967 until early October 1973. It was, however, invoked on two occasions within the next ten months. Spiro T. Agnew resigned as Vice President on 10 October 1973 as part of a plea-bargaining arrangement. Two days later Nixon nominated Ford as Agnew's replacement. On 9 August 1974, Ford became President upon Nixon's resignation. Some eleven days later, Ford proposed Nelson A. Rockefeller to fill the vacancy in the second office. Some confusion concerning the proper standard occurred in both instances. But section two, in admirable fashion, allowed the President and Congress to fill the vice-presidential vacancies.[27]

The First Application: Ford

The first occasion to use section two came in circumstances novel in American history and unanticipated by those who had drafted and approved the Twenty-fifth Amendment. The framers of the procedure had expected application of section two to follow the death of a Vice President or President. Instead, the first usage allowed a President under threat of impeachment to replace a Vice President whose resignation had followed revelations of his past criminal activity. The peculiar situation affected the implementation of section two.

The possibility of impeachment raised strategic considerations for both President and Congress. Nixon was in a position of weakness. Some doubted the legitimacy of a President in his position to nominate his likely successor. Indeed, a number of Democratic members of Congress urged that impeachment proceedings take precedence over confirmation of a new Vice President.[28] Any succession would have elevated the Democratic Speaker of the House, Carl Albert, to the presidency.

Further, the new Vice President was likely either to become President before Nixon's term ended in 1976 or to be in a strong position to win the Republican nomination that year. Nixon seemed unlikely to complete his term; even if he did, he could not seek another. Some called for a vice-presidential nominee unlikely to seek the presidency in 1976.[29] Democrats did not relish the possibility of running against an incumbent Republican President; Republicans did not wish to see a member of a different wing of the party given the advantages a President or Vice President enjoys. In his precarious position, Nixon could ill afford to alienate any congressional supporters. Finally, the novelty of the section two procedure added to the uncertainty. No one knew how it would operate; procedural questions had first to be resolved.[30]

These factors all gave Nixon incentive to find a nominee likely to win confirmation with relative ease. John Connally, not Ford, was apparently Nixon's first choice. Opposition to Connally quickly surfaced; the certainty of congressional scrutiny prevented his nomination.[31] Other possible choices also had liabilities. Selection of Rockefeller would alienate the Republican right and upset Democrats not eager to face him in the next election; nomination of Governor Ronald Reagan would upset moderates in Nixon's party. Attorney General Elliot L. Richardson eliminated himself from consideration; as the "Government accuser" of Agnew he felt he should not be considered as his replacement.[32]

Ford possessed several assets and none of these liabilities. He was well liked in Congress. He was not seen as a presidential candidate in 1976. Albert told Nixon that Ford would win easy confirmation; Representatives Jack Kemp (R. N.Y.) and Dan Kuykendall (R. Tenn.) began circulating petitions among their colleagues on Ford's behalf only moments after Agnew's resignation. The nomination was widely praised; Gallup found that 66 percent of the public approved it while only 7 percent disapproved.[33]

Despite clear congressional sentiment in favor of confirmation, both Houses conducted a thorough examination. The FBI assigned more than 350 of its agents to probe Ford's background. They interviewed more than 1,000 people and produced more than 1,700 pages of reports. Other investigative bodies of the executive and legislative branches also participated.[34]

Both Houses conducted hearings during which members indicated the seriousness of their task. Senator Cannon urged the Rules Committee to "view its obligations as no less important than the selection of a potential President of the United States." The chairman of the House Judiciary Committee, Representative Peter Rodino, characterized the hearings as "an examination of a man's qualification and fitness to hold the highest office in America, that of President of the United States."[35]

The questions members of the relevant committees asked Ford can be divided into three categories. Some involved personal information—tax returns, associations, and past political conduct. Others solicited Ford's views on the proper operation of political institutions. These "good government" questions included queries concerning openness, executive privilege, the extent of a government's right to lie and so on. The final area consisted of "bread and butter" issues—welfare, civil rights, foreign policy. Oral questions asked in hearings were tabulated and assigned to one of these categories. The results are presented in Table 10.2.

TABLE 10.2
Nature of Questions Asked Ford

	Personal	Institutional	Issues
Senate (N = 121)	33%	50%	17%
House (N = 541)	50	35	15

SOURCE: Compiled by the author from the transcripts of the hearings published by the House and the Senate.

Both committees were more interested in exploring Ford's personal characteristics and learning his institutional views than in hearing his policy preferences. After all, Ford's voting record during his twenty-five years in the House made his general philosophy clear. The aftermath of Watergate made integrity and "good government" concerns more important. Generally, Republicans focused on Ford's personal traits. Democrats asked 95 percent of the "issues" questions in the Senate and 80 percent in the House.

The hearings presented a wealth of information and examined a variety of allegations about Ford. Much attention concentrated on charges made by a Washington lobbyist that Ford had solicited large gifts from him and had been under psychiatric care.[36] Both claims were discredited. Ford's role in initiating the impeachment investigation of Justice William Douglas was explored at length. Clarence Mitchell of the NAACP presented a critical assessment of Ford's record on civil rights. Speaking for the ADA, Rauh urged rejection on the grounds that Ford was unqualified to be President; Representative Bella Abzug (D. N.Y.) and Representative Michael Harrington (D. Mass.) took similar positions.[37]

During the hearings, Ford indicated his disagreement with some practices of the Nixon administration. He denied that any official had the right to disobey a court order. He promised to be accessible to Congress and honest with the public. He defined executive privilege more narrowly than had Nixon.[38] But he reaffirmed his agreement with most substantive policies of the Nixon administration.

In at least two instances, however, Ford's responses provided misleading cues to his future action. Cannon asked Ford if a President by succession would have the "power" to prevent or terminate any investigation or criminal prosecution of his predecessor. Ford replied:

> I do not think the public would stand for it. I think—and whether he has the technical authority or not, I cannot give you a categorical answer.
>
> The Attorney General, in my opinion, with the help and support of the American people, would be the controlling factor.[39]

Ford's response suggested that he would not later pardon Nixon. But Cannon put the question poorly—he did not seek a specific guarantee from Ford and Ford did not offer one. Ford also said repeatedly that he would not be a candidate for any office in 1976.

Ford's nomination won overwhelming support by both committees. The Senate Rules Committee backed him, 9 to 0, on 20 November; the House Judiciary Committee gave Ford its endorsement, 29 to 8, nine days later. Those in the minority were all liberal Democrats. The Senate voted to confirm, 92 to 3 on 27 November, the opposition being three liberal Democrats—Senators Thomas Eagleton, William Hathaway, and Gaylord Nelson. Ford became Vice President upon gaining the approval of the House, 387 to 35, the negative votes all coming from Democrats. Many of those who supported Ford acknowledged that they disagreed with him on many specific issues but contended that ideology was irrelevant to their function.

The Second Application: Rockefeller

Ford was in a much stronger position than Nixon had been to nominate a Vice President of his choice. In the immediate aftermath of his graceful succession he enjoyed the good will of public and Congress. His consideration of a Vice President soon narrowed to Rockefeller and party chairman George Bush.[40] Bush was preferred by many Republican officials as most likely to unite the party. Rockefeller's assets included his vast experience and appeal to more moderate elements of the electorate. The announcement by Melvin Laird, long a Ford ally, that he preferred Rockefeller, failed to produce the expected protest from the Republican right. Indeed, Senators Goldwater, Thurmond, and John Tower indicated that they would not oppose Rockefeller although he was not their preference.[41] Ford's selection of Rockefeller thus met with much acclaim and little opposition.

The congressional inquiry again produced a massive federal investigation of the nominee. More than 300 FBI agents interviewed more than 1,400 people and produced reports in excess of 2,000 pages. Rockefeller made available extensive financial records including his recent tax returns and statements of his net worth.[42]

The committees in both Houses concentrated on the financial affairs of the nominee and his family. As Rodino announced at the outset of the House inquiry:

. . . The use of money in a political system, for political purposes, is a highly relevant subject, and will bear on these proceedings.

We will therefore wish to inquire of the nominee regarding a history of gifts, loans and of forgiven loans; we must attempt to measure the network of Rockefeller wealth, family wealth, and place it into the perspective of both the American economy and the American political system.[43]

The nomination of Rockefeller raised "a very fundamental philosophical question," said Representative Paul Sarbanes (D. Md.), "and that is that we have as a fundamental principle in this country the concept that public power will be available to check and restrain and limit and control private economic wealth and power."[44] Rockefeller's succession to the presidency, Sarbanes continued, would represent "the melding together . . . of great public power and probably the most significant concentration of private economic power in the Nation."

Questioning in both committees focused on "personal" matters. These generally concerned the Rockefeller family wealth, the substantial gifts Rockefeller had made to government officials, Rockefeller's handling of the Attica prison tragedy and the involvement of Rockefeller and his brother Laurance in financing a derogatory book about his opponent in the 1970 gubernatorial campaign, Arthur J. Goldberg. The interest in Rockefeller's record as opposed to the other two categories is suggested in Table 10.3.

TABLE 10.3
Nature of Questions Asked Rockefeller

	Personal	Institutional	Issues
Senate (N = 721)	77%	7%	16%
House (N = 419)	63	13	24

SOURCE: See Table 10.2.

The hearings produced some concessions from Rockefeller regarding the future conduct of his financial affairs. He agreed to place his holdings in a blind trust if confirmed. He pledged not to make gifts to federal employees with two exceptions— he would continue to give "relatively nominal amounts" to friends on various holidays and personal occasions and he would assist friends "in the event of special hardships of a compelling human character."[45] He promised to place the public welfare above his private interest.

Although the Ford confirmation required less than two months from nomination to confirmation, Rockefeller's lasted twice that long. Senate Minority Leader Hugh Scott accused Democrats of delaying the process because "the designee has undertaken not to campaign during the confirmation proceedings." Following the election he denounced the majority for "sabotaging" the Twenty-fifth Amendment by its "unconscionable" conduct. Senator Robert Griffin said "Congress is really on trial" for its "dillydallying."[46] As the proceedings continued, public support for confirmation declined. In October, the Roper Poll found that 37 percent approved of Ford's nomination of Rockefeller while 39 percent disapproved.[47] Still, the nomination was approved by decisive majorities of 90 to 7 in the Senate and 287 to 128 in the House.

Significantly, Bayh was among those opposing Rockefeller. As the principal framer of section two, his comments are instructive in understanding its proper application. Bayh concluded that Rockefeller "does not command and would not command the public confidence of large numbers of American people" if he became President. Bayh described the legislators' role as "surrogate electors" and as "the vehicle through which our constituents' feelings were to be made known . . ." Public sentiment, he said, was to be "a critical element in the decision-making process for those of us called upon to vote."[48]

An Assessment

The first two implementations of section two reveal several problems inherent in the procedure. The standard for voting is vague. The process calls for something more than the perfunctory treatment often associated with advise and consent. Congressmen generally defer to the President in the selection of his associates in the executive branch. But choice of a Vice President properly requires a more exacting test. Still, the process is not an election; legislators are not intended to give the same weight to policy as might citizens voting for a presidential ticket. The section-two standard falls somewhere between these two operations. As it involves a balance, it is necessarily less clear.

Further, legislators may be tempted, especially when the control of Congress and the presidency is divided, to put partisan advantage above national interest. They may be inclined to delay confirmation or to insist that the nominee not be a likely presidential candidate in subsequent campaigns. Future use of the standard may suggest ways in which Presidents, too, can abuse their responsibility.

The procedure also raises questions about invasion of the privacy of the nominee and his family. Congressional committees have not always been sensitive to the rights of individuals. They may seek to ferret out personal information which is interesting to the public but not germane to their undertaking. Finally, the procedure allows someone to become Vice President and perhaps President without ever facing the voters. That presents an uncomfortable situation for a nation that prides itself on being democratic.

It would, of course, be preferable if these problems did not exist. Still, section two remains a valuable feature of American institutional arrangements. It closes previous loopholes in the provisions for handling presidential succession. It worked well in its first two implementations. Section two allows a detailed examination of the background of a nominee. In so doing, it provides citizens with more information about the second officer than would a presidential campaign. Those who become Vice President under section two are not elected, but neither, really, are those chosen in the usual manner. The ambiguity of the standard is a necessary byproduct of combining the two values implicit in section two—compatibility between President and Vice President and participation in the selection. Section two allows the President a successor of his choice; since that individual may become President the congressional scrutiny is appropriate. Invasions of privacy and dilatory tactics may occur. But any procedure is subject to abuse. Institutional engineering cannot guarantee that human beings will always behave in a proper manner. At some point, political procedures must rely on the good will and judgment of individuals.

Adoption of section two recognized the increased importance of the vice presidency. Other less formal developments in American political practice suggest the same conclusion. In recent years, Vice Presidents have received more serious consideration as presidential candidates, the subject of the next chapter.

11

★ ★ ─────────────────────────────────

Springboard to the Presidency

For most of its history the vice presidency has justifiably been regarded as a political graveyard. Its occupant might become President upon the death of the Chief Executive; otherwise he was unlikely to advance. Changes in American politics since the New Deal have enhanced the value of the office as a stepping stone. Rather than being a burial ground for presidential ambitions, it has recently provided a reliable incubator for them.[1] The springboard value varies with different personalities and times. As a general though not absolute rule, it has recently been an asset in gaining the nomination but a liability in winning the election.[2]

Early experience suggested that the vice presidency might become the standard training ground of Presidents. The original constitutional scheme provided a single election for the two highest offices with each elector having two votes. The architects of the system hoped thereby to encourage electors to support the two most outstanding public figures.[3]

Initially, the plan succeeded. John Adams and Thomas Jefferson, the first two Vice Presidents, each later won election as President. But the growth of political parties and adoption of a new electoral method adversely affected the quality of Vice Presidents. Of subsequent nineteenth-century Vice Presidents, only Martin Van Buren was ever elected Chief Executive. No other holder of the office won nomination; few were even considered.[4]

In the twentieth century, Vice Presidents again began to be

viewed as presidential possibilities. Those elected were more impressive men than their nineteenth-century predecessors. Often they represented some important party faction which provided a base for their subsequent candidacies. Yet they lacked sufficient strength to capture the prize. Charles Fairbanks, Thomas Marshall, and Charles Dawes all had support but were blocked by the incumbent who preferred someone else.[5] John Nance Garner and Alben Barkley sought the honor without success. Roosevelt's interest in a third term and opposition from liberals defeated Garner; labor leaders vetoed Barkley as too old. Henry Wallace was unable even to secure a second term as Vice President.[6]

It was not, then, until the 1950s that the office really emerged as a sure springboard. Since then, two Vice Presidents—Nixon and Humphrey—have been nominated to seek the presidency. Indeed, since 1956, the party controlling the White House has nominated only the President or the Vice President.

Standing alone, two cases would provide thin support for an argument. But other evidence also suggests the value of the vice presidency as a stepping stone. Public opinion polls have consistently indicated strong backing for Vice Presidents as prospective Presidents. Since its creation in 1935, the Gallup Poll has often asked voters who identify with a major party whom they prefer as their party's candidate in the next presidential campaign. As illustrated by the following table, Vice Presidents run strongly in those surveys which exclude the name of the incumbent Chief Executive.

Nixon trailed Chief Justice Earl Warren in early polls measuring the preferences of Republican voters as Eisenhower's successor. By 1955, however, he was the clear front-runner. In surveys taken during the second term, he comfortably outdistanced Senator William Knowland, his main competitor before the elections in November, 1958, and Governor Nelson A. Rockefeller, his chief rival thereafter. An unsuccessful

TABLE 11.1
Standing of Vice Presidents in Gallup Presidential Preference Polls of
Voters of Their Party

Vice President	No. of Polls	First	Second	Other
Garner (1937-1940)	16	10	5	1 (5th)
Wallace	n.a.	—	—	—
Truman	n.a.	—	—	—
Barkley	3	0	2	1 (3rd)
Nixon (1954-1956)	9	6	3	0
(1957-1960)	19	19	0	0
Johnson	n.a.	—	—	—
Humphrey	3	2	1	0
Agnew (1971)	1	0	1	0
(1973)	3	2	0	1 (4th)
Ford	1	1	0	0
Rockefeller	n.a.	—	—	—
Mondale	n.a.	—	—	—

(Standing columns: First, Second, Other)

SOURCE: Joel K. Goldstein, "An Overview of the Vice-Presidency," *Ford. L. Rev.* 45 (1977):788; data taken from *The Gallup Poll: Public Opinion, 1935-71*, *The Gallup Poll: Public Opinion, 1972-77*, and *The Gallup Opinion Index*.

NOTE: "N.a." means that there were no published Gallup Polls measuring the party preferences for the presidential nomination that did not include the incumbent President. The dates listed next to the Vice Presidents' names refer to the years in which relevant polls were taken.

race for governor of California eliminated Knowland from further consideration. Rockefeller was briefly inclined to challenge Nixon. He withdrew, however, late in 1959 after discovering that the party's political and financial leaders backed Nixon.[7] The Republicans nominated Nixon on the first ballot, with only ten votes going to Senator Barry M. Goldwater.

Humphrey's nomination, though achieved with greater difficulty than Nixon's in 1960, was hardly strenuous by usual standards. Humphrey had not expected to run for President in 1968.[8] Accordingly, he had relatively little time to plan his campaign. He entered the presidential race only after Johnson announced on 31 March 1968 that "I shall not seek, and I will not accept, the nomination of my party for another term as your President."[9] Two others—Senators Eugene McCarthy and Robert F. Kennedy—were candidates before Humphrey declared his availability on 27 April 1968. A *Newsweek* delegate poll in early April found Humphrey trailing Kennedy (541 to 858) though leading McCarthy (272) with 951 delegates either leaning to favorite sons or uncommitted.[10] But seven weeks later, *Newsweek* reported a dramatic change.[11] Its latest delegate count gave Humphrey 1,279½ "solid" or "leaning" votes compared to 713½ for Kennedy and 280 for McCarthy. It is impossible to predict with certainty the outcome had Kennedy lived. Still, Humphrey seemed within reach of the nomination at the time of Kennedy's death on 6 June 1968.

Interest in drafting Senator Edward M. Kennedy posed the major threat to Humphrey at the convention. Negotiations involved McCarthy, Kennedy's brother-in-law Stephen E. Smith, and the two politicians controlling the largest blocs of delegates, Mayor Richard J. Daley of Illinois and Jesse Unruh of California. Whether enough delegates would have coalesced to nominate Kennedy is uncertain. Most evidence suggests that Kennedy could not have gained the necessary majority.[12] Kennedy issued a statement disclaiming interest, and Humphrey (1,760¼ delegates) won the nomination easily over McCarthy (601) and McGovern (146½), with 114¼ votes going to other candidates.[13]

Agnew would probably have been the front-runner for the Republican nomination in 1976 had not revelations of his criminal activity forced his resignation in October 1973. A relative unknown when chosen for the ticket in July 1968, Agnew quickly became a Republican favorite. Late in April 1971 a Gallup Poll found that Agnew trailed only Reagan as the preference of Republican (25 percent to 31 percent) and independent (18 percent to 25 percent) voters for the 1972 presidential nomination should Nixon not run.[14] Agnew became the front-runner following the 1972 election. Between 30 March and 2 April 1973, Gallup asked a sampling of Republicans to indicate from a list of ten names their first and second choice for the 1976 nomination. Agnew emerged the clear favorite.[15]

TABLE 11.2
Republican Presidential Preferences, April 1973

Candidate	First Choice	Second Choice
Agnew	35%	21%
Reagan	20	21
Connally	15	1?
Rockefeller	11	14
Percy	8	9

SOURCE: *The Gallup Opinion Index*, May 1973, p. 12.

Agnew's support had declined by August, following disclosure of the investigation of possible wrongdoing on his part. Reagan now ran even with him when Republican preferences were measured, each claiming the support of 22 percent.[16] By early October, only days before he resigned as Vice President as part of a plea-bargaining arrangement, Agnew had fallen to fourth place behind Reagan (24 percent), Rockefeller (16 percent), and Connally (15 percent); tied with Percy (13 percent).[17]

The value of the vice presidency as a springboard is shown even more clearly in Ford's experience. Ford had never been considered a presidential prospect. Gallup had never included his name on the lists submitted to its samples. Yet in February 1974, Gallup reported that "Ford's selection as Vice President has projected him into the national spotlight as a possible GOP nominee in 1976."[18]

TABLE 11.3
Preferences Among Republican Presidential Candidates, January 1974

Candidate	Republicans	Independents
Ford	24%	16%
Reagan	20	17
Rockefeller	18	14
Connally	9	6
Percy	8	10
Baker	5	8

SOURCE: Gallup, *The Gallup Poll: Public Opinion, 1972-77*, 1:230.

Some knowledgeable observers believe the vice presidency has given Mondale a headstart toward winning the nomination for the top spot on the Democratic ticket in 1984.

The value of the vice presidency has not gone unrecognized by presidential hopefuls. Once prominent political figures avoided the office. No longer—many major politicians now make themselves available to run in the second spot on tickets with a reasonable chance of success. Those that have recently let such opportunities pass—Rockefeller in 1960 and 1968 (with Humphrey), Kennedy in 1968, and Ford in 1980—stood in unique positions that lessened the appeal of the office.

Nor have Vice Presidents been anxious to relinquish their offices. In 1956 Eisenhower advised Nixon to "'chart out his own course" and suggested that a cabinet position might provide a better base from which to seek the presidency.[19] Eisenhower's motives are unclear; he may simply have wanted Nixon off his ticket. If the President did hope to advance Nixon's career, his advice was misguided. Nixon realized that the office he held offered his best chance of reaching the White House.

The reasons the vice presidency has become an advantageous springboard are not obscure. Larger changes in American politics have contributed to that development. Parties now tend to place better candidates in the second slot on the ticket. No longer can a party give its vice-presidential nomination to someone with the meager experience of a Chester Arthur or Garret Hobart. The importance of the presidency forces parties to offer plausible successors; the inevitability of media coverage and the need to wage a national campaign provide incentives to pick able candidates. Those who become Vice President today are more capable of later launching a presidential bid.

The Twenty-second Amendment, ratified in 1951, changed the eligibility requirements for presidential candidates in a manner potentially helpful to some Vice Presidents. Regarding Presidents after Truman, it provided: "No person shall be elected to the office of the President more than twice, and no person who has held the office of President, or acted as President, for more than two years of a term to which some other person was elected President shall be elected to the office of President more than once. . . ." The amendment represented an attempt to restrain the growth in presidential power. As one scholar points out, it "was adopted with almost no thought for its potential effects on the Vice Presidency."[20] Yet the term restriction on Presidents can help some ambitious second men. Uncertainty about whether the Chief Executive would seek a third term had constrained previous Vice Presidents from actively soliciting support. The term limitation allows the Vice President to plan his future without such doubts. Of course other aspirants can also act with greater knowledge, but the restriction helps the President's lieutenant most. His chance to win the nomination depends most heavily on his ability to maintain the good will of the chief. Further, his office possesses resources that become most valuable when the President is not planning another term.

Name Recognition

A presidential hopeful must be known to the electorate. Generally, that process takes years. The vice presidency provides a short cut. It guarantees its occupant instant name recognition. Many senators and cabinet members, and most governors and members of the House of Representatives toil in obscurity, never in danger of losing their national anonymity. But, as Donald R. Matthews observes, "The Vice-Presidency is an especially advantageous position from which to receive publicity within a presidential context."[21]

The Vice President has profited from the increased attention focused on the executive branch and from his relatively new association with it. He has been given more to do. Owing to the growth of mass media, his activity has become more evident. As such, the Vice President has become highly visible and widely recognized.

The presidential campaign begins the process of making national figures of the eventual Vice President and his counterpart on the rival ticket. During the campaign, the second candidates receive far greater attention than most have previously experienced. The emergence of defeated candidates as presidential contenders suggests its impact. Of the seven unsuccessful vice-presidential aspirants from 1952 to 1976, five later showed some support as a prospective standard-bearer for their party. Three—Kefauver, Lodge, and Muskie— were front-runners at some stage and led in some polls.[22] Mondale, too, will no doubt fall into this category.

Service as Vice President enhances the individual's public recognition. Occupants of the office receive far greater media coverage than most other public officials. The vice presidency pays dividends in increased publicity for those long active in public life.

Table 11.4 suggests the magnitude of the advantage. It attempts to measure the publicity value of the vice presidency by presenting figures for the average number of references per month behind the names of Vice Presidents and vice-presidential candidates in the *New York Times Index* over three time periods: the first five months of the year in which

TABLE 11.4
Average Monthly References to Vice-Presidential Candidates

Candidate	Precandidacy Jan. 1- May 31	Candidacy Sept. 1- Election	Year after Election
Nixon*	4.0	70.0	22.0
Sparkman	5.0	72.0	6.0
Kefauver	47.0[a]	80.0	13.0
Johnson*	31.5	52.0	34.0
Lodge	13.5	84.0	3.0
Humphrey*	28.0	80.0	38.0
Miller	2.0	70.5	2.0
Agnew*	3.5	80.0	31.5
Muskie	1.5	65.0	13.5
Eagleton	4.0	—[b]	4.0
Shriver	0	70.5	2.0
Ford*	3.5	84.0[c]	66.0[d]
Rockefeller*	28.0	225.0[e]	66.0[e]
Mondale*	4.5	60.0	31.0
Dole	1.0	70.5	4.5

SOURCE: Compiled by author from *New York Times* indexes.

NOTE: This table presents a rough measure of publicity given Vice Presidents and vice-presidential candidates since it presents not the number of times an individual's name was mentioned in the *New York Times* per month but the number of cross-references to his name. Thus one story in the newspaper may receive several references in the index. The table's value lies in the comparison between the columns.

* Became Vice President.

[a] Kefauver's total in the first column is inflated by the fact that he was a candidate in presidential primaries during the period.

[b] Eagleton withdrew prior to 1 September.

[c] Second-column figures for Ford and Rockefeller cover the period of their confirmation hearings; they were never, strictly speaking, candidates.

[d] Ford's third column covers just the first six months of his vice presidency; after that his succession appeared very likely.

[e] The *Times* gave greater coverage to Rockefeller as a former governor of New York.

the candidate first sought the office, the nine weeks between 1 September and election day during which the campaign was in full swing, and the year beginning with the day after the election.

This table suggests that the candidacy period provides a significant boost in recognition. Vice Presidents receive fewer references than they did during their candidacy for the position. Still, they enjoy greater media attention than they had previously experienced. For Johnson and Humphrey the gains were modest. They had been unusually active and prominent senators and had been discussed frequently during the early part of the year as a prospective presidential and vice-presidential candidate respectively. But others experienced a dramatic surge in the amount of publicity they received. By contrast, defeated candidates subsequently attracted relatively modest attention. The candidacy period allows the politician to become known. The vice presidency enables its occupant to maintain a high measure of visibility and further increase his recognition.

TABLE 11.5
Republican Name Recognition, Spring 1973

Public Figure	Name Recognition
Agnew	90%
Reagan	85
Rockefeller	85
Connally	71
Buckley	55
Percy	54
Brooke	36
Baker	20
Brock	17
Evans	12

SOURCE: Gallup, *The Gallup Poll: Public Opinion, 1972-77*, 1:115.

Not surprisingly, Vice Presidents become widely known fairly quickly. Some 82 percent could identify Nixon after his first term in office had barely started. Four years later, 96 percent recognized his name.[23] The day he was first nominated as the Republican candidate for Vice President, Agnew conceded that his was not a household name. It was by the spring of 1973. Rockefeller and Connally had held important public offices far longer than had Agnew. Reagan, Percy, Brooke, and Baker were first elected governors or senators in 1966, the same year Agnew was chosen governor of Maryland. Greater voter familiarity with Agnew resulted from the high visibility of the vice presidency. Although precise data is not easily available, it seems obvious that the office has provided instant fame for its other recent occupants.

Presidential Context

For a politician, publicity of virtually any sort is preferable to indifference. Coverage is especially helpful, however, when it comes "within a presidential context." The vice presidency provides such publicity. As Vice Presidents perform duties quasi-presidential in nature they appear more plausible as prospective Chief Executives. One perceptive journalist rightly observed, "A Vice President takes on some of the glamour and prestige of the Presidency."[24]

Perhaps nowhere is this so pronounced as in foreign policy. Experience in international affairs has become an important criterion in evaluating presidential candidates. This change has generally hurt governors and helped the Vice President and senators. The Vice President is in a particularly auspicious position to appear expert in diplomatic matters. He receives the same briefings as the President and participates in conferences of at least symbolic value. His frequent travels abroad where he is received in a manner similar to a head of state are widely publicized. The promise of diplomatic assignments was one attraction the second spot held for Johnson. His trips "gave him an opportunity to build himself up" in an area in which he had been "conspicuously weak."[25]

Foreign travel seems to have helped Humphrey's standing. A Harris survey conducted for the White House traced Humphrey's popularity for more than a year.[26] In April 1966, 54 percent had favorable attitudes toward him while 46 percent were unfavorable. A year later, Humphrey's standing had improved to 60 percent to 40 percent. Harris measured voter preferences between Humphrey and his leading rival, Senator Robert Kennedy, during the same period.[27] Harris reported that Humphrey's trip to Europe in the spring of 1967

TABLE 11.6
Humphrey versus Kennedy, 1966-1967

Date of Poll	Humphrey Preference	Kennedy Preference
Mar. '66	44%	56%
Sept. '66	42	58
Oct. '66	40	60
Nov. '66	39	61
Jan. '67	47	53
Mar. '67	47	53
Apr. '67	51	49

SOURCE: L. Harris, *The Harris Survey* (New York: The Chicago Tribune-New York News Syndicate, 1 May 1967).

was a major factor in his comeback. Some 17 percent of the electorate indicated that they had a higher opinion of Humphrey than before. Only 4 percent held him in less esteem.

The vice presidency offers advantages in the domestic sphere, too. Its occupants can curry the favor of important groups by taking popular stands on issues. Johnson, for instance, improved his standing with civil rights leaders as Vice President. Agnew became a hero to right-wing groups. And Vice Presidents are not as vulnerable to public dissatisfaction with some policy as governors or cabinet members, as they cannot be assigned total responsibility.

Available information suggests that voters tend to hold Vice Presidents in high regard. In measures spaced two years apart,

Gallup found that 51 percent and 59 percent of the electorate gave Nixon a favorable rating.[28] Late in 1957, 53 percent believed Nixon would be "better" or "about the same" as Eisenhower as President; only 26 percent thought he would be worse.[29] Eisenhower was popular, suggesting general confidence in his Vice President. Other measures support this conclusion. In the summer of 1959, 66 percent believed Nixon had "the background and experience to be President." Only 18 percent dissented. Gallup found that the public perceived Nixon more as a politician than a statesman, 49 percent to 26 percent. Yet 42 percent felt he was "the kind of person" they "would like to have at the head of the country" if the international situation worsened, while 34 percent disagreed.[30]

After his first sixteen months in office, Agnew received favorable ratings from 49 percent and unfavorable evaluation from 32 percent.[31] Even after allegations of criminal wrongdoing on his part had surfaced, Agnew was still held in esteem by more than half the electorate. Some 56 percent gave Agnew a positive rating of some sort while 39 percent viewed him negatively.[32]

These polls do not suggest that either Nixon or Agnew, or any other recent Vice President, was regarded by the majority as the person they would most like to see as the next President. The two Vice Presidents who ran for President both lost, though narrowly. At different stages, Gallup found that Earl Warren, Adlai Stevenson, Estes Kefauver, and John Kennedy all ran ahead of Nixon in presidential preference polls.[33] Humphrey trailed Nixon and Rockefeller in similar tests in 1968, and Agnew and Ford ran behind Senator Edward Kennedy.[34]

Toward the end of Humphrey's first year as Vice President, only 23 percent said they would "like to see him become President sometime" while 58 percent did not. A similar question asked after Agnew had held the office for sixteen months found that but 19 percent hoped he would be Chief Executive "someday" while 61 percent did not.[35]

The surveys indicate only that Vice Presidents enjoy considerable public esteem. They suggest that the office is an efficacious position in which to develop a favorable public image.

Party Leader

The role the Vice President inherits as a chief party spokesperson and campaigner offers a third resource of no small importance. Vice Presidents are most visible in this function during elections. Nixon, Humphrey, Agnew, and Mondale assumed primary responsibility for helping candidates of their party at all levels during off-year campaigns. Vice Presidents who seek reelection with the Chief Executive emerge as the party's major salesmen. In fact, Vice Presidents perform a variety of political duties throughout the term. In the process, Vice Presidents collect assorted IOUs from other party figures. These are often redeemable in the form of delegate support when the Vice President seeks to move up. In recent years, the work a Vice President has done for the party has produced considerable convention support.

Nixon, in 1960, had accumulated so many debts from leading Republicans as to make any challenge for the nomination futile.[36] Humphrey's efforts for Democrats—as Vice President, he campaigned in every state—enabled him to amass widespread party support without contesting any primaries.[37] Agnew, too, had captured impressive party support before his political demise. A poll of delegates to the 1972 Republican Convention conducted by the *Miami Herald* found that 36 percent considered him the party's best candidate for 1976.[38] That the Vice President is the first successor helps him here. Party leaders do not wish to alienate someone who may become President at any time.

Of course, party work is not a sure route to the nomination. At best, it can help win favor. It may not be sufficient to overcome other obstacles confronting a Vice President. It is not at all certain that Johnson could ever have won the presidential nomination had Kennedy served two terms. The extent of the Republican opposition to Rockefeller suggests strongly that he would not have been the candidate had Ford chosen not to stand.

Further, the proliferation of presidential primaries since 1968 lessens the value of party service as a source of delegate support. Political leaders now play a reduced role in delegate selection and in convention decision-making. Vice Presidents can no longer hope to achieve sufficient first-ballot support to gain the nomination by relying solely on the good will of party leaders. They, like others, must compete in presidential primaries.

Here, the Vice President may be disadvantaged. Turnout in presidential primaries is generally low; those that do vote often are not representative national samples, and may not include a Vice President's likely supporters.[39] The primary system minimizes the advantage of the Vice President's name recognition. States holding early primaries are small enough to allow well-organized unknowns to do surprisingly well. The national media coverage given early primaries allows a previously obscure politician to gain instant fame. Accordingly, the Vice President's wide recognition no longer gives him such a boost. Indeed, in certain cases, it may even prove a hindrance. By virtue of his position, he is likely to be considered a front-runner. Expectations are high. A defeat, or even an unconvincing win, may prove disastrous to an early favorite, initiating a negative bandwagon effect.[40]

The changes in nominating rules which assign more importance to primaries are relatively recent. Vice Presidents have yet to feel their effects. Judgments about their impact are necessarily speculative. It is conceivable, though unlikely, that the proliferation of primaries and proportional allocation of delegates will result in deadlocked conventions at which party leaders will turn to the Vice President. Indeed, some Democrats and journalists disenchanted with the Carter-Kennedy choice in 1976 spoke of Mondale as an alternative.

General Election Problems

More concrete observations can be made elsewhere. Although the vice presidency carries advantages, it also encumbers its occupant with problems uncommon to others. His association with the administration makes him vulnerable to attack for its failures. He cannot so easily criticize existing programs or propose new departures as can others. Further, he is largely dependent on the good will of the Chief Executive. These factors hurt Nixon in 1960, and especially Humphrey in 1968.

Nixon, no doubt, benefited from his association with Eisenhower. Even as he completed his second term, Eisenhower maintained high public approval ratings. Membership in the administration was not, however, an unmixed blessing. Nixon reasoned that a more progressive posture would enhance his electoral appeal. He tried unsuccessfully to persuade administration figures to design more liberal programs regarding civil rights, aid to education, and medical care for the elderly. He could not easily criticize Eisenhower's policies or offer alternatives he preferred.[41] Kennedy could promise to "get the country moving again." Such a pledge from Nixon would have seemed an attack on Eisenhower. In at least one instance, Nixon may have suffered from his involvement in administration planning. During the campaign, Kennedy recommended American participation in an invasion of Cuba. Knowing that a covert operation to do just that was being planned, Nixon felt compelled to denounce Kennedy's suggestion.[42] Eisenhower clearly supported Nixon. He fulfilled the campaign assignments given him and apparently was irritated at not being asked to do more.[43] In one instance, however, he inadvertently damaged Nixon's campaign.

Nixon attempted to make his experience as Vice President one of the main selling points of his campaign.[44] A careless answer Eisenhower gave in his press conference on 24 August 1960 damaged the credibility of this strategy. Asked for "an example of a major idea" of Nixon's that had become policy, Eisenhower replied, "If you give me a week, I might think of one. I don't remember." To Nixon's embarrassment, the line was quoted widely in the print media and in a question asked during the nationally televised first debate. Eisenhower's reply was surely impolitic, but taken in proper context was not nearly so hurtful. It was the final answer of the press conference. Eisenhower had responded to two similar questions in some detail, and with some irritation. He had referred to Nixon as "one of the principal" advisers who had participated "in all of the consultative meetings that have been held." But, he had argued, "no one can make a decision except me if it is in the national executive area."[45] The earlier answers suggested that Nixon had played an important role. Pique apparently produced the harmful rejoinder. Taken alone, it misrepresents Eisenhower's position. To Nixon's detriment, it generally was taken alone.

The problems Nixon faced owing to his association with the administration seem minor when compared to Humphrey's predicament. Humphrey became the primary target for public dissatisfaction with the handling of the war in Vietnam. Further, Johnson showed little disposition to help him. The war in Vietnam had lost popularity by 1968. Those most opposed included many traditional Democratic voters. Humphrey was vulnerable to attack as a representative of the administration responsible for American involvement in the conflict. Further, he had accepted assignment as an active advocate of that war. His speeches defending American participation litter the public record.

Longtime friends suggested that Humphrey distance himself from Johnson's handling of the war. Senator Joseph Clark indicated that Humphrey opposed the war in administration councils and urged him to make public these feelings. Governor Richard J. Hughes wrote Johnson that "the Vice President must emerge clearly and decisively as his own man, as a fresh and creative candidate for the Presidency." Bill Moyers, once Johnson's closest aide, said Humphrey should "say publicly what he has been feeling privately."[46]

Humphrey acknowledged the presence of constraints. "Hubert Humphrey as Vice President is a member of the team," he said. "Hubert Humphrey as President is captain of the team. There's a lot of difference."[47] But he declined to criticize the administration. The diffidence that prevented Humphrey from breaking with Johnson reflected constraints imposed by the vice presidency and by Humphrey's personality. Excerpts from a memo James R. Jones, a White House aide, sent Johnson summarizing a telephone conversation with the Vice President suggest the mix.

> VP said he is proud of his association with the President and is proud of his part in the Johnson Administration. He said he has no intention of repudiating any of this or breaking in any way with the President. He said he would like to get nominated and elected—and he knows well that he couldn't do either if he turned his back on the Administration.
>
> VP said there are a number of reporters trying to stir up a split between the President and VP; and also, trying to say VP is candidate of the bosses.
>
> VP said he feels heartbroken. He said he hasn't had chance to talk to the President in a long time, but wants us to know

that he would rather lose the election than to let anything appear he is double-crossing or repudiating the President he has been proud to serve.[48]

Success at the convention depended on not incurring Johnson's wrath. Humphrey quietly promoted a compromise plank on Vietnam for the party platform. Initially, Dean Rusk and Walt Rostow approved it. Subsequently, Marvin Watson informed Humphrey of Johnson's displeasure.[49] An announcement by Governor John Connally, a close ally of the President, that he might nominate Johnson underscored the importance of this report. Humphrey relented.

Humphrey did not deviate publicly from administration policy on Vietnam until just five weeks remained in the campaign. On 30 September 1968, he supported cessation of bombing to expedite the peace talks. The proposal did not constitute a major break with existing policy. Secretary of State Dean Rusk urged Johnson to minimize the confrontation. White House aide Charles F. Murphy found Humphrey's speech ambiguous. Secretary of Defense Clark Clifford believed Humphrey was trying "to reach out as far as he can to the doves without actually breaking on anything" Johnson had said publicly.[50] Humphrey did distance himself from Johnson but his break was too little too late. His tie to the administration made him a ready target of dissidents. It also constrained him from establishing an independent stand.

Nor did Johnson help Humphrey as much as he might have.[51] In the speech announcing his withdrawal, Johnson had stated his belief "that I should not permit the Presidency to become involved in the partisan divisions that are developing in this political year."[52] He refrained from endorsing any candidate for the Democratic nomination, a decision probably helpful to Humphrey. But Johnson apparently attempted to dissuade members of his administration from endorsing the Vice President, too. In the days immediately following the announcement of his decision not to run, Johnson indicated that he had no policy on political activities of his subordinates.[53] Accordingly, Secretary of Agriculture Orville Freeman, a Humphrey protégé, advised Johnson on 23 April 1968 of his intention to endorse his mentor that day. He promised that his government duties "will, of course, command priority in my time and energies." But, he reasoned that "the fifteen hours a day on the job since 1961 can be slowed some, as was done in 1964." He would also use "some of the other nine hours" for Humphrey.[54] Following Freeman's action, Johnson instructed his associates not to participate in the campaigns. Joseph Califano, a top White House aide, told cabinet members that administration policy was "that there were to be no statements of support or staff work for any of the candidates for office."[55] Secretary of HUD Robert Weaver had planned to support Humphrey publicly but agreed to hold off. Transportation Secretary Alan Boyd promised to try to convince his wife not to become active.[56] White House assistant Harry McPherson assured Johnson that published reports that he supported Humphrey actively were mistaken.[57] Califano told Johnson that nine cabinet members had promised compliance in their departments. Attorney General Ramsey Clark and Secretary of Commerce C. R. Smith, though neutral themselves, indicated that the policy would create some problems in their agencies.[58] And Califano reported that "Freeman is clearly quite distressed" and "has a great deal of difficulty not continuing to support Humphrey openly."[59]

Once the campaign began, Johnson did make efforts on Humphrey's behalf in areas where his support would be useful. He contacted members of the Texas Democratic party and urged them to help the national ticket. In several public statements he praised Humphrey and Muskie profusely and challenged Nixon's and Agnew's fitness to lead the country.[60] Yet his insensitivity to the needs of Humphrey's campaign in ways discussed above contributed to the Republican victory.

To some extent, personality traits of Eisenhower and Johnson rather than institutional factors damaged their Vice Presidents' chances. Had Eisenhower been more patient and careful in his press conference and had Johnson been more tolerant of dissent generally, Nixon and Humphrey would have been stronger candidates. Future Chief Executives may be more responsive to the problems their Vice Presidents face.

Former Vice Presidents

On two occasions since 1952, a former Vice President—Nixon (1968) and Humphrey (1972)—has sought the presidential nomination. A Mondale candidacy in 1984 may present a third instance. The name recognition, exposure in a presidential context, and favor with party leaders that former Vice Presidents gained while in office may help them, though the passage of time may attenuate that benefit. Moreover, they seem less likely than sitting Vice Presidents to be associated with the popularity or unpopularity of their President's administration. Their major advantage probably lies in the absence of restraints the vice presidency imposes. They are freer to develop their own programs and to criticize those of the incumbent than are occupants of the second office.

Conclusion

The vice presidency is likely to continue as a mixed blessing. The growth of the office and the valuable resources it provides have made its occupants plausible successors. Reliance on an extensive series of presidential primaries, however, has recently undercut the advantage the office offers as a springboard to the nomination, for they reduce the value of the Vice President's name recognition and ties to party leaders.

Further, as government has assumed responsibility for solving more complex problems, administrations may be hard pressed to emerge with their popularity intact. The public will assign a share of the blame for government failures to the Vice President. He cannot escape responsibility as easily as most other party members. Nor can he implement new programs, as can a President, to help his chances. It is likely that many future Vice Presidents will be presidential contenders; yet they will probably encounter obstacles that will make winning the office difficult.

12

★ ★

Evaluating Reform Proposals

*F*ew aspects of the vice presidency have escaped the attention of reformers. More than two dozen proposals suggesting some change in the office have been offered. Yet it is ironic that an institution so susceptible to legitimate criticism remains so resistant to successful reform. Most proposals offer false cures. Although they would enhance the vice presidency they would inflict unwarranted damage on other parts of the political system.

To be acceptable, a reform of the vice presidency should pass a fourfold test. It should 1) have a desirable effect on the office itself without 2) unduly damaging other political institutions or 3) undermining important values like public participation, leader competence, and stability. And 4) it should be better than all other alternatives. Most suggested changes fail to meet at least one criterion.

Some reforms commonly encounter opposition not because they are ill advised but rather because they stand no chance of adoption. Efforts to improve the vice presidency face obstacles of this sort. The presence of a written Constitution imposes an institutional constraint. Changes that would require amending that document are unlikely to secure the necessary support. Reform of the second office also must overcome a political impediment. It is not an issue uppermost in the minds of many citizens. Cries for change are heard only in the aftermath of some incident that calls attention to the office or of some crisis that reveals inadequacies.

Even then, discussion is subdued and short-lived. Politicians have little incentive to invest much time in pursuing reform in areas that offer such meager rewards. Nor should they be expected to concentrate on such questions when more immediate problems exist.

There is reason, however, to evaluate even those reforms whose enactment seems improbable. First, discussion may eventually generate sufficient support to achieve reform. As Arthur M. Schlesinger, Jr. put it:

> I think that the only way any constructive change is ever going to be brought about is if it makes sense and if people begin to discuss it, and if it wins the backing of eminent committees and eminent people, and so on, so that it enters the bloodstream, so to speak, and maybe some time, maybe not in this generation but some time in the future, something will happen. So I don't think the fact of the temporary or the contemporary futility of a suggestion should necessarily mean that we should not consider it and try to do a little pioneering.[1]

Second, the vice presidency, like other institutions, lends itself to normative as well as descriptive discussion. Political scientists should be interested not only in what is and what can be but also in what ought to be. Discussion of all serious proposals promotes knowledge of problems relating to the office. Finally, a wide consideration of proposed changes allows a more complete appreciation of political institutions generally. It helps locate the vice presidency as part of a political system by exposing ways in which that office relates to other aspects of the American system of government and politics. Moreover, an examination of an array of proposed changes in the vice presidency instructs in the process of reform generally.

This chapter considers various possible reforms. It discusses, in turn, those regarding the selection, election, duties, and successor role of the Vice President.

Selection

Some observers identify the method of choosing vice-presidential candidates as the major problem. They believe the selection process is not conducive to producing Vice Presidents qualified to serve as Chief Executive. The question for such students is, as Hubert Humphrey put it, "how to have the most qualified person available to assume the powers and responsibilities of the Presidency, should such an emergency arise."[2] This aspect received little attention until the early 1970s. The withdrawal of Senator Thomas Eagleton from the second spot on the Democratic ticket in 1972 and the forced resignation of Agnew as Vice President awakened observers to defects in the manner of selecting the running mates. The Democratic National Committee appointed a commission with Humphrey as its chairman to examine selection procedures. The next few years brought several short studies of the topic.[3] Reforms addressed to alleged ills in the nomination process fall into two groups. Some identify limited participation as the chief villain. Others maintain that the presidential candidate has too little time to make an informed choice.[4]

A number of proposals would use primaries to help select vice-presidential candidates. Endicott Peabody has suggested establishing vice-presidential primaries to operate like the presidential preconvention tests.[5] Another plan pushed by former Senator Margaret Chase Smith would nominate the second candidate through a national vice-presidential primary.[6] A third would hold a national presidential primary in which each voter would be allowed two votes.[7] The runner-up would be designated the vice-presidential candidate. Finally, some suggest having presidential aspirants choose their running mates before the primaries. These tests would then feature slates, not individual candidates.[8]

This type of reform has received significant popular support. In the spring of 1972, Gallup showed that 63 percent of those polled favored direct voter participation in vice-presidential selection.[9] Significantly, the survey took place even before the Eagleton and Agnew incidents.

Such a primary has several attractions. It would promote participation in the choice. Turnout in presidential primaries is disappointing; presumably, it would be even lower in those for the vice-presidential nomination.[10] Even so, such a system would involve more citizens than does the present method. It might also help resolve the problem of haste. It would focus attention on candidates over a longer period of time and stimulate investigation and discussion of their backgrounds and views. Finally, such a process would probably raise public perceptions of the vice presidency by giving its occupant an independent electoral base.

A number of problems lessen the appeal of some or all of these reforms. Four are common to all but the runner-up plan. They would, in effect, narrow the range of possible vice-presidential nominees by forcing political leaders to decide at an early date which office to seek. The most prominent figures would probably compete for the first spot unless prevented by the ambitions of a popular incumbent. It is unlikely that Kefauver in 1956, Johnson in 1960, or Bush in 1980 would have foregone a presidential race to compete for the second place. Others might not seek the second place owing to their involvement in some presidential campaign; Mondale, for instance, might have felt too committed to a possible Humphrey candidacy in 1976.

By restricting the choice of vice-presidential nominees, the three plans would produce a second, more serious problem. Those effectively excluded would often be the most able and popular members of the party. Those willing to make themselves available would frequently be the party's second echelon leaders. Accordingly, the proposals would adversely affect the quality of some vice-presidential candidates.

Any format that would require consideration of vice-presidential candidates alongside assessment of presidential aspirants would create at least two further problems. It would distract some attention from those seeking the first spot. Citizens often know little about those running in presidential primaries. Including the second spot in the process would increase the number of candidates, thereby compounding confusion. Nor would such a system be conducive to making an informed choice for the lower half of the ticket. Voters would probably pay relatively little attention to that question.

Three of the plans using primaries would deny the presidential candidate any formal role in the selection of his running mate. These might produce tickets consisting of politicians who are politically or personally incompatible. A vice-presidential candidate with an independent constituency might advance views quite different from those the standard-bearer held. Ideological differences between tickets might accordingly become even more obscure. Further, a Chief Executive would be less likely to delegate assignments to a Vice President of different views or uncongenial temperament.

Finally, three of the plans might complicate the task of unifying the party following the selection of the standard-bearer. The second spot often can be used to placate elements of the party who are not enthralled with the presidential nominee. Such a use abuses the vice presidency if it fills the ticket with a candidate who is unqualified to become President or one who differs markedly from the standard-bearer. Otherwise, it can help preserve the party cohesion necessary to a two-party system. The procedures for selecting the vice-presidential candidates under discussion here would disregard this important byproduct.

Table 12.1 summarizes the weaknesses of the plans just discussed:

TABLE 12.1
Drawbacks of Participatory Reforms

Drawback	Runner-up	National Primary	VP Primaries	Slates
Options Excluded		x	x	x
Quality Decline		x	x	x
Compatibility Decline	x	x	x	
Unity Decline	x	x	x	
Attention Distracted		x	x	x
Uninformed Choice		x	x	x

NOTE: X indicates which of the drawbacks identified in the text apply to each plan discussed in the text.

Other objections are peculiar to one or another of the plans. For instance, a national primary would eliminate the convention or retain it only with the perfunctory purpose of approving the platform written by the presidential nominee. The proposal to select vice-presidential delegates in a series of primaries would create other difficulties for the convention. It would mean having separate sets of presidential and vice-presidential delegates.

Slight modifications in the four plans outlined above could help. Peabody, for instance, has improved his proposal for vice-presidential primaries by stipulating that the convention could consider on the first ballot anyone who had competed in a presidential or vice-presidential primary, or anyone who was recommended by a presidential candidate or announced his availability at least two weeks before the convention. Subsequent ballots would be open to anyone at all.[11] Some, though not all, of the objections to the slates plan might be met if they applied only in the later primaries. Any of the four plans might be used, but strictly on an advisory basis, which would not deny the presidential candidate and convention the right to make a different selection. A vice-presidential primary might be held, but after the convention. These changes make the general plans more appealing but fail to obviate other inherent problems.

A second set of reformers also sees limited participation as the major defect in the current selection process. But rather than involving voters in the choice they would assign the convention a larger role. Most dramatic is the proposal that the convention use its discretion to select the vice-presidential candidate rather than rubber-stamp a decision made by the standard-bearer.[12] Of course, such a method would require only a change in behavior rather than in rules. The current practice by which both parties accept the choice of their presidential nominee is founded in custom rather than dictated by some provision. An "open" convention, in the truest sense, would require that the presidential nominee not suggest a running mate. The 1956 Democratic convention in which Stevenson did not recommend a partner provides the most recent model for this process. One prominent journalist proposed a plan similar in goal though with a different format. It would give the runner-up in the presidential voting the second spot.[13]

Other plans call for the delegates to select a vice-presidential candidate from a list submitted to them. James Mac-Gregor Burns is among those who have suggested that the convention choose from three or four names proposed by the presidential nominee. Others would limit those eligible to persons nominated for the presidency. Professor Charles Hyneman has recommended that a party committee chaired by the presidential nominee offer the convention a name to be considered alongside others.[14]

These plans, if they functioned as intended, have some welcome effects. They would allow wider participation than is now common. Further, unlike the proposal for primaries, they would allow party activists a role. They would focus greater attention on the vice presidency and provide its occupant with a larger constituency.

These virtues come at a price. All might impose a second divisive fight on the convention that would impede the process of unifying the party for the autumn campaign. Further, since the second person would not owe his selection to the presidential candidate he might be less inclined to accept direction once in office. If the plans operated as expected, all but the Burns proposal could produce incompatible candidates. As Nelson Rockefeller argued:

> The President has enough problems to worry about in this really impossible job without having to cope with a recalcitrant or conniving Vice President at his side—which might be the case if the Vice President were chosen separately by the delegates of the party at the convention, on the basis of political expediency. This could end up in a disaster.[15]

In fact, it seems unlikely that the presidential nominee would stand aloof as his ticket-partner was being selected. Rather, he would influence the selection publicly or privately. A party could hardly afford to repudiate the first recommendation of its nominee. The Burns plan could most easily be subject to manipulation. As George Reedy suggested:

> . . . suppose the President had to submit a list of candidates for Vice-President. If I were Mr. Carter, what I would have done is to send the following list: Otto Passman, George Wallace, Wayne Hayes [sic], Walter Mondale. You have got to have a certain amount of realism about this, because assuming you can get around the other problems, that is what is going to happen to them.[16]

Presidential candidates would probably be far more subtle in structuring the choice than Reedy conjectured. Still, the point is well taken.

After the 1976 primaries but before the presidential nomination, Ronald Reagan designated Senator Richard Schweiker as his choice of a running mate, and suggested that President Ford also indicate his selection before the presidential balloting. Although political considerations inspired Reagan's action, some have suggested regular application of that procedure. It would allow convention delegates to nominate a ticket, not just a presidential candidate. Moreover, it would prevent a presidential candidate from garnering convention votes by using the second spot to entice support from several prospective running mates. The Reagan-Schweiker plan suffers from other defects, however. In a competitive convention a presidential candidate would probably be unable to select his most serious convention rivals or perhaps their leading backers. If the outcome of the presidential balloting were certain in advance, however, the Reagan-Schweiker approach would add little, if anything, to current practice.

Other reformers believe the selection process could be helped by changing the circumstances surrounding the deliberations. They attempt to establish mechanisms to ensure full scrutiny of possible running mates. Former Senator William Brock introduced legislation in 1974 to require a check by the Federal Bureau of Investigation of all potential vice-presidential nominees.[17] The Humphrey Commission considered a recommendation that the Democratic party establish a committee to collect information on prospective running mates.[18] The Special Committee on Election Reform of the American Bar Association proposed that presidential candidates be required to release a list of prospective running mates prior to the convention.[19] The media would presumably investigate the backgrounds of those included. The Harvard Study Group included all three plans in its recommendations.[20]

These plans are susceptible to a number of objections. Americans are sensitive to the possibility that data collection activities might violate civil liberties. Schlesinger enunciated this fear:

> I honestly think that this whole notion that we should es-
> tablish a form of scrutiny of potential Vice-Presidential
> candidates is a terrible idea. I mean, from what we know
> about the FBI, first about the use to which it has been put
> and second about its own incompetence, why should we
> assume this is going to give some kind of sacred judgment
> on the merits of candidates? . . . This notion of confiding
> anything to the FBI or any other governmental investigative
> agency is very wrong. This is something where we have to
> stand or fall on the democratic process. The democratic
> process is not infallible. . . . But through most of American
> history the electoral process, the adversary process has been
> perfectly adequate.

Schlesinger went on to "deplore the demeaning notion of why we should do more about Vice-Presidents in this regard than we do about Presidents."[21] The answer to this latter point is relatively straightforward. Presidential candidates receive extensive scrutiny by press and public alike before the election. But no such attention is accorded the second man. Still, Schlesinger does highlight weaknesses in proposals that would bring the FBI into the elective process. A great possibility of abuse would arise if that bureau were formally authorized to investigate numerous leading politicians. The plan to create a party advisory committee to play such a role is less dangerous, but still troubling. It would give the party a larger role; yet it, too, would establish a store of information subject to misuse.

The ABA proposal would avoid the civil liberties objection. It does not seem likely to prove harmful. But it is not clear that it would provide much useful information either. In past years presidential candidates have leaked lists of prospective running mates prior to the convention. Yet until the presidential choice is resolved the media exhibit little interest in the vice-presidential nomination. Nor is it clear that the press has the resources necessary to investigate a number of prospective candidates.

All three proposals concentrate solely on providing the presidential nominee with more background material on potential running mates. But such information is only one element in making a rational choice. Time to consider these inputs is a second necessary ingredient. "How can you entrust such a choice to a man with a hangover from the biggest celebration of his life?" asks one pundit rhetorically.[22] Accordingly, another set of reforms attempts to improve deliberation by allowing the presidential nominee a longer period to make a choice.

One proposal of this sort would rearrange the convention schedule to insert extra time between the presidential and vice-presidential nominations. Such a change could be achieved by moving the presidential nomination up to the second day, dropping the platform consideration to the third day and selecting a running mate on the fourth day. Or, the parties could extend their quadrennial meetings by a day.[23]

This rather modest revision has won the support of a variety of politicians and academics, especially in the aftermath of the Eagleton episode. It would allow the presidential candidate and his staff additional time to investigate prospective running mates, consult other party figures, and reach a decision. The drawbacks—the increased cost of extending the convention and the possible decline in public interest if the presidential nomination occurred so early—are relatively trivial.

The major objection to these schemes lies in their modesty. So short an extension will often not provide the presidential candidate sufficient time to consider possible running mates. Accordingly, some reformers propose postponing selection of the vice-presidential candidate until after the convention.

282 ★ *Evaluating Reform Proposals*

Senator Thomas Eagleton would allow the presidential candidate alone to choose his running mate.[24] Others suggest convening the party national committee perhaps a month after the convention to act on a recommendation by the presidential candidate[25] or to make a less structured decision.[26] Such a procedure would be similar to that used to select Shriver as McGovern's running mate following Eagleton's withdrawal. A proposal by Senator Birch Bayh would have delegates vote on the recommendation of the standard-bearer by mail-in secret ballot some time after the convention.[27]

These plans would allow the presidential nominee and his advisers time to consider, discuss, and investigate possible choices. They would help ensure compatibility by allowing the presidential candidate a leading role; they would also assure consultation with party factions as represented on the national committee. They would probably focus greater attention on the office. One scholar predicted that ". . . by giving the vice presidential nominee his separate day in the sun, this method could add to the dignity and prestige of that office without in any way curbing the discretion of the presidential nominee."[28] Further, they would allow prospective running mates to wage campaigns to show their support.

Critics of postconvention choice raise a number of objections. Some note that choice of the vice-presidential candidate at the convention allows the party to leave its meeting united. A postponed selection might send factions defeated in the presidential balloting away disgruntled. Others argue that additional time in itself can sometimes be harmful. Kirbo, for instance, noted the importance of having ample time. But he observed:

> Now, at the same time you can have too much time to make a judgment. . . . I was glad when the time ran out, frankly. Because you can just go on and on, and every day you are going to get some new names coming in.[29]

Reedy argues that selection at the convention provides a useful test of the judgment of the presidential candidate. He contends:

> I think we get a little too obsessed with orderly procedure sometimes and assume virtues to orderly methods of doing things that may not necessarily be there. Because to me the conditions under which the Presidential nominee must act at the convention bear a very strong resemblance to the conditions under which he must act as President. If the man, if the Presidential nominee, the night of the convention . . . is incapable of making a prudent judgment on his running mate, I would have very strong reservations as to how he would handle himself in a conference with Mr. Brezhnev or if there were a series of crises around the world.[30]

Other objections apply to some of the postconvention plans. The Eagleton proposal would preclude the party from any formal role in the selection. Plans requiring a mini-convention meeting might be difficult to fit into the overcrowded schedules of political events. Use of the secret ballot in the Bayh plan runs against the notion that delegates, as public trustees, should be accountable for their actions.

Election

A second set of proposals attempts to improve the vice presidency by changing the method of electing its occupant. Their advocates assume that reform of the selection process alone cannot reach the major ills. Rather, they suppose that defects in the office are closely related to the system that precludes separate consideration of, and vote for, presidential and vice-presidential candidates. The line of argument supporting these reforms points out that citizens generally vote based on their

preference for President.[31] This produces unhappy results—
the Vice President is selected in an undemocratic fashion;
and his background and qualifications receive little scrutiny.
Reformers have proposed few changes here. Three plans bear
examining.

One proposal calls for the separate election of the President and Vice President. It would seem the most democratic
means of choosing the second officer. An independent choice
would focus more attention by press and public alike on the
relative qualifications of competing candidates for the second
post. The victor would have a greater legitimacy and security; he would owe his position to popular decision, not the
choice of one person. Further, separate election would probably enhance the appeal of the office and the caliber of candidates seeking it. As Peabody argued:

> It will put all the more pressure on party nominating con-
> ventions to come up with someone who is electable to
> office and so we don't get a drone or someone who does
> not have the capacity to be President, so parties will put
> their good people forward as Vice-President as well, and
> with the very good likelihood that they will be elected
> President at a later time.[32]

These advantages come at a high price. Such a system could
produce a President and Vice President of different parties.
Peabody sees this as no great defect. He argues:

> Compatibility of the Vice-President with the President . . .
> is not that important, because the Vice-President has no
> powers. He is in waiting. He can be put in the deep-freeze
> and left there. But we want someone who is responsive to
> the vote of the people and who is there because the people
> put him there. That is a foundation on which everything is
> built.
> So I would say it makes not that much difference if he is

compatible. It makes not that much difference if he is of a different party.[33]

In fact, it makes a great deal of difference. Election of a President and Vice President from opposite parties could produce at least three unfortunate consequences. It would, first of all, present a threat to executive power. Presidential decisions would often be subjected to immediate criticism from within the executive branch. Of course presidential initiatives often provoke rebuke by opposition leaders. But the spectacle of dissent from an elected Vice President would be a unique experience with serious ramifications. His appraisals would carry the weight provided by his separate election and by his position as successor. The presence of such a Vice President would present yet another constraint on presidential power. Rockefeller believed such an arrangement "could create a situation in which there would be the danger of splitting the loyalties of the officers and employees in the executive branch."[34]

Further, the problem of presidential succession would become more complicated with a Vice President of the opposing party.[35] Death or resignation of the President could lead to a radical shift of government policy and personnel. Calculations of partisan advantage would attend to a greater degree consideration of impeachment of a President. Operation of the procedures for handling presidential inability would become difficult. The President would be indisposed to turn power over to a political rival; his cabinet would be reluctant to act with a political adversary.

Finally, the vice presidency would lose some of the influence it has now gained. Presidents would not be inclined to take a political rival into executive councils. The Vice President accordingly might not be privy to some information a successor should have.

Similar consequences, though to a far lesser degree, could

attend the separate election of a President and Vice President of the same party. The second officer would no longer owe his position to the Chief Executive. He would be in a position to take divisive actions. He might not only oppose the administration on various issues, but also present a threat to the renomination of the President, a situation that would further exacerbate their relations.

A second plan attempts to maintain some of the advantages of the Peabody proposal without the drawbacks. It would give citizens two votes, with the ticket receiving most support the winner.[36] This scheme would probably induce parties to pick vice-presidential candidates of high caliber. It seems likely, however, that rational voters would simply cast both of their votes for the ticket whose presidential candidate they found most appealing. The system would thus become a sham.

The third plan rests on far different premises. It would remove the vice presidency from the electoral process entirely. Presidential candidates would seek office alone. The President-elect would then nominate a Vice President subject to confirmation of both Houses of Congress.[37] In other words, all Vice Presidents would be chosen by the process prescribed in section two of the Twenty-fifth Amendment.

Such a scheme would represent a sharp break with tradition. Yet it offers several attractions. First, it would delay the selection of a vice-presidential nominee to a time when considerations of competence and fitness for office were more likely to prevail. Presidential candidates now have good reasons to weigh political factors heavily in their choice, for they select their running mate when electoral success is foremost in their minds. A President-elect is not encumbered with these concerns. "A President secure in the White House will have undergone a metamorphosis from his earlier self," predicted then Representative Charles McC. Mathias in opposing section two of the proposed Twenty-fifth Amendment in 1965.[38]

Yet that metamorphosis would seem likely to contribute to the quality of Vice Presidents.

Second, it would allow greater scrutiny of prospective Vice Presidents. Senator Robert Griffin, the architect of the plan, has put this argument well. He reasoned: "In contrast to the hurried, harried, haphazard way a Vice President is now selected, almost as an afterthought at the political convention, my proposal would allow the President-elect—as well as Congress—ample time for sober reflection, thorough investigation and deliberate consideration in choosing the Vice President."[39] The media would be likely to focus a considerable amount of attention on the Vice-President-designate.

Third, institution of Griffin's plan would be at no great cost to the democratic character of the system. The Vice President is not really elected under the present system. Indeed, consideration by the members of Congress might in practice give citizens a larger say even while honoring the constraints which the framers of the Twenty-fifth Amendment spelled out in its legislative history.

Finally, use of the Griffin scheme might elevate the vice presidency. Presidents would be more likely to nominate someone with whom they felt politically and personally compatible. Accordingly, they might well delegate meaningful duties to their Vice Presidents.

Yet the system Griffin suggests poses some troubling problems. Removal of the vice-presidential candidates from the campaign might jeopardize the two-party system. The second candidate is often chosen to help unify diverse wings of the parties. As Professor Paul Freund has argued:

> My judgment is that the presence of a Vice Presidential candidate on the ticket helps to show the capaciousness of a political party. It helps to avoid the splintering of the major political parties. It helps to moderate ideological cleavages. My guess is, if a President ran alone without a

> Vice President on the ticket, we would have more Presidential candidates, we would have more sharply ideological cleavages and splinter parties, and at any rate, the effect of the absence of a vice presidential candidate ought to be carefully explored in its political ramifications before we turn seriously to the change proposed by Senator Griffin.[40]

The effects Professor Freund identifies would be particularly likely if the proposed constitutional amendment to replace the Electoral College with a direct election plan ever won ratification.

Second, selection of the Vice President under the Griffin plan might divert the President and Congress from beginning to fashion new programs. John D. Feerick has made this point most clearly. He observes:

> It also seems to me on January 20, after a Presidential election, it is time for our national officers to get down to business and the business is, as I see it, to govern this country. A President at that point should have his administration intact and he should be effectively beginning his programs and plans to govern this country for a 4-year period.[41]

Congress might not have approved a Vice President by the inauguration.

That possibility suggests a third problem with the Griffin plan. It would probably preclude the Vice President from participating in the formation of the administration. Mondale was able to influence the course of the Carter administration by his involvement in the selection of high-level personnel. Future occupants of his job could not play the same role if they were busy at that time defending themselves to Congress.

Finally, postelection choice of the Vice President would leave hiatuses in the machinery handling presidential succession. A President-elect might die or fail to qualify before the

Vice President was confirmed. That would install in office some other successor, with only at best a tangential relationship to the results of the election.[42]

That these difficulties should arise is not surprising. The section two procedure was designed to fill a vice-presidential vacancy occurring during a term when many of the above considerations would not be so relevant. It is striking that a number of those most instrumental in drafting the provision and most persuasive in defending it—Bayh,[43] Feerick, and Freund—oppose extending its use as Griffin suggests.

Duties

A variety of reforms propose institutional changes in the responsibilities of the vice presidency. Two strategies would add to its duties in either the legislative or executive branch. Other reformers, believing these approaches misguided, call for the abolition of the office.

Theodore Roosevelt was among those who suggested strengthening the role of the Vice President in the Senate.[44] To accomplish this goal, he favored giving the Vice President a vote on all occasions, a voice in debates, and power to appoint committees of the Senate. Peabody echoes the first two proposals. He argues:

> I suggest that one way to bring the Vice-President along is to give him further duties in the Senate of the United States, to give him a full legislative vote, to let him express the national conscience on Capitol Hill, writing the legislation he deems needed by the nation which may be obstructed by regionalism or the chairman, legislation which he deems important, and let him work and strive in that direction.
>
> The Speaker of the House is third in line for the Presidency and does have the opportunity; why do we deny it to the second in line?[45]

Peabody makes this recommendation in conjunction with his proposal for separate election of the Vice President. Thus, the expresser of "the national conscience on Capitol Hill" would have his own identifiable national constituency.

No doubt these proposals would add appeal to the office. The Vice President would become powerful indeed if he possessed power to appoint committees. Even without it, the changes Roosevelt and Peabody have suggested would give the second officer the same duties as a senator, assuming he was allowed to serve on committees. He would have higher status, however, as a nationally elected officer and as the successor.

Several difficulties present themselves. First, the proposal, by separating the Vice President from the executive branch, would deny him the direct contact with the administration and its policies that is desirable in a successor.[46] Second, unless the Vice President was elected separately, he would have little independent authority in exercising his Senate roles. As Allan P. Sindler points out, "the vice-president would have neither electoral nor moral mandate to 'be his own man' rather than the president's man."[47] He would probably vote as instructed by the White House. Third, the Vice President's regular exercise of his voice and vote in the Senate would serve no governmental purpose other than giving him something to do. Appointment of committees presents a problem uncommon to the vice presidency: it might make it too powerful. Those assignments are prized possessions of senators. The Vice President would have excessive patronage if they were his to allot. He might use this power to force administration programs through the Senate; such an exercise would abridge the spirit of the separation of powers principle. Or he might use that responsibility to bargain with the Chief Executive, for he could frustrate administration measures by his construction of committees. It would seem improper to give someone who is not responsible to the Senate so much power over the conduct of its business.

Others have offered a variety of schemes for enhancing the power of the Vice President within the executive branch. One proposal would require the President to appoint the Vice President to one of the leading cabinet positions. Indeed, by some accounts, Reagan made such an offer to Ford in 1980. Other plans would entrust him with some lesser executive responsibilities. Clinton Rossiter was among those who advocated transfer of certain administrative chores from the President to the Vice President.[48] Henry Cabot Lodge has proposed that the Vice President coordinate the activity of the White House, departments of State and Defense, CIA, and Arms Control and Disarmament Agency. Nixon had promised him such a role.[49] Others would involve the second officer more formally in legislative liaison. Former Representative Thomas B. Curtis believes Presidents should allow their Vice Presidents to distribute all patronage. Since the Senate has power to confirm top echelon federal appointments and to ratify treaties, such a grant, Curtis suggests, would make the Vice President's role as president of the Senate meaningful.[50] Another believed the second officer should serve as executive chairman of a council to harmonize legislative policy.[51] Still others would institutionalize the Vice President as a senior legislative adviser. Negotiations between Reagan and Ford associates at the 1980 Republican convention drew on various of these plans. Ford would have coordinated much of the daily conduct of the executive branch, including activities of the National Security Council and Office of Management and Budget. He also would have directed Reagan's legislative liaison.[52]

Generally these reforms would give the Vice President a meaningful role. The proposals to appoint him to a cabinet position and the Curtis plan would make him particularly important. All have the advantage of involving the Vice President in the activities of the executive branch.

Yet consideration of the defects suggests that none are realistic. Any plan to institutionalize a meaningful role for the Vice President encounters a fatal objection. The Vice President is the one officer in the executive branch who cannot be removed at will by the President. A plan that would tie specified functions to the second office would remove a portion of the executive responsibility from the President.

Even the proposal that the President name his successor to a cabinet post provides little flexibility. Political factors would constrain a Chief Executive who was dissatisfied with the performance of the Vice President from removing him. Further, a Vice President might be a capable successor without being an optimal choice to handle any of the major departments. Finally, such specific responsibilities would distract him from the broader involvement desirable in a successor.

Nor would it be possible to make the Vice President the major adviser to the Chief Executive. Presidents take their advice from those whose counsel they value. A President might listen to his partner if he respected his views. But the Vice President can only become a valued consultant if the President chooses to make him one.

Some Presidents might give the Vice President some patronage. But no President would, as Curtis suggests, bestow this great source of his own power upon a subordinate.

Recognizing the futility of these proposals, others make no effort to augment the responsibilities of the vice presidency. Rather, they propose its abolition.[53] In part, that case rests on the argument, often proven true, that the second officer performs no meaningful chores that could not easily be transferred to some other member of the executive branch. Thus, former Representative James G. O'Hara writes, "too many good men have wasted their time and effort in seeking it and in holding it."[54] Accordingly, the office is seen as dispensable.

Succession

The argument for abolition of the vice presidency does not rest primarily on the idea that the office is hollow. It relies instead on the conclusion that the vice presidency fails to resolve in a satisfactory manner problems of presidential succession. The attack on the office rests first on the notion that succession of the Vice President contravenes principles of democracy. As Schlesinger puts it, "No one votes for a Vice President per se. He is a part of a package deal . . ."[55] Accordingly, it is inappropriate for the Vice President to succeed to the nation's foremost elective position in the event of presidential vacancy.

Further, Schlesinger and others argue, elevation of the Vice President is likely to produce unwelcome results. Presidential candidates choose their running mates with political considerations in mind. As O'Hara nicely put it, presidential candidates "will not, in the final analysis, choose their Vice-Presidential candidate to succeed them. They will choose them to help them succeed."[56] The Vice President is thus apt to be ill equipped to be Chief Executive. Nor do opponents of the office concede it any advantage in preparing someone to succeed. Rather, they argue, Presidents give their Vice Presidents little opportunity to grow in office. Nor do they keep them advised of important developments. Vice Presidents, Schlesinger argues, see "things as an ill-informed, impotent, and often sullen outsider." Accordingly, they "will very likely 'learn' the wrong things."[57]

Further, these critics see the office as inevitably frustrating. They believe that this frustration will erode or destroy the Vice President's capacity to be an effective President. Eric F. Goldman, a former Johnson assistant, writes, "If a man of ability and spirit is chosen, he is being placed in a role that is certain to be miserable, likely to be demeaning, and may well—depending on the personalities and circumstances— seriously corrode his potential for effective leadership in the future."[58] Moreover, Eugene McCarthy argues that a quali- fied public servant is wasted in the vice presidency. "Good and able men and women are too scarce to permit the reg- ular removal of one of them from the field of active govern- ment just to fulfill an archaic, constitutional provision."[59]

Those who favor abolition of the vice presidency generally suggest designating an interim successor, usually the secre- tary of state, pending the results of a special election.[60] Some propose holding a special election within ninety days of the vacancy unless it occurs during the fourth year of the term. Others would conduct the special presidential race along with the midterm congressional elections if the vacancy happened during the first two years of the term.[61] Prominent journalist Tom Wicker suggests scheduling the event ten months after the demise of the Chief Executive.[62] Some plans would pre- vent the caretaker from standing in the special election.[63]

A special election would inject a strong dose of democracy into the system of succession. It would allow the people to choose directly the person who would guide their fortunes. The collective ballots provide a better means of selecting a leader than the promotion of someone not explicitly ap- proved by the people for the presidency. As Senator Edward Kennedy put it, "I would feel more confident about the future if the President had earned his way to the Oval Office along the campaign trail."[64] Special elections would probably pro- vide high-quality successors.

Many of the arguments commonly used against special elections are misconceived. Some doubt that the campaign could be abbreviated sufficiently to permit a special election. "National elections can hardly be held in a matter of weeks," argued Senator Roman Hruska. "There must be a little more time to develop a presentation of the issues and qualifications and so on."[65] Others believe an appeal to the public would be unwise under some circumstances. Representative John M. Robsion argued in 1945:

> We do not want to have the country thrown into the chaos of a special election after the death of a President. . . . It cannot help the country but must result in harm.[66]

Still others complain that special elections would be "a new and drastic departure from our historic system of quadrennial presidential elections . . ."[67]

These arguments are not persuasive. In France, elections follow a presidential vacancy by three to five weeks. The French chose a new President without complication in 1969 and 1974. Although the American system could not be abbreviated to that extent, campaigns could be pared considerably. Special elections would not require "the elaborate foreplay of the quadrennial orgy," Schlesinger rightly observes.[68] The national committees could choose their candidates as they would if death, withdrawal, or inability visited the ticket during a regular campaign. A series of broadcast debates might telescope the campaign. Nor would tragic events prohibit special elections. War or the mourning of presidential death are perhaps not the best times to choose a leader. But presidential elections have been conducted during war and within a year of a President's death.

Use of special elections might constitute a dramatic departure from past practice but not from the intent of the Constitution. The Constitution was written to make such an event possible. For most of American history, succession has been governed by statutes which either explicitly or implicitly called for an intermediate election in case both the presidency and vice presidency fell vacant.[69]

Even so, other objections cast doubt on the wisdom of instituting special elections. Such a system might threaten the stability of government. Schlesinger rightly argues that France operated without detriment a system like that envisioned by the American founding fathers. But there are limits to comparison. France does not have international responsibilities of the same magnitude as does the United States. World economics depends heavily on American policy. Western defense relies on the certainty of American response. A caretaker government might not be strong enough to provide such stability. Special elections might bring several changes of policy and personnel within a brief period. As Aaron Wildavsky argues, "Weakness, indecision, futility, even challenges of the right of a temporary occupant to act like a President would be the most likely consequences of failing to allow a successor to serve until the end of the established presidential term."[70]

Institutional variations make special elections more problematic for the United States. Parliamentary systems conduct such events with relative ease. Legislative debate sharply defines issue differences. Standing in the parliamentary party helps identify candidates. A longer campaign is more appropriate, however, to the American system. The lack of programmatic parties requires more time to develop and expose positions on the issues. Further, America takes its candidates from diverse sources. More time is necessary to allow them to demonstrate their strengths. Finally, an American President needs a longer period to construct his administration. He cannot rely on party leaders to run government departments and act as his cabinet. Nor can he look to a neutral civil service to handle major administrative chores.

In some circumstances, special elections could pose real inconvenience. If a vacancy occurred right before the midterm congressional elections, America might have to follow them with another major campaign some weeks later. If it came near the end of the term, the special election would presumably overlap with the presidential primaries. Moreover, special elections help little in the case of inability. Current provisions allow a transfer of power to last only the length of the incapacity of the Chief Executive. A system of special elections would presumably abort his term.

The suggestions that the special elections only coincide with the midterm campaign or that they follow the vacancy by ten months do not meet many of the problems sketched above. These might just provide for a longer caretaker period. They would promote uncertainty and instability. They would produce clashes with other institutions.

Some proponents of special elections are slightly more generous to the vice presidency. They would retain the office. Their target is rather section two of the Twenty-fifth Amendment. Former Senator John Pastore proposed holding a special election whenever a Vice President chosen through that procedure became President with more than one year remaining in the term. Former Representative Bella Abzug favored abolishing section two altogether.[71]

These plans deal with more remote contingencies. They would schedule a special election only if both the elected President and Vice President were unable to serve for any reason as Chief Executive. Still, they are vulnerable to the same objections made earlier against special elections. Further, they fail to acknowledge the successful manner in which section two has operated to date. If used as intended, it provides a compatible successor quickly after a thorough review. Finally, section two is necessary to make the inability provisions function, for they depend on the presence of a Vice President.

Former Senator Kenneth Keating approached the vice presidency quite differently than those whose ideas have been discussed in the last few pages.[72] He initially opposed the Twenty-fifth Amendment. Rather than abolish the office he favored creating an extra Vice President. One would act as the President's right-hand officer, the other as president of the Senate. Both would stand with the presidential candidate.

This plan, too, would assure compatibility. It might enable the standard-bearer to unify his party to a greater degree by placating two factions instead of just one. Indeed, some other countries do have multiple Vice Presidents. But Senator Keating's suggestion does not provide a happy solution. The second vice presidency, with its meager duties and low prestige, would be unlikely to attract outstanding individuals. The presence of an additional candidate on each ticket would further complicate campaigns. The third-stringer would probably receive little scrutiny but would distract some attention from the standard-bearer and his proposed successor.

Finally, others attack the disability provisions of the Twenty-fifth Amendment. They argue that it might allow unelected officials to oust an unpopular Chief Executive by declaring him disabled. As Representative Henry B. Gonzalez put it, the amendment issues "a standing invitation to overthrow the President, through the operation of the disability clause."[73] This attack seems implausible. Such a use of the amendment would violate its purpose. John Feerick, who studied the subject in detail, found that "at various times in the debates and hearings of 1964 and 1965, it was made clear that unpopularity, incompetence, impeachable conduct, poor judgment, and laziness do not constitute an 'inability' within the meaning of the Amendment."[74] Moreover, the unelected officials empowered to declare a President disabled are the members of the cabinet. As the President's appointees, they would seem unlikely to force his removal unless he was unable to discharge his duties. Moreover, the Twenty-fifth Amendment provides further protection by allowing Congress to supervise the exercise of that power.

Those who would reform the vice presidency score high for ingenuity. The plans discussed above cover much ground, and this critique does not include all. Yet almost all are ill-advised. Political engineering is a tricky business. One astute political scientist observed that "the actual consequences of party reform are, in the future as in the past, likely often to disappoint their advocates, relieve their opponents, and surprise a lot of commentators."[75] Uncertainty pervades attempts to reform the vice presidency, too. Some proposed changes would appear to damage the vice presidency. More often, reforms are unsuitable because they fail to appreciate the relationship of the vice presidency to other political institutions. The doubtful benefits to the vice presidency are outweighed by the potential harm to other parts of the system.

13

★ ★ ★

The Vice Presidency in Perspective

For most of its history the vice presidency has been occupied by men of modest talents who gained their lofty station in the absence of any serious appraisal of their ability to govern, and who subsequently faded into deserved obscurity. Party leaders chose vice-presidential candidates based on assorted political considerations—to placate a disgruntled wing of the party, to give the ticket ideological or geographical balance, to carry an important state. Voters paid little attention to those competing for the second spot. When they were so disposed, Vice Presidents presided over the Senate, their sole ongoing duty but one devoid of power or interest. A few became President upon the death of the incumbent. Otherwise, the second spot represented the last stop in their careers. A familiar fable captured the poverty of the office. It went: There were two brothers; one ran off to sea, the other became Vice President; neither was ever heard from again. The vice presidency is no longer the humble station that aphorism lampoons. Modern Vice Presidents commonly perform duties of some significance. Their office has become the surest springboard to the White House. The qualifications of some recent candidates have not been immediately evident, but the office has become attractive to politicians with impressive credentials.

The recent rise of the vice presidency is occasionally traced to the improved relations between Presidents and Vice Presidents or to the increased salience of presidential succession.

Both factors have influenced its development, but alone they provide only part of the answer.

The amiable relations some earlier Presidents and Vice Presidents enjoyed produced no lasting growth in the second office. Three nineteenth-century pairs—Jackson and Van Buren, Polk and Dallas, McKinley and Hobart—proved compatible. Each Vice President exercised some influence. Yet their service left the office no stronger.

Further, politicians and public alike were fully cognizant of the possibility of presidential succession in the past, especially following the death of a Chief Executive. Six Vice Presidents became the nation's leader in that manner before the New Deal. Yet these reminders of the potential importance of the second man brought no improvement in the office or in those chosen to seek it.

The Rise of the Vice Presidency

The vice presidency owes its recent growth primarily to larger changes in American politics and government since the New Deal. That event began a redefinition of the American political context. The new domestic and international demands made on federal government increased the power and responsibility of the Chief Executive. The Vice President was a beneficiary of the new presidential eminence. He was drawn into the executive branch where attractive duties were available.

The expanded role of the President was most responsible for promoting the modern vice presidency. But changes in the parties in the same period also shaped the office. The importance of party declined and the bases of Democratic and Republican support changed. These developments affected the selection of vice-presidential candidates, their campaign roles, their electoral impact and the nature of their duties. Traditionally party leaders had assumed the major role in filling the second spot on the ticket. The presidential nominee played a minor, and often acquiescent, part in that decision. The New Deal transformed the relative strength of these actors. Local bosses became dependent on the President. They did not wish to alienate a potential dispenser of federal patronage by challenging his preference for a running mate. Delegates had other reasons not to oppose his first major decision. The growth of mass media ensured that a repudiation of his choice would receive immediate national attention, thus hurting the party's prospects in the election.

The standard-bearer now generally does consult party leaders before suggesting a running mate. He does so to retain the good will of local leaders, which will help assure their active efforts in the campaign. The spread of presidential primaries since 1968 has provided recent nominees greater incentive to consider the sense of the convention before making a choice. The first growth of these preconvention tests reduced the number of delegates the political bosses controlled and increased those whose loyalty ran directly to the candidate on whose slate they had been elected. The more recent proliferation has filled the convention with delegates who favor the presidential nominee but who behave more independently than did their predecessors. Recent presidential nominees have solicited the views of others but the final choice is theirs.

The new selection process has transformed the relationship between the two. It has made the standard-bearer responsible for the conduct of his partner. He cannot blame party leaders for the faux pas the second officer commits. Further, it has made the Vice President more clearly the subordinate of the President. Since the second officer owes his place to the President (or presidential candidate) he accepts direction from him during the campaign and in office. Finally, the two are more likely to be compatible. A presidential candidate may not always be able to place his true first choice on the ticket.

But he is in a position to select someone whose views he deems palatable and whose personality he finds agreeable.

Changes in the political universe have also made ideological balancing less common. The number of competitive states has increased since the 1940s. Members of national tickets find it necessary to conduct national campaigns, something air travel and the growth of mass media have made possible. But these technological changes prevent candidates from tailoring their positions to please the diverse sentiments of each region in which they campaign. Presidential and vice-presidential candidates must synchronize their views. Subtle forms of ideological balance continue to occur. Eisenhower and Nixon (1952), Kennedy and Johnson, Carter and Mondale, and Reagan and Bush being recent examples. But a ticket that bridges the ideological spectrum is no longer credible.

The changed political context modified the nature of presidential campaigns as well. From the New Deal onwards, the outcomes of presidential elections depended to a greater degree on the personalities of the competing presidential candidates. Of course that conclusion must rest largely on intuition rather than on solid empirical evidence; the survey research techniques on which psephologists now rely only originated in the 1930s. Yet three factors allow that premise to be advanced with some confidence. First, the presidency has become more important since the New Deal; voters would be highly irrational not to consider more carefully the attributes of those seeking the office. Second, the development of mass media and air travel has made information about candidates more accessible. Third, party has recently become less significant in voting.

The new emphasis on the presidential contenders has changed the role of the vice-presidential candidate. He is no longer commonly expected to provide independent electoral advantage in only one particular state or region. Rather, the second candidate has become part of a national campaign team. Like others in the effort his role is to promote the prospects of the standard-bearer. The running mate seeks to enhance the ticket's fortunes by soliciting the active support of various media, party organizations, and interest groups. Further, the vice-presidential candidate generally performs four roles in which he appeals directly to voters on behalf of the head of his ticket. He serves as the most visible salesman for the presidential candidate. He echoes the themes which the standard-bearer emphasizes. He assumes primary responsibility for attacking the opposition. And although the second candidate campaigns nationally, he may concentrate on a particular region.

The vice-presidential candidate may contribute to the electoral outcome by his skill at performing these assignments. He may also affect the result if his presence on the ticket influences the way some citizens vote. Evidence cited earlier suggests that Nixon cost Eisenhower votes in 1956 and that the choice between Agnew and Muskie in 1968 and between Dole and Mondale in 1976 helped the Democrats on both occasions. The increased significance of the presidency has added importance to the choice between vice-presidential candidates. Presidential vacancy occurs with disturbing frequency. Citizens should be concerned with the characteristics of the successor. Yet the choice between vice-presidential candidates generally has little impact on the election returns. Voters often know little about nominees for the second office. Campaigns offer little information about them. Parties rarely emphasize qualities of their second candidate; more often they castigate the rival. These attacks are most common when the opposing standard-bearer is popular, when his running mate is controversial or when the possibility of presidential succession is unusually salient. The media give the vice-presidential candidates relatively little coverage. Few citizens mention the vice-presidential candidates as an influence on their votes.

As it is, the Vice President is not really an elected official. He owes his position largely to the public's preference for the standard-bearer of his party. In part, however, ticket-building strategies of presidential nominees encourage voter indifference toward the running mates. Experience suggests that the choice between the second candidates is likely to prove most important when at least one is controversial. Presidential candidates will generally avoid running mates with high propensity for alienating voters. They seek partners whose campaign skills will enhance the appeal of the standard-bearer but whose presence on the ticket will not dissuade potential supporters. Vice-presidential candidates would probably have greater impact on the outcome if presidential nominees were less conservative in selecting them.

The rise of the presidency since the New Deal has not made the second office unduly taxing but it has added some substance to it. Since the Chief Executive chooses his partner he has incentive to find functions for him to perform. Relations between the two often are not excessively cordial but neither do they reflect the personal animosity and ideological distance common in the past. Further, the President has become responsible not only for the quality of government during his incumbency but also for its conduct should he die before his term ends. If he ignores his running mate voters may think he has provided them with a poor successor. More important, citizens might regard as irresponsible a Chief Executive who excludes the Vice President from government activity.

The increased activity of government has provided Presidents opportunities to give the second officer institutional duties. They have named Vice Presidents to head various commissions, have sent them abroad as their emissaries and have solicited their advice. The enlarged role of the President and decline of the parties have allowed the Vice President to contribute in political roles, too. The Chief Executive now makes extensive legislative proposals. The second officer helps lobby for these programs. Administrations have come to appreciate the expediency of communicating directly with the people. The contact with citizens that the media and airplane make possible decreases dependence on party organizations which, in any event, are no longer able to mobilize support so effectively. The Vice President has become a prominent administration spokesman, adapting the campaign roles of salesman, echo, and "hit man" to the circumstances of incumbency. The administration cannot, however, ignore party politicians. It needs their support in legislative and electoral battles. The Vice President has assumed much of the responsibility for preserving the loyalty of the party's local leaders and their organizations. He may also become the President's chief surrogate campaigner in the presidential primaries.

The changed political context has given Presidents incentive and opportunity to delegate activities to their Vice Presidents in these roles. The gravitational pull the strengthened presidency exerts has drawn the second officer into the executive orbit. Vice Presidents have reason to accept this position and the assignments it entails. The selection process suggests a subordinate role. The Vice President has little choice but to accept the chores the President gives him; even insignificant duties are better than none at all. Further, Vice Presidents have performed important assignments.

Yet the main attraction of these duties is prospective. Politicians accept the second office because they hope some day to occupy the first. Other positions offer more power and interest than the vice presidency. Yet politicians relinquish these, often eagerly, for the uncertainty it promises.

The vice presidency is no longer the political dead end it long was. Modern Vice Presidents are invariably considered potential presidential nominees. The new importance of the presidency has forced parties to nominate people of higher caliber for the second spot. They are better able to seek the presidency than were their predecessors. Further, the office offers resources valuable to one interested in promoting himself as a presidential possibility.

Vice-presidential activity receives substantial coverage relative to that given other politicians. Campaign publicity allows him to shed his anonymity; attention as Vice President keeps him in the public eye. Accordingly, the Vice President enjoys wide recognition. Much of the coverage of the second officer comes within a presidential context—chairing presidential commissions, representing the nation abroad, attending White House meetings. He thus seems to have familiarity with the national issues with which the Chief Executive deals. As a party worker he collects debts from other politicians which often are convertible into future support.

The Twenty second Amendment was intended to curb the President's power by restricting his tenure in office. Unforeseen, however, was the manner in which it helps a Vice President serving during the second term of a Chief Executive. He can manuever more freely to promote his prospects for winning the nomination and election.

Yet most Vice Presidents who become Chief Executive owe their advance to succession rather than election. Presidential vacancy or the threat of it has occurred with alarming frequency. The method of replacing a fallen leader assumes greater importance in the post-New Deal world. Any evaluation of the vice presidency must depend largely on its ability to provide a solution to that problem. Changes since 1933 have made the office a more efficacious means of filling that role.

First, recent Vice Presidents have generally been more competent political figures. Most have brought wide experience to the office. Many were considered presidential timber prior to their selection for the second spot; most were subsequently so regarded. Further, succession of the Vice President is now less likely to produce shifts in policy or personnel. Vice Presidents are more closely identified with the Chief Executive, his programs and associates. They are more likely to be familiar with the information a Chief Executive must have. Modern Presidents are more willing to trust the successor they have chosen. The growth of the presidency creates an obligation to keep the second officer current.

Indeed, the office was held in sufficiently high regard in the 1960s that the Twenty-fifth Amendment included a provision to allow the President and Congress to fill a vice-presidential vacancy. Section two represented a compromise between conflicting approaches. The price of consensus was a mechanism that provides legislators with no clear standard for determining the merit of a particular nomination. Still, the procedure worked well in its two tests. The Vice Presidents it produces must undergo a thorough examination more rigorous in many respects than the electoral process.

The Problems Remaining

The developments sketched above have given the vice presidency far greater significance. It is no longer the empty office which provided so appropriate a target for derision for most of American history. Yet if the office is not so frail as it was, neither is it very robust. The vice presidency now attracts public figures of greater accomplishment and skill who have more opportunities for meaningful activity and greater prospect for future advance. Despite the clear growth of their office, Vice Presidents continue to suffer through unhappy incumbencies. "I detested every minute of it," Johnson confided.[1] In his memoirs, Humphrey contends that he "liked being Vice President" but portrays an office of uncommon frustration. Elsewhere he said:

> It's like being naked in the middle of a blizzard with no one to even offer you a match to keep you warm—that's

the vice presidency. You are trapped, vulnerable and alone
. . .[2]

Rockefeller told the Senate when he presided for the last time:
"For me, these past two years, in all candor, cannot be said
to have sorely tried either my talents or my stamina."[3]

The disillusionment these Vice Presidents express cautions
against being too sanguine about the office. Although it has
grown markedly, the vice presidency remains an awkward
aspect of American constitutional design.

Some problems are inherent in the office. The developments that allowed the vice presidency to advance have treated
but not cured these afflictions. The standard of Vice Presidents has improved, but the system of selection and election
still is likely to produce occasional Vice Presidents of inferior
quality. Presidential candidates have great incentive to choose
running mates with political assets and little reason to seek
those most able to govern. It is not always feasible or desirable for voters to reject a ticket because the successor is unsuited for the role he might play.

Vice Presidents typically have more to do. But they depend
on the generosity of the Chief Executive for any useful duties.
The sum of those assignments often does not amount to much.
Further, the delegations are not permanent; as Humphrey put
it, "He who giveth can taketh away and often does."[4]

Structural factors, in part, constrain the involvement of the
Vice President. He is the one major subordinate the Chief
Executive cannot remove at will from office. The President is
understandably reluctant to trust significant continuing responsibilities to an officer over whom he lacks this leverage.

Ironically, the increased importance of the presidency which
has contributed most to the growth of the second office is
also the source of new problems. Fewer people now participate in the selection of the vice-presidential candidate. It is,
of course, fitting that a potential Chief Executive should have

a large role in choosing members of his administration. But it also is appropriate that others should join in the selection of a person who may succeed to the presidency.

Further, Vice Presidents pay a price for becoming part of the executive branch. In the past they had little to do but were independent. They did not owe their position to the Chief Executive nor did they look to him to embellish it. Not only is the second person indebted to the President for his station. He looks to the Chief Executive for the assignments that might add substance and dignity to his office. He is eager to please to procure those gifts. Accordingly, Vice Presidents are often willing to undertake assignments which demean their person and debase the conduct of politics. Of course, the acts of any public figure may fall below standards of proper political etiquette. Yet the Vice President is particularly vulnerable to this failing. He is well-placed to perform chores the Chief Executive would not dare undertake himself. He also has special incentive to respond to presidential instruction.

Political scientists have lately come to appreciate the importance of studying presidential personalities.[5] Performance in the White House depends largely on character traits as well as experience and policy preferences. The way a Chief Executive treats the lieutenant, too, relates largely to the presidential psyche. It has become fashionable to criticize Presidents for mistreating their Vice Presidents. Indeed, recent Chief Executives have often behaved miserably toward the second officer. Johnson inflicted numerous indignities on Humphrey; Nixon was no more kind to Agnew.

But the President is not always to blame for not taking the Vice President into his confidence or involving him intimately in consultations leading to important decision-making. The personality of the Vice President also shapes the relationship. Humphrey may have been excluded in part because of his loquacity. Presidents necessarily value advisers who are able to discuss issues succinctly. Further, Presidents invite the participation of those not likely to let their confidences slip. Humphrey no doubt could have offered much more as Vice President had Johnson not so abused him. But the exclusion was probably not entirely Johnson's fault. Kennedy and Ford both treated their Vice Presidents well. And, for their part, Johnson and Rockefeller carried themselves in a circumspect manner. But both Presidents might have been more inclined to confide in their Vice Presidents had the latter not had such overpowering personalities and reputations.

The damage a Vice President may do should concern students of American politics. The harm a presidential successor may cause provides a real source of worry. Recent occupants of the vice presidency have seemed better equipped to become President than their predecessors. Yet unqualified men may still inhabit the office. The assignments they receive may do little to prepare them to succeed. Further, the experience may erode their abilities rather than enlarge them.

The Futile Search for Solutions

In short, the vice presidency remains a dangerous office. Its recent growth has mitigated but not removed its harmful potential. On balance, the office continues to merit a negative assessment. This would make the case for abolition of the vice presidency compelling if some preferable arrangement for handling presidential succession existed. None is evident.

The appeal of various options depends not only, or indeed primarily, on their probable impact on the vice presidency. More important is the likely effect on the total system of politics and government. Evaluations of different proposals will diverge according to the characteristics a particular reformer wishes to accentuate. Many reformers, especially in recent years, have proposed changes that would directly involve more people in the selection of a presidential replacement. The concept of participation is an intrinsic value of the American system. It is not, however, the only criterion relevant in appraising the wisdom of a particular proposal. A method for filling a sudden presidential vacancy should also be likely to elevate a competent leader in a manner conducive to maintaining stability in government.

The virtue of proposals for special elections is that they would allow the citizenry to choose directly their new Chief Executive. They would be likely to produce a President essentially as competent as those chosen in the regular quadrennial contests. Yet they would create instability in a number of ways. There would be a brief period under a caretaker in which government policy would be uncertain. The introduction of special elections might interfere with other events on the political calendar. Election of the candidate of the opposition party might provoke comprehensive changes in policy and personnel. Presumably, the new leader would assume office immediately. He would thereby lack the transition period that allows Presidents time to select their associates and plan their programs.

Other democracies may be able to afford these inconveniences but their circumstances are not analogous to those of the United States. They do not carry comparable responsibilities for international and economic leadership. Their parliamentary systems allow their parties to produce candidates more quickly than the complicated American machinery. They rely on professional civil servants to ease the transition by providing continuous neutral administration.

The threat to stability that special elections would pose make them unsuitable methods for replacing a President. Other alternatives are even worse. The succession might be vested in some other officer, the Speaker of the House or the secretary of state for instance, for the remainder of the term. Neither position seems likely to provide a better solution than the Vice President. A Speaker or secretary might be unsuited to be Chief Executive. Their selections have a far more remote relationship to the popular will than does that of the Vice President. Succession of the former might give control of the executive branch to the opposition party; elevation of the latter might produce a leader with little political experience.

The vice presidency has several virtues as the station of the first successor. It provides a quick replacement who is widely accepted as a legitimate heir. It virtually assures that succession will not change party control of the executive branch; it allows general continuity of policy and personnel. Given developments since the New Deal, the Vice President is likely to be qualified to be President. Recent occupants of the office have been able men; their incumbency generally provides them some opportunity to familiarize themselves with current issues. Further, the Vice President is likely to understand how politics operates through past participation in democratic contests. Although the Vice President is not elected directly, he is likely to be acceptable to large segments of the population. Other provisions for succession could supply some of these virtues. But none can satisfy so many so well as the vice presidency.

If the vice presidency is worth retaining it is worth improving. Three considerations can helpfully guide efforts to strengthen the office. How can the system be designed to place good people in the office? What arrangements can enable the Vice President to play a useful role while in that office? How can the vice presidency enhance the ability of its occupant to serve as Chief Executive? Reformers generally do not purport to address just one question. Although the three raise separate objectives they may have common solutions. For instance, a change which brought more able people to the office might also allow them a more useful role and better prepare them to succeed to the presidency.

Some proposals attempt to improve the quality of Vice Presidents by introducing more participation into their selection and/or election. Vice-presidential primaries, open conventions, and separate elections are prominent among the plans with this objective. Other recommendations leave the selection processes untouched. They attempt to vivify the office and enable it to produce better successors. These plans would commonly institutionalize a larger role for the Vice President, usually within the executive branch.

Here again sweeping reforms encounter sound objections. The plans sketched above fail in two ways to appreciate the proper relationship of the presidency and vice presidency. The second office has grown because it has achieved a closer association with the executive branch. Indeed, it seems entirely appropriate that a permanent presidential successor in a system that separates branches of government should come from the administration. The reforms under discussion might well impose on the Chief Executive a successor he did not want in roles he did not approve. Presidents would be likely to ostracize Vice Presidents chosen and operating in the manner these reforms envision. Ultimately, the vice presidency would suffer.

The damage to the second office which these reforms would entail is not so serious as their consequences for the presidency. Proposals to institutionalize a larger role for the Vice President within the executive branch pose an ominous threat to the conduct of the presidency. A Chief Executive should not be encumbered with subordinates whose duties he cannot control. His power of dismissal provides him with a check on the activities of members of his administration. It also allows the Congress, courts, and ultimately the electorate to hold him accountable for the policy and performance of the executive branch. Since the President cannot remove the second officer, proposals to grant the Vice President a larger role by statute would undermine the notion of presidential responsibility.

The other reforms are less damaging but still objectionable

on similar grounds. The chief advantage of allowing a potential Chief Executive the major role in choosing his Vice President is that it creates incentives for preparing the possible successor for the role he might have to assume. Presidents do not always discharge their responsibilities in this regard. But they would be far less likely to take these precautions if ideology and/or party identification separated the two officers. Other members of the administration would be less likely to cooperate should presidential vacancy advance an incompatible successor.

The criticisms of these reforms do not presuppose a notion of a strong presidency. Those who advance these proposals do not usually purport to do so to weaken the presidency. It is conceivable, however, that these approaches may appeal to those with that objective. It would be unfortunate, however, if these plans were used to constrain the presidency. There are other ways of achieving that end which would reduce the President's power without denying him responsibility or jeopardizing the succession.

The paradox of the vice presidency is that although its serious defects are apparent solutions are elusive. A large corpus of ingenious plans is available. Yet the more ambitious reforms invariably involve substantial dislocation in other aspects of the political system.

Prospects for the Office

Reform of the vice presidency must rely on more modest forms of institutional engineering. Three rather minor changes might produce some improvement in the quality of those chosen to seek the office. First, parties could require candidates for the presidential nomination to release some time before the convention a list of people who have agreed to be considered as their running mate. Such a list need not include competitors for the nomination; they should be assumed to be possible running mates. Such a procedure might provoke some discussion and media scrutiny of the backgrounds and credentials of those involved. Little attention ensues now when presidential candidates "float" names of possible running mates before and during the convention as they invariably do. Some marginal gains might be achieved by formalizing the process.

Second, parties should allow the presidential nominees more time to consider their choice of running mate. They could give them an extra day by either scheduling the presidential balloting earlier or by allowing them to extend the convention for twenty-four hours. In some cases, a longer extension with the choice being submitted to the national committee might be appropriate. Presidential candidates should not await their own nomination before beginning to consider whom they would prefer as their running mate. Yet some aspects of the evaluation cannot occur until the identity of the standard-bearer is conceded by all. A presidential candidate cannot really approach some party members regarding their availability or credentials until his nomination is secured. He cannot discuss with them their concepts of the vice presidency. The time after the presidential nomination is determined is most valuable, yet it is often too scarce to allow the standard-bearer to make an evaluation. Forcing him to make a rushed decision may, of course, indicate how he reacts under pressure. But campaigns are full of such tests. There is no reason to create an artificial test that involves so important a decision.

A third change, the inclusion of at least one vice-presidential debate in the campaign, would contribute to the selection of more able running mates and would introduce more democracy into the election of the Vice President. Vice-presidential candidates are rarely seen in a presidential context. They receive little campaign attention relative to the presidential contenders. Since voters have little chance to assess the second candidate, the presidential candidates have less incentive to choose a running mate with qualities likely to impress the electorate. A televised debate would provide the electorate with more information about the second people. It might lead the presidential nominees to choose more wisely and voters to attach more importance to the merits of their running mates.

These reforms leave untouched the problem of structuring the vice presidency to provide its occupant a more meaningful role and better preparation should he succeed to the presidency. In these areas reforms are even more inadequate. Here it is advisable to recommend a form of conduct for Presidents and Vice Presidents to follow, but not to engage in any institutional architecture.

Presidents should continue to give the Vice President duties within the categories described in chapters six through eight—commission chairman, foreign envoy, general adviser, legislative liaison, party worker, administration spokesperson, and primary surrogate. But they should make these grants under different conditions than those often present in the past. They should avoid loading the second officer with meaningless but time-consuming tasks. They should not commonly use the Vice President for chores they would consider beneath their dignity. The Chief Executive should include the Vice President in important administration councils, give him frequent and easy access to the President and to the information the President receives.

Three of these roles pose special problems for Vice Presidents. Vice Presidents should generally be wary of assuming commission chairmanships or other line responsibilities. Occupants of the second office who undertake significant operational duties will probably antagonize the department (and especially its leader) that formerly did or otherwise would handle those functions. Moreover, Vice Presidents will generally lack the staff support sufficient to discharge such duties. They will be forced to rely on the existing bureaucracy, the very entity that resents the vice-presidential intrusion on its turf, to perform the assigned task. Conversely, if the operational assignment is insignificant a Vice President will waste his time and demean his office by assuming it. Occasionally, Presidents may offer a Vice President a commission or operational responsibility worth accepting. But, for the reasons stated above, Vice Presidents should at least proceed cautiously. Two other roles—administration spokesman and primary surrogate—present different pitfalls. These roles have appeal for Vice Presidents. They provide visibility and allow the second officer to win the favor of the President for whom, and the groups to whom, he speaks. But Presidents have incentive to use the Vice President as a vocal public advocate of administration programs and as a vociferous critic of administration foes. Such activity may cause the public to view the Vice President as a champion of controversial positions he does not even support and as a political hatchet man unsuited for the presidency. Vice Presidents should continue to speak and campaign for the President they serve but should recognize, and guard against, the dangers these roles entail.

Of the vice-presidential roles, that of general adviser is potentially most useful to the conduct of government and most important in assuring an informed successor. Increasingly, Presidents have surrounded themselves with technocrats. They fill fewer important positions with politicians. Presidents reach the White House with fewer debts to political figures. Accordingly, they have less obligation to appoint them to major posts. Further, the increasing complexity of issues and managerial problems has made attractive the expertise people from other fields can supply. The cost of this change is that the President receives less advice from those schooled in democratic procedures whose approach is primarily a political one. The Vice President is well suited to help fill this void. His perspective may be slightly different from that of the Chief

Executive, but at least he is accustomed to considering the political ramifications of actions. The Vice President can also best prepare for the succession by acting as a general adviser, acquainting himself with information on a wide range of issues and on the decision-making processes that at least one President employed.

Whether Presidents will allow their Vice Presidents such a role depends largely on the relationship between the two officers. Accordingly, the presidential candidate must maintain control over the choice of the running mate. Once in office, the success of the relationship will turn on the extent to which the two officers are politically and personally compatible, and mutually dependent. A Vice President on amicable terms with the White House staff will encounter less resistance to playing a significant role.

The discussion of the proper role of the Vice President and the factors likely to produce it follows closely the experience of Carter and Mondale during their term in office. The two and their staffs established a cooperative relationship. Further, Mondale brought important assets to the administration—his knowledge of Washington and Congress, his ties to traditional Democratic groups—in areas in which it was otherwise weak. Carter, apparently, was secure enough not to feel threatened by his Vice President; Mondale was sufficiently self-effacing and did not possess an overshadowing reputation. Carter gave Mondale extensive access and meaningful responsibilities far beyond those any previous Vice President had enjoyed. The success of their association did not, of course, work any formal change in the second office. But it may create expectations for Presidents to treat their Vice Presidents in similar fashion.

One conclusion my study of the vice presidency suggests is that institutional engineering cannot always be used to achieve a desired result. Changes that may correct the particular fault a reformer addresses are likely to have repercussions across the system. These often make the costs of the proposal prohibitive. Reformers cannot possibly anticipate all consequences of the changes they advance. But much damage has been done to political systems, including America's, by imposing structural changes on institutions independent of a careful consideration of their larger implications.

Institutional changes in other aspects of American politics will often reach the vice presidency without so intending. The Twenty-second Amendment sought merely to limit the tenure of a Chief Executive, yet it also enhanced the vice presidency as a stepping stone to the White House. The proliferation of primaries occurred because reformers sought to introduce more participation into the selection of presidential nominees. But they seem likely to make it more difficult for future Vice Presidents to win the nomination when the Chief Executive is retiring. Ironically, they make it more possible for the Vice President to challenge the President for renomination. Discussions of replacing the Electoral College with a system of direct popular vote rarely, if ever, consider the effects of such a change on the second officer. In fact, the need to win votes nationally would probably lessen even further the temptation to seek regional balance; rather, the party standard-bearer would probably seek a popular national figure as his running mate. Any change that would make presidential nominations likely to require more than a single ballot would probably give new strength to another common ticket-building strategy of the past, the deal.

Further, the need to respond to short-term events and the consequences of those responses will no doubt change major political institutions. The vice presidency will adapt to these changes. The effects of those events are impossible to predict. The continuation of recent trends that have made the President more vulnerable may cause future Vice Presidents to seek more independence from the executive branch. Or, they may cause the Chief Executive to rely more heavily on the second officer. Or they may bring both changes at once.

The experience of the vice presidency since 1953 serves as a reminder that political institutions are not independent entities. They belong to a system of political and governmental arrangements. Changes in that larger context redefine the nature of its parts just as the evolution of any important component alters the general framework. The importance of different Vice Presidents will continue to vary largely according to their relationships with the President. But just as the current status of the vice presidency is the product of changes in American politics since the New Deal, its future will depend on subsequent developments in the political context.

Appendix: Characteristics of Prospective Vice-Presidential Candidates, 1952-1980

It is not always possible to determine whether a presidential candidate sought a particular type of ticket-balance by looking at the characteristics of his running mate. Preferred choices may not have agreed to run. Or the eventual candidate may have been chosen despite having certain characteristics. Better judgments about the balancing the standard-bearer desired can be made by studying the features of all the prospective candidates he gave serious consideration.

It is, however, difficult in many cases to ascertain who those persons were. No formal list is generally available; published accounts often differ. In some cases, it is easy to identify the relevant individuals. Those Democrats listed in 1956 were the five who received most delegate votes when Adlai Stevenson asked the convention to make the choice. Democratic names from 1960 are taken from memoirs of Kennedy associates, Theodore Sorensen and Arthur M. Schlesinger, Jr. Hubert Humphrey's memoirs provide the basis for judgments about those he considered; accounts provided by several McGovern associates generally agree on those whose selection he weighed. Carter's list of seven was made public.

The judgments are more difficult on the Republican side. Eisenhower's memoirs give five names he supposedly included on a list of acceptable running mates; I have added the name of William Knowland because a number of other accounts report that he, too, was considered. In 1960 accounts differ slightly. Little information exists on Goldwater's selection; Ford was certainly considered but it is not clear how seriously Scranton was taken. Accounts of 1968 and 1976 generally agree.

In 1964, Johnson floated many names; I have omitted those like Senator Thomas Dodd, Mayor Robert Wagner, Governor Pat Brown, and Agriculture Secretary Orville Freeman, whose inclusion seems implausible. Little authoritative information exists concerning the 1952 Democratic selection. Newspaper speculation differed; I have included those commonly mentioned.

Other judgments may also be in doubt. On ideology, for instance, I have classified individuals according to my perception of their position on the political spectrum at the time of the campaign. On background, I have indicated major experience in different areas; whether balance exists depends on how important a particular background was in shaping the candidate's experience.

Tables A.1 and A.2 present the names and characteristics of the prospective candidates I have included.

TABLE A.1
Characteristics of Prospective Republican VP Candidates

Contender	Region	Ideology	Religion	Experience
1952				
Nixon	W	C	P	L
Halleck	M	C	P	L
Judd	M	C	P	L
Knowland	W	C	P	L
Langlie	W	M	P	S
Thornton	W	M	P	S
1956				
Nixon	W	M	P	C-L
1960				
Lodge	N	M	P	E-L
Anderson	S*	C	P	E
Ford	M	C	P	L
Judd	M	C	P	L
Mitchell	N*	M	C	E
Morton	B	M	P	L-E
Rockefeller	N	L	P	S-E
Seaton	M	C	P	E-L
1964				
Miller	N	C	C	L
Ford	M	C	P	L
Scranton	N	M	P	S-L
1968				
Agnew	B	M	P	S
Baker	S	C†	P	L
Finch	W	L	P	S

TABLE A.1 *(cont.)*

Contender	Region	Ideology	Religion	Experience
Volpe	N	M	C	S
1972				
Agnew	B	C	P	E-S
1976				
Dole	M	C	P	L
Armstrong	S*	C	P	E
Baker	S	C†	P	L
Ruckelshaus	M	M	C	E
1980				
Ford	M	M	P	E-L
Bush	S	M	P	E-L
Kemp	N	C	P	L
Baker	S	M	P	L
Laxalt	W	C	C	L-S
Simon	N*	C	C	E
Rumsfeld	M	M	P	E-L
Lugar	M	M†	P	L-U
Van der Jagt	M	C	P	L

NOTE: Region—N = North, S = South, M = Midwest, B = Border State, W = West.

* indicates subject had never run for a major office in his home state; residence is then used.

Ideology—L = Liberal, M = Moderate, C = Conservative; † indicates I am uncertain about the classification.

Religion—P = Protestant, C = Catholic, J = Jewish.

Experience—L = Legislative, E = Executive, S = State Governor, U = Urban (Mayor). When more than one letter is used following a name, the first indicates the individual's most recent position prior to the time of consideration. Tables in the text reflect those letters.

TABLE A.2
Characteristics of Prospective Democratic VP Candidates

Contender	Region	Ideology	Religion	Experience
1952				
Sparkman	S	M	P	L
Barkley	B	M	P	E-L
Chapman	W*	M	P	E
Fulbright	S	M	P	L
Kefauver	S	L	P	L
Kerr	B	C	P	L
Magnuson	W	L	P	L
Monroney	B	M	P	L
Russell	S	C	P	L
1956				
Kefauver	S	L	P	L
Gore	S	M	P	L
Humphrey	M	L	P	L
J. Kennedy	N	M	C	L
Wagner	N	L	C	U
1960				
Johnson	S	C	P	L
Freeman	M	L	P	S
Humphrey	M	L	P	L-U
Jackson	W	M	P	L
Symington	B	M	P	L-E
1964				
Humphrey	M	L	P	L-U
R. Kennedy	N*	L	C	E
McCarthy	M	L	C	L
McNamara	M*	M†	P	E
Mansfield	W	M†	C	L
Shriver	B*	L	C	E
1968				
Muskie	N	M	C	L-S
Harris	B	M	P	L
R. Hughes	N	L	C	S
E. Kennedy	N	L	C	L
Rockefeller	N	L	P	S-E
Sanford	S	M	P	S
Shriver	B*	M	C	E
1972₁				
Eagleton	B	L	C	L
Askew	S	L	P	S
Church	W	L	P	L

TABLE A.2 (*cont.*)

Contender	Region	Ideology	Religion	Experience
E. Kennedy	N	L	C	L
Mondale	M	L	P	L
Nelson	M	L	P	L-S
O'Brien	N*	M†	C	E
Ribicoff	N	L	J	L-E-S
Shriver	B*	L	C	E
White	N	L	C	U
1972$_2$				
Shriver	B*	L	C	E
Askew	S	L	P	S
Humphrey	M	M	P	L-E-U
E. Kennedy	N	L	C	L
Muskie	N	M	C	L-S
O'Brien	N*	M†	C	E
Ribicoff	N	L	J	L-E-S
1976				
Mondale	M	L	P	L
Church	W	L	P	L
Glenn	M	M	P	L
Jackson	W	M	P	L
Muskie	N	L	C	L-S
Rodino	N	L	C	L
Stevenson	M	L	P	L
1980				
Mondale	M	L	P	E-L

NOTE: See Table A.1.

Abbreviations

Am. Hist. Rev.	American Historical Review
Am. L. Rev.	American Law Review
Am. Pol. Sci. Rev.	American Political Science Review
Br. J. Pol. Sci.	British Journal of Political Science
Cong. Rec.	Congressional Record
Cur. Hist.	Current History
Ford. L. Rev.	Fordham Law Review
Govt. & Opp.	Government and Opposition
J. Pol.	Journal of Politics
Law & Contemp. Probs.	Law and Contemporary Problems
Mo. Hist. Rev.	Missouri Historical Review
Parlia. Affs.	Parliamentary Affairs
Pol. Sci. Q.	Political Science Quarterly
Pol. Stds.	Political Studies
Pres. Stds. Q.	Presidential Studies Quarterly
Pub. Op. Q.	Public Opinion Quarterly
Rev. Pol.	Review of Politics
S. C. L. Rev.	South Carolina Law Review
UCLA L. Rev.	University of California at Los Angeles Law Review
W. Pol. Q.	Western Political Quarterly

Notes

1. Interview with Nixon, *U.S. News and World Report*, 16 May 1960, p. 102.
2. M. Farrand, ed., *Records of the Federal Convention of 1787*, 4 vols. (New Haven, 1911), 2:536-37.
3. A. Hamilton, J. Madison, and J. Jay, *The Federalist Papers*, ed. C. Rossiter (New York, 1961), No. 68, p. 414.
4. J. D. Feerick, "The Vice-Presidency and the Problems of Presidential Succession and Inability," *Ford. L. Rev.* 32 (1964):457, 460-62.
5. Farrand, ed., *Records*, 2:537.
6. Hamilton, Madison, and Jay, *The Federalist*, No. 68, p. 415.
7. Farrand, ed., *Records*, 2:537.
8. *Ibid.*, p. 427.
9. A. M. Schlesinger, Jr., "On the Presidential Succession," *Pol. Sci. Q.* 89 (1974):489.
10. Farrand, ed., *Records*, 2:113-14.
11. *Ibid.*, p. 537.
12. For a concise account of the election of 1800, see R. Hofstadter, *The Idea of a Party System* (Berkeley and Los Angeles, 1969), pp. 128-40.
13. See L. Wilmerding, Jr., "The Vice Presidency," *Pol. Sci. Q.* 68 (1953):17, 21-31.
14. See J. D. Feerick, *From Failing Hands* (New York, 1965), pp. 72-75.
15. U.S., Congress, *Annals*, 8th Cong., 1st sess., 1803-1804, pp. 733; 672; 155; 674; and 84, 682.
16. Burr, Calhoun, Richard M. Johnson, Hannibal Hamlin, Schuyler Colfax, and Levi P. Morton.
17. Clinton, Gerry, King, Henry Wilson, Thomas Hendricks, and Hobart.
18. John Tyler, Millard Fillmore, Andrew Johnson, and Arthur.
19. I. G. Williams, *The Rise of the Vice Presidency* (Washington,

D.C., 1956), p. 25; Feerick, *From Failing Hands*, p. 82; Williams, p. 60; D. Young, *American Roulette* (New York, 1972), pp. 70-72; pp. 25-37; Williams, p. 66.

20. See Young, *American Roulette*, pp. 12-20, 41, 64, 85-87, and *passim*.
21. J. N. Garner, "This Job of Mine," *American*, July 1934, p. 23.
22. Williams, *The Rise of the Vice Presidency*, p. 162.
23. C. Rossiter, *The American Presidency*, 2nd ed. (New York, 1960), p. 135.
24. H. C. Hoover, *Memoirs: The Cabinet and the Presidency: 1920-1933* (New York, 1951).
25. J. M. Burns, *Roosevelt: The Lion and the Fox* (New York, 1956), pp. 413-14; J. M. Burns, *Roosevelt: The Soldier of Freedom* (New York, 1970), pp. 341-42.
26. Feerick, *From Failing Hands*, p. 199.
27. A. W. Barkley, *That Reminds Me* (Garden City, N.Y., 1954).
28. W. Wilson, *Congressional Government* (Gloucester, Mass., 1973), p. 162.
29. Rossiter, *The American Presidency*, pp. 134-35.
30. Quoted from *The Journal of William Maclay* in Feerick, *From Failing Hands*, p. 66.
31. J. K. Goldstein, "An Overview of the Vice-Presidency," *Ford. L. Rev.* 45 (1977):786.
32. See chapter 9, especially Table 9.1.
33. See chapter 11.
34. See chapters 6-8.
35. Williams, *The Rise of the Vice Presidency*; Young, *American Roulette*; M. D. Natoli, "The Vice Presidency Since World War II" (Ph.D. diss., Tufts University, 1975).
36. Barkley, *That Reminds Me*; R. M. Nixon, *Six Crises* (Garden City, N.Y., 1962); H. H. Humphrey, *The Education of a Public Man* (Garden City, N.Y., 1976); L. Baker, *The Johnson Eclipse* (New York, 1966); J. Witcover, *White Knight: The Rise of Spiro Agnew* (New York, 1972); M. Turner, *Finding a Policy Role for the Vice President: The Case of Nelson A. Rockefeller* (Ann Arbor, 1978); F. Lewis, *Mondale* (New York, 1980).
37. Feerick, *From Failing Hands* and *The Twenty-Fifth Amendment* (New York, 1976).

38. Williams, *The Rise of the Vice Presidency*, p. 71; N. W. Polsby, *Political Promises* (New York, 1974), p. 156; Rossiter, *The American Presidency*, p. 135.
39. Williams's *The Rise of the Vice Presidency* ends just prior to the 1956 campaign.

NOTES, CHAPTER 2

1. W. E. Leuchtenburg, *The Perils of Prosperity, 1914-32* (Chicago, 1958), p. 103.
2. Quoted in G. E. Mowry, *The Urban Nation* (New York, 1965), p. 45.
3. J. D. Hicks, *The Republican Ascendancy 1921-1933* (New York, 1960), p. 91.
4. W. E. Leuchtenburg, *Franklin D. Roosevelt and the New Deal* (New York, 1963), pp. 41-62, 143-66.
5. E. F. Goldman, *The Crucial Decade—And After* (New York, 1960), p. 292.
6. See Leuchtenburg, *Franklin D. Roosevelt and the New Deal*, pp. 231-38.
7. United States v. Carolene Products Co., 304 U.S. 144, 152 n. 4 (1938).
8. H. Kaufman, "The Growth of the Federal Personnel System," in *The Federal Government Service*, ed. W. Sayre (Englewood Cliffs, N.J., 1965), p. 42.
9. See S. H. Beer, "In Search of a New Public Philosophy," in *The New American Political System*, ed. A. King (Washington, D.C., 1978), pp. 6-9.
10. *Public Papers of the Presidents 1949*, p. 2.
11. *Public Papers of the Presidents 1953*, p. 785.
12. *U.S. News and World Report*, 3 August 1959, p. 71; *Vital Speeches* 25 (1958-1959):677-78.
13. See e.g., Goldman, *The Crucial Decade—And After*, pp. 64-66, 280-83, on Truman and Eisenhower; A. M. Schlesinger, Jr., *A Thousand Days* (Boston, 1965) on Kennedy.
14. M. Fiorina, *Congress—Keystone of the Washington Establishment* (New Haven, 1977), p. 92.

15. H. Heclo, "Issue Networks and the Executive Establishment," in *The New American Political System*, ed. King, pp. 89-91.
16. Leuchtenburg, *Franklin D. Roosevelt and the New Deal*, pp. 229-30.
17. G. Gallup, *The Gallup Poll: Public Opinion 1935-71*, 3 vols. (New York, 1972), 1:3, 35, 71, 144.
18. *Ibid.*, pp. 145, 154, 180, 184, 186, 220.
19. Quoted in F. R. Dulles, *America's Rise to World Power 1898-1954* (New York, 1955), p. 229.
20. *Public Papers of the Presidents 1947*, pp. 176-80.
21. N. H. Nie, S. Verba, and J. R. Petrocik, *The Changing American Voter* (Cambridge, 1976), pp. 100-103.
22. R. Wiebe, *The Segmented Society* (New York, 1975), p. 200.
23. *Public Papers of the Presidents 1961*, p. 1.
24. G. Reedy, "The Presidency in 1976: Focal Point of Political Unity?" *J. Pol.* 38 (1976):229.
25. See J. H. Ely, *Democracy and Distrust: A Theory of Judicial Review* (Cambridge, 1980).
26. Wiebe, *Segmented Society*, p. 200.
27. F. Greenstein, "What the President Means to Americans," in *Choosing the President*, ed. J. D. Barber (Englewood Cliffs, N.J., 1974), pp. 125-26, 129.
28. *Gallup Opinion Index*, January 1973, pp. 18-23; January 1974, pp. 16-17; January 1975, pp. 26-27; Gallup Poll news releases, 21 December 1978, 23 December 1979, 28 December 1980. No survey was issued for 1975 and 1976.
29. Gallup, *Public Opinion 1935-71*, 2:1560.
30. R. E. Neustadt, *Presidential Power* (New York, 1980), p. 44.
31. W. Johnson, "The American President and the Art of Communications," Inaugural Lecture at University of Oxford, England, 13 May 1958.
32. *Public Papers of the Presidents 1948*, pp. 1-10; *Public Papers of the Presidents 1955*, pp. 19, 167, 243-50; T. C. Sorensen, *Kennedy* (New York, 1965), pp. 427-33, 496-506; J. L. Sundquist, *Politics and Policy* (Washington, D.C., 1968).
33. A fifth new department was created in 1979, when Congress transferred HEW's education programs into a separate Depart-

ment of Education. The former HEW was reconstituted as the Department of Health and Human Services.

34. Neustadt, *Presidential Power*, p. 7.
35. S. Kelley, Jr., "Patronage and Presidential Legislative Leadership," in *The Presidency*, ed. A. Wildavsky (Boston, 1969), pp. 268-77.
36. R. G. Tugwell, "The President and His Helpers: A Review Article," *Pol. Sci. Q.* 82 (1967):253, 256.
37. S. Hess, *Organizing the Presidency* (Washington, D.C., 1976), pp. 27, 30-31.
38. President's Committee on Administrative Management, *Administrative Management in the Government of the United States*, p. 5.
39. R. Rose, *Managing Presidential Objectives* (New York, 1976), p. 41.
40. Hess, *Organizing the Presidency*, p. 9.
41. C. Rossiter, "The Constitutional Significance of the Executive Office of the President," *Am. Pol. Sci. Rev.* 43 (1949):1206, 1216.
42. Quoted in H. Seidman, *Politics, Position and Power*, 2nd ed. (New York, 1975), p. 77.
43. Tugwell, "The President and His Helpers," pp. 264-65.
44. See Seidman, *Politics, Position and Power*, pp. 1-37.
45. V. Vale, "The Collaborative Chaos of Federal Administration," *Govt. & Opp.* 8 (1973). See R. P. Nathan, *The Plot That Failed: Nixon and the Administrative Presidency* (New York, 1975), pp. 59-61.
46. See A. M. Schlesinger, Jr., *The Imperial Presidency* (Boston, 1973).
47. See H. C. Mansfield, Sr., ed., *Congress Against the President* (New York, 1975).
48. See D. Mayhew, *Congress—The Electoral Connection* (New Haven, 1974); T. Mann, *Unsafe at Any Margin* (Washington, D.C., 1978), pp. 3-4.
49. S. G. Patterson, "The Semi-Sovereign Congress," in *The New American Political System*, ed. King, pp. 169-71.
50. Fiorina, *Congress—Keystone*, pp. 56-67. See generally Patterson, "The Semi-Sovereign Congress," pp. 125-77.

51. Mayhew, *Congress—The Electoral Connection*, p. 62.
52. S. Kelley, Jr., *Professional Public Relations and Political Power* (Baltimore, 1956), p. 209.
53. *Ibid.*, pp. 202-35.
54. G. Pomper, "The Decline of the Party in American Elections," *Pol. Sci. Q.* 92 (1977):21, 39. See also Neustadt, *Presidential Power*, p. 176.
55. Sorensen, *Kennedy*, pp. 122-53.
56. See generally A. Ranney, *Participation in American Presidential Nominations, 1976* (Washington, 1977), pp. 20-26; A. Ranney, "Turnout and Representation in Presidential Primary Elections," *Am. Pol. Sci. Rev.* 66 (1972):21-37. Primaries are, however, as Ranney shows, unrepresentative in some respects.
57. See W. R. Keech and D. R. Matthews, *The Party's Choice* (Washington, D.C., 1976), pp. 22-27.
58. See L. Sabato, *Goodbye to Good-Time Charlie: The American Governor Transformed, 1950-1975* (Lexington, Mass., 1978).
59. See generally J. D. Barber, ed., *Race for the Presidency: The Media and the Nominating Process* (Englewood Cliffs, N.J., 1978).
60. W. G. Carleton, "The Revolution in the Presidential Nominating Convention," *Pol. Sci. Q.* 72 (1957):224, 233-35.
61. D. S. Collat, S. Kelley, Jr., and R. Rogowski, "Presidential Bandwagons" (Paper delivered at Annual Meeting of the American Political Science Association, Chicago, Ill., September 1976).
62. H. Nicholas, "The Insulation of the Presidency," *Govt. & Opp.* 8 (1973):158-63.
63. Quoted in O. L. Graham, Jr., *Toward a Planned Society* (New York, 1976), p. 319.
64. S. Lubell, *The Future of American Politics*, 2nd ed. (Garden City, N.Y., 1955), p. 37.
65. The Republicans controlled both Houses of Congress from 1947 to 1949 and from 1953 to 1955. They gained control of the Senate, though not the House of Representatives, in the 1980 elections.
66. R. L. Rubin, *Party Dynamics* (New York, 1976), pp. 107-43.
67. Nie, Verba, Petrocik, *The Changing American Voter*, p. 102.

68. P. Williams and G. K. Wilson, "The 1976 Election and the American Political System," *Pol. Stds.* 25 (1977):189.
69. Nie, Verba, Petrocik, *The Changing American Voter*, p. 83.
70. A. Campbell, P. E. Converse, W. E. Miller, and D. E. Stokes, *The American Voter* (New York, 1964).
71. Nie, Verba, Petrocik, *The Changing American Voter*, p. 47. See, for examples, R. W. Boyd, "Electoral Trends in Postwar Politics," in *Choosing the President*, ed. Barber; J. J. Kirkpatrick, "Changing Patterns of Electoral Competition," in *The New American Political System*, ed. King, pp. 268-74.
72. Nie, Verba, Petrocik, *The Changing American Voter*, p. 96.
73. S. Kelley, Jr. and T. W. Mirer, "The Simple Act of Voting," *Am. Pol. Sci. Rev.* 68 (1974):572-91.
74. Nie, Verba, Petrocik, *The Changing American Voter*, pp. 47-73.
75. W. D. Burnham, "Insulation and Responsiveness in Congressional Elections," *Pol. Sci. Q.* 90 (1975):411, 427-29.

NOTES, CHAPTER 3

1. See, for instance,· "Report of the Study Group on Vice-Presidential Selection," mimeographed (Institute of Politics, John F. Kennedy School of Government, Harvard University, 1976); A. M. Schlesinger, Jr., "On the Presidential Succession," *Pol. Sci. Q.* 89 (1974):484-85 (political considerations dominate).
2. For an excellent account, see J. M. Burns, *Roosevelt: The Lion and the Fox* (New York, 1956), pp. 428-30, 432.
3. *New York Times*, 30 July 1956, p. 1; letter, Humphrey to Representative Eugene McCarthy, 23 July 1956, Prepresidential Papers, Kennedy Library, Boston, Mass.
4. H. Humphrey, *The Education of a Public Man* (Garden City, N.Y., 1976), p. 188.
5. See T. C. Sorensen, *Kennedy* (New York, 1965), pp. 80-92; C.A.H. Thomson and F. M. Shattuck, *The 1956 Presidential Campaign* (Washington, D.C., 1960), pp. 154-55; H. S. Parmet, *Jack: The Struggles of John F. Kennedy* (New York, 1980), pp. 358-64.
6. Sorensen, *Kennedy*, pp. 82-83.

7. Letter, Sorensen to Schlesinger, 1 August 1956; letter, Sorensen to Kenneth Hechler, 31 July 1956; Prepresidential Papers, Kennedy Library, Boston, Mass.
8. Letter, Schlesinger to J. F. Kennedy, 6 July 1956, Prepresidential Papers, Kennedy Library, Boston, Mass. According to Nixon, John Kennedy privately supported him against Douglas, and gave him a $1000 contribution on behalf of Joseph P. Kennedy, Sr. (R. M. Nixon, *RN: The Memoirs of Richard Nixon* [New York, 1978], p. 75).
9. Letter, Shriver to J. P. Kennedy, Sr., 18 July 1956, Prepresidential Papers, Kennedy Library, Boston, Mass.
10. Sorensen, *Kennedy*, pp. 81, 88.
11. Letter, Thompson to Stevenson, 26 July 1956; letter, Boland to Stevenson, 31 July 1956; Prepresidential Papers, Kennedy Library, Boston, Mass.
12. Interview with Sidney M. Davis, former Kefauver aide, New York, N.Y., 1 October 1976.
13. See J. B. Gorman, *Kefauver: A Political Biography* (New York, 1971), pp. 249-65.
14. *Public Papers of the Presidents 1956*, p. 289.
15. E. J. Hughes, *The Ordeal of Power: A Political Memoir of the Eisenhower Years* (New York, 1963), p. 173.
16. *Time*, 5 March 1956, p. 22; *New York Times*, 27 July 1956, p. 5; *ibid.*, 28 July 1956, p. 1. For Nixon's account, see *RN: Memoirs*, pp. 166-76 and *Six Crises* (Garden City, N.Y., 1962), pp. 158-67; for Eisenhower's, see *Waging Peace* (Garden City, N.Y., 1965), pp. 6-10.
17. See G. Pomper, "The Nomination of Hubert Humphrey for Vice-President," *J. Pol.* 28 (1966):639; A. Eisele, *Almost to the Presidency* (Blue Earth, Minn., 1972), pp. 197-223.
18. P. Tillett, "The National Conventions," in *The National Election of 1964*, ed. M. C. Cummings, Jr. (Washington, D.C., 1966), p. 23; *New York Times*, 17 August 1964, p. 1.
19. *New York Times*, 4 August 1964, p. 1.
20. Corbin apparently was acting independently of Kennedy's wishes; see A. M. Schlesinger, Jr., *Robert Kennedy and His Times* (Boston, 1978), pp. 651-52.
21. Letter to Democratic members of the House of Representatives

from Representatives Mario Biaggi and Charles Rangel, 8 June 1976.

22. Letter to Republican members of House of Representatives from Representative Paul K. Findley, 22 July 1976.

23. See J. B. Martin, *Adlai Stevenson and the World* (Garden City, N.Y., 1978), pp. 349-52.

24. See Gorman, *Kefauver*, pp. 255-63; Thomson and Shattuck, *1956 Presidential Campaign*, p. 161.

25. *Public Papers of the Presidents 1955*, pp. 556-58; S. Adams, *Firsthand Report: The Story of the Eisenhower Administration* (New York, 1961), pp. 34-36.

26. J. B. Martin, *Adlai Stevenson of Illinois* (Garden City, N.Y., 1977), pp. 606-607.

27. See I. Hinderaker, "The 1960 Republican Convention: Chicago and Before," in *Inside Politics: The National Conventions, 1960,* ed. P. Tillett (Dobbs Ferry, N.Y., 1962). Representative Gerald R. Ford was among those backing Senator Thruston Morton. He concluded that Nixon had decided on Lodge in advance but pretended to be undecided; *A Time to Heal* (New York, 1979), pp. 72-73.

28. See T. H. White, *The Making of the President 1968* (New York, 1969); L. Chester, G. Hodgson, and B. Page, *An American Melodrama: The Presidential Campaign of 1968* (New York, 1969); J. Witcover, *White Knight: The Case of Spiro Agnew* (New York, 1972); The Ripon Society, *The Lessons of Victory* (New York, 1969).

29. Nixon, *RN: Memoirs*, pp. 312-13. Nixon claims that he offered the second spot to Finch and to Representative Rogers Morton of Maryland. Both declined.

30. U.S., Congress, Senate, Subcommittee on Constitutional Amendments of the Committee of the Judiciary, *Hearings on Examination of the First Implementation of Section Two of the Twenty-fifth Amendment*, 94th Cong., 1st sess., 1975, p. 127.

31. Nixon, *RN: Memoirs*, pp. 311-12.

32. Transcript of interview with J. Lindsay Almond, Jr., 5 February 1969, pp. 15-16, LBJ Oral History Project, Johnson Library, Austin, Texas.

33. See P. Potter, "How L.B.J. Got the Nomination," *The Reporter*, 18 June 1964, pp. 26-30.
34. L. F. O'Brien, *No Final Victories* (Garden City, N.Y., 1974), p. 84; A. M. Schlesinger, Jr., *A Thousand Days* (Boston, 1965); Schlesinger, *Robert Kennedy*, p. 208; P. Salinger, *With Kennedy* (Garden City, N.Y., 1966), p. 44; transcript of interview with Representative Hale Boggs, 13 March 1969, LBJ Oral History Project, Johnson Library, Austin, Texas.
35. Interview with Lawrence F. O'Brien, Johnson campaign manager, New York, N.Y., 29 September 1976; E. F. Goldman, *The Tragedy of Lyndon Johnson* (New York, 1969), pp. 201-202. Humphrey apparently had doubts; see *The Papers of Adlai E. Stevenson*, ed. W. E. Johnson, 8:584, 610.
36. Interview with William R. White, administrative assistant to Senator John Glenn, Washington, D.C., 22 September 1976.
37. *Newsweek*, 26 July 1976, p. 26; R. Reeves, *Convention* (New York, 1977), pp. 96-98; M. Schram, *Running for President 1976: The Carter Campaign* (New York, 1977), p. 208.
38. J. Witcover, *Marathon: The Pursuit of the Presidency 1972-1976* (New York, 1977), pp. 504-10.
39. See Griffin's comments in "Symposium on the Vice-Presidency," *Ford. L. Rev.* 45 (1977):725-26.
40. *St. Louis Post-Dispatch*, 5 December 1976, p. 7. See generally Ford, *A Time to Heal*, pp. 399-404; Witcover, *Marathon*, p. 505.
41. On the Eagleton selection, see R. Dougherty, *Goodbye, Mr. Christian* (Garden City, N.Y., 1973), pp. 150-58; G. W. Hart, *Right from the Start* (New York, 1973), pp. 238-45; G. L. Weil, *The Long Shot: George McGovern Runs for President* (New York, 1973); G. McGovern, *Grassroots: The Autobiography of George McGovern* (New York, 1977), pp. 188-201.
42. O'Brien, *No Final Victories*, p. 253.
43. Humphrey, *Education*, pp. 490-91; interview with Hon. Endicott Peabody, Humphrey associate, New York, N.Y., 3 December 1976. Peabody was the conduit for one of the messages.
44. Humphrey, *Education*, p. 391.
45. *Ibid.*, p. 491. T. C. Sorensen, *The Kennedy Legacy* (New York,

1969), p. 287. The Kennedys apparently were upset with Shriver for not actively supporting his brother-in-law, Robert Kennedy, for President that year.
46. Humphrey, *Education*, p. 391; G. Christian, *The President Steps Down* (New York, 1970), p. 156.
47. *Time*, 7 August 1972, p. 19. Reprinted by permission. Copyright Time Inc. 1972.
48. Nixon, *RN: Memoirs*, pp. 215-16.
49. *Public Papers of the Presidents 1963-64*, 2:919; L. B. Johnson, *The Vantage Point* (New York, 1971), pp. 98-101, 576-77; Humphrey, *Education*, pp. 298-99.
50. Nixon, *RN: Memoirs*, pp. 674-75.
51. *Newsweek*, 21 June 1976, pp. 18-19.
52. *Newsweek*, 26 July 1976, p. 26. See generally Witcover, *Marathon*, pp. 361-68.
53. Schlesinger, *Robert Kennedy*, pp. 206-207; H. Fairlie, *The Kennedy Promise: The Politics of Expectation* (Garden City, N.Y., 1973), pp. 49-50; Schlesinger, *A Thousand Days*, pp. 19, 27, 29.
54. Transcript of interview with Clark Clifford, 7 August 1969, pp. 2-4, LBJ Oral History Project, Johnson Library, Austin, Texas.
55. Transcript of interview with Orville Freeman, 14 February 1969, p. 8, LBJ Oral History Project, Johnson Library, Austin, Texas.
56. Transcript of interview with Senator Clinton Anderson, 14 April 1967, p. 27, JFK Oral History Project, Kennedy Library, Boston, Mass.
57. Schlesinger, *Robert Kennedy*, pp. 206-11.
58. Sorensen, *Kennedy*, pp. 163-64.
59. Transcript of interview with Representative Thomas "Tip" O'Neill, 28 January 1976, pp. 4-6, JFK Oral History Project, Kennedy Library, Boston, Mass. See also transcript of interview with Representative John McCormack, 30 March 1977, p. 29, JFK Oral History Project, Kennedy Library, Boston, Mass. (McCormack told Joseph Kennedy, Sr. that Johnson would accept the vice-presidential nomination.)
60. Schlesinger, *A Thousand Days*, p. 41. See also Schlesinger, *Robert Kennedy*, p. 206. Two other Kennedy aides have written that John Kennedy selected Johnson in order to remove him

from his position as Senate Majority Leader, see K. O'Donnell and D. Powers, *"Johnny, We Hardly Knew Ye"* (Boston, 1972), pp. 191-93. Schlesinger convincingly refutes this explanation in *Robert Kennedy*, p. 208.

61. Humphrey, *Education*, pp. 390-91.
62. Dougherty, *Goodbye, Mr. Christian*, p. 197; Hart, *Right from the Start*, pp. 242-43.
63. Hart, *Right from the Start*, pp. 238-43; Dougherty, *Goodbye, Mr. Christian*, pp. 150-58.
64. *New York Times*, 7 August 1976, p. 6; 14 August 1976, p. 14.
65. *St. Louis Post-Dispatch*, 20 August 1976, p. 11A. See generally Ford, *A Time to Heal*, pp. 401-404; Witcover, *Marathon*, pp. 504-10.
66. *New York Times*, 18 July 1980, p. 1; 17 July 1980, p. 1; *St. Louis Post-Dispatch*, 16 July 1980, p. 1; *Wall Street Journal*, 18 July 1980, p. 1.
67. "The Role of the Vice Presidency: On Choosing a Vice President," *Current*, October 1972, pp. 51-52. (Transcript of CBS News Special Report: Campaign '72—The Election Year: "On Choosing a Vice President," 6 August 1972. Reprinted by permission.)
68. Sorensen, *Kennedy*, pp. 162-65.
69. Interview with O'Brien, 29 September 1976.
70. Nixon, *Six Crises*, p. 317.
71. Nixon, *RN: Memoirs*, p. 216.
72. *Public Papers of the Presidents 1963-1964*, 2:1009; see also Goldman, *Tragedy of Lyndon Johnson*, pp. 231-32 on why Johnson did not select Robert Kennedy.
73. E. Hughes, *Newsweek*, 7 September 1964, p. 15; see also S. Alsop, *Saturday Evening Post*, 2 May 1964, p. 12.
74. *Life*, 14 August 1964, p. 68. Only Robert Kennedy and Stevenson were named more often as likely to be the best president.
75. "The Role of the Vice Presidency," *Current*, October 1972, p. 51.
76. Governor Richard Hughes, for instance, was a Catholic governor of an urban state.
77. *Newsweek*, 26 July 1976, p. 28. See generally Witcover, *Marathon*, pp. 359-68.

78. Henry Wallace of Iowa in 1940.
79. Ford did eliminate Ruckelshaus, however, partly because he came from Indiana, a neighboring state to Michigan; Ford, *A Time to Heal*, p. 402.
80. D. Young, *American Roulette: The History and Dilemma of the Vice Presidency* (New York, 1972), p. 311.
81. Interview with O'Brien, 29 September 1976.
82. *Newsweek*, 7 September 1964, p. 15.
83. Letter to the author from Roan Conrad, manager NBC News Election Coverage, 6 October 1976.
84. Of course, Eisenhower's military career gave him valuable experience in foreign and defense matters.
85. Agnew in 1968 was the exception.
86. Agnew and Shriver had not.
87. Muskie, Agnew, Eagleton, and Mondale.
88. Lodge, Shriver, and Bush.
89. Humphrey and Agnew.

NOTES, CHAPTER 4

1. R. M. Nixon, *Six Crises* (Garden City, N.Y., 1962), p. 76. Nixon acknowledges that the second candidate helps "to stir up the party faithful."
2. B. N. Timmons, *Garner of Texas* (New York, 1948), pp. 168-70, 210.
3. T. C. Reeves, "Chester A. Arthur and the Campaign of 1880," *Pol. Sci. Q.* 84 (1969):628-37.
4. S. Kelley, Jr., "Campaign Propaganda in Perspective," in *The President: Rex, Princeps, Imperator?*, ed. J. M. Ray (El Paso, 1969), p. 60.
5. See e.g., R. Bendiner, *The Reporter*, 9 February 1956, p. 11.
6. See e.g., *Newsweek*, 8 August 1960, pp. 18-20.
7. See, for instance, *New Republic*, 8 August 1964, pp. 3-4; E. Hughes, *Newsweek*, 7 September 1964, p. 15.
8. L. Chester, G. Hodgson, B. Page, *American Melodrama* (New York, 1969), p. 718; see also M. H. Bloom, *Public Relations and Presidential Campaigns: A Crisis in Democracy* (New York, 1973), p. 234.

9. H. Humphrey, *The Education of a Public Man* (Garden City, N.Y., 1976), p. 392.
10. *New York Times*, 29 September 1968, p. 10E.
11. *Washington Post*, 18 July 1976, p. C7.
12. See e.g., *Wall Street Journal*, 31 August 1976, p. 10; *Newsweek*, 25 October 1976, p. 36.
13. The Democrats chose octagenarian Henry Davis in 1904 because they hoped he would contribute a sizeable part of his fortune to the party's cause. He did not. I. G. Williams, *The Rise of the Vice Presidency* (Washington, D.C., 1956), pp. 87-88; D. Young, *American Roulette* (New York, 1972), p. 124.
14. See D. Adamany and G. Agree, "Election Campaign Financing: The 1974 Reforms," *Pol. Sci. Q.* 90 (1975):201-20.
15. Interview with William Josephson, Shriver vice-presidential campaign manager, New York, N.Y., 28 September 1976.
16. *Washington Post*, 23 August 1976, p. A9. See also D. Broder, *Washington Post*, 26 September 1976, p. C7. P. Williams and G. K. Wilson, "The 1976 Election and the American Political System," *Pol. Stds.* 25 (1977):188. See, for instance, comments of Clarence Mitchell in "Symposium on the Vice-Presidency," *Ford. L. Rev.* 45 (1977):748; *Wall Street Journal*, 31 August 1976, p. 10.
17. N. W. Polsby and A. Wildavsky, *Presidential Elections*, 3rd ed. (New York, 1971), p. 148; Nixon, *Six Crises*, p. 76; Nixon, *RN: Memoirs* (New York, 1978), p. 112.
18. J. B. Gorman, *Kefauver* (New York, 1971), p. 343.
19. *St. Louis Post-Dispatch*, 19 August 1976, p. 13A.
20. *New York Times*, 10 September 1980, p. B7; see also *St. Louis Post-Dispatch*, 18 September 1980, pp. 1, 10 (meeting with Kennedy supporters).
21. T. C. Sorensen, *Kennedy* (New York, 1965), pp. 187-88; C. M. Brauer, *John F. Kennedy and the Second Reconstruction* (New York, 1977), pp. 53-54; transcript of interview with Charles Boatner, special aide to Vice President Johnson, 17 December 1968, LBJ Oral History Project, Johnson Library, Austin, Texas.
22. Interview with Josephson.
23. See also acceptance speech of R. Sargent Shriver, delivered

before Democratic National Committee, Washington, D.C., 8 August 1972.

24. *New York Times*, 24 September 1972, p. 46; see also *ibid.*, 21 October 1972, p. 17 (Representative Wayne Hays, though critical of McGovern, backs Shriver).

25. Sorenson, *Kennedy*, p. 187

26. Louis Harris, A Study of the Presidential Election in Texas in 1960, 14 September 1960; A Study of the Presidential Election of 1960 in Tennessee, 20 September 1960, Robert F. Kennedy Pre-Administration Political Files, Kennedy Library, Boston, Mass.

27. S. Kelley, Jr., "The Presidential Campaign," in *The National Election of 1964*, ed. M. C. Cummings, Jr. (Washington, D.C., 1966), pp. 66, 76; Kelley, "The Presidential Campaign," in *The Presidential Election and Transition, 1960-61*, ed. P. David (Washington, D.C., 1961), p. 72.

28. L. F. O'Brien, *No Final Victories* (Garden City, N.Y., 1974), p. 90; A. M. Schlesinger, Jr., *A Thousand Days* (Boston, 1965), p. 703; Brauer, *John F. Kennedy and the Second Reconstruction*, p. 58.

29. R. Amper, *New York Times*, 30 September 1956, V:5. See generally, C.A.H. Thomson and F. M. Shattuck, *The 1956 Presidential Campaign* (Washington, D.C., 1960), pp. 253, 352; Gorman, *Kefauver*, pp. 269-272, 282.

30. Kelley, "The Presidential Campaign," in *The National Election of 1964*, p. 66.

31. *Ibid.*, pp. 66, 76; Kelley, "The Presidential Campaign," in *The Presidential Election and Transition 1960-61*, p. 72.

32. *New York Times*, 10 October 1980, p. 9.

33. Interview with Josephson.

34. See e.g., "Acceptance Speech of Walter F. Mondale," 15 July 1976, *Congressional Quarterly*, 17 July 1976, pp. 1935, 1939; *New York Times*, 15 September 1976, p. 33 (Mondale generally follows Carter's lead although he and Carter differed regarding some Supreme Court decisions).

35. *New York Times*, 13 September 1980, p. 10.

36. See N. H. Nie, S. Verba, J. R. Petrocik, *The Changing American Voter* (Cambridge, 1976).

37. M. Greenfield, *Newsweek*, 16 August 1976, p. 80.

38. 19 *Vital Speeches* 11, 14-15 (1952-53).
39. *New York Times,* 7 September 1956, pp. 1, 10.
40. W. Blair, *New York Times,* 7 October 1956, p. 67.
41. *New York Times,* 31 October 1956, p. 26.
42. *New York Times Magazine,* 23 October 1960, pp. 19, 114.
43. See P. E. Converse, A. Campbell, W. E. Miller, and D. E. Stokes, "Stability and Change in 1960: A Reinstating Election," *Am. Pol. Sci. Rev.* 55 (1961):269-80; V. O. Key, Jr., "Interpreting the Election Results," in *Presidential Election and Transition 1960-61,* ed. David, pp. 174-75.
44. Transcript of interview with Orville Freeman, 14 February 1969, LBJ Oral History Project, Johnson Library, Austin, Texas.
45. R. Evans, Jr. and R. D. Novak, *Lyndon B. Johnson: The Exercise of Power* (New York, 1966), pp. 301, 299.
46. *New York Times,* 18 October 1964, p. 58; *ibid.,* 18 September 1964, p. 21; *ibid.,* 15 September 1964, p. 20; *ibid.,* 6 September 1964, p. 1.
47. *Ibid.,* 27 September 1964, p. 66; *ibid.,* 18 October 1964, p. 56.
48. *Ibid.,* 29 September 1968, p. 74; *ibid.,* 13 October 1968, p. 68.
49. *Ibid.,* 6 August 1972, p. 28; *Newsweek,* 16 October 1972, p. 29. See also *New York Times,* 25 October 1972, p. 33; 30 October 1972, p. 22.
50. "Acceptance Speech of Spiro T. Agnew," Republican National Convention, Miami Beach, Fla., 23 August 1972, *New York Times,* 24 August 1972, p. 47.
51. *New York Times,* 16 October 1976, p. 8; *ibid.,* 27 October 1976, p. 1.
52. *Ibid.,* 16 September 1976, p. 32; *Wall Street Journal,* 31 August 1976, p. 10.
53. A. Hunt, *Wall Street Journal,* 24 September 1980, p. 30; *New York Times,* 2 September 1980, p. B8; *ibid.,* 11 September 1980, p. D18 (Carter's refusal to debate Reagan and Anderson together).
54. *New York Times,* 1 November 1980, p. 9.
55. See D. A. Graber, "Press Coverage and Voter Reaction in the 1968 Presidential Election," *Pol. Sci. Q.* 89 (1974):80.

56. Nixon, *Six Crises*, p. 77. See also Nixon, *RN: Memoirs*, p. 112. ("Everywhere I went I blasted the Democrats, linking Stevenson with Truman and Acheson and asking how the same people who had created the mess in Washington could be expected to clean it up.")
57. *New York Times*, 3 September 1952, p. 19.
58. Quoted in S. Kelley, Jr., *Professional Public Relations and Political Power* (Baltimore, 1956), p. 186.
59. *New York Times*, 10 October 1952, p. 19; *ibid.*, 11 October 1952, p. 11; *ibid.*, 9 October 1952, p. 25.
60. *Ibid.*, 12 October 1952, p. 68. Quoted in E. Mazo and S. Hess, *Nixon: A Political Portrait* (New York, 1968), p. 92.
61. G. Gallup, *The Gallup Poll: Public Opinion, 1935-71*, 2:1115.
62. *New York Times*, 13 September 1956, p. 22.
63. Press Release, Republican National Committee, 8 October 1956. See generally Nixon, *RN: Memoirs*, pp. 176-79. *New York Times*, 3 October 1956, p. 1; *ibid.*, 31 October 1956, p. 26; *ibid.*, 1 November 1956, p. 34.
64. *New York Times*, 18 August 1956, p. 1.
65. *Ibid.*, 26 September 1956, p. 1.
66. Gorman, *Kefauver*, pp. 268-72.
67. *New York Times*, 30 October 1956, p. 32.
68. *Ibid.*, 20 September 1956, p. 25.
69. *Ibid.*, 26 October 1960, p. 31.
70. *Ibid.*, 23 September 1964, pp. 1, 24; *ibid.*, 27 September 1964, p. 66 (linking Johnson and Bobby Baker); *ibid.*, 17 October 1964, p. 14.
71. *Ibid.*, 9 September 1964, p. 25. See also *ibid.*, 6 September 1964, p. 44 (Senator Mike Mansfield and Speaker John Mc-Cormack criticizing Miller).
72. *Ibid.*, 16 October 1964, p. 24; *ibid.*, 18 September 1964, p. 21; *ibid.*, 13 September 1964, p. 68; *ibid.*, 18 September 1964, p. 21; see also 1 October 1964, p. 22; *ibid.*, 2 October 1964, p. 20; *ibid.*, 15 September 1964, p. 20.
73. *Ibid.*, 11 September 1968, p. 1; *ibid.*, 10 August 1968, p. 1.
74. J. Wooten, *New York Times*, 26 September 1972, p. 36.
75. *New York Times*, 9 September 1972, p. 10; *ibid.*, 19 October 1972, p. 53.

76. Referred to in letter of Senator Robert Dole to Senator George McGovern, 7 October 1972. See also *New York Times*, 29 October 1972, p. 53 (Nixon had "dillydallied" regarding Vietnam peace prospects).
77. *New York Times*, 3 October 1976, p. 33; *International Herald Tribune*, 18 October 1976, pp. 6-7; *New York Times*, 26 October 1976, p. 27. See also *ibid.*, 16 October 1976, pp. 1, 8-9. Dole later modified his stand; see *ibid.*, 27 October 1976, p. 1.
78. *St. Louis Post-Dispatch*, 5 August 1980, p. 1. See also Germond and Witcover, *Boston Globe*, 21 August 1980, p. 19. *New York Times*, 2 September 1980, p. B8; see Hunt, *Wall Street Journal*, 24 September 1980, p. 30; *New York Times*, 25 September 1980, p. B10; *ibid.*, 26 September 1980, p. A18; *ibid.*, 10 October 1980, p. 9.
79. *Ibid.*, 10 September 1980, p. B7; *ibid.*, 11 September 1980, p. D18; *ibid.*, 24 September 1980, p. 26; *ibid.*, 27 September 1980, p. 8; see also *ibid.*, 3 September 1980, p. B10 (accusing Mondale of being a hatchet man).

NOTES, CHAPTER 5

1. See, for instance, H. Humphrey, "On the Threshold of the White House," *Atlantic Monthly*, July 1974, p. 65.
2. N. Polsby and A. Wildavsky, *Presidential Elections*, 3rd ed. (New York, 1971), p. 157.
3. A. M. Schlesinger, Jr., "On the Presidential Succession," *Pol. Sci. Q.* 89 (1974):483-84.
4. G. Gallup, *The Gallup Poll: Public Opinion, 1935-71*, 3 vols. (New York, 1972), 3:2284. The poll also reported that 71 percent could identify Mayor John V. Lindsay, 42 percent Senator George McGovern, 23 percent Senator Birch Bayh, and 11 percent Senator Harold Hughes.
5. *Ibid.*, 2:1175, 1508, 1525, 1428.
6. *Ibid.*, pp. 1508, 1525.
7. See C. Thomson, "Mass Media Activities and Influence," in *The Presidential Election and Transition, 1960-61*, ed. P. David (Washington, D.C., 1961), p. 94.

8. Gallup, *Public Opinion, 1935-71*, 2:1580.
9. *Ibid.*
10. Miller was so little recognized that he has been able to trade on his anonymity in American Express television commercials. Mondale's recognition ranged from 26 percent to 37 percent in Gallup Polls taken between June 1973 and May 1975; G. Gallup, *The Gallup Poll: Public Opinion, 1972-77*, 2 vols. (Wilmington, Del., 1978), 1:137, 384, 499.
11. Muskie's 76 percent recognition in the January 1971 poll was due largely to exposure in the 1968 campaign.
12. *Wall Street Journal*, 15 October 1976, p. 1.
13. Gallup, *Public Opinion, 1935-71*, 1:467. A poll taken two months earlier found that 64 percent of British citizens could identify Truman and 62 percent, Bricker; see *ibid.*, pp. 457, 754, 2:1085.
14. Quoted in Kelley, "The Presidential Campaign," in *The Presidential Election and Transition 1960-61*, p. 67.
15. T. H. White, *The Making of the President 1968* (New York, 1969), p. 419.
16. *Public Papers of the Presidents 1968*, 2:1027.
17. T. Lippman, Jr. and D. Hansen, *Muskie* (New York, 1971), p. 18.
18. M. Schram, *Running for President 1976: The Carter Campaign* (New York, 1977), p. 330.
19. *New York Times*, 29 October 1976, p. 18.
20. I am grateful to Mr. Tony Schwartz, the producer of this commercial, for playing the commercial for me and discussing it with me. Excerpts are reprinted here with his permission.
21. Gallup, *Public Opinion, 1935-71*, 2:1437. Some 30 percent thought Eisenhower likely to have another heart attack within four years while another 38 percent thought it impossible to predict.
22. *New York Times*, 14 August 1956, pp. 1, 14; *ibid.*, 18 August 1956, p. 1; *ibid.*, 18 October 1956, p. 1.
23. *Ibid.*, 4 November 1956, p. 1; *ibid.*, 6 November 1956, p. 1.
24. *Ibid.*, 6 September 1964, p. 1; *ibid.*, 15 October 1964, p. 25.
25. Press Release, Republican National Committee, 30 October 1964.

26. *Ibid.*, 28 October 1964.
27. I am grateful to Mr. Tony Schwartz, the producer of these commercials, for playing them for me and discussing them with me. Excerpts are reprinted here with his permission.
28. See *New York Times*, 29 October 1968, p. 31; *ibid.*, 30 October 1968, p. 34; *ibid.*, 31 October 1968, p. 37; *ibid.*, 1 November 1968, p. 27; *ibid.*, 2 November 1968, p. 19.
29. Quoted in Schram, *Running for President 1976*, p. 267.
30. See *Time*, 7 August 1972; *Newsweek*, 7 August 1972.
31. *New York Times*, 3 December 1960, p. 13.
32. See C.A.H. Thomson and F. M. Shattuck, *The 1956 Presidential Campaign* (Washington, D.C., 1960), pp. 339-40.
33. Transcript, "Meet the Press," 3 January 1960.
34. C. D. Tubbesing, "Vice Presidential Candidates and the Home State Advantage: Or 'Tom Who?' Was Tom Eagleton in Missouri," *W. Pol. Q.* 26 (1973):702-16.
35. L. Harris, "A Survey of the Presidential Election in Texas in 1960," 14 September 1960, Robert Kennedy Pre-Administration Political Files, Kennedy Library, Boston, Mass.
36. Survey Research Center, 1964 and 1972 National Election Studies, University Consortium for Political Research.
37. E. J. Hughes, *The Ordeal of Power: A Political Memoir of the Eisenhower Years* (New York, 1963), p. 183.
38. Gallup, *Public Opinion, 1935-71*, 2:1415-16. (Interviews occurred in the spring before the tickets were established.)
39. *Newsweek*, 7 October 1968, p. 32.
40. *Time*, 7 August 1972, p. 12; *Newsweek*, 7 August 1972, p. 13.
41. *New York Times*, 29 October 1976, p. 18. P. Williams and G. K. Wilson, "The 1976 Election and the American Political System," *Pol. Stds.* 25 (1977):187. Gallup, *Public Opinion, 1972-77*, 2:911, 922.
42. *New York Times*, 5 September 1964, p. 6; *Time*, 15 November 1976, p. 35; *Newsweek*, 4 November 1968, p. 29; *Washington Post*, 4 October 1972, pp. A1, 20.

NOTES, CHAPTER 6

1. I do not discuss those duties that are essentially ceremonial.

2. C. F. Adams, ed., *The Works of John Adams*, 10 vols. (Boston, 1850-1856), 1:460.
3. J. D. Feerick, *From Failing Hands* (New York, 1965), p. 70.
4. Thomas Jefferson, *The Writings of Thomas Jefferson*, ed. P. L. Ford (New York, 1896), 7:120, 98-99.
5. Feerick, *From Failing Hands*, p. 115 (Wilson); D. Young, *American Roulette* (New York, 1972), p. 119 (Roosevelt).
6. See C. O. Paullin, "The Vice-President and the Cabinet," *Am. Hist. Rev.* 29 (1924):496-500; C. Coolidge, *The Autobiography of Calvin Coolidge* (New York, 1929), p. 163.
7. J. M. Burns, *Roosevelt: The Soldier of Freedom* (New York, 1970), pp. 341-42; C. Hull, *The Memoirs of Cordell Hull* (New York, 1948), 2:1585-86.
8. H. S. Truman, *Year of Decisions, 1945* (Garden City, N.Y., 1955), p. 55.
9. U.S., Congress, Senate, Subcommittee on Reorganization of the Committee on Government Operations, *Hearings on Administrative Vice President*, 84th Cong., 2nd sess., 1956, p. 60 (testimony of Clark Clifford).
10. See A. W. Barkley, *That Reminds Me* (Garden City, N.Y., 1954).
11. Jefferson, *Writings*, 7:120.
12. Quoted in Williams, *The Rise of the Vice-Presidency*, p. 93.
13. *New York Times*, 11 December 1918, p. 1.
14. Truman, *Year of Decisions, 1945*, p. 197.
15. D. D. Eisenhower, *Waging Peace* (Garden City, N.Y., 1965), p. 6.
16. R. M. Nixon, *Six Crises* (Garden City, N.Y., 1962), pp. 184-85.
17. Quoted in B. N. Timmons, *Garner of Texas* (New York, 1948), p. 176.
18. Press release, Walter F. Mondale's Office, February 18, 1981, p. 4 (edited text of lecture at University of Minnesota on the Vice Presidency).
19. See generally Williams, *The Rise of the Vice-Presidency*, pp. 24-26, 34, 40-43, 52-53, 64-67, 69-70, 81-83, 88-90, 133-40, 145-47.
20. T. R. Marshall, *Recollections of Thomas R. Marshall, Vice President and Hoosier Philosopher* (Indianapolis, 1925), p. 368.

21. A. M. Schlesinger, Jr., "On the Presidential Succession," *Pol. Sci. Q.* 89 (1974):479.
22. Quoted in Williams, *The Rise of the Vice-Presidency*, p. 82.
23. See chapter two.
24. Interview with Nixon, *U.S. News and World Report*, 16 May 1960, pp. 98-99; interview with Agnew, *U.S. News and World Report*, 6 October 1969, p. 33.
25. U.S., Congress, 121 *Cong. Rec.* 639 (1975).
26. *National Journal*, 11 March 1978, p. 383. Johnson generally presided over the Senate for a brief period during the "morning hour." P. T. David, "The Vice-Presidency," *J. Pol.* 29 (1967):737. See also H. McPherson, *A Political Education* (Boston, 1972), p. 184.
27. See U.S., Congress, Senate, Committee on Rules and Administration, *Standing Rules of the United States Senate.*
28. 109 *Cong. Rec.* 1214 (1963).
29. H. B. Learned, "Casting Votes of the Vice-Presidents, 1789-1915," *Am. Hist. Rev.* 20 (1915):571-76.
30. See comments of George Reedy, "Symposium on the Vice-Presidency," *Ford. L. Rev.* 45 (1977):740-41.
31. For a historical discussion, see 113 *Cong. Rec.* 910-18 (1967).
32. 103 *Cong. Rec.* 178 (1957); 107 *Cong. Rec.* 9, 920 (1961) (remarks of Senators Kuchel and Javits). For two different views on the importance of Nixon's opinion, see "Symposium on the Vice-Presidency," pp. 740-41 (see comments of G. Reedy and C. Mitchell). 105 *Cong. Rec.* 8-9 (1959); 107 *Cong. Rec.* 9 (1961).
33. 109 *Cong. Rec.* 186 (1963).
34. 109 *Cong. Rec.* 1411, 1218, 1229, 1412, 1219, 2062 (1963).
35. 113 *Cong. Rec.* 918 (1967).
36. 115 *Cong. Rec.* 593, 995 (1969).
37. 117 *Cong. Rec.* 618 (1971).
38. See *Congressional Quarterly*, 1 March 1975, pp. 448-61.
39. H. H. Humphrey, "Changes in the Vice Presidency," *Cur. Hist.* 67 (1974):58-59.
40. E. F. Goldman, *Tragedy of Lyndon Johnson* (New York, 1969), pp. 261-64.
41. H. Kissinger, *White House Years* (Boston, 1979), p. 713.

42. Quoted in D. Kearns, *Lyndon Johnson and the American Dream* (New York, 1976), p. 164. Kennedy, according to his friend, Benjamin C. Bradlee, liked and respected Johnson, "[b]ut there are times . . . when LBJ's simple presence seems to bug him." B. C. Bradlee, *Conversations with Kennedy* (New York, 1975), p. 194.
43. Schlesinger, "On the Presidential Succession," p. 479.
44. See chapter eleven.
45. For a discussion of Nixon's and Johnson's personalities, and of presidential personality generally, see J. D. Barber, *Presidential Character*, 2nd ed. (Englewood Cliffs, N.J., 1977).
46. Interview with Senator Birch Bayh, Washington, D.C., 27 September 1977; telephone interview with Richard Moe, Mondale's chief of staff, 29 January 1981 (attributing Mondale's role to "the relationship between the two principals"). See also Humphrey's comments in "The Role of the Vice Presidency: On Choosing a Vice President," *Current*, October 1972, p. 51.
47. Schlesinger, *Robert Kennedy and His Times* (Boston, 1978), pp. 621-22; "Symposium on the Vice-Presidency," p. 750 (comments of Schlesinger and Reedy). Letter, Johnson to J. F. Kennedy, 9 January 1962; letter, Johnson to J. F. Kennedy, 30 August 1963; memo, Ralph A. Dungan to J. F. Kennedy, 3 October 1962; letter, Philip Graham to J. F. Kennedy, 5 October 1962, President's Office File, Kennedy Library, Boston, Mass. McPherson, *A Political Education*, p. 191; Kearns, *Lyndon Johnson*, pp. 160-69; "Symposium on the Vice-Presidency," p. 750 (comments of Schlesinger and Reedy); T. C. Sorensen, *Kennedy Legacy* (New York, 1969), p. 109. Schlesinger, *A Thousand Days* (Boston, 1965), pp. 703-704.
48. See Humphrey, *The Education of a Public Man* (Garden City, N.Y., 1976), p. 427; telephone interview with Moe, 29 January 1981.
49. S. Hess, *Organizing the Presidency* (Washington, D.C., 1976), p. 94. The relationship between Johnson and Attorney General Robert Kennedy was cool. See e.g., Schlesinger, *Robert Kennedy*, pp. 646-49.
50. Humphrey, *Education*, pp. 408, 427.
51. D. Rather and G. Gates, *The Palace Guard* (New York, 1974),

p. 256; H. S. Dent, *The Prodigal South Returns to Power* (New York, 1978), pp. 267-68.

52. M. Turner, *Finding a Policy Role for the Vice President: The Case of Nelson A. Rockefeller* (Ann Arbor, 1978), pp. 296-99; J. J. Casserly, *The Ford White House* (Boulder, 1977), p. 160; R. Nessen, *It Sure Looks Different From the Inside* (Chicago, 1978), p. 154; G. R. Ford, *A Time to Heal* (New York, 1979), pp. 234-35; R. T. Hartmann, *Palace Politics: An Inside Account of the Ford Years* (New York, 1980), pp. 306-10.

53. *Washington Post*, 30 December 1976, p. A2; *Time*, 23 May 1977, p. 32; Brower, *The New York Times Magazine*, 5 June 1977, pp. 39-40; *National Journal*, 8 January 1977, p. 78.

54. Interview with Moe, Washington, D.C., 28 September 1977.

55. Telephone interview with Moe, 29 January 1981.

56. *Ibid.*; telephone interview with Albert A. Eisele, Mondale's press secretary, 13 January 1981. There was one exception; see chapter seven.

57. Telephone interview with Moe, 29 January 1981; *National Journal*, 3 February 1979, p. 189; 31 March 1979, p. 538; 1 December 1979, p. 2014.

NOTES, CHAPTER 7

1. A. M. Schlesinger, Jr., "On the Presidential Succession," *Pol. Sci. Q.* 89 (1974):481.

2. See D. Kearns, *Lyndon Johnson* (New York, 1976), p. 163.

3. D. D. Eisenhower, *Mandate for Change* (Garden City, N.Y., 1963), p. 236.

4. Memorandum, Bill Moyers and G. W. Siegel to Lyndon Johnson, 22 December 1960, Civil Rights, Papers of LBJ as VP, Johnson Library, Austin, Texas.

5. R. M. Nixon, *Six Crises* (Garden City, N.Y., 1962) and *RN: Memoirs* (New York, 1978); *U.S. News and World Report*, 16 May 1960, pp. 98-106.

6. *Public Papers of the Presidents 1961*, p. 150.

7. *The Reporter*, 17 January 1963, p. 29.

8. *Public Papers of the Presidents 1962*, pp. 8, 826; *Public Papers of the Presidents 1961*, pp. 256-57.

9. Transcript of interview with Hobart Taylor, Jr., 6 January 1969, p. 14, LBJ Oral History Project, Johnson Library, Austin, Texas.
10. Memorandum, Moyers and Siegel to Johnson, p. 3.
11. Transcript of interview with Roy Wilkins, 1 April 1969, p. 5, LBJ Oral History Project, Johnson Library, Austin, Texas.
12. Letter, James E. Webb to Johnson, 13 April 1961; letter, Harris L. Wofford to Johnson, 21 April, 1961, Civil Rights File, Vice Presidential Papers, Johnson Library, Austin, Texas.
13. Transcript of interview with Whitney Young, 18 June 1969, p. 4, LBJ Oral History Project, Johnson Library, Austin, Texas.
14. Letter, Horton to R. F. Kennedy, 4 June 1963, Burke Marshall Papers, Kennedy Library, Boston, Mass.
15. Schlesinger, *Robert Kennedy and His Times* (Boston, 1978), pp. 312-13, 335-36.
16. *The Reporter*, 17 January 1963, p. 29.
17. Transcript of interview with Taylor, p. 21. Robert Kennedy regarded Johnson and Taylor as ineffective; see Schlesinger, *Robert Kennedy*, p. 313.
18. Transcript of interview with W. Young, p. 4.
19. *Public Papers of the Presidents 1961*, pp. 253-54.
20. J. Deakin, *New Republic*, 29 May 1965, p. 10.
21. H. H. Humphrey, *The Education of a Public Man* (Garden City, N.Y., 1976), pp. 407-408.
22. Speech reprinted in 113 *Cong. Rec.* 6316 (1967).
23. *Public Papers of the Presidents 1965*, 2:1017-19.
24. 111 *Cong. Rec.* 25141 (1965).
25. Transcript of interview with W. Young, p. 11.
26. Humphrey, *Education*, p. 408.
27. *New York Times*, 18 January 1969, p. 13; *Public Papers of the Presidents 1969*, p. 96.
28. Interview with Agnew, *U.S. News and World Report*, 6 October 1969, p. 35; interview with Rockefeller, *ibid.*, 13 October 1975, p. 53. H. Seidman, *Politics, Position and Power* (New York, 1975), p. 181.
29. R. Reeves, *A Ford, Not a Lincoln* (London, 1975), pp. 44-58. See generally, G. R. Ford, *A Time to Heal* (New York, 1979), pp. 113-23.
30. See generally M. Turner, *Finding a Policy Role for the Vice*

President: The Case of Nelson A. Rockefeller (Ann Arbor, 1978), pp. 100-122.

31. *Congressional Quarterly,* 26 July 1975, p. 1617.
32. Interview with Rockefeller, *U.S. News and World Report,* 13 October 1975, p. 52.
33. Turner, *Finding a Policy Role for the Vice President,* pp. 254-57.
34. *Ibid.,* pp. 252-54. Rockefeller's chairmanship of the Water Quality Commission antedated his vice presidency.
35. Interview with Richard Moe, Mondale's chief of staff, 28 September 1977. Mondale did chair a high-level task force on youth unemployment; see *Public Papers of the Presidents 1978,* pp. 960-61.
36. Interview with Mondale, *National Journal,* 11 March 1978, p. 379.
37. "Symposium on the Vice-Presidency," *Ford. L. Rev.* 45 (1977):738.
38. Quoted in B. Brower, "The Remaking of the Vice President," *New York Times Magazine,* 5 June 1977, p. 42. Rockefeller also foresaw this danger; see Turner, *Finding a Policy Role for the Vice President,* pp. 251-52, 255-56.
39. C. M. Brauer, *John F. Kennedy and the Second Reconstruction* (New York, 1977), p. 80.
40. Letter, McGeorge Bundy to Bowles, 31 January 1965; memorandum, Jack Valenti to Johnson, 24 February 1965; memorandum, Valenti to Johnson, 7 March 1966; memorandum, Johnson to Valenti, 5 March 1966; memorandum, Hayes Redman, 17 November 1966, WHCF, Ex C.F. 440, FG 440, Sp/WE9, Johnson Library, Austin, Texas.
41. Humphrey, "Changes in the Vice Presidency," *Cur. Hist.* 67 (1974):59.
42. See interview with Nixon, *U.S. News and World Report,* 16 May 1960, pp. 100-101; Humphrey, *Education,* p. 415; *New York Times,* 21 December 1980, p. 32 (Mondale).
43. For Nixon's account, see Nixon, *Six Crises,* pp. 235-91 and *RN: Memoirs,* pp. 203-13.
44. *New York Times,* 9 August 1962, p. 6; *ibid.,* 9 September 1962, pp. 1, 18.

45. *Newsweek*, 17 April 1967, pp. 56-57.
46. *Washington Post*, 9 January 1977, p. A1.
47. *Ibid.*, 24 January 1977, p. 1.
48. *Washington Post*, 18 May 1977, p. A17; 22 May 1977, p. A2; 21 May 1977, p. A7.
49. *Time*, 16 July 1956, p. 14.
50. Nixon, *RN: Memoirs*, pp. 181-83.
51. U.S., Department of State, *Bulletin*, 4 September 1961, pp. 391-95.
52. 107 *Cong. Rec.* 16708, 16710, 16434 (1961).
53. Nixon, *RN: Memoirs*, pp. 119-37.
54. M. Panter-Downes, "Frontiersman in Asia," *New Yorker*, 13 December 1958, p. 120.
55. R. Trumbull, *New York Times*, 20 May 1961, p. 3. On Johnson's popularity on his trip to Asia, see Kearns, *Lyndon Johnson*, p. 168.
56. W. Lippmann, *Newsweek*, 24 April 1967, p. 23.
57. *Newsweek*, 4 January 1954, pp. 17-18.
58. *Public Papers of the Presidents 1961*, p. 354.
59. *New York Times*, 12 May 1961, p. 2; *ibid.*, 13 May 1961, p. 1.
60. Halberstam, *The Best and the Brightest* (New York, 1969), p. 134; memorandum, Johnson to J. F. Kennedy, 23 May 1961; President's Office File, Kennedy Library, Boston, Mass.
61. Humphrey, *Education*, pp. 332, 335, 336-37; Halberstam, *The Best and the Brightest*, pp. 535-36; see memorandum, Humphrey to Johnson, 3 March 1966, U.S., Department of State, *Bulletin*, 28 March 1966, pp. 489-91.
62. Memorandum, Mike Manatos to Johnson, 19 February 1966, WHCF, Ex FG 440, Johnson Library, Austin, Texas.
63. See chapter eight.
64. Schlesinger, "On the Presidential Succession," p. 481.
65. *New York Times*, 2 April 1961, p. 3. *Public Papers of the Presidents 1961*, p. 633.
66. See U.S., Department of State, *Bulletin*, 14 October 1963, pp. 583-94; *New York Times*, 4 September 1963, p. 16; U.S., Department of State, *Bulletin*, 2 December 1963, pp. 850-54. Doris Kearns has concluded that Johnson "seemed to learn

little or nothing about international relations from [his] trips."
Kearns, *Lyndon Johnson*, p. 168.

67. *Public Papers of the Presidents 1969*, pp. 1041-42.

68. *Newsweek*, 19 January 1970, p. 20; *Time*, 5 January 1970,
p. 19.

69. J. Witcover, *White Knight* (New York, 1972), p. 420.

70. *Newsweek*, 31 January 1977, p. 28.

71. See comments of Reedy in "Symposium on the Vice-Presidency," p. 751; E. L. Richardson, *The Creative Balance* (New
York, 1976), pp. 74-75.

72. Interview with Nixon, *U.S. News and World Report*, 16 May
1960, pp. 99, 105-106. See Eisenhower's comments in *Public
Papers of the Presidents 1960-1961*, pp. 653, 657.

73. Nixon, *RN: Memoirs*, pp. 139-44; S. Adams, *Firsthand Report*
(New York, 1961), pp. 139-46.

74. Eisenhower, *Waging Peace* (Garden City, N.Y., 1965), p. 316;
Nixon, *RN: Memoirs*, pp. 193-99.

75. P. David, "The Vice Presidency: Its Institutional Evolution and
Contemporary Status," *J. Pol.* 29 (1967):741; Kearns, *Lyndon
Johnson*, p. 163.

76. Transcript of interview with Douglas Dillon, 29 June 1969,
LBJ Oral History Project, Johnson Library, Austin, Texas.

77. T. C. Sorensen, *Kennedy* (New York, 1965), pp. 265-66. See
also Sorensen, *The Kennedy Legacy* (New York, 1969), pp.
109-12. But Sorensen wrote *Decision-Making in the White
House* (New York, 1963) without mentioning Johnson. "Symposium on the Vice-Presidency," p. 750.

78. Interview with L. F. O'Brien, New York, N.Y., 30 September
1977. Transcript of interview with Dillon, p. 5. Transcript of
interview with Roswell Gilpatrick, 5 May 1970, p. 5; 30 June
1970, p. 95, JFK Oral History Project, Kennedy Library, Boston, Mass. Sorensen, *The Kennedy Legacy*, p. 108.

79. G. Christian, *The President Steps Down* (New York, 1970), p.
148; "Symposium on the Vice-Presidency," p. 750; transcript
of interview with Charles Boatner, 17 December 1968, pp.
22-23, LBJ Oral History Project, Johnson Library, Austin, Texas.
See also L. B. Johnson, *The Vantage Point* (New York, 1971),
p. 4.

80. Transcript of interview with W. Young, p. 5.
81. Sorensen, *Kennedy*, p. 266; L. J. Paper, *The Promise and the Performance* (New York, 1975), pp. 267-68.
82. Transcript of interview with Dillon, p. 6; L. Baker, *Johnson Eclipse* (New York, 1966), p. 112; transcript of interview with Freeman, pp. 12-13.
83. *Public Papers of the Presidents 1965*, 2:903.
84. Letter, Johnson to Humphrey, 3 September 1965, WHCF, Ex FG 440, Johnson Library, Austin, Texas.
85. Humphrey, *Education*, p. 427.
86. See e.g., E. F. Goldman, *Tragedy of Lyndon Johnson* (New York, 1969), p. 313; memoranda: Humphrey to Califano, 22 January 1966; Humphrey to Johnson, 12 January 1968; Humphrey to Moyers, 20 September 1965; Humphrey to Califano, 22 January 1966; Humphrey to Johnson, 9 May 1966; Humphrey to Johnson, 12 January 1968; Valenti to Humphrey, 20 September 1965 and 7 December 1965, WHCF, Ex 442, LG, FG 505/ 4, C.F. 440, FG 440, Johnson Library, Austin, Texas. Halberstam, *Best and Brightest*, pp. 531, 534. See also Goldman, *Tragedy of Lyndon Johnson*, p. 263. Johnson remembered Humphrey as being of "mixed emotions" but opposing the bombing while Soviet premier Kosygin was in Hanoi. See Johnson, *The Vantage Point*, p. 130. Humphrey, *Education*, pp. 319-25, 328-29; see also Goldman, *Tragedy of Lyndon Johnson*, p. 263.
87. Memorandum, Humphrey to Johnson, 9 November 1965, WHCF, Ex NO 19/CO 312, Johnson Library, Austin, Texas.
88. Christian, *The President Steps Down*, p. 148.
89. Interview with Agnew, *U.S. News and World Report*, 6 October 1969, pp. 32-33. See Schlesinger, "On the Presidential Succession," p. 478; Reeves, *A Ford*, pp. 41-43; Witcover, *White Knight*, p. 291.
90. J. S. Magruder, *An American Life* (New York, 1974), p. 128.
91. *Washington Post*, 16 May 1973, p. A1.
92. Interview with Rockefeller, *U.S. News and World Report*, 13 October 1975, p. 50; Ford, *A Time to Heal*, p. 327.
93. For this account I have relied on Turner, *Finding a Policy Role for the Vice President*, pp. 152-249.

94. Interview with Mondale, *U.S. News and World Report*, 28 March 1977, p. 62.
95. *New York Times*, 29 September 1977, p. B15; 30 September 1977, p. 8.
96. Interview with Moe, 28 September 1977; *National Journal*, 1 December 1979, p. 2012.
97. F. Lewis, *Mondale* (New York, 1980), pp. 235, 249.
98. *New York Times*, 29 September 1977, p. B15.
99. *Newsweek*, 18 April 1977, p. 26; interview with Moe, 2 September 1977; Mondale observed: "In these four years, never once did President Carter embarrass me . . ." *New York Times*, 21 January 1981, p. B3.
100. *Time*, 23 May 1977, p. 32.
101. Interview with Moe, 29 January 1981; *National Journal*, 1 December 1979, pp. 2014-15.
102. Interview with Mondale, *New York Times*, 21 December 1980, p. 32; *San Francisco Chronicle*, 19 January 1981, p. 11 (Mondale: "an unprecedented close relationship").
103. Interview with Albert A. Eisele, Mondale's press secretary, 13 January 1981.
104. Interview with Moe, 29 January 1981.
105. By contrast, Johnson as Vice President apparently requested an office next to President Kennedy's. " 'I have never heard of such a thing,' said Kennedy, and gave [Johnson] an office in the Executive Office Building across the way." Schlesinger, *Robert Kennedy*, p. 622.
106. *National Journal*, 11 March 1978, p. 380; *ibid.*, 1 December 1979, p. 2014; interview with Moe, 29 January 1981. See e.g., *Public Papers of the Presidents 1978* for listings of Mondale's meetings with Carter.
107. On the importance of this role, see R. E. Neustadt, "Staffing the Presidency: Premature Notes on the New Administration," *Pol. Sci. Q.* 93 (1978):1, 8-9; Neustadt, "A January 1978 Postscript," *Pol. Sci. Q.* 93 (1978):12, 14.
108. Interview with Moe, 29 January 1981; interview with Eisele, 13 January 1981.

NOTES, CHAPTER 8

1. Nixon, Johnson, Humphrey, and Mondale came to the vice presidency from the Senate; Ford from the House of Representatives. Bush had served two terms in the House. Agnew and Rockefeller had no legislative background.

2. Garner was Speaker of the House before becoming Vice President; Truman and Barkley had been senators; Wallace had not served in Congress.

3. See generally, R. M. Nixon, *RN: Memoirs* (New York, 1978), pp. 139-50, 195; S. Adams, *Firsthand Report* (New York, 1961), pp. 139-46; E. Mazo and S. Hess, *Nixon: A Political Portrait* (New York, 1968), pp. 130-39; R. H. Rovere, *Senator Joe McCarthy* (New York, 1959), p. 169; R. Griffith, *The Politics of Fear: Joseph R. McCarthy and the Senate* (Lexington, 1970), p. 248; D. D. Eisenhower, *Waging Peace* (Garden City, N.Y., 1965), p. 316; Eisenhower, *Mandate for Change* (Garden City, N.Y., 1963), p. 283.

4. Transcript of interview with McCormack, 23 September 1968, p. 26, LBJ Oral History Project, Johnson Library, Austin, Texas.

5. Transcript of interview with Charles Boatner, 21 May 1969, p. 27, LBJ Oral History Project, Johnson Library, Austin, Texas. L. Baker, *Johnson Eclipse* (New York, 1966), p. 29; T. C. Sorensen, *Kennedy* (New York, 1965), p. 341. Transcript of interview with McGovern, 30 April 1969, p. 3, JFK Oral History Project, Kennedy Library, Boston, Mass. Transcript of interview with Anderson, 14 April 1967, p. 51, JFK Oral History Project, Kennedy Library, Boston, Mass.; interview with L. F. O'Brien, New York, N.Y., 30 September 1977.

6. *Time*, 14 November 1969, p. 19. Letters: Humphrey to Senator Edward Kennedy, 30 April 1965; Humphrey to Representative Michael Feighen, 30 April 1965; memoranda: Humphrey to Johnson, 13 August 1965; Jones to Watson, 27 April 1966; Watson to Johnson, 27 April 1966; William Connell to Watson, 11 May 1966, WHCF, Ex LE/IM, LE/WE 7, WH 10, LE/LG, FI 4/FG 170, Johnson Library, Austin, Texas.

7. *Time*, 31 October 1969, p. 12.

8. R. Reeves, *A Ford, Not a Lincoln* (London, 1975), pp. 45, 48.

9. Interview with Rockefeller, *U.S. News and World Report*, 13 October 1975, p. 53.
10. M. Turner, *Finding a Policy Role for the Vice President* (Ann Arbor, 1978), pp. 209-12.
11. Interview with Congressman Robert Young, Washington, D.C., 25 September 1977; *People*, 27 February 1978, p. 23. See also E. L. Davis, "Legislative Liaison in the Carter Administration," *Pol. Sci. Q.* 94 (1979):297.
12. Interview with Richard Moe, 28 September 1977; *National Journal*, 11 March 1978, p. 381.
13. Quoted in Tolchin, "The Mondales," *New York Times Magazine*, 26 February 1978, p. 61.
14. Interview with Moe, 28 September 1977.
15. Quoted in *Newsweek*, 18 April 1977, p. 25.
16. Interview with Senator Birch Bayh, Washington, D.C., 22 September 1976.
17. *Time*, 14 November 1969, p. 19.
18. Interview with O'Brien, 30 September 1977.
19. L. F. O'Brien, *No Final Victories* (Garden City, N.Y., 1974), p. 165.
20. Transcript of interview with Humphrey, 17 August 1971, p. 39, LBJ Oral History Project, Johnson Library, Austin, Texas.
21. Interview with O'Brien, 30 September 1977; O'Brien, *No Final Victories*, pp. 165-66. See also Kearns, *Lyndon Johnson*, pp. 164-65.
22. Interview with Hon. Thomas Curtis, former Congressman, St. Louis, Mo., 9 September 1977.
23. Interview with O'Brien, 30 September 1977.
24. *Ibid.*
25. Interview with Mondale, *U.S. News and World Report*, 28 March 1977, p. 63.
26. H. H. Humphrey, *The Education of a Public Man* (Garden City, N.Y., 1976), p. 431.
27. Interview with Bayh.
28. Adams, *Firsthand Report*, p. 167.
29. R. J. Donovan, *Eisenhower: The Inside Story* (New York, 1956), p. 280.
30. *Newsweek*, 15 November 1954, p. 34.

31. *Public Papers of the Presidents 1954*, pp. 975-76.
32. For a different view, see Nixon, *RN: Memoirs*, pp. 199-200. Nixon argues that his "campaigning had had little visible effect, had gained [him] little thanks or credit, and had tarred [him] with the brush of partisan defeat at a time when . . . potential rivals for the nomination, Rockefeller and Barry Goldwater, were basking in the glory of victory."
33. P. T. David, "The Vice Presidency: Its Institutional Evolution and Contemporary Status, *J. Pol.* 29 (1967):740. Many of these speeches are reprinted in the Congressional Record. See e.g., 109 *Cong. Rec.* 799-800, 3537-38, 3669-70, 5548-50, 8420 (1963).
34. Humphrey, *Education*, p. 367.
35. Memorandum, Humphrey to Watson, 2 December 1965; memorandum, Watson to Humphrey, 4 December 1965, WHCF, Ex PL 7, Johnson Library, Austin, Texas.
36. Memorandum, Humphrey to Johnson, "The Vice President's Year, 1965," 28 January 1966, WHCF, Ex FG 440, Johnson Library, Austin, Texas.
37. Memorandum, Humphrey to Johnson, 31 March 1966, WHCF, Ex FG 100 MC, Johnson Library, Austin, Texas.
38. Letter, Humphrey to Harry McPherson, 27 August 1965; memoranda: Humphrey to Jake Jacobson, 8 October 1965; Humphrey to Watson, 25 May 1966; Humphrey to Johnson, 29 April 1966, WHCF, Ex ND 11/FG 125, Ex FG 440, Ex PL/ST 27, Ex MC, Johnson Library, Austin, Texas.
39. Memorandum, Humphrey to Johnson, 16 February 1967, WHCF, Ex PL/ST 5, Johnson Library, Austin, Texas.
40. Memorandum, Roche to Johnson, 13 November 1967, WHCF, Ex FG 440, Johnson Library, Austin, Texas.
41. *Time*, 14 November 1969, pp. 17-18.
42. J. Witcover, *White Knight* (New York, 1972), p. 393.
43. D. Halberstam, *The Best and the Brightest* (New York, 1969), p. 663; Nixon, *RN: Memoirs*, p. 491.
44. Reeves, *A Ford*, p. 45.
45. *New York Times*, 2 May 1976, IV:3.
46. Interview with Robert Young.

47. *National Journal*, 1 December 1979, p. 2012; *ibid.*, 11 March 1978, p. 380.
48. See *U.S. News and World Report*, 1 September 1953, pp. 28-31; 2 September 1955, pp. 106-107.
49. *Public Papers of the Presidents 1954*, pp. 299-300.
50. *Time*, 22 March 1954, p. 28.
51. See e.g., *Vital Speeches* 20, no. 8 (1953-54); *Vital Speeches* 22, no. 546 (1955-56).
52. Reprinted, 109 *Cong. Rec.* 8321-22 (1963).
53. Transcript of interview with Whitney Young, p. 4.
54. 109 *Cong. Rec.* 10005, 10006, 10035, 13184 (1963).
55. *Ibid.*, p. 10005 (Reprinted).
56. *Washington Post*, 27 July 1963, p. A6. Copyright *The Washington Post*.
57. Reprinted, 111 *Cong. Rec.* 8355 (1965).
58. Reprinted, 111 *Cong. Rec.* 20620 (1965).
59. C. Fritchey, "Washington Insight," *Harpers*, July 1966, p. 30; 112 *Cong. Rec.* 5911 (1966); *Newsweek*, 6 November 1967, p. 25.
60. *Newsweek*, 17 November 1969, p. 38; *Time*, 7 November 1969, p. 24.
61. *New York Times*, 14 November 1969, p. 24; *ibid.*, 21 November 1969, p. 1.
62. *Public Papers of the Presidents 1969*, pp. 1004-5; Nixon, *RN: Memoirs*, pp. 411-12.
63. Reeves, *A Ford*, pp. 44-58.
64. *New York Times*, 26 January 1975, p. 34.
65. *Ibid.*, 9 February 1975, IV:5.
66. Transcript of Mondale Remarks to National Council of Senior Citizens Biennial Legislative Conference, 6 June 1977, Mondale Press Office; Mondale Press Release, 18 June 1977; *Washington Post*, 9 July 1979, p. A1; Mondale Press Release, 19 August 1977. Transcript of Mondale Remarks to American Bar Association Annual Meeting, 8 August 1977, Mondale Press Office; *Washington Post*, 6 March 1979, p. A4.
67. *Washington Post*, 22 July 1979, p. A7. See also Transcript of Mondale Remarks to World Affairs Council of Northern California, 17 June 1977, Mondale Press Office; *New York Times*,

25 May 1978, p. 1 (speech to United Nations General Assembly disarmament session suggesting "regional arms-control efforts"); *Washington Post*, 11 October 1979, p. A2; transcript of Mondale Remarks to Brotherhood of Railway and Airline Clerks, AFL-CIO, 21 September 1977, Mondale Press Office. See Tolchin, "The Mondales," *New York Times Magazine*, 26 February 1978, p. 63 (Quoting Jody Powell); *National Journal* 1 December 1979, p. 2012.

68. See Nixon's comments in *Public Papers of the Presidents 1971*, pp. 548-49.
69. Interview with Rockefeller, *U.S. News and World Report*, 13 October 1975, p. 51.
70. *Public Papers of the Presidents 1954*, pp. 610-12.
71. *Public Papers of the Presidents 1969*, pp. 1004-5; Nixon, *RN: Memoirs*, pp. 411-12.
72. *Life*, 28 November 1969, p. 35.
73. *New York Times*, 18 May 1980, p. 30.
74. See Broder, *Washington Post*, 7 October 1979, p. C7.
75. *Washington Post*, 31 October 1980, p. A2; *New York Times*, 11 January 1980, p. 12; 12 January 1980, p. 9; 17 May 1980, p. 10.

NOTES, CHAPTER 9

1. W. Wilson, *Congressional Government* (Gloucester, Mass., 1973), p. 162.
2. U.S., *Constitution*, art. II. sec. 1, cl. 6.
3. See M. Farrand, ed., *Records of the Federal Convention of 1787* (New Haven, 1911), 2:575; J. D. Feerick, *From Failing Hands* (New York, 1965), pp. 50-51, 89-98; R. C. Silva, *Presidential Succession* (Ann Arbor, 1951), pp. 4-13; E. S. Corwin, *The President: Office and Powers*, 4th ed. (New York, 1957), p. 54; R. Hansen, *The Year We Had No President* (Lincoln, 1962), pp. 13-20; R. P. Longaker, "Presidential Continuity: The Twenty-Fifth Amendment," *UCLA L. Rev.* 13 (1966):532, 537. [In fairness to Tyler, it should be noted that he lacked access to sources available to modern scholars.]
4. *Public Papers of the Presidents 1957*, pp. 213-14.

5. *Public Papers of the Presidents 1958*, pp. 196-97; *Public Papers of the Presidents 1961*, pp. 561-62; *Public Papers of the Presidents 1963-1964*, 1:65-66. McCormack as Speaker of the House was the first successor, 22 November 1963 to 20 January 1965, when Humphrey became Vice President. *Public Papers of the Presidents 1965*, 2:1044.

6. *Public Papers of the Presidents 1958*, p. 189. (Eisenhower spoke on 26 February 1958, before his agreement with Nixon had been made public but apparently after it had been formulated.)

7. 104 *Cong. Rec.* 2879 (1958).

8. D. D. Eisenhower, *Waging Peace* (Garden City, N.Y., 1965), p. 235.

9. See J. Feerick, *The Twenty-Fifth Amendment* (New York, 1976), pp. 197-207.

10. The President could declare his inability by transmitting a letter to that effect to the offices of the Speaker of the House and president pro tempore of the Senate. See *S. Rep. 66*, p. 2 (1965); Feerick, *The Twenty-Fifth Amendment*, pp. 89-90, 199.

11. The phrase "principal officers of the executive departments" refers to the cabinet secretaries. 111 *Cong. Rec.* 3283, 15383 (1965).

12. See Feerick, *The Twenty-Fifth Amendment*, pp. 197-207.

13. U.S., *Constitution*, art. II, sec. 1, cl. 6; Amend. 20 sec. 3, 4.

14. 3 U.S.C. 19 (1976). The statute was passed in 1947; it has been revised to reflect changes in the executive departments. Earlier laws created different lines. A 1792 law placed the president pro tempore of the Senate and Speaker of the House in line with a special election to follow; an 1886 statute placed the cabinet only in line. See Feerick, *From Failing Hands*, pp. 57-62, 140-46.

15. See Feerick, *From Failing Hands*, pp. 294-309.

16. See J. K. Goldstein, "An Overview of the Vice-Presidency," *Ford. L. Rev.* 45 (1977):786.

17. See R. E. Neustadt, *Presidential Power* (New York, 1980), pp. 216-20.

18. See generally L. Henry, *Presidential Transitions* (Washington, D.C., 1960).

19. G. Gallup, *The Gallup Poll: Public Opinion, 1935-71*, 3 vols. (New York, 1972), 3:1850-51.
20. Feerick, *The Twenty-Fifth Amendment*, p. 157; *New York Times*, 6 August 1974, p. 1.
21. R. Reeves, *A Ford, Not a Lincoln* (London, 1975) p. 57.
22. Feerick, *The Twenty-Fifth Amendment*, pp. 159-60, Reeves, *A Ford*, pp. 51-52, 57-58; *New York Times*, 26 August 1974, p. 1; G. R. Ford, *A Time to Heal* (New York, 1979), pp. 129-31.
23. Gallup, *Gallup Poll: Public Opinion, 1972-77*, 2 vols. (Wilmington, Del., 1978), 1:293, 322.
24. L. A. Sobel, ed., *Presidential Succession* (New York, 1975), p. 177.
25. *New York Times*, 8 August 1974, pp. 1, 22.
26. C. A. Arthur, *State Papers of Chester A. Arthur* (Washington, 1885), p. 11.
27. *Newsweek*, 2 December 1963, p. 26. (Emphasis in original.)
28. See L. B. Johnson, *The Vantage Point* (New York, 1971), pp. 14-15, 18-21; D. Kearns, *Lyndon Johnson* (New York, 1976), pp. 174-76. One close Johnson associate observed that Robert Kennedy seemed to resent Johnson. Transcript of interview with Clark Clifford, 2 July 1969, p. 4, LBJ Oral History Project, Johnson Library, Austin, Texas.
29. Neustadt, *Presidential Power*, p. 233.
30. See Ford, *A Time to Heal*, pp. 131-33, 234-40.
31. *New York Times*, 9 August 1974, p. 4.
32. Interview with L. F. O'Brien, New York, N.Y., 30 September 1977.
33. See S. Hess, *Organizing the Presidency* (Washington, D.C., 1976), pp. 93-94; Johnson, *The Vantage Point*, pp. 14-15, 18-21. See also Kearns, *Lyndon Johnson*, pp. 174-76.
34. Comments of Schlesinger and Reedy, "Symposium on the Vice-Presidency," *Ford. L. Rev.* 45 (1977):750; Johnson, *The Vantage Point*, p. 4. Transcript of interview with Douglas Dillon, 29 June 1969, p. 17, LBJ Oral History Project, Johnson Library, Austin, Texas.
35. L. F. O'Brien, *No Final Victories* (Garden City, N.Y., 1974), p. 164. See also A. M. Schlesinger, Jr., *Robert Kennedy* (Boston, 1978), pp. 626-28.

36. Transcript of interview with Clifford, 7 August 1969, p. 14; transcript of interview with Dillon, p. 17.
37. The exception was Ron Ziegler, Nixon's vocal press secretary. See Ford, *A Time to Heal*, pp. 147-48; *New York Times*, 9 August 1974, p. 4 and 10 August 1974, pp. 1, 5.
38. See Ford, *A Time to Heal*, pp. 186-87, 239-40.
39. *Public Papers of the Presidents 1963-64*, p. 9.
40. U.S., Congress, House of Representatives, Committee on the Judiciary, *Hearings on Nomination of Gerald R. Ford to be the Vice President of the United States*, 93rd Cong., 1st sess., 1973, p. 9.
41. Ford, *A Time to Heal*, pp. 139-42, 156-57.
42. T. Wicker, *J.F.K. and L.B.J.* (Baltimore, 1968), pp. 182-85, 198-99.
43. Gallup, *Public Opinion, 1935-71*, 2:1535, 3:1647, 1681.
44. *Ibid.*, 3:1976.
45. *Ibid.*, p. 2253.
46. See generally R. A. Dahl, *A Preface to Democratic Theory* (Chicago, 1956), pp. 124-51.
47. H. S. Truman, *Year of Decisions, 1945* (Garden City, N.Y., 1955), p. 53.
48. *Public Papers of the Presidents 1957*, p. 132.
49. Economy, Papers of Lyndon B. Johnson as Vice President, Johnson Library, Austin, Texas.
50. Interview with Richard Moe, Mondale's chief of staff, Washington, D.C., 28 September 1977.
51. Schlesinger, "On the Presidential Succession," *Pol. Sci. Q.* 89 (1974):485-86.
52. Neustadt, *Presidential Power*, pp. 156-57.
53. *New York Times*, 1 October 1955, p. 1; 9 October 1955, pp. 1, 78.
54. R. M. Nixon, *Six Crises* (Garden City, N.Y., 1962), pp. 143-44.
55. U.S., *Constitution*, Amend. 12. The only Vice President elected in such a manner was Richard M. Johnson in 1837.

NOTES, CHAPTER 10

1. See generally J. D. Feerick, *From Failing Hands* (New York, 1965) and *The Twenty-Fifth Amendment* (New York, 1976) and B. Bayh, *One Heartbeat Away* (Indianapolis, 1968).
2. 110 *Cong. Rec.* 22986 (1964). See also Bayh's comments in introducing the measure, 109 *Cong. Rec.* 24421 (1963); 110 *Cong. Rec.* 22987 (1964).
3. 110 *Cong. Rec.* 22992-22994 (1964) (Comments of Senators Leverett Saltonstall, Hiram Fong and Jacob Javits).
4. The second vote occurred because Senator John Stennis did not believe the Senate should propose a constitutional amendment based on the preferences of just nine of its members in a voice vote.
5. 111 *Cong. Rec.* 30 (1965).
6. *Public Papers of the Presidents 1965*, 1:100-103.
7. For the best discussions of the legislative history, see Feerick, *The Twenty-Fifth Amendment*, pp. 59-113, and B. Bayh, *One Heartbeat Away*.
8. 111 *Cong. Rec.* 7932-7933, 7959-7961 (1965) (Remarks of Representatives Clarence J. Brown, John Dingell, and John O'Hara).
9. House Rep. No. 203, 89th Cong., 1st sess., 1965. (Dissenting views of Representative Charles McC. Mathias.) See also 111 *Cong. Rec.* 7932 (1965) (Comments of Representative Clarence J. Brown) ("Under certain conditions and certain circumstances, . . . a President could name a billy goat as Vice President and some Congresses would approve of that nomination and that selection.").
10. 110 *Cong. Rec.* 22990 (1964). See also G. Haimbaugh, Jr., "Vice-Presidential Succession: A Criticism of the Bayh-Cellar Plan," *S. C. L. Rev.* 17 (1965):315.
11. 111 *Cong. Rec.* 3275, 3281, 3279, 3282 (1965). See Feerick, *The Twenty-Fifth Amendment*, pp. 93-94.
12. See 110 *Cong. Rec.* 22988 (1964); 111 *Cong. Rec.* 3255 (1965) (Remarks of Senators Ervin and Bayh).
13. U.S., Congress, Senate, Subcommittee on Constitutional Amendments of the Committee on the Judiciary, *Hearings on*

Presidential Inability and Vacancies in the Office of Vice President, 88th Cong., 2d sess., 1964, pp. 16-21 [Hereinafter *1964 Senate Hearings*]. S.J. Res. 147, 88th Cong., 2d sess. (1964) (Ervin). H.J. Res. 140 (Lindsay); H.J. Res. 264 (Mathias); 89th Cong., 1st sess. (1965). *1964 Senate Hearings*, pp. 78-82 (Church); S.J. Res. 148, 88th Cong., 2d sess. (1964) (Church). S.J. Res. 149, 89th Cong., 2d sess. (1964) (Young).

14. S.J. Res. 140, S.J. Res. 143, 88th Cong., 2d sess. (1964).
15. *1964 Senate Hearings*, pp. 21-29, 234-52; U.S., Congress, Senate, Subcommittee on Constitutional Amendments of the Committee on the Judiciary, *Hearings on Presidential Inability and Vacancies in the Office of Vice President*, 89th Cong., 1st sess. (1965), pp. 105-106 [Hereinafter *1965 Senate Hearings*]; S.J. Res. 25, 89th Cong., 1st sess. (1965).
16. 111 *Cong. Rec.* 3255 (1965).
17. 110 *Cong. Rec.* 22994 (1964).
18. *1964 Senate Hearings*, pp. 130-31.
19. *1965 Senate Hearings*, p. 11.
20. 110 *Cong. Rec.* 22988, 22996 (1964).
21. 120 *Cong. Rec.* 41452 (1974).
22. U.S., Congress, Senate, Committee on Rules and Administration, *Hearings on Nomination of Nelson A. Rockefeller of New York to be Vice President of the United States*, 93d Cong., 2d sess. (1974), p. 1025 [Hereinafter *Senate Hearings on Rockefeller*]. House of Representatives, Committee on the Judiciary, *Hearings on Nomination of Gerald R. Ford to be the Vice President of the United States*, 93d Cong., 1st sess. (1973), p. 183. [Hereinafter *House Hearings on Ford*].
23. U.S., Congress, Senate, Committee on Rules and Administration, *Hearings on Nomination of Gerald R. Ford of Michigan to be Vice President of the United States*, 93d Cong., 1st sess. (1973), pp. 159, 344, 171 [Hereinafter *Senate Hearings on Ford*].
24. *House Hearings on Ford*, p. 18.
25. 119 *Cong. Rec.* 34381 (1973).
26. *Senate Hearings on Ford*, p. 5.
27. For excellent discussions of these events, see Feerick, *The Twenty-Fifth Amendment*, pp. 117-90.
28. *House Hearings on Ford*, pp. 6, 18, 21 [Remarks of Repre-

sentatives Conyers, Kastenmeier, and Edwards]; 119 *Cong. Rec.* 37961 (1973) [Remarks of Senator Hathaway].

29. R. M. Nixon, *RN: Memoirs* (New York, 1978), p. 925; G. D. Aiken, *Senate Diary: January 1972-January 1975* (Brattleboro, Vt., 1976), p. 228.

30. See Feerick, *The Twenty-Fifth Amendment*, pp. 132-35.

31. Nixon, *RN: Memoirs*, pp. 925-36; H. Dent, *The Prodigal South Returns to Power* (New York, 1978), pp. 279-80; R. K. Price, Jr., *With Nixon* (New York, 1977), pp. 253-54.

32. *New York Times*, 12 October 1973, p. 26.

33. C. Albert, "The Most Dramatic Events of My Life," *Outreach*, March 1974, p. 6. R. Reeves, *A Ford, Not a Lincoln* (London, 1975), p. 36; *New York Times*, 15 October 1973, p. 1.

34. Feerick, *The Twenty-Fifth Amendment*, pp. 135-36.

35. *Senate Hearings on Ford*, p. 4; *House Hearings on Ford*, p. 1.

36. *House Hearings on Ford*, pp. 380-474.

37. *Ibid.*, pp. 270-326, 175-207, 713-20.

38. *Senate Hearings on Ford*, pp. 41, 31, 33.

39. *Ibid.*, p. 124.

40. G. R. Ford, *A Time to Heal* (New York, 1979), pp. 42-43. One close Ford aide suggests that Donald Rumsfeld was also among those under strongest consideration. See R. T. Hartmann, *Palace Politics: An Inside Account of the Ford Years* (New York, 1980), pp. 227-28.

41. *New York Times*, 9 August 1974, p. 4; 11 August 1974, p. 43.

42. *Senate Hearings on Rockefeller*, pp. 3-4

43. U.S., Congress, House of Representatives, Committee on the Judiciary, *Hearings on Nomination of Nelson A. Rockefeller to be Vice President of the United States*, 93rd Cong., 2nd sess., 1974, p. 2.

44. *Ibid.*, p. 132.

45. *Ibid.*, p. 65; *Senate Hearings on Rockefeller*, p. 617.

46. 120 *Cong. Rec.* 31349 (1974); "Statement of Hugh Scott," 11 November 1974; *Senate Hearings on Rockefeller*, p. 592.

47. *Current Opinion*, November 1974, p. 132.

48. 120 *Cong. Rec.* 38922 (1974).

NOTES, CHAPTER 11

1. See D. R. Matthews, "Presidential Nominations," in J. D. Barber, ed., *Choosing the President* (Englewood Cliffs, N.J., 1974); J. K. Goldstein, "An Overview of the Vice-Presidency," *Ford. L. Rev.* 45 (1977):787-88.
2. See H. H. Humphrey, *The Education of a Public Man* (Garden City, N.Y., 1976), p. 427.
3. See U.S., *Constitution*, art. II, sec. 1, cl. 3; see also chapter 1.
4. G. Pomper, *Nominating the President* (New York, 1966), p. 170.
5. Theodore Roosevelt favored William Howard Taft instead of Fairbanks; Wilson and Coolidge apparently hoped the conventions would draft them for another term.
6. See generally I. G. Williams, *The Rise of the Vice Presidency* (Washington, D.C., 1956).
7. T. H. White, *The Making of the President 1960* (New York, 1961), pp. 73-77.
8. Humphrey, *Education*, p. 358.
9. *Public Papers of the Presidents 1968-69*, p. 476.
10. *Newsweek*, 15 April 1968, p. 48B.
11. *Ibid.*, 3 June 1968, pp. 28-29.
12. White, *The Making of the President 1968* (New York, 1969), pp. 328-32; L. Chester, G. Hodgson, B. Page, *American Melodrama* (New York, 1969), pp. 564-76; but see T. C. Sorensen, *The Kennedy Legacy* (New York, 1969), p. 300.
13. White, *The Making of the President 1968*, Appendix C.
14. G. Gallup, *The Gallup Poll: Public Opinion, 1935-71*, 3 vols. (New York, 1972), 3:2307.
15. Gallup, *The Gallup Poll: Public Opinion, 1972-77*, 2 vols. (Wilmington, Del., 1978), 1:115; *The Gallup Opinion Index*, May 1973, p. 12.
16. Gallup, *Public Opinion, 1972-77*, 1:173.
17. *Ibid.*, p. 197.
18. *The Gallup Opinion Index*, February 1974, pp. 20-22; Gallup, *Public Opinion, 1972-77*, 1:230.
19. *Public Papers of the Presidents 1956*, p. 287; D. D. Eisen-

hower, *Waging Peace* (Garden City, N.Y., 1965), pp. 6-9; R. M. Nixon, *Six Crises* (Garden City, N.Y., 1962), pp. 158, 160.

20. P. David, "The Vice Presidency: Its Institutional Evolution and Contemporary Status," *J. Pol.* 29 (1967):721, 748.
21. Matthews, "Presidential Nominations," p. 44.
22. Gallup, *Public Opinion, 1935-71*, 2:1470, 3:1878, 2273.
23. *Ibid.*, 2:1175, 1508, 1525.
24. W. Shannon, "Humphrey and 1972," *Commonweal*, 4 March 1966, p. 629.
25. A. M. Schlesinger, Jr., *A Thousand Days* (Boston, 1965), p. 705.
26. L. Harris, *The Harris Survey* (New York: The Chicago Tribune-New York News Syndicate, 1 May 1967).
27. *Ibid.*
28. Gallup, *Public Opinion, 1935-71*, 2:1535, 3:1647. See also 3:1681.
29. *Ibid.*, 2:1535.
30. *Ibid.*, 3:1622.
31. *Ibid.*, p. 2253.
32. *Gallup Opinion Index*, September 1973, p. 15.
33. See e.g., Gallup, *Public Opinion, 1935-71*, 2:1309, 1328, 1325, 1509.
34. *Ibid.*, 3:2122, 2126; Gallup, *Public Opinion, 1972-77*, 1:115-16, 271-72.
35. Gallup, *Public Opinion 1935-71*, 3:1975-76, 2253.
36. See White, *The Making of the President 1960*.
37. *Newsweek*, 29 April 1968, p. 24.
38. *U.S. News and World Report*, 4 September 1972, p. 20.
39. A. Ranney, "Turnout and Representation in Presidential Primary Elections," *Am. Pol. Sci. Rev.* 66 (1972):21, 37; Ranney, *Participation in American Presidential Nominations, 1976* (Washington, D.C., 1977), p. 20.
40. See generally D. S. Collat, S. Kelley, Jr., and R. Rogowski, "Presidential Bandwagons" (Paper delivered at the Annual Meeting of the American Political Science Association, Chicago, Illinois, September 1976).
41. See E. L. Richardson, *The Creative Balance* (New York, 1976), pp. 124-25.

42. Nixon, *Six Crises*, pp. 353-56; S. Kelley, "The Presidential Campaign," in *The Presidential Election and Transition, 1960-61*, ed. P. David (Washington, D.C., 1961), pp. 82-83.
43. White, *The Making of the President 1960*, pp. 308-309.
44. Kelley, "The Presidential Campaign," pp. 65, 67.
45. *Public Papers of the Presidents 1960-1961*, pp. 653, 657-58.
46. *Nation*, 17 June 1968, pp. 783-84; *Time*, 28 June 1968, p. 13; letter, Hughes to Johnson, 30 July 1968, WHCF, C.F. N.D. 19/CO 312, Johnson Library, Austin, Texas.
47. *Time*, 28 June 1968, p. 13.
48. Memorandum, Jones to Johnson, 18 July 1968, WHCF, Ex FG 440, Johnson Library, Austin, Texas.
49. Humphrey, *Education*, pp. 387-90.
50. Memoranda: W. W. Rostow to Johnson, 30 September 1968; Murphy to Johnson, 1 October 1968; WHCF, Ex PL/Humphrey, Hubert, Johnson Library, Austin, Texas. The words quoted are Rostow's. See also R. M. Scammon and B. J. Wattenberg, *The Real Majority* (New York, 1970), pp. 165-66.
51. See generally H. McPherson, *A Political Education* (Boston, 1972), pp. 448-49. Johnson may have hoped the Democratic Convention would draft him despite his withdrawal. See D. Kearns, *Lyndon Johnson* (New York, 1976), pp. 350-51.
52. *Public Papers of the Presidents 1968-69*, 1:476.
53. *Ibid.*, p. 480.
54. Letter, Freeman to Johnson, 23 April 1968, Ex PU 1/FG 150, Johnson Library, Austin, Texas.
55. Memorandum, Califano to Johnson, 25 April 1968, WHCF, Ex PL 2, Johnson Library, Austin, Texas.
56. Memorandum, Califano to Johnson, 24 April 1968, WHCF, Ex PL/Humphrey, Hubert, Johnson Library, Austin, Texas.
57. Memorandum, McPherson to Johnson, 24 April 1968, WHCF, Ex PL/Humphrey, Hubert, Johnson Library, Austin, Texas.
58. Memorandum, Califano to Johnson, 25 April 1968, WHCF, Ex PL 2, Johnson Library, Austin, Texas.
59. Memorandum, Califano to Johnson, 24 April 1968, WHCF, Ex PL/Humphrey, Hubert, Johnson Library, Austin, Texas.
60. *Public Papers of the Presidents 1968-69*, 2:963, 977, 1026-28.

NOTES, CHAPTER 12

1. "Symposium on the Vice-Presidency," *Ford. L. Rev.* 45 (1977):759.
2. Press Release, Democratic National Committee, 18 October 1973.
3. A. P. Sindler, *Unchosen Presidents* (Berkeley and Los Angeles, 1976); "Report of the Study Group on Vice-Presidential Selection," mimeographed (Cambridge: Institute of Politics, J. F. Kennedy School of Government, Harvard University, 1976); "Symposium on the Vice-Presidency."
4. See "Statement of Laurence I. Radway to the Vice-Presidential Selection Commission," mimeographed (Concord, N.H., 1975), p. 1.
5. "Symposium on the Vice-Presidency," p. 711.
6. *Ibid.*, p. 727.
7. S. Eizenstat, "Alternative Possibilities of Vice Presidential Selection," prepared for the Democratic National Committee Commission on the Selection of the Democratic Nominee for Vice President, 5 October 1973, reprinted 119 *Cong. Rec.* 34235-34239 (1973).
8. *Ibid.* Carter, in effect, did designate Mondale as his running mate for 1980 before the primaries.
9. G. Gallup, *The Gallup Poll: Public Opinion, 1972-77*, 2 vols. (Wilmington, Del., 1978), 1:42.
10. A. Ranney, "Turnout and Representation in Presidential Primary Elections," *Am. Pol. Sci. Rev.* 66 (1972):21-37.
11. "Symposium on the Vice-Presidency," p. 711.
12. Transcript of speech of Senator Mike Gravel before the Democratic National Convention, 13 July 1972; statement by Senator Mike Gravel to the Vice Presidential Selection Commission of the Democratic National Committee, 28 September 1973, mimeographed, Working Papers, Study Group on Vice-Presidential Selection.
13. D. Lawrence, *U.S. News and World Report*, 25 April 1952, p. 92; see also B. Weisberger, *New York Times*, 10 August 1972, p. 35.
14. Eizenstat, "Alternative Possibilities"; C. Hyneman, "Selection

374 ★ Notes to Pages 278-84

of Vice Presidential Candidates," mimeographed, Working Papers, p. 3.

15. Letter, Rockefeller to R. Rosenbaum, reprinted, *New York Times*, 1 February 1979, p. B3.

16. "Symposium on the Vice-Presidency," p. 751.

17. S.2741, 93d Cong., 1st sess., 26 November 1973.

18. 119 *Cong. Rec.* 40649 (1973) [Remarks by Senator Humphrey].

19. "Recommendation and Report of the Special Committee on Election Reform," *Ford. L. Rev.* 45 (1977):779-85; see also 120 *Cong. Rec.* 26513-26515 (1974) [Remarks of Representative Esch]; *New York Times*, 13 August 1972, p. 39 [Reporting views of Senator Mathias].

20. "Report of the Study Group on Vice-Presidential Selection," pp. 12, 15, 17-19.

21. "Symposium on the Vice-Presidency," pp. 734-35. See also T. Wicker, *New York Times*, 20 June 1976, Sec. IV, p. 17.

22. Quoted in J. H. Parris, *The Convention Problem* (Washington, D.C., 1972), p. 103.

23. See 120 *Cong. Rec.* 26513-26515 (1974) [Remarks of Representative Esch]; Press Release of Senator Jacob Javits, 14 August 1972, p. 6.

24. T. F. Eagleton, "How I'd Pick the Vice President." I am grateful to Senator Eagleton for supplying me with this statement of his views.

25. Statement of D. G. Herzberg before the Commission on the Selection of the Democratic Nominee for Vice President, 7 November 1973 (mimeo).

26. Letter from G. M. Pomper to Senator H. Humphrey, 20 August 1973.

27. "Symposium on the Vice-Presidency," pp. 715-16.

28. "Statement of L. Radway," p. 5.

29. "Symposium on the Vice-Presidency," p. 723.

30. *Ibid.*

31. Under the current electoral system, citizens in each state vote for a single slate of electors pledged to a presidential and vice-presidential candidate. Although the electors vote separately for each office, they are chosen based on a vote for the ticket.

32. *Ibid.*, p. 770.
33. *Ibid.*, pp. 769-70.
34. Letter, Rockefeller to Rosenbaum, reprinted in *New York Times,* 1 February 1979, p. B3.
35. See L. Wilmerding, "The Vice Presidency," *Pol. Sci. Q.* 68 (1953):34-35.
36. V. Righter, *New York Times,* 9 September 1972, p. 23.
37. S.J. Res. 166, 93d Cong., 1st sess., 1973.
38. H. Rep. 203, 89th Cong., 1st sess., 1965 (Dissenting views of Representative Charles McC. Mathias, Jr.).
39. 119 *Cong. Rec.* 34795 (1973).
40. U.S., Congress, Senate, Subcommittee on Constitutional Amendments of the Committee on the Judiciary, *Hearings on Examination of the First Implementation of Section Two of the Twenty-Fifth Amendment,* 94th Cong., 1st sess., 1975, p. 138.
41. *Ibid.*, p. 146.
42. *Ibid.*
43. "Symposium on the Vice-Presidency," p. 715. Bayh would prefer involving citizens in the selection.
44. T. Roosevelt, "The Three Vice-Presidential Candidates and What They Represent," *Review of Reviews* 14 (1896):289.
45. "Symposium on the Vice-Presidency," p. 752.
46. Some analogies can be drawn between the vice presidency and lieutenant governorship. The author of the leading work on the American governorship observes that that office has been improved in states where the lieutenant governor does not preside over the state senate, thus bringing that officer into the executive branch. L. Sabato, *Goodbye to Good-Time Charlie: The American Governor Transformed, 1950-1975* (Lexington, Mass., 1978), p. 75.
47. A. Sindler, *Unchosen Presidents,* p. 62.
48. C. Rossiter, "The Reform of the Vice-Presidency," *Pol. Sci. Q.* 63 (1948):393-403.
49. Lodge, letter to the editor, *New York Times,* 4 March 1979, p. 18E. Dean Acheson thought Nixon's promise was merely a campaign tactic to appeal to those who preferred Lodge to Nixon. Moreover, Acheson believed that "interposing bodies between the President . . . and the responsible Cabinet officers . . . does

nothing for either" but "only confuses and hampers both."
Transcript of interview with Acheson, 27 April 1964, p. 4, JFK
Oral History Project, Kennedy Library, Boston, Mass. (quoting
from letter to JFK, 15 September 1960).
50. Interview with Hon. Thomas B. Curtis, former congressman, St.
Louis, Mo., 9 September 1977; letter, Curtis to author, 6 April
1981.
51. G. H. Durham, "The Vice Presidency," *W. Pol. Q.* 1 (1948):311-
14.
52. *Wall St. Journal,* 18 July 1980, pp. 1, 26.
53. Schlesinger, "On the Presidential Succession," pp. 475-505;
Wilmerding, "The Vice Presidency," pp. 17-41; T. E. Cronin,
The State of the Presidency (Boston, 1975), pp. 211-35; E. F.
Goldman, "Do We Really Need a Veep?" *This Week,* 29 June
1969, pp. 2, 4; E. J. McCarthy, "Memories of Hubert: A Politician too Good to be Vice President," *New Republic,* 18 February 1978, p. 23.
54. Letter from O'Hara to the author, 13 August 1976.
55. Schlesinger, "On the Presidential Succession," pp. 483-84. See
also Cronin, *The State of the Presidency,* pp. 229-33.
56. "Testimony before the Vice Presidential Selection Commission
of the Democratic National Committee," 7 November 1973
(mimeo), p. 10.
57. Schlesinger, "On the Presidential Succession," p. 485.
58. E. F. Goldman, *The Tragedy of Lyndon Johnson* (New York,
1969), p. 264.
59. McCarthy, "Memories of Hubert," p. 23.
60. Schlesinger, "On the Presidential Succession," p. 475; W. E.
Christopher, "A Special Election to Fill a Presidential Vacancy," *Record of the Association of the Bar of the City of New
York* 30 (1975):47-54.
61. Wilmerding, "The Vice Presidency," p. 39.
62. T. Wicker, *New York Times,* 20 December 1974, p. 37.
63. Letter from Goldman to the author, 5 August 1976.
64. E. M. Kennedy, *New York Times,* 21 October 1974, p. 33.
65. U.S., Congress, Senate, Committee on Rules and Administration, *Hearings on Nomination of Nelson A. Rockefeller of New*

York to be Vice President of the United States, 93rd Cong., 2nd sess., 1975, p. 239.

66. 91 *Cong. Rec.* 7020 (1945).

67. U.S., Congress, Senate, Subcommittee on Constitutional Amendments of the Committee on the Judiciary, *Hearings on Presidential Inability and Vacancies in the Office of Vice President,* 89th Cong., 1st sess., 1965, p. 62 (testimony of Lewis F. Powell, Jr., then president-elect of the American Bar Association).

68. Schlesinger, "On the Presidential Succession," p. 504.

69. J. D. Feerick, *From Failing Hands* (New York, 1965), pp. 60, 146; Wilmerding, "The Vice Presidency," pp. 37-41; Schlesinger, "On the Presidential Succession," pp. 496-97.

70. A. Wildavsky, "Presidential Succession and Disability: Policy Analysis for Unique Cases," in *The Presidency,* ed. A. Wildavsky (Boston, 1969), p. 781.

71. S.J. Res. 26, 94th Cong., 1st sess., 1975; H.R. 11230, 93d Cong., 1st sess., 1973.

72. U.S., Congress, Senate, Subcommittee on Constitutional Amendments of the Committee on the Judiciary, *Hearings on Presidential Inability and Vacancies in the Office of Vice President,* 88th Cong., 2nd sess., 1964, pp. 27-28.

73. 127 *Cong. Rec.* H932-933 (daily ed. March 12, 1981).

74. J. D. Feerick, *The Twenty-Fifth Amendment* (New York, 1976), p. 202. For a discussion of the legislative history on this point see *ibid.,* pp. 200-202.

75. A. Ranney, *Curing the Mischiefs of Faction* (Berkeley and Los Angeles, 1975), p. 191.

NOTES, CHAPTER 13

1. D. Kearns, *Lyndon Johnson and the American Dream* (New York, 1976), p. 164.

2. H. H. Humphrey, *The Education of a Public Man* (Garden City, N.Y., 1976), p. 407; but see pp. 314-429 for a different picture; *Time,* 14 November 1969, p. 19.

3. 123 *Cong. Rec.* 1587 (1977).
4. Humphrey, "Changes in the Vice Presidency," *Cur. Hist.* 67 (1974):59.
5. See J. D. Barber, *The Presidential Character*, 2nd ed. (Englewood Cliffs, N.J., 1977).

Selected Bibliography

ARCHIVES

Austin, Texas. Lyndon Baines Johnson Library.
  Papers of Lyndon B. Johnson as Vice President.
  WHCF, Ex FG 440 (The Vice Presidency).
  WHCF, Ex C.F. 440 (Confidential, The Vice Presidency).
  Transcripts of interviews, Oral History Project.
Boston, Massachusetts. John F. Kennedy Library.
  Presidents Office File.
  Prepresidential Papers.
  Robert F. Kennedy Pre-Administration Political Files.
  Burke Marshall Papers.
  Transcripts of interviews, Oral History Project.
Cambridge, Massachusetts. Institute of Politics, John F. Kennedy
  School of Government, Harvard University. Working Papers, Study
  Group on Vice-Presidential Selection.
Washington, D.C. National Archives. Presidential Libraries Divi-
  sion.
  Hearings before the Commission on Vice Presidential Selection,
  Democratic National Committee, Concord, New Hampshire, 25
  September 1973.
  Hearings before the Commission on Vice Presidential Selection,
  Democratic National Committee, Boston, Massachusetts, 26 Sep-
  tember 1973.
  Hearings before the Commission on Vice Presidential Selection,
  Democratic National Committee, Washington, D.C., 7 Novem-
  ber 1973.

GOVERNMENT DOCUMENTS

Doyle, Vincent A. "The Twenty-Second Amendment—Its Effect on
  Eligibility for the Presidency." Mimeographed. Legislative Refer-
  ence Service, Library of Congress, 21 January 1964.
Gorman, Joseph. "Suggested Alternatives to the Present Method of

Selecting Nominees for the Vice-Presidency." Mimeographed. Congressional Research Service, Library of Congress, 7 August 1973.

Public Papers of the Presidents. Washington, D.C.: Government Printing Office, 1945-1978.

U.S., Congress, *Annals*, 8th Cong., 1st sess., 1803-1804.

U.S., Congress, *Congressional Record*, 1953-1981.

U.S., Congress, Senate, Subcommittee on Reorganization of the Committee on Government Operations, *Hearings on Administrative Vice President*, 84th Cong., 2nd sess., 1956.

U.S., Congress, Senate, Subcommittee on Constitutional Amendments of the Committee on the Judiciary, *Hearings on Presidential Inability and Vacancies in the Office of Vice President*, 88th Cong., 2nd sess., 1964.

U.S., Congress, House of Representatives, Committee on the Judiciary, *Hearings on Presidential Inability and Vice Presidential Vacancy*, 89th Cong., 1st sess., 1965.

U.S., Congress, Senate, Subcommittee on Constitutional Amendments of the Committee on the Judiciary, *Hearings on Presidential Inability and Vacancies in the Office of Vice President*, 89th Cong., 1st sess., 1965.

U.S., Congress, Senate, Subcommittee on Constitutional Amendments of the Committee on the Judiciary, *Selected Materials on the Twenty-Fifth Amendment*, 93rd Cong., 1st sess., 1973.

U.S., Congress, House of Representatives, Committee on the Judiciary, *Application of the Twenty-fifth Amendment to Vacancies in the Office of the Vice President*, 93rd Cong., 1st sess., 1973.

U.S., Congress, House of Representatives, Committee on the Judiciary, *Hearings on Nomination of Gerald R. Ford to be the Vice President of the United States*, 93rd Cong., 1st sess., 1973.

U.S., Congress, Senate, Committee on Rules and Administration, *Hearings on Nomination of Gerald R. Ford of Michigan to be Vice President of the United States*, 93rd Cong., 1st sess., 1973.

U.S., Congress, Senate, Committee on Rules and Administration, *Report on Nomination of Gerald R. Ford of Michigan to be the Vice President of the United States*, S. Exec. Rep. 93-26, 93rd Cong., 1st sess., 1973.

U.S., Congress, Senate, *How Can the Federal Political System be Improved?*, 93rd Cong., 2nd sess., 1974.

U.S., Congress, Senate, Committee on Rules and Administration, *Hearings on Nomination of Nelson A. Rockefeller of New York to be Vice President of the United States*, 93rd Cong., 2nd sess., 1974.

U.S., Congress, House of Representatives, Committee on the Judiciary, *Hearings on Nomination of Nelson A. Rockefeller to be Vice President of the United States*, 93rd Cong., 2nd sess., 1974.

U.S., Congress, Senate, Committee on Rules and Administration, *Report on Nomination of Nelson A. Rockefeller of New York to be Vice President of the United States*, S. Exec. Rep. 93-34, 93rd Cong., 2nd sess., 1974.

U.S., Congress, Senate, Subcommittee on Constitutional Amendments of the Committee on the Judiciary, *Hearings on Examination of the First Implementation of Section Two of the Twenty-fifth Amendment*, 94th Cong., 1st sess., 1975.

U.S., Department of State, *Bulletin*, 1953-1981.

INTERVIEWS

Interview with Senator Birch Bayh, Washington, D.C., 27 September 1977.

Interview with Hon. Thomas B. Curtis, former U.S. congressman, St. Louis, Mo., 9 September 1977.

Interview with Sidney M. Davis, former Kefauver aide, New York, N.Y., 1 October 1976.

Interview with Albert A. Eisele, press secretary of Vice President Mondale, Washington, D.C., 28 September 1977. Telephone interview with Eisele, 13 January 1981.

Interview with William Josephson, Shriver vice-presidential campaign manager, New York, N.Y., 30 September 1976.

Interview with Richard Moe, chief of staff for Vice President Mondale, Washington, D.C., 28 September 1977. Telephone interview with Moe, 29 January 1981.

Interviews with Lawrence F. O'Brien, former special assistant to Presidents Kennedy and Johnson, Postmaster General, and chairman of the Democratic National Party, New York, N.Y., 29 September 1976 and 30 September 1977.

Interview with Hon. Endicott Peabody, former governor of Massachusetts and candidate for the Democratic vice-presidential nomination, New York, N.Y., 3 December 1976.

Interview with William R. White, administrative assistant to Senator John Glenn, Washington, D.C., 22 September 1976.

Interview with Congressman Robert Young, Washington, D.C., 25 September 1977.

NEWSPAPERS AND MAGAZINES

Boston Globe, 1978-1981.
Congressional Quarterly, 1952-1981.
Gallup Opinion Index, 1972-1979.
Nation, 1952-1978.
National Journal, 1969-1981.
New Republic, 1952-1981.
New York Times, 1952-1981.
Newsweek, 1952-1981.
St. Louis Post-Dispatch, 1974-1981.
San Francisco Chronicle, 1979-1980.
The Reporter, 1952-1972.
Time, 1952-1981.
U.S. News and World Report, 1952-1981.
Wall Street Journal, 1976-1981.
Washington Post, 1952-1981.

BOOKS AND ARTICLES

Adamany, David; and Agree, George. "Election Campaign Financing: The 1974 Reforms." *Pol. Sci. Q.* 90 (1975):201-220.

Adams, C. F., ed. *The Works of John Adams.* 10 vols. Boston: Little, Brown, 1850-1856.

Adams, Sherman. *Firsthand Report: The Story of the Eisenhower Administration.* New York: Harper and Brothers, 1961.

Aiken, George D. *Senate Diary: January, 1972-January, 1975.* Brattleboro, Vt.: Stephen Greene Press, 1976.

Arthur, Chester A. *State Papers of Chester A. Arthur.* Washington, D.C.: U.S. Government Printing Office, 1885.

Baker, Leonard. *The Johnson Eclipse: A President's Vice President's Vice Presidency.* New York: Macmillan, 1966.

Barber, James D. *The Presidential Character: Predicting Performance in the White House.* 2d ed. Englewood Cliffs, N.J.: Prentice-Hall, 1977.

————, ed. *Choosing the President.* Englewood Cliffs, N.J.: Prentice-Hall, 1974.

————, ed. *Race for the Presidency: The Media and the Nominating Process.* Englewood Cliffs, N.J.: Prenctice-Hall, 1978.

Barkley, Alben W. *That Reminds Me.* Garden City, N.Y.: Doubleday, 1954.

Bayh, Birch. *One Heartbeat Away.* Indianapolis: Bobbs-Merrill, 1968.

Blackman, Paul. "Presidential Disability and the Bayh Amendment." *W. Pol. Q.* 20 (1967):440-455.

Bloom, Melvyn H. *Public Relations and Presidential Campaigns: A Crisis in Democracy.* New York: Thomas Y. Crowell, 1973.

Bradlee, Benjamin C. *Conversations with Kennedy.* New York: W. W. Norton, 1975.

Brams, Steven J.; and Davis, Morton D. "The 3/2's Rule in Presidential Campaigning." *Am. Pol. Sci. Rev.* 68 (1974):113-134.

Brauer, Carl M. *John F. Kennedy and the Second Reconstruction.* New York: Columbia University Press, 1977.

Burnham, Walter Dean. "Insulation and Responsiveness in Congressional Elections." *Pol. Sci. Q.* 90 (1975):411-435.

Burns, James MacGregor. *Roosevelt: The Lion and the Fox.* New York: Harcourt Brace Jovanovich, 1956.

————. *Presidential Government.* Boston: Houghton Mifflin, 1965.

————. *Roosevelt: The Soldier of Freedom.* New York: Harcourt Brace Jovanovich, 1970.

Campbell, Angus; Converse, Philip E.; Miller, Warren E.; and Stokes, Donald E. *The American Voter.* New York: John Wiley and Sons, 1964.

Caraley, Demetrios et al. "American Political Institutions after Watergate—A Discussion." *Pol. Sci. Q.* 89 (1974-1975):713-749.

Carleton, William G. "The Revolution in the Presidential Nominating Convention." *Pol. Sci. Q.* 72 (1957):224-240.

Casserly, John J. *The Ford White House: The Diary of a Speech-writer.* Boulder: Colorado Associated University Press, 1977.

Chester, Lewis; Hodgson, Godfrey; and Page, Bruce. *An American Melodrama: The Presidential Campaign of 1968.* New York: Viking Press, 1969.

Christian, George. *The President Steps Down.* New York: Macmillan, 1970.

Christopher, Warren E. "A Special Election to Fill a Presidential Vacancy." *The Record* (of the Association of the Bar of the City of New York) 30 (1975):47-54.

Clausen, Aage R.; Converse, Philip E.; and Miller, Warren E. "Electoral Myth and Reality: The 1964 Election." *Am. Pol. Sci. Rev.* 59 (1965):321-336.

Cohen, Richard M.; and Witcover, Jules. *A Heartbeat Away: The Investigation and Resignation of Vice President Spiro T. Agnew.* New York: Viking Press, 1974.

Collat, Donald S.; Kelley, Stanley Jr.; and Rogowski, Ronald. "Presidential Bandwagons." Paper delivered at the Annual Meeting of the American Political Science Association, Chicago, Ill. September 1976.

Converse, Philip E.; Campbell, Angus; Miller, Warren E.; and Stokes, Donald E. "Stability and Change in 1960: A Reinstating Election." *Am. Pol. Sci. Rev.* 55 (1961):269-280.

———; Miller, Warren E.; Rusk, Jerrold G.; and Wolfe, Arthur C. "Continuity and Change in American Politics: Parties and Issues in the 1968 Election." *Am. Pol. Sci. Rev.* 63 (1969):1083-1105.

Coolidge, Calvin. *The Autobiography of Calvin Coolidge.* New York: Cosmopolitan Book Company, 1929.

Corwin, Edward. *The President: Office and Powers.* 4th ed. New York: New York University Press, 1957.

Cronin, Thomas E. *The State of the Presidency.* Boston: Little, Brown. 1975.

Cummings, Milton C., Jr., ed. *The National Election of 1964.* Washington, D.C.: The Brookings Institution, 1966.

Dahl, Robert. *A Preface to Democratic Theory.* Chicago: University of Chicago Press, 1956.

David, Paul T. "Reforming the Presidential Nominating Process." *Law & Contemp. Probs.* 27 (1962):159-177.

————. "The Vice Presidency: Its Institutional Evolution and Contemporary Status." *J. Pol.* 29 (1967):721-748.

————; Moos, Malcolm; and Goldman, Ralph M. *Presidential Nominating Politics in 1952.* Baltimore: The Johns Hopkins University Press, 1954.

————; and Goldman, Ralph M. "Presidential Nominating Patterns." *W. Pol. Q.* 9 (1956):465-480.

————; Goldman, Ralph M.; and Bain, Richard C. *The Politics of National Party Conventions.* Washington, D.C.: The Brookings Institution, 1960.

————, ed. *The Presidential Election and Transition, 1960-61.* Washington, D.C.: The Brookings Institution, 1961.

Davis, Eric L. "Legislative Liaison in the Carter Administration." *Pol. Sci. Q.* 94 (1979):287-301.

Dent, Harry. *The Prodigal South Returns to Power.* New York: John Wiley and Sons, 1978.

Di Salle, Michael V. *Second Choice.* New York: Hawthorn Books, 1966.

Donovan, Robert J. *Eisenhower: The Inside Story.* New York: Harper and Brothers, 1956.

Dorman, Michael. *The Second Man.* New York: Delacorte Press, 1968.

Dougherty, Richard. *Goodbye, Mr. Christian.* Garden City, N.Y.: Doubleday, 1973.

Dulles, Foster Rhea. *America's Rise to World Power 1898-1954.* New York: Harper and Brothers, 1955.

Durham, G. Homer. "The Vice Presidency." *W. Pol. Q.* 1 (1948): 311-314.

Eisele, Albert A. *Almost to the Presidency.* Blue Earth, Minn.: The Piper Co., 1972.

Eisenhower, Dwight D. *Mandate for Change: The White House Years, 1953-56.* Garden City, N.Y.: Doubleday, 1963.

————. *Waging Peace: The White House Years, 1956-61.* Garden City, N.Y.: Doubleday, 1965.

Ely, John H. *Democracy and Distrust: A Theory of Judicial Review.* Cambridge: Harvard University Press, 1980.

Evans, Rowland Jr.; and Novak, Robert D. *Lyndon B. Johnson: The Exercise of Power.* New York: New American Library, 1966.

Evans, Rowland Jr.; and Novak, Robert D. *Nixon in the White House.* New York: Random House, 1971.

Fairlie, Henry. *The Kennedy Promise: The Politics of Expectation.* Garden City, N.Y.: Doubleday, 1973.

Farrand, Max, ed. *Records of the Federal Convention of 1787.* 4 vols. New Haven: Yale University Press, 1911.

Feerick, John D. "The Problem of Presidential Inability—Will Congress Ever Solve It?" *Ford. L. Rev.* 32 (1963):73-134.

———. "The Vice-Presidency and the Problems of Presidential Succession and Inability." *Ford. L. Rev.* 32 (1964):457-498.

———. *From Failing Hands.* New York: Fordham University Press, 1965.

———. "The Proposed Twenty-Fifth Amendment to the Constitution." *Ford. L. Rev.* 34 (1965):173-206.

———. "Vice Presidential Succession: In Support of the Bayh-Celler Plan." *S. Caro. L. Rev.* 18 (1966):226-236.

———. *The Twenty-fifth Amendment.* New York: Fordham University Press, 1976.

Field, Oliver P. "The Vice Presidency of the United States." *Am. L. Rev.* 56 (1922):365.

Fiorina, Morris. *Congress—Keystone of the Washington Establishment.* New Haven: Yale University Press, 1977.

Ford, Gerald R. *A Time to Heal.* New York: Harper & Row and The Reader's Digest Association, Inc., 1979.

Ford, Paul Leicester, ed. *The Writings of Thomas Jefferson.* Vol. VII. New York: G. P. Putnam's Sons, 1896.

Fotheringham, Peter. "Changes in the American Party System." *Govt. & Opp.* 8 (1973):217-241.

Galbraith, John Kenneth. *Ambassador's Journal: A Personal Account of the Kennedy Years.* Boston: Houghton Mifflin, 1967.

———. *A Life in Our Times.* Boston: Houghton Mifflin, 1981.

Gallup, George. *The Gallup Poll: Public Opinion, 1935-71.* 3 vols. New York: Random House, 1972.

———. *The Gallup Poll: Public Opinion, 1972-77.* 2 vols. Wilmington, Del.: Scholarly Resources, Inc., 1978.

Garner, John Nance. "This Job of Mine," *American*, July 1934.

Goldman, Eric F. *The Crucial Decade—And After.* New York: Vintage Books, 1960.

———. *The Tragedy of Lyndon Johnson*. New York: Alfred A. Knopf, 1969.

———. "Do We Really Need a Veep?" *This Week*, 29 June 1969, pp. 2, 4.

Goldstein, Joel K. "Presidential Succession and Inability: America's Inadequate Provisions." Senior thesis, Woodrow Wilson School of Public and International Affairs, Princeton University, 1975.

———. "An Overview of the Vice-Presidency." *Ford. L. Rev.* 45 (1977):786-799.

Goldwater, Barry M. *With No Apologies: The Personal and Political Memoirs of United States Senator Barry Goldwater*. New York: William Morrow, 1979.

Gorman, Joseph Bruce. *Kefauver: A Political Biography*. New York: Oxford University Press, 1971.

Graber, Doris A. "Press Coverage and Voter Reaction in the 1968 Presidential Election." *Pol. Sci. Q.* 89 (1974):68-100.

Graham, Otis L., Jr. *Toward a Planned Society: From Roosevelt to Nixon*. New York: Oxford University Press, 1976.

Griffith, Robert. *The Politics of Fear: Joseph R. McCarthy and the Senate*. Lexington: University of Kentucky Press, 1970.

Griffith, Winthrop. *Humphrey: A Candid Biography*. New York: William Morrow, 1965.

Haimbaugh, George Jr. "Vice Presidential Succession: A Criticism of the Bayh-Cellar Plan." *S. C. L. Rev.* 17 (1965):315-333.

———. "Vice Presidential Succession: A Brief Rebuttal." *S. C. L. Rev.* 18 (1966):237-239.

Halberstam, David. *The Best and the Brightest*. New York: Random House, 1969.

Hamilton, Alexander; Madison, James; and Jay, John. *The Federalist Papers*. Edited by C. Rossiter. New York: Macmillan, 1961.

Hansen, Richard. *The Year We Had No President*. Lincoln: University of Nebraska Press, 1962.

Hargrove, Erwin C. *Presidential Leadership: Personality and Personal Style*. New York: Macmillan, 1966.

Harris, Louis. "Why the Odds Are Against a Governor's Becoming President." *Pub. Op. Q.* 23 (1959):361-370.

Hart, Gary W. *Right from the Start*. New York: Quadrangle, 1973.

Hart, John. "Presidential Power Revisited." *Pol. Stds.* 25 (1977):48-61.

Hartmann, Robert T. *Palace Politics: An Inside Account of the Ford Years.* New York: McGraw-Hill, 1980.

Harwood, Michael. *In the Shadow of Presidents.* Philadelphia: J. B. Lippincott Company, 1966.

Hatch, Louis C. *A History of the Vice-Presidency of the United States.* Revised by Earl L. Shoup. New York: American Historical Society, 1934.

Henry, Laurin L. *Presidential Transitions.* Washington, D.C.: The Brookings Institution, 1960.

Hess, Stephen. *Organizing the Presidency.* Washington, D.C.: The Brookings Institution, 1976.

Hicks, John D. *The Republican Ascendancy, 1921-1933.* New York: Harper and Brothers, 1960.

Hofstadter, Richard. *The Idea of a Party System.* Berkeley and Los Angeles: University of California Press, 1969.

Hoover, Herbert C. *Memoirs: Vol. 2, The Cabinet and the Presidency, 1920-1933.* New York: Macmillan, 1951.

Hoxie, R. Gordon, ed. *The White House: Organization and Operations.* New York: Center for the Study of the Presidency, 1971.

Hughes, Emmet John. *The Ordeal of Power: A Political Memoir of the Eisenhower Years.* New York: Atheneum, 1963.

Huitt, Ralph K. "Congress: Retrospect and Prospect." *J. Pol.* 38 (1976):209-227.

Hull, Cordell. *The Memoirs of Cordell Hull.* New York: Macmillan, 1948.

Humphrey, Hubert H. "Changes in the Vice Presidency." *Cur. Hist.* 67 (1974):58-59, 89-90.

———. *The Education of a Public Man.* Garden City, N.Y.: Doubleday, 1976.

Johnson, Lyndon B. *The Vantage Point.* New York: Holt, Rinehart and Winston, 1971.

Johnson, Walter. "The American President and the Art of Communications." Inaugural Lecture at University of Oxford, England, 13 May 1958. Offprint in Rhodes House Library, Oxford, England.

————; Evans, Carol; and Sears, C. Eric. *The Papers of Adlai E. Stevenson.* Vol. VIII. Boston: Little, Brown, 1979.

Kallenbach, Joseph E. *The American Chief Executive: The Presidency and the Governorship.* New York: Harper & Row, 1966.

Kearns, Doris. *Lyndon Johnson and the American Dream.* New York: Harper & Row, 1976.

Keech, William R.; and Matthews, Donald R. *The Party's Choice.* Washington, D.C.: The Brookings Institution, 1976.

Kelley, Stanley, Jr. *Professional Public Relations and Political Power.* Baltimore: The Johns Hopkins University Press, 1956.

————. "Afterthoughts on Madison Avenue Politics." *Antioch Review* 17 (1957):173.

————. *Political Campaigning.* Washington, D.C.: The Brookings Institution, 1960.

————. "Elections and the Mass Media." *Law & Contemp. Probs.* 27 (1962):307-326.

————; and Mirer, Thad W. "The Simple Act of Voting." *Am. Pol. Sci. Rev.* 68 (1974):572-591.

King, Anthony, ed. *The New American Political System.* Washington, D.C.: American Enterprise Institute for Public Policy Research, 1978.

Kissinger, Henry. *White House Years.* Boston: Little, Brown, 1979.

Koenig, Louis W. *The Chief Executive.* New York: Harcourt, Brace and World, 1964.

Lamb, Karl A.; and Smith, Paul A. *Campaign Decision-Making: The Presidential Election of 1964.* Belmont, Cal.: Wadsworth Publishing Company, 1968.

Leach, Paul R. *That Man Dawes.* Chicago: Really and Lee Company, 1930.

Learned, Henry B. "Casting Votes of the Vice-Presidents, 1789-1915." *Am. Hist. Rev.* 20 (1915):571-576.

Leuchtenburg, William E. *The Perils of Prosperity, 1914-32.* Chicago: University of Chicago Press, 1958.

————. *Franklin D. Roosevelt and the New Deal.* New York: Harper & Row, 1963.

Lewis, Finlay. *Mondale.* New York: Harper & Row, 1980.

Lippman, Theo, Jr.; and Hansen, Donald C. *Muskie.* New York: W. W. Norton, 1971.

Longaker, Richard P. "Presidential Continuity: The Twenty-Fifth Amendment." *UCLA L. Rev.* 13 (1966):532-562.

Lubell, Samuel. *The Future of American Politics.* 2nd ed. Garden City, N.Y.: Doubleday, 1955.

McClure, Arthur F.; and Costigan, Donna. "The Truman Vice Presidency: Constructive Apprenticeship or Brief Interlude?" *Mo. Hist. Rev.* 65 (1971):318-341.

McConnell, Grant. *The Modern Presidency.* 2nd ed. New York: St. Martin's Press, 1976.

McGovern, George. *Grassroots: The Autobiography of George McGovern.* New York: Random House, 1977.

McPherson, Harry. *A Political Education.* Boston: Little, Brown, 1972.

Magruder, Jeb Stuart. *An American Life: One Man's Road to Watergate.* New York: Atheneum, 1974.

Manchester, William. *The Death of a President.* New York: Harper & Row, 1967.

Mann, Thomas E. *Unsafe at Any Margin: Interpreting Congressional Elections.* Washington D.C.: American Enterprise Institute for Public Policy Research, 1978.

Mansfield, Harvey C., Sr., ed. *Congress Against the President.* New York: Praeger, 1975.

Marshall, Thomas R. *Recollections of Thomas R. Marshall, Vice President and Hoosier Philosopher.* Indianapolis: Bobbs-Merrill, 1925.

Martin, John Bartlow. *Adlai Stevenson of Illinois.* Garden City, N.Y.: Doubleday Anchor Books, 1977.

————. *Adlai Stevenson and the World.* Garden City, N.Y.: Doubleday Anchor Books, 1978.

May, Ernest R.; and Fraser, Janet, eds. *Campaign '72: The Managers Speak.* Cambridge: Harvard University Press, 1973.

Mayhew, David. *Congress—The Electoral Connection.* New Haven: Yale University Press, 1974.

Mazo, Earl; and Hess, Stephen. *Nixon: A Political Portrait.* New York: Harper & Row, 1968.

Menez, Joseph F. "Needed: A New Concept of the Vice-Presidency." *Social Science* 30 (1955):143.

Miller, Arthur H. "Partisanship Reinstated? A Comparison of the

1972 and 1976 U.S. Presidential Elections." *Br. J. Pol. Sci.* 8 (1978):129-152.

Miller, Merle. *Lyndon: An Oral Biography.* New York: G. P. Putnam's Sons, 1980.

Minow, Newton; Martin, John Bartlow; and Mitchell, Lee. *Presidential Television.* New York: Basic Books, 1973.

Mowry, George E. *The Urban Nation.* New York: Hill and Wang, 1965.

Nathan, Richard P. *The Plot That Failed: Nixon and the Administrative Presidency.* New York: John Wiley & Sons, 1975.

Natoli, Marie D. "The Vice Presidency Since World War II." Ph.D. dissertation, Tufts University, 1975.

———. "The Mondale Vice Presidency: Is the Die Cast?" *Pres. Stds. Q.* 7 (1977):101.

———. "The Vice Presidency: Gerald Ford as Healer." *Pres. Stds. Q.* 10 (1980):662-664.

Nessen, Ron. *It Sure Looks Different from the Inside.* Chicago: Playboy Press, 1978.

Neustadt, Richard E. "The Constraining of the President: The Presidency after Watergate." *Br. J. Pol. Sci.* 4 (1974):383-397.

———. "Staffing the Presidency: Premature Notes on the New Administration." *Pol. Sci. Q.* 93 (1978):1-12.

———. "A January 1978 Postscript." *Pol. Sci. Q.* 93 (1978):12-14.

———. *Presidential Power.* Rev. ed. New York: John Wiley & Sons, 1980.

Nicholas, Herbert. "The Insulation of the Presidency." *Govt. & Opp.* 8 (1973):156-176.

Nie, Norman H.; Verba, Sidney; and Petrocik, John R. *The Changing American Voter.* Cambridge: Harvard University Press, 1976.

Nixon, Richard M. *Six Crises.* Garden City, N.Y.: Doubleday, 1962.

———. *RN: The Memoirs of Richard Nixon.* New York: Grosset & Dunlap, 1978.

O'Brien, Lawrence F. *No Final Victories.* Garden City, N.Y.: Doubleday, 1974.

O'Donnell, Kenneth P.; and Powers, David F. *"Johnny, We Hardly Knew Ye": Memories of John Fitzgerald Kennedy.* Boston: Little, Brown, 1972.

Orfield, Gary. *Congressional Power: Congress and Social Change.* New York: Harcourt Brace Jovanovich, 1975.

Paper, Lewis J. *The Promise and the Performance: The Leadership of John F. Kennedy.* New York: Crown Publishers, 1975.

Parmet, Herbert S. *Jack: The Struggles of John F. Kennedy.* New York: Dial Press, 1980.

Parris, Judith H. *The Convention Problem.* Washington, D.C.: The Brookings Institution, 1972.

Paullin, Charles O. "The Vice-President and the Cabinet." *Am. Hist. Rev.* 29 (1924):496-500.

Peabody, Robert L.; Ornstein, Norman J.; and Rohde, David W. "The United States Senate as a Presidential Incubator: Many Are Called but Few Are Chosen." *Pol. Sci. Q.* 91 (1976):237-258.

Pious, Richard M. *The American Presidency.* New York: Basic Books, 1979.

Polsby, Nelson W. "Decision-Making at the National Conventions." *W. Pol. Q.* 13 (1960):609-619.

———. *Political Promises.* New York: Oxford University Press, 1974.

———. "Presidential Cabinet Making: Lessons for the Political System." *Pol. Sci. Q.* 93 (1978):15-25.

———; and Wildavsky, Aaron. *Presidential Elections.* 3rd ed. New York: Charles Scribner's Sons, 1971.

Pomper, Gerald. *Nominating the President.* New York: W. W. Norton, 1966.

———. "The Nomination of Hubert Humphrey for Vice-President." *J. Pol.* 28 (1966):639-659.

———. "The Decline of the Party in American Elections." *Pol. Sci. Q.* 92 (1977):21-41.

———, ed. *The Election of 1976.* New York: David McKay Company, 1977.

Price, Raymond K. *With Nixon.* New York: Viking Press, 1977.

Ranney, Austin. "Turnout and Representation in Presidential Primary Elections." *Am. Pol. Sci. Rev.* 66 (1972):21-37.

———. *Curing the Mischief of Faction: Party Reform in America.* Berkeley and Los Angeles: University of California Press, 1975.

———. *Participation in American Presidential Nominations, 1976.* Washington, D.C.: American Enterprise Institute for Public Policy Research, 1977.

Rather, Dan; and Gates, Gary Paul. *The Palace Guard*. New York: Harper & Row, 1974.

Ray, Joseph M., ed. *The President: Rex, Princeps, Imperator?* El Paso: Texas Western Press, 1969.

Reedy, George E. *The Twilight of the Presidency*. New York: New American Library, 1970.

————. "The Presidency in 1976: Focal Point of Political Unity?" *J. Pol.* 38 (1976):228-238.

Reeves, Richard. *A Ford, Not a Lincoln*. London: Hutchinson and Company, 1975.

————. *Convention*. New York: Harcourt Brace Jovanovich, 1977.

Reeves, Thomas C. "Chester A. Arthur and the Campaign of 1880." *Pol. Sci. Q.* 84 (1969):628-637.

"Report of the Study Group on Vice-Presidential Selection." Mimeographed. Cambridge: Institute of Politics, John F. Kennedy School of Government, Harvard University, 1976.

Richardson, Elliot L. *The Creative Balance: Government, Politics and the Individual in America's Third Century*. New York: Holt, Rinehart and Winston, 1976.

Ripon Society. *The Lessons of Victory*. New York: Dial Press, 1969.

Rose, Richard. *Managing Presidential Objectives*. New York: The Free Press, 1976.

Roosevelt, Theodore. "The Three Vice-Presidential Candidates and What They Represent." *Review of Reviews* 14 (1896):289.

Rossiter, Clinton. "The Reform of the Vice-Presidency." *Pol. Sci. Q.* 63 (1948):383-403.

————. "The Constitutional Significance of the Executive Office of the President." *Am. Pol. Sci. Rev.* 43 (1949):1206-1217.

————. *The American Presidency*. 2nd ed. New York: Harcourt Brace Jovanovich, 1960.

Rovere, Richard H. *Senator Joe McCarthy*. New York: Harper & Row, 1959.

Rubin, Richard L. *Party Dynamics*. New York: Oxford University Press, 1976.

Sabato, Larry. *Goodbye to Good-Time Charlie: The American Governor Transformed, 1950-1975*. Lexington, Mass.: D. C. Heath, 1978.

Salinger, Pierre. *With Kennedy*. Garden City, N.Y.: Doubleday, 1966.

Sayre, Wallace, ed. *The Federal Government Service.* Englewood Cliffs, N.J.: Prentice-Hall, 1965.

Scammon, Richard M.; and Wattenberg, Ben J. *The Real Majority.* New York: Coward-McCann, 1970.

———; and McGillivray, Alice V., eds. *America Votes 12.* Washington, D.C.: Election Research Center, 1977.

Schlesinger, Arthur M., Jr. *A Thousand Days.* Boston: Houghton Mifflin, 1965.

———. *The Imperial Presidency.* Boston: Houghton Mifflin, 1973.

———. "On the Presidential Succession." *Pol. Sci. Q.* 89 (1974):475-505.

———. *Robert Kennedy and His Times.* Boston: Houghton Mifflin, 1978.

———; and Israel, Fred L., eds. *History of American Presidential Elections.* Vols. III & IV. New York: Chelsea House, 1971.

Schram, Martin. *Running for President 1976: The Carter Campaign.* New York: Stein and Day, 1977.

Seidman, Harold. *Politics, Position and Power: The Dynamics of Federal Organization.* 2nd ed. New York: Oxford University Press, 1975.

Shaw, Malcolm. "Reinstatement: The American Presidential Election of 1976." *Parlia. Affs.* 30 (1977):241-257.

Silva, Ruth C. *Presidential Succession.* Ann Arbor: University of Michigan Press, 1951.

Sindler, Allan P. *Unchosen Presidents.* Berkeley and Los Angeles: University of California Press, 1976.

Sobel, Lester A., ed. *Presidential Succession.* New York: Facts on File, 1975.

Sorensen, Theodore C. *Decision-Making in the White House.* New York: Columbia University Press, 1963.

———. *Kennedy.* New York: Harper & Row, 1965.

———. *The Kennedy Legacy.* New York: Macmillan, 1969.

Special Committee on Election Reform of the American Bar Association. "Recommendation and Report." *Ford. L. Rev.* 45 (1977):779-785.

Stathis, Stephen W.; and Moe, Ronald C. "America's Other Inauguration." *Pres. Stds. Q.* 10 (1980):550-570.

Sundquist, James L. *Politics and Policy: The Eisenhower, Kennedy and Johnson Years*. Washington, D.C.: The Brookings Institution, 1968.

"Symposium on the Vice-Presidency." *Ford. L. Rev.* 45 (1977):707-778.

Thomson, Charles A. H. *Television and Presidential Politics*. Washington, D.C.: The Brookings Institution, 1956.

———; and Shattuck, Frances M. *The 1956 Presidential Campaign*. Washington, D.C.: The Brookings Institution, 1960.

Tillett, Paul, ed. *Inside Politics: The National Conventions, 1960*. Dobbs Ferry, N.Y.: Oceana Publications, 1962.

Timmons, Bascom N. *Garner of Texas*. New York: Harper and Brothers, 1948.

———. *Portrait of an American: Charles G. Dawes*. New York: Henry Holt and Company, 1953.

Truman, Harry S. *Year of Decisions, 1945*. Garden City, N.Y.: Doubleday, 1955.

———. *Years of Trial and Hope*. Garden City, N.Y.: Doubleday, 1956.

Tubbesing, Carl D. "Vice Presidential Candidates and the Home State Advantage: Or, 'Tom Who?' Was Tom Eagleton in Missouri." *W. Pol. Q.* 26 (1973):702-716.

Tugwell, Rexford G. "The President and His Helpers: A Review Article." *Pol. Sci. Q.* 82 (1967):253-267.

———. "The Historians and the Presidency: An Essay Review." *Pol. Sci. Q.* 86 (1971):183-204.

Turner, Michael. *Finding a Policy Role for the Vice President: The Case of Nelson A. Rockefeller*. Ann Arbor: University Microfilms, 1978.

Vale, Vivian. "The Collaborative Chaos of Federal Administration." *Govt. & Opp.* 8 (1973):177-194.

Wallace, Henry L. "The Campaign of 1948." Ph.D. dissertation, Indiana University, 1970.

Waugh, Edgar. *Second Consul*. Indianapolis: Bobbs-Merrill, 1956.

Weil, Gordon L. *The Long Shot: George McGovern Runs for President*. New York: W. W. Norton, 1973.

White, Theodore H. *The Making of the President 1960*. New York: Atheneum, 1961.

White, Theodore H. *The Making of the President 1964.* New York: Atheneum, 1965.

———. *The Making of the President 1968.* New York: Atheneum, 1969.

———. *The Making of the President 1972.* New York: Atheneum, 1973.

Wicker, Tom. *J.F.K and L.B.J.* Baltimore: Penguin Books, 1968.

Wiebe, Robert. *The Segmented Society.* New York: Oxford University Press, 1975.

Wildavsky, Aaron. "The Goldwater Phenomenon: Purists, Politicians, and the Two Party System." *Rev. Pol.* 27 (1965):386-413.

———, ed. *The Presidency.* Boston: Little, Brown, 1969.

Williams, Irving G. *The American Vice-Presidency: New Look.* New York: Doubleday, 1954.

———. *The Rise of the Vice Presidency.* Washington, D.C.: Public Affairs Press, 1956.

———. "The American Vice Presidency." *Cur. Hist.* 66 (1974):254-258, 273-274.

Williams, Philip; and Wilson, Graham K. "The 1976 Election and the American Political System." *Pol. Stds.* 25 (1977):182-200.

Wilmerding, Lucius, Jr. "The Vice Presidency." *Pol. Sci. Q.* 68 (1953):17-41.

———. "Presidential Inability." *Pol. Sci. Q.* 72 (1957):161-181.

Wilson, Woodrow. *Congressional Government.* Gloucester, Mass.: Peter Smith, 1973.

Witcover, Jules. *White Knight: The Rise of Spiro Agnew.* New York: Random House, 1972.

———. *Marathon: The Pursuit of the Presidency, 1972-1976.* New York: Viking Press, 1977.

Young, Donald. *American Roulette: The History and Dilemma of the Vice Presidency.* New York: Holt, Rinehart and Winston, 1972.

Index

Rayburn, Sam, 49, 54, 62
Reagan, Ronald, 57; as President, 207-8, 210, 223; as presidential candidate, 38, 64, 80, 83, 99, 103, 111, 125, 252-54, 303, 344n; selection of Bush as running mate, 53, 63, 65, 83, 291; selection of Schweiker as running mate (1976), 73, 78, 80-81, 279; as vice-presidential contender, 55, 60, 80, 241
Reedy, George, 23, 169, 278, 283
Reuther, Walter, 56, 122
Ribicoff, Abraham, 50, 56, 144, 326
Richardson, Elliot L., 241
Roberts, Dennis, 50
Robsion, John M., 295
Roche, John P., 188
Rockefeller, Nelson A., 11, 57, 108, 359n, 361n; as presidential candidate, 37, 250-51, 253, 254, 257-59, 261, 263; relations with Ford, 147, 311; selection as Ford's Vice President, 228, 239, 244-46; on the Vice Presidency, 278, 285, 309; as Vice President, 142, 145, 148, 149, 156-57, 158, 159, 171-72, 176, 179-80, 189, 195, 197, 200, 257; as vice-presidential contender, 60, 63, 64, 81, 241, 323
Rodino, Peter, 53, 61, 241, 244-45, 326
Roosevelt, Franklin D., 25, 102; death of, 13, 19; electoral coalition, 17, 24, 40, 82; as President, 14, 17, 26-27, 29, 30, 31, 207; Vice Presidents of, 8-9, 47, 80, 90, 118, 136
Roosevelt, Theodore, 8, 10, 16, 135, 139-40, 212-13, 216, 229, 289-90, 370n
Roper Poll, 67-68, 246
Rose, Alex, 56

Rossiter, Clinton, 9, 13, 30, 291
Rostow, Walt W., 267
Rowe, James, 60
Ruckelshaus, William, 64, 81, 341n
Rumsfeld, Donald, 149, 156, 172, 195, 216, 324, 369n
Rusk, Dean, 213, 214, 267
Russell, Richard, 49, 55, 144, 325

Salinger, Pierre, 216
Sanders, Carl, 58
Sanford, Terry, 58
Sarbanes, Paul, 245
Schlesinger, Arthur M., Jr., 50, 62, 168-69, 322; on the vice presidency, 113, 139, 146-47, 164, 221-22, 272, 280, 293, 295-96
Schlesinger, James, 213
Schultze, Charles, 173
Schwartz, Tony, 347n, 348n
Schweiker, Richard, 73, 80-81, 85, 86, 88, 279
Scott, Hugh, 246
Scowcroft, Brent, 216
Scranton, William, 322, 323
Seaton, Fred, 60, 323
Sherman, James S., 11, 137, 229
Sherman, Roger, 4
Short, Robert E., 50
Shriver, R. Sargent, 50, 216; qualifications of, 86, 87, 88, 341n; selection as McGovern's running mate, 53, 66, 70, 73, 76, 79, 81, 282, 326; as vice-presidential candidate, 94, 95, 96, 99, 102-3, 110, 117, 120, 125, 126, 128, 129, 132, 257, 343n; as vice-presidential contender, 57-58, 60, 325, 339n
Simon, William, 213, 214, 324
Sindler, Allen P., 290
Smathers, George, 50
Smith, Al, 40, 71
Smith, C. R., 268

Joel Goldstein began his research on the vice presidency while an undergraduate at Princeton University. As a Rhodes Scholar at Oxford University, he expanded it for his doctoral thesis. A recent graduate of Harvard Law School, Dr. Goldstein is currently a law clerk in Boston.

Library of Congress Cataloging in Publication Data

Goldstein, Joel K. (Joel Kramer), 1953-
   The modern American vice presidency.

   Bibliography: p.
   Includes index.
   1. Vice-Presidents—United States.   I.   Title.
JK609.5.G64   353.03'18   81-47918
ISBN 0-691-07636-7   AACR2
ISBN 0-691-02208-9 (pbk.)